797,885

are availabl[e]

www.ForgottenBooks.com

Forgotten Books' App

Available for mobile, tablet & eReader

ISBN 978-1-331-04152-8
PIBN 10137214

This book is a reproduction of an important historical work. Forgotten Books uses state-of-the-art technology to digitally reconstruct the work, preserving the original format whilst repairing imperfections present in the aged copy. In rare cases, an imperfection in the original, such as a blemish or missing page, may be replicated in our edition. We do, however, repair the vast majority of imperfections successfully; any imperfections that remain are intentionally left to preserve the state of such historical works.

Forgotten Books is a registered trademark of FB &c Ltd.
Copyright © 2015 FB &c Ltd.
FB &c Ltd, Dalton House, 60 Windsor Avenue, London, SW19 2RR.
Company number 08720141. Registered in England and Wales.

For support please visit www.forgottenbooks.com

1 MONTH OF FREE READING

at

www.ForgottenBooks.com

By purchasing this book you are eligible for one month membership to ForgottenBooks.com, giving you unlimited access to our entire collection of over 700,000 titles via our web site and mobile apps.

To claim your free month visit:

www.forgottenbooks.com/free137214

* Offer is valid for 45 days from date of purchase. Terms and conditions apply.

Similar Books Are Available from

www.forgottenbooks.com

Beautiful Joe
An Autobiography, by Marshall Saunders

Theodore Roosevelt, an Autobiography
by Theodore Roosevelt

Napoleon
A Biographical Study, by Max Lenz

Up from Slavery
An Autobiography, by Booker T. Washington

Gotama Buddha
A Biography, Based on the Canonical Books of the Theravādin, by Kenneth J. Saunders

Plato's Biography of Socrates
by A. E. Taylor

Cicero
A Biography, by Torsten Petersson

Madam Guyon
An Autobiography, by Jeanne Marie Bouvier De La Motte Guyon

The Writings of Thomas Jefferson
by Thomas Jefferson

Thomas Skinner, M.D.
A Biographical Sketch, by John H. Clarke

Saint Thomas Aquinas of the Order of Preachers (1225-1274)
A Biographical Study of the Angelic Doctor, by Placid Conway

Recollections of the Rev. John Johnson and His Home
An Autobiography, by Susannah Johnson

Biographical Sketches in Cornwall, Vol. 1 of 3
by R. Polwhele

Autobiography of John Francis Hylan, Mayor of New York
by John Francis Hylan

The Autobiography of Benjamin Franklin
The Unmutilated and Correct Version, by Benjamin Franklin

James Mill
A Biography, by Alexander Bain

George Washington
An Historical Biography, by Horace E. Scudder

Florence Nightingale
A Biography, by Irene Cooper Willis

Marse Henry
An Autobiography, by Henry Watterson

Autobiography and Poems
by Charlotte E. Linden

THOMAS DRUMMOND

UNDER-SECRETARY IN IRELAND 1835-40

LIFE AND LETTERS

BY

R. BARRY O'BRIEN

OF THE MIDDLE TEMPLE, BARRISTER-AT-LAW

AUTHOR OF "FIFTY YEARS OF CONCESSIONS TO IRELAND"

LONDON

KEGAN PAUL, TRENCH & CO., 1 PATERNOSTER SQUARE

1889

PREFACE.

MRS DRUMMOND having recently found among her husband's papers a number of interesting letters, throwing fresh light on his work and character, placed them in my hands with a view to publishing a new life.

Through the courtesy of Sir Bernard Burke, Ulster King-of-Arms, I have been able to examine the papers in the Record Tower, Dublin Castle, relating to Drummond's administration of Ireland.

I have drawn upon Hansard, the contemporary press, Parliamentary Committees, and other sources of information little used before.

The sketch of Drummond's early days is based on Mr McLennan's "Memoir" (now out of print), from which I have also taken some useful letters.

I have had the advantage of many conversations with Mrs Drummond, whose recollection of her husband's work in Ireland is vivid, and with Sir C. Gavan Duffy, whose memory goes back to those days, and who met Drummond in Dublin.

I beg to express my indebtedness to Earl Spencer, for permitting me to read the *Althorp Correspondence*, and to Mrs Kay and Miss Drummond for important facts and suggestions.

The work has been a labour of love.

It is the record of a noble life.

R. BARRY O'BRIEN.

January 1889.

CONTENTS.

CHAPTER IX.

CHAPTER X.

CHAPTER XI.

CHAPTER XII.

LIST OF PLATES.

THOMAS DRUMMOND.

CHAPTER I.

EARLY DAYS.

THOMAS DRUMMOND was born in Castle Street, Edinburgh, on October 10, 1797. His father, who was a Writer to the Signet, belonged to a Scotch family of ancient lineage.

When Edgar Atheling fled from England, he took refuge, under stress of weather, in the Firth of Forth. He was accompanied in his flight by Maurice, the first of the name of Drummond,[1] who was himself a member of the Royal House of Hungary.

King Malcolm welcomed the fugitives, and, in an especial manner, showed favour to Maurice, on whom he bestowed honours, offices, and lands. So runs the story of the foundation of the house of Drummond.

But we come to more settled historical facts, when, in 1445, we find Sir Malcolm Drummond of Cargill and Stobball, head of that house, and owner of vast estates in Perth, Dumbarton, and Stirling. In 1487 Sir Malcolm's eldest son was raised to the Peerage as Lord Drummond. In 1605 the fourth Lord Drummond was created Earl of Perth; and in 1686 the fourth Earl of

[1] Maurice assumed the name of Drummond.—Malcolm, "Genealogical Memoir of the House of Drummond."

Perth became Lord Justice-General, and Lord High Chancellor of Scotland.

The house of Drummond was divided into three branches—Invermay, Drummondernoch, and Comrie. The founder of the Drummondernoch branch was Thomas, the fourth son of Sir Malcolm Drummond of Stobhall.[1] From him was lineally descended James, "the seventh of Drummondernoch." His grandson, Patrick, who succeeded to the estates and title of Comrie, as well as of Drummondernoch, was the grandfather of the subject of this Memoir. Patrick died in embarrassed circumstances—the Drummondernoch estates having been sold to meet his liabilities. He left two sons and a daughter—James, John, and Beatrice. James succeeded to the Comrie estate, and married in 1792 "the beautiful Betsy Somers," daughter of James Somers of Edinburgh, a woman of remarkable character and energy; John became a major in the East India Service; and Beatrice married James Drummond of Strageath. In the lifetime of James Drummond, who was a generous man, and an improving landowner of large views, the family property became still further impaired, and after his death the Comrie estates were sold to the son of Viscount Melville. So the inheritance of the Drummonds of Drummondernoch and Comrie passed away.

James Drummond died on February 1, 1800. He left three sons and one daughter—James Patrick, Thomas, John, and Elizabeth. Mrs Drummond survived her husband many years, and lived to witness the fame and mourn the untimely death of her gifted child.

[1] Thomas Drummond, fourth son of Sir Malcolm Drummond, was at Drummond Castle when the house refused to surrender to King James IV. Thomas fled to Ireland and subsequently to England, where, at the intercession of Henry VII., he was pardoned by King James; and returning to Scotland he received from Lord Graham the lands of Drummondernoch, which signifies the Irish Drummond's lands.—Malcolm, "Genealogical Memoir of the House of Drummond," p. 51.

Thomas Drummond began life the inheritor of an historic name, but the possessor of no fortune. With an annual income of about £120, Mrs Drummond had to face the world with her helpless family. When his father died, Thomas was about three years old; and we have a touching account of an incident in his life at that early period, written nearly forty years afterwards by the mother whose comfort, pride, and hope he was from infancy to manhood. While Under Secretary at Dublin Castle, and then suffering from the malady which ended in his death, his mother wrote to him:

"*Thursday*,[1] MOUNT PLEASANT.

"MY DEAREST TOM,—Your letter and recollections of the time gone by, were as refreshing to my mind as the scenes I sketched to you. The Sunday morning you describe, Eliza says she recollects well; and when you and I returned from our long and early walk, the rest were either not up, or newly arisen, but Eliza felt sore the disappointment in not having been awake to join us in our morning walk. No doubt it was for retirement I chose that early hour on a Sabbath morning, whose hallowed morn gives joy to all who love God's blessed day. I am glad it seems so deeply impressed, my dear Tom, upon your mind. Early impressions sink deep. When I am gone, you may, perhaps, and very possibly will, take the same range, and point to your son or daughter what I did to you. You were a dear little boy. Once when your beloved father was ill, the servants all occupied, you were in my arms. I kissed you, placed you on a chair at the foot of the bed, and bid you be a good boy and sit there till I had time to take you again. I was so much taken up attending your dear papa that I quite forgot you, and long after found you patiently sitting waiting till I was to

[1] Written probably in 1838 or 1839.

take you again in my arms as mamma's lambie. Well do I recollect this proof of your early love for me, and your docile temper; and since you have grown up, many a day you have been my treasure and my comfort, and God will return it all to you, though in a different way. He will give you comfort and delight in your children, for of all God's mercies this is the choicest, good, kind children. . . —Your attached mother,

"E. DRUMMOND."

During the years following her husband's death, Mrs Drummond took a house on the bank of the Esk, near Musselburgh, and there—from 1801 to 1810—Drummond's boyhood days were spent. We have no graphic picture of him in these days. Here and there we get glimpses of him in his sister's and mother's letters or conversations, but only in faint outline. He seems to have been a thoughtful, serious boy, with kindly blue eyes and dark eyelashes; short, even for his years, but energetic, practical, docile, and affectionate. The weight of the great sorrow which fell upon his mother, when he was yet an infant in arms, appears to have pressed on him too. He felt her troubles, lad as he was, and tried to lighten them. He was always busy about the house, "making things," as his sister expresses it. "About the house," says Eliza Drummond, "his power of contrivance made him exceedingly useful. And whatever went wrong, from the roasting jack upwards, the appeal was to Tommy to put it right." Nor, there is every reason for thinking, was this done merely because it amused the boy, but also because it pleased the mother whom he "idolised."

He took a great interest in cannons and ships. These were his toys, and he was an adept at "mounting batteries," and rigging all sorts of craft. In later years Mrs Drummond described these youthful traits. Writing in 1838, when her son was ill in Dublin, to Mrs Sharp,[1] she says:—

"*4th October* 1838.

"MY DEAR MRS SHARP,—I received your last; I wish I could say, with pleasure. Alas! your account of my dear son is most painful; I fear indeed his constitution is deeply impaired.

"Except a cut, or bruise, or hurt, my boys never had any other sore; and when I saw them safe in bed at night, I used often to say, thank God they are all safe and sound. My great fear in those days was gun powder, for which boys have such an itching for their little cannons. Squibs, rockets, &c., were a perpetual cause of alarm, for an encampment was near where we were, and the boys were often getting cartridges from the soldiers. With all my care I could not prevent this. I used often to threaten that I would write to the commanding officer to put a stop to it. Tom had then a little battery of cannon, machinery for a bridge, little ships nicely rigged out, &c.—in short, his time was completely occupied, never a moment idle. But his lessons were first despatched. From his infancy he was busied, often neglecting food—his mild and generous temper often leading him to espouse quarrels to help the weaker party—for he was very heroic. Pardon all this egotism. I think you don't dislike hearing this, as you love him with a sincere affection. . . .—Your affectionate friend,

"E. DRUMMOND."

The first school—a day school—to which Drummond went, was kept by a brutal master named Taylor. Taylor seems to have taken an aversion to the boy, and to have treated him infamously. One day Drummond came home

[1] *post.*

with his ears pierced by Taylor's nails, and his dress besmeared with blood. This produced a crisis; and the Taylors—for Taylor senior was assisted in the management of the school by his son Colin—were soundly rated by a friend of the family, Mr Aitchison of Drummore. Drummond describes the scene. Writing in September 1807 to his eldest brother, he says:—"Mr Aitchison gave him (Colin Taylor) a terrible scold about partiality, which he told to his father, and Mr Taylor's tongue has never lain. One time when he was speaking, he said, 'I shall be accused of partiality by none.' I have not told you the half of it. At one time we thought he was going out of his senses." But the tortures of the Taylors did not prevent Drummond from enjoying his favourite pastimes at home. In this letter he adds, "We are sailing our ships yet. I am sure you will not sail the Dutch ship any more. My mother and aunt think you might give it to me, and I will give mine to John." After Mr Aitchison's onslaught on the Taylors, Drummond fared better at their hands; but he soon left their establishment, and came under the tuition of more appreciative masters.

Professor Jardine, an old friend of Mrs Drummond, spent the summers of 1808 and 1809 at Portobello. He took a fancy to Drummond, and insisted on the lad becoming his pupil during these summer months. In the winters, when the professor returned to Glasgow, Drummond had another tutor provided by his friend Mr Aitchison, Mr Roy.

In 1810 he became a resident pupil of Mr Scott, a mathematical teacher at Edinburgh, and in the same year entered the Edinburgh University. Freed from the blighting influences of the Taylors, his intellect quickly ripened, and his genial temperament showed itself to all around him. "John Wilson and your sons," said Professor

Jardine to Mrs Drummond, "are the cleverest boys I had ever under my charge." "His knowledge of geometry," wrote Mr Scott in 1812 (Drummond had then been with him two years), "I have never seen equalled in one of his years; and the progress he is now making in the higher branches of mathematics and natural philosophy, is such as might be expected from one who possesses a sound judgment combined with uncommon application."[1] "I have no hesitation," wrote Professor Leslie (whose classes he attended at the University), "in saying that no young man has ever come under my charge with a happier disposition, or more promising talents."[2]

In 1812 Drummond's school and college days ended. In 1813, favoured by the influence of Mr Aitchison, he became a cadet at the Royal Military Academy, Woolwich.

Students of biography are sometimes curious to know if the qualities for which in later life a man becomes remarkable, show themselves in early youth. In Drummond's case the child was certainly the father of the man. As a lad, he was of a practical and inquiring turn of mind; affectionate and sympathetic; distressed at suffering; and, in his boyish ways, eager to avenge wrong.

There is a story told of how once he watched for days to thrash a boy who had plundered a bird's nest and drowned the little occupants.

Mrs Drummond pathetically tells us that "his mild and generous temper often led him to espouse quarrels to help the weaker party—for he was very heroic." He was anxious to know the ins and outs of things; the why and wherefore. Once he made himself miserable because he could not guess why a new roasting jack ticked. At length he undid the jack and got at the secret.

At school and college his proficiency was greatest in

[1] Letter to Mrs Drummond, November 24, 1812.—M'Lennan.

[2] Letter to Mr M'Farlane, December 26, 1812.—M'Lennan.

mathematics; his mind was essentially of a scientific bent. Professors Leslie and Barlow testify to his aptitude for scientific studies; and his mathematical exercise books, which have been preserved, bear the marks of their commendation. "Concise;" "Remarkably neat, and ably solved;" "Most curious;" "Most ingenious," are their judgment on his work. Twenty-three years afterwards, when Drummond was drawn into politics, Faraday deplored the loss which science sustained by this departure.

CHAPTER II.

WOOLWICH.

ON October 3, 1812, Drummond wrote to his friend Mr Aitchison ·—

"I feel a strong inclination for the profession of a military engineer. I have studied for these two years those branches preparatory for such a line, and have received a satisfactory certificate from Mr Leslie, professor of mathematics in Edinburgh. Could I only be so fortunate as to obtain a strong recommendation to Lord Mulgrave,[1] I would soon obtain the wished-for appointment."

The appointment was obtained, and in February 1813 Drummond went to Woolwich to stand his examination.

The examination was fixed for February 24, at eleven o'clock in the morning. Drummond sailed from Leith to Gravesend, reaching Gravesend at 2 A.M. on the day of the examination. He had told the steward the night before to call him early in the morning. The steward forgot the message, and Drummond did not wake until 7 A.M. He reached shore just to hear that the coach had started ten minutes previously. He gave chase to it, running along the road for three miles, but did not overtake it. A return chaise came up and he got into it. The chaise stopped within two miles of Woolwich at twenty minutes to eleven o'clock, eleven being the hour for examination. The driver would go no farther, he wanted to rest his horses. Drummond again started off on foot; ran

[1] Then Master of Ordnance.

all the way; arrived at the Academy at five minutes to eleven; presented himself for examination; and passed with flying colours. This incident is characteristic of the energy and determination of the man. Through life, what Drummond wanted to do, he did.

His days at Woolwich were not happy, though his progress was great. It is doubtful if he had chosen a congenial profession. It is certain that the system at the Academy was irksome and deterrent to study. Drummond did not tell his troubles to his mother lest it might make her unhappy, but he unburdened himself to his aunt, Mrs M'Farlane.

DRUMMOND TO HIS AUNT.

"ROYAL ARSENAL, *March* 26, 1813.

"MY DEAR AUNT,—You will be greatly surprised, and will, I daresay, sympathise with me when you read this. I have been here now upwards of a month, and from one of my mother's letters I gather you all think I like the place very well. God knows, I never told you this in any of my letters. Now you must promise to keep my mother ignorant of what I am about to tell you. From the moment I entered this place, till the present time, I have been miserable, and what I shall do, I know not. I expected to have seen Mr Aitchison, and to have told him all this, but from some cause I have not seen him; but perhaps he has not left London, and I may yet see him. I trust I may. I have hesitated long with myself whether or not to tell you this, but my situation becoming everv day more irksome, at last compels me to write to you; and you are the best person to give me advice, as I should not like my mother to know, she being so unwell. I would give worlds, if I had them, to get my discharge. But when I think of the enormous expense she has been at in sending me here, and how ill she can afford it, added to my last winter's expense, and when I consider her illness, I know not what to do. Upon no account show her this letter; you know what effect these things have upon her. But if I got my discharge I might follow some profession in which I might make it up to her, and in which I might be happy. You see how I am situated; as my mother is so unwell I am afraid to tell her. If I delay till July, it will be too late, and I will never get out. You will think this most unaccountable conduct, but the unhappy situation I am in must plead my excuse. After being ready for a commission, there are many chances against getting into the Engineers; promotion is so slow in the Artillery, that all try to get into the Engineers. In the Artillery, one may be a lieutenant for twenty years, living on 5s. 6d. per day. Had I known all this before I came, had I only had a trial of this place! Write to me as soon as you can, and tell me what to do. Should I write to Mr Aitchison, entreating him to apply to General Hope to get me my discharge? O that I was only in Edinburgh in person to tell you all! Colonel Mudge, to whom I was recommended, tries always to prevent those that are good at mathematics from getting their discharge. Whether should I keep it a secret from him, or try and engage him to help me? He could get my discharge if he asked it. You may think it most foolish in me talking thus, and that I may like it better after I have been longer here. But I have seen the life I have to lead, and though I was offered a commission in the Engineers just now, I would be most thankful to give it up. There are a great many wanting to be discharged. I am afraid to delay. I will get it far easier now than after I have been longer here. Write to me immediately if you can, and tell me what to do. O that I had had a trial of this place! Do not show this letter to my mother. General Hope may apply for my discharge, and surely they would not refuse him. . . . I will look every day for your answer. Remember me to Mr M'Farlane. Farewell. I remain, my dear aunt, your affectionate nephew,

"THOMAS DRUMMOND."

But Drummond's unhappiness did not prevent him from doing his work. He entered the Academy in February. In April he passed his first examination for a place in the school. "At the last examination here," he writes to Mr Aitchison, "I got from the bottom of the sixth academy to be fifth in the fifth academy, by which I took fifty-five places, and was made by Captain Gow head of a room." In less than three months afterwards a vacancy occurred in the senior department. Drummond competed for the place. He tells the result in a letter to his mother on July 1. "The examination is over, and everything has succeeded according to my wishes. I am first on the mathematical list, and second in the academy. . . . When I return (after the vacation) I shall be at the upper barracks, or, to speak so as you may understand me better, at the senior department."

He went home for the summer holidays of 1813. While at home he received a letter from Professor Jardine, showing the affectionate esteem in which his old tutor held him.

PROFESSOR JARDINE TO DRUMMOND.

"HALLSIDE, *4th August* 1813.

"MY DEAR THOMAS,—I received your letter, and I need not inform you that I am highly pleased with the information it contains, and with the very flattering accounts I have had of your conduct and progress at Woolwich from other quarters. I have often seen Colonel Miller, who was in this neighbourhood four or five weeks, and he informed me that Colonel Mudge said to him that you were just such a student as he wished, and that if you continued your ambition and your industry, there was no doubt of your future success.

"My dear young friend, you are now at a distance from your affectionate and anxious mother, and your other friends whom, I am sure, you will ever gratefully remember; and you must mix with many young persons, and persons who have been brought up, and instructed very differently from you, and you must be exposed to many temptations of various kinds at present, and as you advance in life. I, therefore, most solemnly advise you to adhere strictly to the good instructions you have received, and the good principles of religion in which you have been brought up.

"I do not mean that you are to show yourself a stiff and sour Presbyterian. Religion is a matter betwixt God and your own conscience, and you may do your duty completely both to God and man, either as a Presbyterian or an Episcopalian. What I mean is, that if, when you are still better qualified to determine, you prefer the one to the other, adhere to it, but not rigidly, as the difference is in form, not in substance. You will, no doubt, meet with many young persons who think and talk lightly perhaps irreverently, on these subjects. You need not attempt to correct or reform them unless the occasion be very favourable; but whatever they do, preserve your innocence and integrity; you will find them never-failing sources of comfort and happiness when you most require them. . . . Thomas, you are to be a soldier and a man of honour; and you must preserve that character uniformly. You will best preserve it by avoiding causes of offence, and by taking a cautious part in the offences and differences among your companions and friends. This is essentially necessary. Because, on proper occasion, there must be no doubt of your honour, and there must be regard to your character. Well-disposed, well-bred men, and men of accommodating, obliging dispositions, seldom or never have any occasion for their prudence or resolution. These are better discovered in very different situations. My dear Thomas, I have very little more to say to you at present, but I shall at all times, while I live, be ready to give you my best advice whenever you wish for it. I have only to recommend to you to remember at all times your beloved mother and grandmother.[1] I know you cannot forget them. But let them be present with you. Think of the pleasure you give them when you do well, and think of the tears and misery you would cause them if you were to do otherwise. I am sure your kind affectionate heart could not bear to think of a suffering, miserable mother. God bless you and preserve you from all evil. Fear God, honour your parents, your days shall be long, and your end happy.—I ever am, my dear Thomas, your faithful friend and servant, "GEO. JARDINE."

Drummond returned to Woolwich in August 1813, and resumed his studies with renewed success. In October he got into the third academy, and before Christmas into the second; early in the year 1814 he was advanced to the first. Within twelvemonths of his entrance at Woolwich he had reached the highest point of distinction open to him. In July 1815, he obtained a commission in the Royal Engineers.

Of his career at Woolwich, General Larcom writes:—"Much of his success was doubtless to be attributed to the admirable preliminary education he had received, but much also to a character of determined perseverance, and to the vigorous and well-regulated mind he brought to bear on all subjects. To this it was probably due that he never became exclusively a mathematician, but advanced equally in all the various branches of study,

[1] Mrs Somers.

being at that time, as he continued through life, distinguished for general intelligence, and for aptitude to seize on information of every kind."[1]

Professor Barlow bears like testimony to the abilities of his gifted pupil, and tells us in a few sentences how Drummond won his way at the Academy. "Mr Drummond, by his amiable disposition, soon gained the esteem of the masters under whom he was instructed; with the mathematical masters in particular, his reputation stood very high, not so much for the rapidity of his conception as for his steady perseverance, and for the original and independent views he took of the different subjects which were placed before him. There were among his fellow-students some who comprehended an investigation more quickly than Drummond, but there was none who ultimately understood all the bearings of it so well. While a cadet in a junior academy, not being satisfied with a rather difficult demonstration in the conic sections, he supplied one himself on an entirely original principle, which at the time was published in Leyborn's 'Mathematical Repository,' and was subsequently taken to replace that given in Dr Hutton's course of mathematics, to which he had objected. This apparently trifling event gave an increased stimulus to his exertions, and may perhaps be considered the foundation stone of his scientific fame. After leaving the Academy he still continued his intercourse with his mathematical masters, with whom he formed a friendship which only terminated on his much lamented death."[2]

Carrying with him the esteem and affection of many friends, Drummond, now nearly eighteen years old, began his life as a Royal Engineer.

[1] Memoir of Drummond in "Papers on subjects connected with the duties of the Corps of Royal Engineers," vol. iv.

[2] Quoted in General Larcom's Memoir.

CHAPTER III.

THE ROYAL ENGINEERS.

In 1815 Drummond entered the Royal Engineers, but for the next two years we learn little of his movements. In 1817 he joined the head-quarters at Chatham, and later on made a short trip to France "for the purpose of visiting the army of occupation, and attending one of the great reviews."[1]

In 1818 he was at Chatham, engaged in routine work, and busy besides in directing the attention of the authorities to a pontoon which he had designed. This invention has been described by Captain, afterwards Lieutenant-Colonel, Dawson. "The various inventions to supersede the use of the old pontoon led Drummond to consider the subject, and he made a model of a form like a man-of-war's gig or galley, sharp at both ends, and cut transversely into sections for facility of transport, as well as to prevent it from sinking if injured in any part. Each section was perfect in itself, and the sections admitted of being bolted together, the partitions falling under the thwarts or seats. The dockyard men and sailors to whom he showed it, said it would run better than any boat except a gig; and it was light, and capable of being transported from place to place on horseback."[2]

The fate of this invention is not known. Little encouragement was given at head-quarters to men of genius. On March 27, 1818, Drummond wrote to his

[1] Larcom. [2] Quoted in Larcom's Memoir.

mother: "I shall let you know what success my memoir[1] meets with. But there's no wish at the office to bring forward anything of that kind." Later on he writes again: "When I was at the Engineer office, a few days ago, I found Major Blanchard's model, with his memoir and a letter addressed to General Mann, in the ante-room. The box had been opened, only one of the models taken out; his memoir apparently had not been looked into, for within the first leaves was the letter I have just mentioned, unopened." In May, Drummond brought his model and memoir to London. The model, he tells us in a letter to his mother, written May 31, "experienced a gracious reception." But at this stage we lose sight of the invention. Drummond regarded the matter with his accustomed calm. He wrote to his mother: "If the plan is not approved, I may safely say it will not be laughed at. Whatever, then, may be the result—it may be for good—it cannot do me harm."

An incident in his life at Chatham deserves to be recorded, as showing the presence of mind and generous nature of the man. "He was charged with the construction, for practice, of a bridge of casks in the rapid current of the Medway, at Rochester Bridge, and having previously made piers of the casks in the still water above the bridge, it was necessary to move them through the rapids to get them below the bridge. The piers were, as usual, lashed two and two for security; but one remained, and as its removal was like to involve some danger, Mr Drummond determined to go on it himself. There were two soldiers on the pier, one of whom showed a little apprehension at setting off. Drummond placed this man next himself, and desired them both to sit quite still. They passed through the arch in safety, when the man

[1] It was the custom to send a memoir, with the model of an invention, to the head office.

who had previously shown apprehension, wishing by activity to restore himself to his officer's good opinion, got suddenly up to assist in making fast to the buoy; in an instant the pier upset, all hands were immersed in the water, and the man who had caused the accident, being on his feet, was thrown from the pier and drowned. Mr Drummond and the other man clung to the pier, and Mr Drummond afterwards described his sensations, when finding his body swept by the current against the under side of the pier. His last recollection was a determination to cling to one side of it, in hopes the depression of that side might be noticed. This presence of mind saved him and his comrade; for, as he expected, a brother officer (Fitzgerald) noticing the lowness of one side, sprang from a boat upon the other, and immediately the heads of poor Drummond and the sapper appeared above the water. Drummond was senseless, with the ropes clenched firmly in his hands."[1]

In July 1818 Drummond was stationed at Edinburgh, where he found the time hanging so heavily on his hands, that he resolved to give up the Engineers and join the Bar; "with this view he had actually entered his name at Lincoln's Inn."[2] But in 1819 he met Colonel Colby, who was then engaged on the Ordnance Survey in Scotland. In 1820 Colby was appointed chief of the survey. He asked Drummond to join him in the work. Drummond consented, gave up all notion of joining the Bar, and took the first step in a career which has made his name memorable.

[1] Larcom. [2] *Ibid.*

CHAPTER IV.

THE DRUMMOND LIGHT AND HELIOSTAT—THE ORDNANCE SURVEY IN IRELAND.

THE Ordnance Survey of Great Britain began in Scotland after the rebellion of 1745. The object was to obtain "accurate knowledge" of the Highland districts. The work was badly done, and the results were not published. In 1763 the subject of a general survey of the island was broached, but no steps were taken to carry it out. Finally, in 1783, "a representation was made from France to our Government, of the advantages which the science of astronomy would derive from the connection, through trigonometrical measurements, of the observatories of Greenwich and Paris, and the exact determination of their latitudes and longitudes. The French had by this time carried a series of triangles from Paris to Calais, and what they proposed was that the English should carry a similar series from Greenwich to Dover, when the two might be connected by observations from both sides of the Channel. The scheme was approved of by George III., and the English survey begun by the measurement of an initial base line[1] at Hounslow Heath by General

[1] "A base-line is an initial measured line, whose length is assumed as the unit to which all other distances calculated in the survey are temporarily referred. The exact length of the base in yards, feet, and inches being known, these other distances admit at once of being reduced to yards, feet, and inches. But any error in measuring the base must enter into all of them. For convenience in measuring any large tract of country—in other words, in constructing a Trigonometrical Survey—it is necessary that the length of the base should be a considerable multiple of the standard unit of length, several thousand yards at least; and for the accuracy of the survey, it is necessary that this length should be measured most exactly."—McLennan.

Roy—the foundation of the triangulation[1] since effected of Great Britain."[2]

The work was now entrusted to the Royal Engineers, and from 1783 to 1790 proceeded steadily under the direction of General Roy. In 1790 General Roy died, and was succeeded by Colonel Mudge. In 1791 Hounslow base was re-measured. Between 1792 and 1794 the triangulation was extended southwards to the Isle of Wight. Between 1794 and 1801 it embraced Salisbury Plain—which was taken as the base—Dorset, Devon, Cornwall, and the Scilly Isles. In 1801 a new base was measured on Misterton Carr in North Lincolnshire; and in 1806 part of North Wales was surveyed. In 1817 Scotland was

[1] "The base being measured, the next set of operations, those of the triangulation, commence. Some object is fixed upon, which is considerably farther from either end of the base than the length of the base line. Theodolites, with delicately graduated circles, capable of measuring angles to an extreme nicety, are then placed centrally over the dots which mark the extremities of that line, and their telescopes are directed to one another until, as it has been graphically said, 'they look down the throats of each other.' The telescopes being in this position, are clearly both of them directed along the base line. Each of them being now turned round till it looks straight at the object which has been fixed upon, the instruments are clamped, and the angles through which the telescopes have been turned are read off on the graduated circles. The angles are thus ascertained, which lines, drawn to the object from the extremities of the base, make with the base line. The object, in short, is made the summit of a triangle in which two angles, and the length of the side between them, are known. Its distance from either end of the base can thus be ascertained by computation, and made available as a new and larger base. 'Thus,' says Sir John Herschell, in a paper in which this subject is handled with his usual lucidity, 'the survey may go on throwing out new triangles on all sides, of larger and larger dimensions, till the whole surface of a kingdom, or a continent, becomes covered with a network of them, all whose angular points are precisely determined. The strides so taken, moderate at first, become gigantic at last; steeples, towers, obelisks, mountain cairns, and snowy peaks, becoming in turn the stepping-stones for further progress, the distances being only limited by the range of distinct visibility through the haze of the atmosphere.' In mapping a country, after the network of great triangles has been thrown over it, the great spaces comprehended by them are filled in by a system of smaller triangles so as to carry the survey to any degree of minuteness that may be required." — McLennan. Sir John Herschell, "Familiar Lectures on Scientific Subjects."

[2] McLennan.

reached, and in 1819, while the work was proceeding, Drummond, as we have seen, met Colby in Edinburgh. In 1820 Colby succeeded Mudge as superintendent of the Survey; and, in 1823, we find Colby and Drummond working together in Kent, Surrey, and Hertford. In November 1823 the British survey was dropped,[1] and in 1824 the survey of Ireland commenced. The circumstances which led to the Irish survey are well described by Mr McLennan:—

"[In 1824] a Select Committee was appointed 'to consider the best mode of apportioning more equally the local burthens collected in Ireland.' The object was to obtain a survey sufficiently accurate to enable the valuators, acting under the superintendence of a separate department of the Government, to follow the surveyors, and to apportion correctly the proper amount of the local burthens. These burthens had previously been apportioned by Grand Jury assessments. The assessments had, in some districts of Ireland, been made by the civil division of ploughlands, in others, by the division of townlands; the divisions, in either case, contributing in proportion to their assumed areas, which bore no defined proportion to their actual contents. The result was great, and much complained of, inequality in levying the assessment, which it was a primary object of the survey to remove by accurately defining the divisions of the country. The Committee reported that it was expedient to give much greater despatch to this work than had occurred in the Trigonometrical Survey of England. They recommended that every facility in the way of improved instruments should be given to the Ordnance officers by whom the survey was to be conducted; and concluded with the hope that the great national work which was projected 'will be carried on with energy as well as with skill, and that it will, when completed, be

[1] It was resumed in 1838.

creditable to the nation, and to the scientific acquirements of the age.'"[1]

The Ordnance Survey gave Drummond what he wanted,—a field of action. He was essentially a man of work; and it was his nature to throw himself heart and soul into whatever he undertook. Mechanically to follow others in a routine course was foreign to his genius; boldly to initiate was congenial to his tastes. Originality of mind and energy of character were among his distinguishing traits, and both were put to the test by the Ordnance Survey.

While engaged with Colby in Kent, Surrey, and Hertford, during the autumn of 1823, Drummond found that the great want of the survey was a light which would enable observations to be made at long distances, and prevent the hindrance of the work in murky weather. He promptly applied himself to supply this want; and the result of his labours was the famous "Drummond Light" and heliostat.

We have seen that from boyhood Drummond showed an aptitude for science. At school and college, at Woolwich, and in the Engineers, he was remarkable for proficiency in scientific studies, and for an original and inventive turn of mind. When the duties of the survey brought him to London in 1823, he resolved to devote all the time that could be spared from his professional work to the improvement of his scientific knowledge. He read hard at night, and in the morning attended the chemistry classes of Brande and Faraday at the Royal Institution. It has been said that some observations made at these lectures about the incandescence of lime suggested to Drummond the idea of the invention which bears his name. But it is best to tell the whole story in Drummond's own words.

[1] McLennan.

In a paper published in the "Philosophical Transactions" in 1826, he says:—

"In the beginning of the survey, General Roy on several occasions, but especially in carrying his triangles across the Channel to the French coast, made use of Bengal and white lights prepared at the Royal Arsenal; for these, parabolic reflectors, similar to those with which our lighthouses are supplied, and illuminated by Argand burners, were afterwards substituted as more convenient, but they have been gradually discontinued, the advantages derived from them proving inadequate, from their want of power, to the trouble and expense incident to their employment. In the trigonometrical operations of 1821, carried on by Colonel Colby and Captain Kater, conjointly with MM. Arago and Mathieu, for connecting the meridians of Greenwich and Paris, an apparatus of a very different kind was employed for the first time—a large plano-convex lens, 0·76 metre square, being substituted for a parabolic reflector, and the illuminating body an Argand lamp with four concentric wicks. The lens was composed of a series of concentric rings, reduced in thickness, and cemented together at the edges. This apparatus resulted from an inquiry into the state of the French lighthouses, and was prepared under the direction of MM. Fresnel and Arago. Its construction and advantages are explained in a 'Mémoire sur un Nouveau Systême d'éclairage,' by M. Fresnel. The light which it gave is stated to possess 3¼ times the intensity of that given by the reflector. It was employed, during the operations alluded to, at Fairlight Down and Folkestone Hill, on the English coast; at Cape Blancez and Montlambert, on the French coast; the greatest distance at which it was observed being 48 miles, and its appearance, I have understood from Colonel Colby, was very brilliant.

"But valuable as this apparatus may be when employed

in a lighthouse, the purpose for which it was indeed invented and constructed, the properties of the simple parabolic reflector appeared to give it a preference for the service of the Trigonometrical Survey, provided a more powerful light could be substituted in its focus instead of the common Argand lamp.

"With this object in view, I at first endeavoured to make use of the more brilliant pyrotechnical preparations; then phosphorus burning in oxygen, with a contrivance to carry off the fumes of phosphoric acid, were tried; but at the first attempts with these substances promising but little success, they were abandoned. The flames, besides being difficult and troublesome to regulate, were large and unsteady, little adapted to the nature of a reflecting figure, which should obviously, when used to the utmost advantage, be lighted by a luminous sphere, the size being regulated by the spread required to be given to the light. This form of the focal light, it was manifest, neither could be obtained nor preserved where combustion was the source of light; and it was chiefly this consideration which then led me to attempt applying to the purpose in view the brilliant light emanating from several of the earths when exposed to a high temperature; and at length I had the satisfaction of having an apparatus completed, by which a light so intense was produced, that when placed in the focus of a reflector, the eye could with difficulty support its splendour even at the distance of 40 feet, the contour of the reflector being lost in the brilliancy of the radiation.

"To obtain the requisite temperature, I had recourse to the known effect of a stream of oxygen directed through the flame of alcohol[1] as a source of heat free from danger, easily procured and regulated, and of great intensity.

"[Plate I.] fig. 4 represents the apparatus such as it is

[1] "Annals of Philosophy," vol. ii. p. 99.

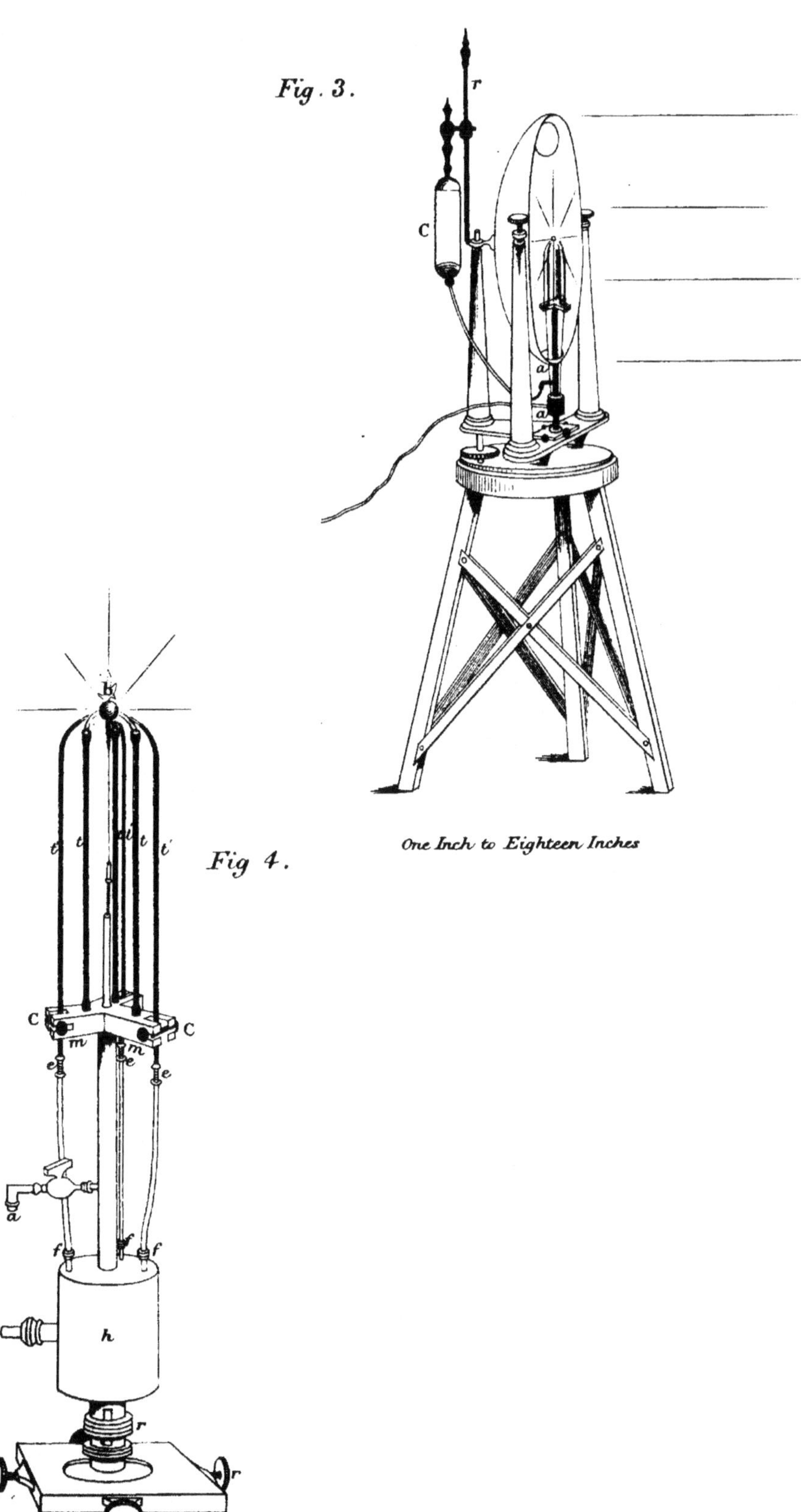

One Inch to Eighteen Inches

now made for the Survey. The spirit entering at *a* ascends through the tubes *t*, while the oxygen entering at *d* is directed by the jets *t′* upon the small ball of lime *b*, the tubes *t* are connected with the cylindrical box *h* by flexible caoutchouc tubes *e*, *f*, and also pass with friction through small cylinders at *c*, which admit of being moved backwards and forwards upon the arms, and are clamped when in the proper position by small mill-beaded screws at the sides. By these means every requisite adjustment is obtained for the jets through which the gas issues. The apparatus is attached by its base to the stand which carries the reflector (fig. 3), and the small ball may then, by means of the horizontal and vertical screws *r* be brought with great accuracy into the focus of the reflector. The cistern *c* containing the alcohol is placed behind the reflector (fig. 3), and being connected with the stem *a* by a flexible caoutchouc tube, may be elevated or depressed on the upright rod *r* (fig 3), and the flame at this point accordingly regulated so as to produce the greatest effect. A flexible tube leads from *d* to the vessel containing the oxygen, which may be either a common gas holder, or perhaps a silk bag with a layer of caoutchouc, such as they are now made, might be conveniently employed for this purpose. The apparatus first made was provided with five jets, and could light up a ball $\frac{3}{8}$ inch in diameter; that now represented has only three, and with it a ball $\frac{1}{4}$ of an inch in diameter may be used sufficiently large to admit of the requisite allowance being made for aberration in the reflector from its true figure, as well as uncertainty of direction arising from terrestrial refraction.

"To ascertain the relative intensities of the different incandescent substances that might be employed, they were referred, by the method of shadows, to an Argand lamp of a common standard, the light from the brightest part of the flame being transmitted through apertures equal in diameter to the small sphere of the different substances submitted to experiment.

"The result of several trials made at the commencement gave for

Lime, ...	37 times,
Zirconia, ...	31 ,,
Magnesia, ...	16 ,,

the intensity of an Argand burner. The oxide of zinc was also tried, but besides wasting away rapidly, it proved inferior even to magnesia.

"Of these substances, and also of their compounds with one another, lime appearing to possess a decided superiority, my subsequent experiments were confined to it alone; and by a more perfect adjustment of the apparatus by bringing the maximum heat, which is confined within narrow limits, exactly to the surface of the ball, and by using smaller balls than those employed in the early experiments, a very material increase of light has been obtained. The mean of ten experiments, made lately with every precaution, gives for the light emitted by lime, when exposed to this intense heat, eighty-three times the intensity of the brightest part of the flame of an Argand burner of the best construction, and supplied with the finest oil. The lime from chalk, and such as is known at the London wharves by the name of flame lime appears to be more brilliant than any that has been tried."[1]

The light soon made a stir in the scientific world. Writing many years afterwards to Drummond's mother, Sir John Herschell says:—

"It is with melancholy pleasure that I recall the impression produced by the view of this magnificent spectacle as exhibited in the vast armoury in the Tower, an apartment

[1] "Philosophical Transactions of the Royal Society for 1826."

three hundred feet long, placed at Mr Drummond's disposal for the occasion. . . . The common Argand burner and parabolic reflector of a British lighthouse were first exhibited, the room being darkened, and with considerable effect. Fresnel's superb lamp was next disclosed, at whose superb effect the other seemed to dwindle, and showed in a manner quite subordinate. But when the gas began to play, the lime being now brought to its full ignition, and the screen suddenly removed, a glare shone forth, overpowering and, as it were, annihilating both its predecessors, which appeared by its side, the one as a feeble gleam, which it required attention to see; the other like a mere plate of heated metal. A shout of triumph and admiration burst from all present. Prisms to analyse the rays, photometric contrivances to measure their intensity, and screens to cast shadows were speedily in requisition, and the scene was one of extraordinary excitement."

In 1825, the survey in Ireland commenced, and the Drummond Light was immediately brought into use. Operations began on Divis Mountain, near Belfast. On August 23 a conspicuous object was placed on the summit of Slieve-Snaght, the highest hill of Innishowen, about 2100 feet above the level of the sea. It became necessary that the object on Slieve-Snaght should be seen from Divis, where a party of observation were encamped. But from August to October Divis remained enveloped in impenetrable mist, and the object on Slieve-Snaght was wholly lost to the observers. Matters now became serious, and the work of the Survey was brought to a standstill. No progress could be made until some object on Slieve-Snaght could be seen by the party on Divis. At this juncture Colonel Colby resolved to try what Drummond could do, and promptly sent him to the front. General Larcom shall tell the rest of the story.

"Mr Drummond took the lamp and a small party of men to Slieve-Snaght, and by calculation succeeded so well in directing the axis of the reflector to the instrument on Divis, that the light was seen, and its first appearance will long be remembered by those who witnessed it. The night was dark and cloudless, the mountain and the camp were covered with snow, and a cold wind made the duty of observing no enviable task. The light was to be exhibited at a given hour, and to guide the observer one of the lamps formerly used, an Argand in a lighthouse reflector, was placed on the tower of Randalstown Church, which happened to be nearly in the line at fifteen miles. The time approached and passed, and the observer had quitted the telescope, when the sentry cried, 'the light'! and the light indeed burst into view, a steady blaze of surpassing splendour, which completely effaced the much nearer guiding beacon. It is needless to add that the observations were satisfactorily completed, the labours of a protracted season closed triumphantly for Drummond, and the Survey remained possessed of a new and useful power."[1]

We have from Drummond himself an interesting letter, written at this period, to his mother, describing the operations on Slieve-Snaght:—

DRUMMOND TO HIS MOTHER.

"SLIEVE SNAGHT, *Friday Night, November* 1825.

"MY DEAR MOTHER,—What has become of Tom? and why does he not write? are questions which you may of late have not unfrequently asked, and, I dare say, without any one being able to give a very satisfactory answer. Why, then, I am perched upon the top of Slieve-Snaght (the snowy mountain), 2100 feet, in the centre of Innishowen, the wildest district in Ireland. Since the 23rd of August,

[1] Larcom, Memoir. "The distance was 60 miles, and the light appeared like a star of the first magnitude, being visible by the naked eye."—Portlock, "Life of Colby," p. 127.

when a pole was placed on this hill, we have endeavoured to observe it from Divis, near Belfast, on which our tent was placed, but in vain. Constituting an important point in the triangulation of Ireland, our sojourning on the hill tops has been prolonged to an unusually late period, in the daily hope that it would have been visible.

"Disappointment, however, was our lot, and the weather becoming broken and tempestuous, the Colonel determined upon breaking up the camp and retiring to winter quarters. Just at that moment a letter was received from one of our officers encamped on Knock Layd, a hill about forty miles distant, giving a splendid description of the solar reflection which I had exhibited to him, and which had been seen through a very hazy atmosphere, and seen for a time with the naked eye; and one of our officers tells me that the country people, whom curiosity had attracted to the spot, on hearing the distance at which it was placed, actually raised a shout of exultation at its brilliant appearance. This being known at Divis, it became a question whether Slieve-Snaght should be attempted at this season; and after due deliberation, it being decided that it should, I made a forced march upon this place, and leaving Belfast on Tuesday forenoon, slept on this mountain on Thursday night, the 27th October, our tents erected and hut constructed, and all the apparatus of the lamp ready for work. For the first week our life was a struggle with tempest—our tents blown down, our instruments narrowly escaping, and ourselves nearly exhausted. At length, by great exertions, we got two huts erected; one for the seven men who are with me, the other for me, a lonely and humble dwelling, it is true; and now that the snow has fallen, so completely covered up that it is not very easily distinguished; nevertheless affording good shelter, warm and comfortable, and at the present moment, with a good peat fire. The weather at length improved, and Wednesday the 9th instant brought our exertions to a successful termination. The Colonel, after making the necessary arrangements, took his departure for London on the very day I arrived here, leaving Murphy and Henderson to keep a constant look-out for the lights. Their assiduity has been unremitting, and their fatigue by incessant watching not a little. This day brought me a letter from Murphy, which begins thus:—'Your light has been most brilliant to-night for three hours and twenty minutes, as was your solar reflection to-day. I began by giving you the pleasing intelligence in a condensed form, but now I must most heartily congratulate you, my dear friend, on the complete success which has thus crowned your very ingenious and laborious exertions for the good of the service. I trust they may eventually prove as beneficial to yourself. I really feel sincere pleasure in making you this communication. I will now give you some details. I first had notice of your appearance from Elliot, who called out that he saw the light, and in fact, though five times more remote, you were much brighter and larger than the Randal's tower reflector.' I have given you a long extract, because I think it will interest and please vou. I have only to inform you now that the distance in a straight line between the two places is about sixty-seven miles.

"I had a letter from the Colonel to-day in London, very anxious to know the result of our labours. To-morrow I commence my retreat; on Monday I shall be in Derry, where I shall have to remain a day. . . . From Derry I proceed to Belfast, where I shall be detained two or three days, and then I make direct for Edinburgh. At Belfast I entreat you to let me hear from you, and I am anxious to hear how Eliza bore the journey from Callander, and how the house is. My last intelligence is her own letter, which I received about the 19th ultimo, on the evening succeeding a gale of wind, which overthrew two of our marquees, and set fire to our cooking-house. I have written you, my dear Mother, a long and gossiping letter, and it being now three o'clock in the morning, it is fit I should stop. To John and Eliza my kindest love, and to Eliza my best thanks for her kind letter. It may amuse my aunt to read this letter to her, and tell her that I add my best regards.—And now, my dear Mother, believe me your affectionate son,

"T. DRUMMOND."

Drummond's work on the Survey seriously impaired his health; and in the winter of 1825 he returned to Edinburgh an invalid. There he remained until the spring of 1826, when he repaired to London to carry out some experiments in connection with the light (which he now designed for use in lighthouses), and to attend to matters relating to the Survey. In the autumn of 1826 he resumed his duties in Ireland. In 1827 and 1828 he was engaged with Colby in measuring the base of Lough Foyle; and in the autumn of 1829 he returned to London to devote himself specially to the improvement of the light so that it might be used in lighthouses.

In a paper "On the Illumination of Lighthouses," published in the "Philosophical Transactions" of the Royal Society for 1830, he described the changes which had been made in the invention since 1826 ·

"[Plate II.,] fig. 1, represents the lamp. The two gases, oxygen and hydrogen,[1] proceeding from separate gasometers, enter at *o* and *h*, but do not mix till they arrive at the small chamber *c*, of which fig. 2 is a section; into this chamber the oxygen gas from the inner tube is projected horizontally through a series of very small apertures, and

[1] It will be observed that Drummond had now substituted hydrogen for alcohol. *Ante* p. 27.

the hydrogen gas rises vertically through a series of similar apertures at *d*. The united gases then pass through two or three pieces of wire-gauze placed at *c*, and being thus thoroughly mixed, issue through the two jets against the ball *b*. To prevent the wasting of the ball opposite the two jets, and at the same time to diffuse the heat more equably, it is made to revolve once in a minute, by means of a movement placed underneath the plate *m*, and with which the wire *f*, carrying the ball and passing through the stem, is connected. Notwithstanding, however, this arrangement, the effect of the heat is such as gradually to cut a deep groove in the ball, so that at the end of about forty-five minutes it becomes necessary to change it.[1] In a lighthouse where it is of essential consequence to maintain a constant light, it would be unsafe to entrust this to an attendant, and hence the necessity of devising some means for remedying this inconvenience. The apparatus represented by fig. 3 is designed for this purpose, and is drawn in the manner in which it is applied to a reflector, the dotted outline of which is shown.

"The wire *a*, *b* passes through the focus of the reflector, and upon it are placed the number of balls at *A*, required for any given time; these, by means of the shears *s*, as shown in fig. 4, are admitted between the plates *p*, *p*, and thence permitted to fall in succession to the focus. No. 1 represents the focal ball; about two minutes before the change, the ball 3 falls into the position 2, where it becomes gradually heated. At the end of that time, the curved support *t*, moving on a pivot, is thrown into the position represented by the dotted line, by the momentary descent of the ring *r*, which, receiving an impulse from the weight *w*, acts upon the extremity *u* of the support. No. 1 falls but is prevented from descending more than its own

[1] When a cylinder is used instead of a ball, a ring of minute crystals is found adhering to the surface above and below this groove.

diameter by the loop *l*, and No. 2 following it, occupies the focus. The support *t*, being immediately released, returns by the action of a spring to its former position, retains No. 2, and suffers No. 1 to escape through the loop into the cistern.

"The wire *a*, *b* and the support *t* revolve together, and carry round the focal ball, which is ignited as in fig. 1 by the two jets *z*, *z*. These jets, which are movable round the joints *d*, *d*, enter through small apertures cut in the sides of the reflector, and are easily adjusted to the proper distance from the ball.

"Wherever the light is required to be diffused equally around, the renewal of the lime may be effected still more easily by using a cylinder as represented in fig. 5, instead of a ball, which being gradually raised while revolving, brings fresh portions in succession opposite the jets. In a reflector, a cylinder occasions partial shadows at the top and bottom; still, however, the simplicity and certainty with which it may be renewed will probably entitle it to a preference even in this case.

"The apparatus for supplying the lamps with gas is represented in fig 6. It consists of two strong cylinders, *A*, 3 feet high, the one for oxygen, the other for hydrogen; the gas is compressed two or three times in each, the latter by being generated under pressure, the former by being pumped in. To each of these gas-holders a governor, *B*, is attached, of one of which a section is shown, by which means, whatever be the variation of pressure in the gas-holder, provided it exceed that of the governor, the gas will issue at *x* with a uniform and constant stream; in the present instance under a pressure of 30 inches of water. . . ."

During the winter of 1829 and the spring of 1830 experiments were tried under the directions of Trinity House, and upon one occasion, before the apparatus was in perfect working order, an explosion took place. Drummond's sister, on hearing of the accident, wrote warning him to be more careful in future. He replied playfully:—

DRUMMOND TO HIS SISTER.

"LONDON, *January* 16*th*, 1830.

"MY DEAR ELIZA,—A week, more than a week, has passed since I ought, and since I intended, to have answered your kind, kind letter; but every day and every evening has brought such constant occupation that I positively have not had time.

"The consequence, no doubt, has been many conjectures and much exercise to my dear mother, if the bell rang about post-time. Now, what have been your conjectures? Another explosion, perhaps, and the heir-presumptive,[1] along with all my beautiful apparatus, sent to the upper, or perhaps the under regions; or everything gone off well, and the Duke extremely delighted, expressed himself highly gratified, and intended conferring upon me some signal mark of his royal approbation! Well, to keep you in suspense no longer. The Duke was not present; he was unwell, and unable to leave his house. We were all prepared, for the messenger did not arrive till the last moment. The next Board day, when he is expected, is the 5th February. Meanwhile, we proceed with the experiments, and it is with them that I have been so much engaged this week. But this is Saturday evening, an evening of repose and enjoyment, and I have taken advantage of it to discharge my debt to you. I was grieved to hear of more colds and plasters, and I fear much that this fierce weather does not agree with you. . . .

"Do you ride? How is the pony? Has John re-

[1] The Duke of Clarence, afterwards William IV., who, in his character of Master of the Trinity Corporation, was expected to witness the experiments. —McLennan.

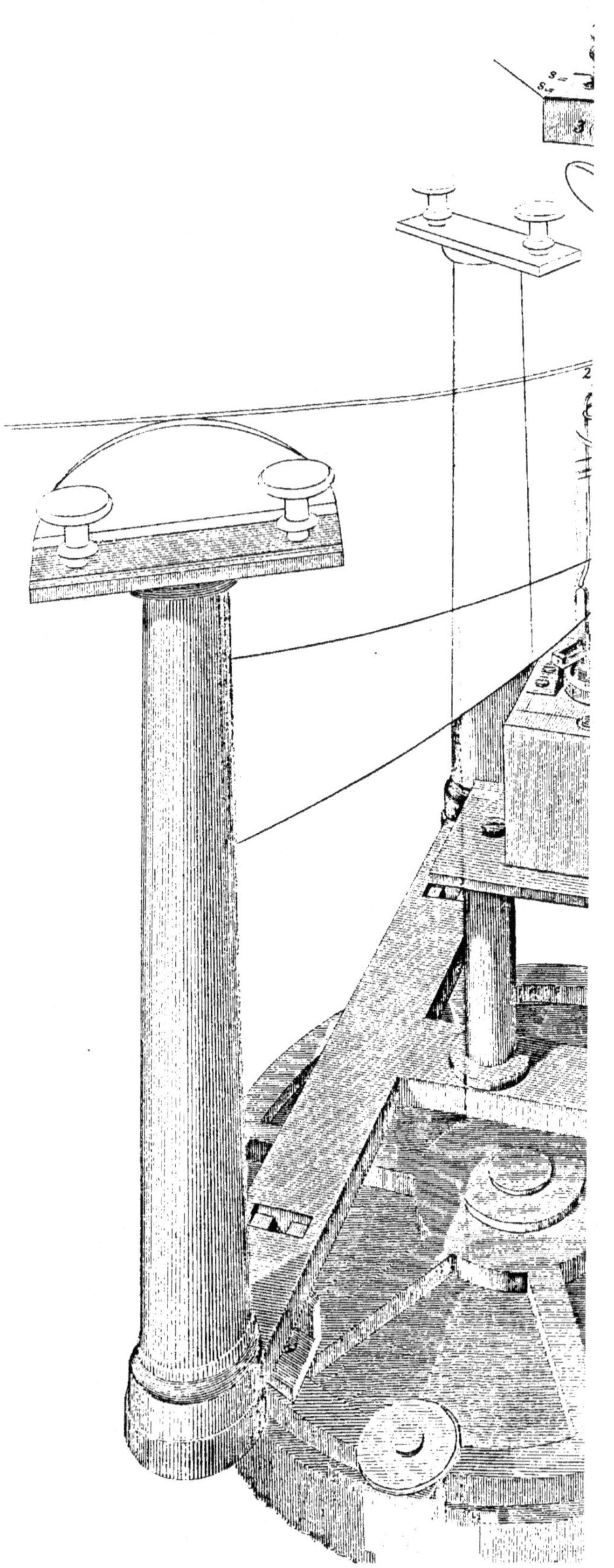
3
2

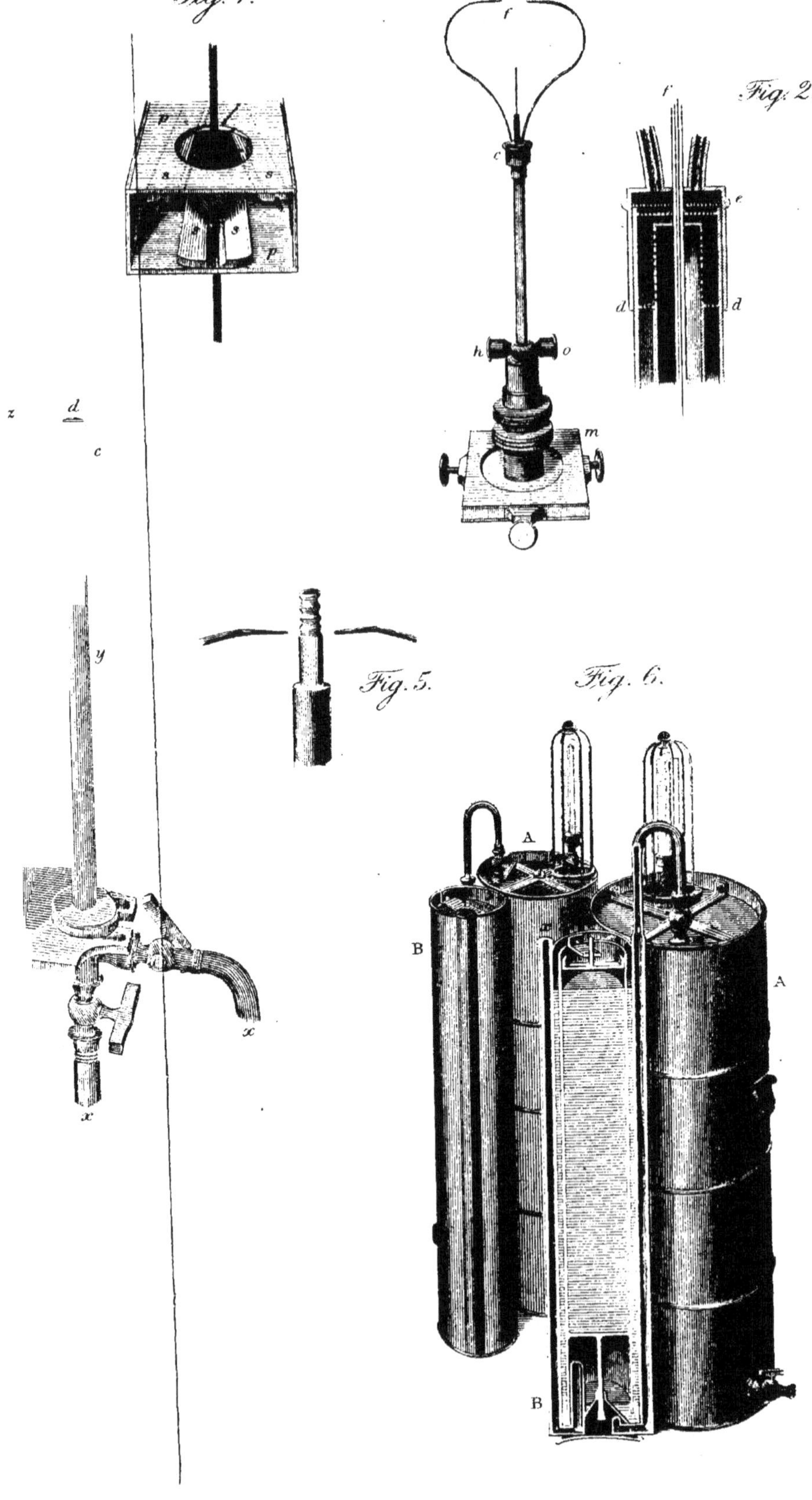

Fig. 2.
Fig. 5.
Fig. 6.
A
B

covered, and has he been laying down the law? I think you might manage among you to write a little oftener. There are some long gaps in our correspondence, and some long intervals during which I hear nothing of you. . . . Almost all my acquaintances have been ill, more or less. I have great reason to be thankful that I have been so well; indeed, notwithstanding all my work, I am in rude health, sleep but one sleep, and no palpitation. All the advice you gave me in your letter I acknowledge to be excellent, yet the exhibition was unavoidable, and so was the explosion. But I think they have got over it; if not, I will tell them the first time I have an opportunity of making a speech, that if I had been making an experiment before men unacquainted with the peculiar nature of such experiments, I should have declined proceeding under such circumstances; but before enlightened and intelligent men, whose indulgence and partiality I had more than once experienced, I could have no hesitation in trying even a first experiment, deeming it the best compliment I could pay them to show them the apparatus under the most disadvantageous circumstances. . . . My best and kindest love to you all at home.—Adieu, my dearest Eliza, and believe me, your affectionate brother,

"T. DRUMMOND."

In May 1830 the light was exhibited at the temporary lighthouse, Purfleet, and we have a graphic account of the experiment from Captain Basil Hall, R.N., in a letter to Drummond. Captain Hall witnessed the exhibition from the Trinity Wharf, Blackwall, a distance of 10¼ miles from Purfleet; and among the observers with him were Sir George Cockburn and Mr Barrow from the Admiralty, the Lord Advocate of Scotland, Sir Thomas Brisbane, Colonel Colby, Captain Beaufort, hydrographer to the Admiralty. Captain Hall wrote:

Captain Basil Hall to Drummond.

"St James's Place, *June* 1, 1830.

"My Dear Sir,—You wished me to take particular notice of last night's experiments with the different kinds of lights exhibited at Purfleet, and observed at the Trinity Wharf, Blackwall; but I have little to add to what I told you respecting those on the evening of the 25th instant; indeed, it is not within the compass of language to describe accurately the details of such experiments, for it is by ocular evidence alone that their merits can be understood.

"Essentially, the experiments of last evening were the same as those of the 25th, and their effects likewise. The degrees of darkness in the evenings, however, were so different, that some particular results were not the same. The moon last night being nine or ten days old, lighted up the clouds so much, that even when the moon herself was hid, there was light enough to overpower any shed upon the spot where we stood by your distant illumination; whereas on the 25th, when the night was much darker, the light cast from the temporary lighthouse at Purfleet, in which your apparatus was fixed, was so great, that a distinct shadow was thrown upon the wall by any object interposed. Not the slightest trace of any such shadow, however, could be perceived when your light was extinguished and any of the other lights were exposed in its place.

"In like manner on the evening of the 25th, it was remarked by all the party at the Trinity Wharf, that, in whatever direction your light was turned, an immense coma or tail of rays, similar to that produced by a beam of sunlight in a dusty room, but extending several miles in length, was seen to stream off from the spot where we knew the light to be placed, although, owing to the reflector being turned too much on one side, the light itself was not visible.

"Now, last night there was none of this singular appearance visible; but whether this was caused by the presence of the moonlight, or by the absence of the haze and drizzling rain which fell during the evening of the 25th, I cannot say. I had hoped that the appearance alluded to was to prove a constant accompaniment to your light, in which case it might, perhaps, have been turned to account for the purposes of lighthouses. If in hazy or foggy weather this curious effect of reflected light from the atmosphere be constant, it may help to point out the position of lighthouses, even when the distance of the observer is so great that the curvature of the earth shall render it impossible for him to see the light itself.

"The following experiments, tried last night, were the same as those of the 25th, and certainly no comparative trials could be more fairly arranged:—

"Exp. I. The first light exposed was the single Argand burner with a reflector. This was quite distinctly seen, and all the party admitted it to be a good light. After several minutes, this was put out.

"Exp. II. The seven Argand burners were next shown, each in its reflector; and this was manifestly superior to the first, but how much so I cannot say—perhaps four times as conspicuous. Both these lights had an obvious tinge of brown or orange.

"Exp. III. The third light which was exposed (on the seven Argands being put out) was that behind the French lens; and I think it was generally admitted by the party present that this light was whiter and more intense than that from the seven Argands, though the size appeared very much the same.

"Exp. IV. The fourth light was that which you have devised, and which, instead of the clumsy word "lime," ought to bear the name of its discoverer. The Drummond light, then, the instant it was uncovered, elicited a sort of shout of admiration from the whole party, as being something much more brilliant than we had looked for. The light was not only more vivid and conspicuous, but was peculiarly remarkable from its exquisite whiteness. Indeed, there seems no great presumption in comparing its splendour to that of the sun; for I am not sure that the eye would be able to look at a disc of such light, if its diameter were made to subtend half a degree.

"The next series of experiments was the most interesting and decisive of all. Each of the lights above enumerated, viz., the single Argand burner, the seven Argands, and the French lens, were exposed, one at a time, in company with your light, in order to try their relative brilliancy.

"First Comparative Experiment.—The single Argand burner was first exposed to this comparative ordeal, and nothing could be more pitiable than the figure it cut. Many of the party could not see the Argand light at all; while others could just detect it 'away in a corner,' as some one described it. It was also of a dusky orange tinge, while your light was of the most intense whiteness.

"Second Comparative Experiment.—The seven Argand burners were now substituted in place of the single light. All the party could now see both lights, but the superiority was not much less obvious. I really cannot affix a proportion either as to size or brilliancy; but I should not hesitate to say that your light was at least six or eight times as conspicuous; while in brilliancy or purity, or intensity of light (for I know not precisely what word to use to describe the extreme whiteness), the superiority was even more remarkable. All this which I have been describing was expressed, and appeared to be quite as strongly felt, by the rest of the company, to the number, I should suppose, of five-and-twenty or thirty persons, who were all closely on the watch.

"Third Comparative Experiment.—The next compara

tive trial was between the French lens and your light. The superiority here was equally undeniable, though the difference in the degree of whiteness was not so remarkable. The French light, however, is so nearly similar to that from the seven Argands, that the comparison of each of them with your light gave nearly the same results, and all equally satisfactory on the score of your discovery.

"Final Experiment.—The flashes with which the experiments concluded were very striking, and might, I think, be turned to great account in rendering lighthouses distinct from one another. The revolutions were not effective, and, as I said before, there was no appearance last night of those enormous comets' tails which swept the horizon on the night of the 25th, to the wonder of all who beheld them: neither could there be detected the slightest trace of any shadow from the light thrown towards us; and I suspect none will ever be seen, when the moon, whether the night be clouded or not, is of so great a magnitude.

"Such is the best account I can give of what we witnessed; and I need only add, that there seemed to be amongst the company but one opinion of the immense superiority of your light over all the others brought into comparison with it.—I am, &c., "BASIL HALL."

Up to the spring of 1831 Drummond continued engaged in trying experiments and improving the invention. The brilliancy of the light was established beyond all doubt, and the only question which remained, as to its suitability for lighthouse purposes, was one of expense. The result of his labours and the experiments he gives in a letter to his mother, dated January 22, 1831. He writes:—

"Truly this same light gives no small trouble. In the last paper which I sent to the Commissioners, I stated that the French light equals, if it does not surpass, the best of the lights in our lighthouses in splendour; while it is superior to them in economy and facility of management. This Stevenson either denies, or has hitherto been negligent in ascertaining. . . . The experiments at Inchkeith have been ordered by the Commissioners (of the Northern Lights), with a view to judge of the point themselves, and not trust to Stevenson's opinion. It is a question between the present method and the French light, not between mine and either. Their relative values have been ascertained by the Trinity House and Blackwall experiments, in a way which admits of no doubt. To recommence similar experiments would be mere trifling. There are obstacles in my way of a different kind, relating to the manufacture of the gas, management, &c., which I am now endeavouring to remove. With respect to brilliancy there can be no doubt."

About this time a copy of Drummond's paper on lighthouses, which had been read before the Royal Society, was presented to the King, William IV. We have an interesting account of this incident in a pleasant letter from Drummond to his mother.

Drummond to his Mother.

January 24, 1831.

"My Dear Mother,—I have begun with a sheet as long as your own, but whether I shall fill it as well is another question. The business part of your letter shall be first answered, and the remainder of the sheet devoted to amuse you. .

"Now, as you sent me a description of the lecture [most probably a lecture delivered in Edinburgh on the Drummond light], I mean to send you a description of another scene which may not gratify you so much, but which, I hope, will nevertheless interest you. Believe me, my dear Mother, the chief, perhaps the only pleasure which I received from the account of the lecture, arose from your being there to hear it; and if with you I mourn the absence of those, from sickness or from death, who would have participated in your feelings, still I am gratified that among those who did witness it, my dearest Mother was one. Now to return to my promised description, for one forgets there are limits to a sheet of paper.

"Among others to whom it was considered proper that a copy of my paper should be presented, was a certain illustrious personage called the King. Now, at the mention of this word away goes your imagination long before my description, and you conclude at once that I am on the high road to honour, rewards, emoluments, and so forth. Not so, however; yet have I had honour to a certain extent—as much as could with propriety be bestowed, and more than was expected. Well, then, the reason for presenting the paper to the King was, that his Majesty is still Master of the Trinity House, and had, as Duke of Clarence, been present at many of the experiments. It was necessary to obtain the King's permission to present the book in question, which he was graciously pleased to give to the Deputy-Master, Captain Woolmore, his old friend. Next came the question, how it was to be presented. I had intended sending a copy in its blue cover to Mr Woolmore for this purpose, but I was given to understand that that would not be according to etiquette; and it was finally resolved that the little pamphlet should be made into a little book, bound in morocco, and stamped with the royal arms; and furthermore, that I should accompany Captain Woolmore to Brighton, when he went to present the monthly report of the Trinity House to the King as Master.

"This being settled, another difficulty arose about uniform. Our uniform has been lately changed; it was considered improper not to go in uniform, and, alas! no alternative remained but that I should get the necessary paraphernalia without delay. Robe [a brother officer who at the time lived with Drummond], being like 'two single gentlemen rolled into one,' his garments are of no use to any one but the owner. With great exertion I got everything ready, and by Monday evening the 9th inst., I found myself at Brighton, where, according to arrangement, I met old Woolmore, who had come from another quarter the same evening. At ten the next morning we walked over to the palace, and put our names in the book of audience. One of the pages carried them to the King, who was still in the breakfast-room, and returned almost immediately, saying that the King desired we should have our breakfast; and that his Majesty would see us afterwards. As we had breakfasted previously, we declined the royal hospitality; but if we had not, we should then have been conducted to the room where the equerries breakfast, and where all strangers and visitors, coming, as we did, of the class of gentlemen and noblemen, are received. We were then conducted into the ante-room of the King's private room, and shortly afterwards he passed through, and we followed him into his room.

"He seated himself at a writing table, Woolmore and I standing at the opposite side. I then presented my book, and accompanied it with some explanation. I had, indeed, prepared a little speech for the occasion, but somehow or other I could not get it in. Nevertheless, I contrived to express the gratification which it afforded us to have had the honour of exhibiting some of the experiments before his Majesty, and to have witnessed the interest which he was pleased to take in them; and furthermore, I told him of the continuation of the experiments afterwards from the lighthouse at Purfleet, knowing full well that he would never look at the book, notwithstanding the above-mentioned interest, and I mentioned the remarkable fact of a shadow being cast at the distance of ten miles. Whereupon his Majesty was pleased to exclaim, 'God bless my soul; that's very wonderful!' Some further conversation ensued, and then he asked what I intended doing when I returned. I replied that having fulfilled the object of my visit to Brighton in being permitted the honour of presenting the paper to his Majesty, I had purposed returning to London that day. 'Are you particularly obliged to be in London to-day?' 'No, sir, only the usual routine of duty!' 'Then you will dine here to-day.' I bowed low. 'Woolmore will show you the way. We dine at seven.' I bowed and withdrew, leaving old Woolmore to finish his business. In the ante-room to which I returned there were several gentlemen waiting, to more than one of whom I heard the unpalatable information given, 'The King, sir, cannot see you to-day.'

"While waiting for Woolmore, one of the pages came and offered to conduct me round the Pavilion—a singular mixture of grandeur and simplicity. One room, spacious and lofty, contained gorgeous furniture, and splendid paintings; but the paintings represented nothing, I should apprehend, ever seen in this planet. Birds, beasts, and fishes glittered in gold, but were very unlike the beasts of the field, or the fowls of the air, such as we are accustomed to see them. Passing from this room—the music-room—which realises the description of the Arabian Nights, we entered a room of a character altogether different—low in the ceiling, neat, but simple, the furniture simple, and having a pretty cheerful appearance, though very different from that of its more gorgeous neighbour. From this we passed into a small music-room, similar to the first in shape, but equally simple in its character with the last; and thence into the drawing-room, commonly used when there is no party; and finally into the dining-room, another magnificent but fantastical room. Preparations were making in the different rooms for the ordinary occupations of the day. In one a portrait of the King, now executing by Sir William Beechy, was brought out. As we were entering one of the rooms, one of the pages whispered to my conductor that the Queen had just entered it, whereupon *we* did not enter.

"Old Woolmore meanwhile rejoined me, pleased with our interview, and gratified at the King having invited me to dinner. He dines on such occasions at the Palace as a matter of course, from his long previous intimacy with the King; but I fancy it is rather an unusual honour to confer on a subaltern. Well, we amused ourselves for the rest of the day walking about the town, calling on some people whom we knew, or rather whom Captain Woolmore knew; and, partly from what I was told, and partly from what I overheard, it was obvious what a matter of mighty moment it was to be received, and well received, at the Pavilion. A. had been invited when B. thought he ought to have been invited. Though the Duchess C. had left her name, no notice had been taken of her call; and so on. The world is the same everywhere, varying only in the scale. Most of these people are of large fortune, and of a station in society to secure them every comfort and happiness; but they are fashion's slaves, and miserable. So passed the day. The Earl of Errol had offered to send his carriage for us, which Captain Woolmore accepted; and having entreated me to be ready in time—though, to tell the truth, there was no great necessity for the caution, seeing I had no wish to have to walk into a room where King, Queen, and Countesses were at dinner, without knowing very well where to go to. However, I can go no further to-night—past twelve—candles smouldering in their sockets, and breakfast to-morrow morning at half-past eight. Good-night.

"Now, to return to the dinner party. My old friend went to his room to dress at half-past five o'clock, and at six o'clock his servant came to me to know if I were ready. He could not overcome his anxiety lest I should not be prepared at the moment, supposing, perhaps, that as one may always take a quarter of an hour at ordinary dinner parties, I might inadvertently, and from habit, do the same on this occasion. However, I relieved all his apprehen sions by entering his room, fully equipped or harnessed, at half-past six o'clock. The hour for the carriage, a quarter to seven—no carriage. Ten minutes to seven—no carriage. What shall we do? Wait three minutes more, and then walk, was my proposal. Enter the waiter—'Lord Errol's carriage is at the door, sir.' Doors fly open—waiters clear the way; enter the carriage, and next moment we are at the Pavilion, a splendid hall, and two rows of servants in the royal livery. We are conducted by a page to a long gallery or room. I have drawn a plan, to make the description more intelligible. In the long room was a single lady. Old Woolmore made his bow, and introduced me to the Countess of Mayo. She is the lady waiting on the Queen.

"Speedily ladies and gentlemen began to enter the room, almost all of them resident in the Palace, for it so happened that there were not above four or five strangers at dinner that day. It might be reckoned almost a family party in point of numbers, though the number amounted to thirty. Presently the Queen enters (by the door marked in the plan), leaning on the arm of her maid-of-honour—a very pretty girl, by-the-by. Ladies and gentlemen form into two rows on each side, to allow her Majesty to pass to the drawing-room. Then the King enters, bows to such of the gentlemen as happen to be near his side, and walks on to the drawing-room. Then the gentlemen enter the drawing-room, or walk about the gallery till dinner is announced.

Whether the King conducts the Queen or not, I cannot tell you, being too distant to notice that part of the ceremony. Be that, however, as it may, the King takes his seat at the middle of the table, ladies of the highest rank on his right and left. On this day the Landgravine of Hesse Homburg, Princess Elizabeth, and Lady Maryborough, were, I believe, the ladies. The Queen on the opposite side, Prince Leopold on her right, Lord Mayo on her left. At the two ends were two officers of the household, Sir Andrew Barnard and Sir Philip Watson.

"Where to go, where to place myself, was the difficulty. There were more gentlemen than ladies, therefore it did not fall to my lot to conduct any of them into the dining-room. Old Woolmore had the last. However, my embarrassment was very soon over, and I found myself very comfortably seated between two ladies—very pretty women; but who might they be — Mrs or Misses, Countesses or Duchesses? From this difficulty I was speedily relieved, by a gentleman on the left of one of these ladies introducing me to both of them. One of them, Miss Mitchell, a beauty, and maid-of-honour to the Queen; the other, Lady Errol, one of the Fitzclarences (daughter of the King and the late celebrated Mrs Jordan). To the gentleman I had been introduced before dinner by Woolmore, but I had not heard his name. I found out afterwards, however, that it was Sir Augustus D'Esté, the son of the Duke of Sussex and Lady Augusta Murray. I was still more indebted to him on our return to the drawing-room. D'Esté is a colonel in the army, and well acquainted with some of our principal officers; and he kept all around him at table in good-humour. He was kind, attentive, and polite to all within his reach. Lady Errol was pleasant and conversible, so that I speedily found myself, if not absolutely at home, yet unconstrained and unembarrassed.

"The King sets an example to the household in his attention to his guests. He asks them all to drink wine with him, from the highest to the lowest. Indeed, he asked me twice—the second time probably because he had forgotten the first. The dishes are brought round by servants, the dessert only being on the table, with magnificent gold candelabra and vases, etc.; the tablecloth is therefore not removed. Plates, silver; servants, of course, in great numbers, and exceedingly attentive. The Queen and the ladies rise, and leave the room; and after no great interval, the King rises, and is followed by the gentlemen, if they please, to the drawing-room.

"After the departure of the ladies, Sir Augustus D'Esté and I had a long chat; and after the King had withdrawn to the drawing-room, I was obliged to remind him that, as the scene was new to me, I was anxious to see what was going on in the drawing-room. 'I had almost forgotten,' he replied; 'but come, and I'll introduce you to some of the ladies.' Well, we entered the drawing-room, where ladies and gentlemen were dispersed much in the way they are in any other room. The ladies—many of them at work, but the conversation was in a low tone, no voice being heard except the King's. In the music-room there was obviously less restraint. The Queen's band occupied the room, and played at intervals. At one table sat the Queen, Lady Mayo, Miss D'Esté, Marchioness Wellesley, and some other lady. They were all employed in embroidering. On the opposite side sat the King and Lady Maryborough on a sofa; and the remainder of the ladies and gentlemen were disposed in groups, in different parts of the room; but it seemed, on entering the music room, as if they had laid aside a mantle of ceremony, and talked and chatted with less reserve. This cannot be a happy state of things, however, though very well to look at once.

"Well, the music ceases; presently the Queen rises.

The ladies form in two lines at the door, and the Queen kisses the cheek of each of her own ladies of honour. They in return kiss her hand. She then disappears. The King follows, and then—the devil take the hindmost.—Your affectionate son, "T. DRUMMOND."

Between 1831 and 1834 the subject of improving the illumination of lighthouses engaged public attention, and in this connection the Drummond light held a foremost place, in the opinion of experts and scientists.

In 1834 a Select Committee of the House of Commons was appointed to inquire into the state and management of lighthouses. Drummond was examined before this Committee, and stated with characteristic frankness the advantages and disadvantages of the light.

DRUMMOND.

"*Q.* State shortly the result of the experiments [which have been made with your light].

"*A.* The result of our experiments was, that a reflector, when lighted up in the manner I proposed, gave a light equal to about 264 times that given by a common Argand lamp.

"*Q.* State what is the principle of attaining that great increase of power.

"*A.* The principle is very different to any other hitherto used in the illumination of lighthouses; it consists in placing a lime ball in the focus of a reflector—

"*Q.* What size?

"*A.* About three-eighths of an inch in diameter, and igniting that ball by a mixture of two gases, hydrogen and oxygen. The light given out by lime, when intensely heated, is of dazzling brightness; it was found to be equal in intensity to about 264 times that of an Argand burner supplied with the best spermaceti oil.

"*Q.* Is the apparatus, by which this is supplied, complex?

"*A.* The apparatus is not itself complex, but there are circumstances attending the combustion which render it difficult to apply this mode at present in lighthouses.

"*Q.* In fact, its application with the men ordinarily kept at lighthouses you do not think could at present be safe?

"*A.* I do not.

"*Q.* It would require double the number of men, would it not?

"*A.* No. I do not think it would require more men, but it would require men of a different description.

"*Q.* It would require two men constantly attending the passing of the lime bodies down the rod?

"*A.* I have given up that mode of supplying the balls, and I have proposed another which I have not yet had an opportunity of trying, though the apparatus is complete. There are, it must be admitted, circumstances of some difficulty to be removed before the use of this method can be safely recommended for lighthouses.

"*Q.* Will you state the circumstances to which you allude.

"*A.* The circumstances to which I allude are, first, the rapid diminution of the ball by the lime becoming fused and volatilized, the difficulty therefore of replacing the lime; it requires some apparatus that shall keep up a constant supply and remove all that portion which has become useless; then if the lime was cracking or breaking, which it is sometimes liable to do, the heat of the mixed gases is so great that it would melt or injure any part of the apparatus which might be exposed by the removal of the lime, and the light would of course be extinguished. These, I think, are the chief circumstances of difficulty attending its management in the lantern;[1] the other cir-

[1] The other witnesses confirmed this opinion.

cumstance relates to the question of economy. The preparation of the gases is easy enough, but the materials from which they are prepared are bulky, and the situation of a lighthouse is very often such as to render the transport of materials of this description expensive."[1]

A few extracts from the evidence of other witnesses examined before the committee deserve to be quoted :—

JACOB HERBERT, *Secretary at Trinity House.*

"*Q.* Have you made any experiment upon Mr Drummond's light?

"*A.* We have.

"*Q.* What has been the result?

"*A.* There has been no decisive result. Mr Drummond was engaged in a course of experiments with a view to simplify, or rather to enable the practical adoption of his system; but I believe that circumstances have prevented his continuing those experiments, and the matter for the present rests.

"*Q.* In the experiments you have made have you found that Mr Drummond's light was visible at a much greater distance than any other you have tried before.

"*A.* The intensity of Mr Drummond's light far surpasses any we have seen."[2]

JAMES JARDINE, *Engineer.*

"*Q.* Drummond's light is seen in weather when you could not see another?

"*A.* Drummond's light will often be seen when no other artificial light has a chance of being seen."[3]

[1] "Parliamentary Papers," Vol. XII. for 1834, pp. 167, 168.
[2] *Ibid.*, p. 29.
[3] *Ibid.*, p. 124.

CHARLES CUNINGHAM, *Secretary to the Commissioners of the Northern Lighthouses.*

"There have been a series of experiments between the Calton Hill and Gullane, from which last station Mr Drummond's light is so strong that it reflects or throws a shadow on the road in Portobello, 12½ miles from the station." [1]

ALAN STEVENSON, *Clerk of Works to the Northern Lights Commissioners.*

"We next tried the Drummond light, which we found to be infinitely superior to any other light in point of power.

"*Q.* Was your object to obtain new results or to prove the result as stated by Lieutenant Drummond?

"*A.* It was partly both, but chiefly to try its effect in penetrating fog.

"*Q.* What did you establish?

"*A.* We established this very important point, that the Drummond light is visible in certain states of the atmosphere in which the reflector and the lens light are not seen. We proved this by showing all three lights—the French, the Drummond, and the reflectors—at one time, and observing them at the distance of 15 miles, as well as at the distance of 12 miles, and about 6 miles; we found that the Drummond light was quite visible when the others were so completely eclipsed as not to be seen at all." [2]

ROBERT STEVENSON, *Engineer to the Board of Commissioners of the Northern Lights.*

"The Drummond light greatly surpasses any other light yet produced by artificial means, in brilliancy and lustre [But] in the present form of the apparatus,

[1] "Parliamentary Papers," Vol. XII. for 1834, p. 94.
[2] *Ibid.*, p. 132.

it seems quite impossible to maintain a steady light of this splendid description for the purposes of the coast. The heat of the united flames of these gases is so intense that any substance yet applied to them is apt to be suddenly destroyed, and even platina, the most infusible of the metals, quickly melts before it. It is from this circumstance chiefly that the difficulty of making practical use of this light arises . . . . . Important advantages might doubtless be obtained by using this light during hazy weather, and the reporter[1] is resolved to spare no pains on his part to bring about its introduction into lighthouses. When the reporter looks back to his early trials with coal gas, which he believes he was the first to exhibit in an experimental form in Edinburgh, and contrasts the conceptions formed by himself and others regarding its general application to economical purposes, with the ease of managing it at the present day, he does not despair of the Drummond light being made applicable to lighthouses. All other lights seem, in any comparative view of intensity, to sink into insignificance; and this light approaches, in its properties, more nearly to solar light, than any other produced by artificial means."[2]

Finally, the Committee reported—

"[Lieutenant] Drummond stated to the Committee all the objections to the present use of his light in lighthouses; but your Committee are so strongly impressed with its importance, and with the merits and ability of Lieutenant Drummond, that they recommend that means should be adopted without delay for prosecuting still further the experiments recommended by him, and under his direction if possible; or if he cannot superintend them, then under some other fit person."[3]

[1] Mr Stevenson made a special report on the light.

[2] "Parliamentary Papers," Vol. XII. for 1834, Appendix, p. 117.

[3] *Ibid.*, Report, p. xxxiii.

But while the fate of the light was yet uncertain, and even when success seemed near at hand, Drummond glided into politics, and, in fact, abandoned the invention. This new departure of Drummond, at the crisis of his career as an inventor and a scientist, General Larcom has, in an eloquent passage, deplored. He says, "This abstraction of Mr Drummond's attention at the moment when he was nearest to success, must, so far as the light is concerned, be matter of regret; with its projector it has dropped; but if it be practicable, ingenuity will, doubtless, sooner or later, be directed to render it available, and the Drummond light may yet cheer the home-bound mariner from the Great Skelley, or the Tuskar."[1]

Two other inventions, which were used in the Irish Survey, deserve to be mentioned. They were a heliostat, designed by Drummond; and measuring bars, designed by Colby, and executed by Drummond.

In the paper published by the Royal Society in 1826, Drummond described the heliostat.

"[Plate III.,] fig. 1, represents [the instrument]; *ab* is a telescope of twelve-inch focal length, and serves as the axis of the instrument; the bars *bd* and *bc* form a right angle; and the bar *gg*, placed so that *bf* (fig. 2) shall be equal to *fg*, works between *bd* and *bc*, carrying a small telescope such as is usually attached to sextants, and provided with a rectangular eye-piece. The mirror *mm*, of which different sizes may be used, according to circumstances, is connected with the instrument by three adjusting screws *r*. The bars *bc*, and *b' c'*, being now made to coincide with *ab*, a movable spirit-level is placed across them in the position

[1] Memoir.

Dr Sullivan, President of the Queen's College, Cork, writes, under date April 1888:—"The Drummond light continues to be still used, though the name of the inventor is not usually associated with it. People speak of it generally under the name of the 'Lime Light,' the 'Oxyhydrogen Lamp,' &c." Letter *penès me*.

ll (fig 2), and rendered horizontal by the foot screws; by the same means the axis *ab*, to which a level is permanently attached, is also brought into a horizontal position. The movable spirit-level being now transferred to the surface of the mirror, the three adjusting screws *r* are employed to render it horizontal. The mirror will then be parallel to *ab* and *ll*, and will have the required position on the instrument. The telescope *ab* being now directed on the object to which the reflection is to be thrown, and the small telescope *gg* turned towards the sun, its rays will be reflected parallel to the axis of the instrument *ab*. The head of the screw *R* (fig 2) is graduated, so that by means of it, and the spirit-level attached to the axis, the required elevation or depression may be given to the instrument when the object towards which it is directed happens to be invisible, its direction only being known relatively to some nearer object; and which, it may be remarked, has been the case in every instance in which it has been employed on the Survey. When packed for travelling, the mirror *mm* is detached, and the bar *gg* turned till it coincides with *bf*. The instrument once directed, its management was usually confided to one of the non-commissioned officers."[1]

The measuring bars were an ingenious contrivance for measuring a base, and were first tried in the measurement of the base of Lough Foyle; the most accurately measured base in the world, according to Sir John Herschell.[2] It was for some time uncertain what share Drummond took in the invention. But the matter has been cleared up by General Larcom. He writes:—

"My conviction with regard to the relative shares of Colby and Drummond in the design and execution of

[1] "Philosophical Transactions for 1826." Drummond improved the heliostat, so that the telescope was finally dispensed with. Larcom, Memoir, "Enc. Brit."

[2] McLennan.

Fig. 1.

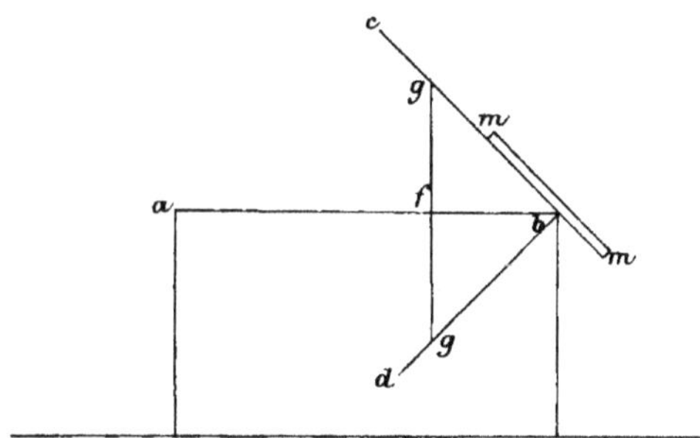

Fig. 2.

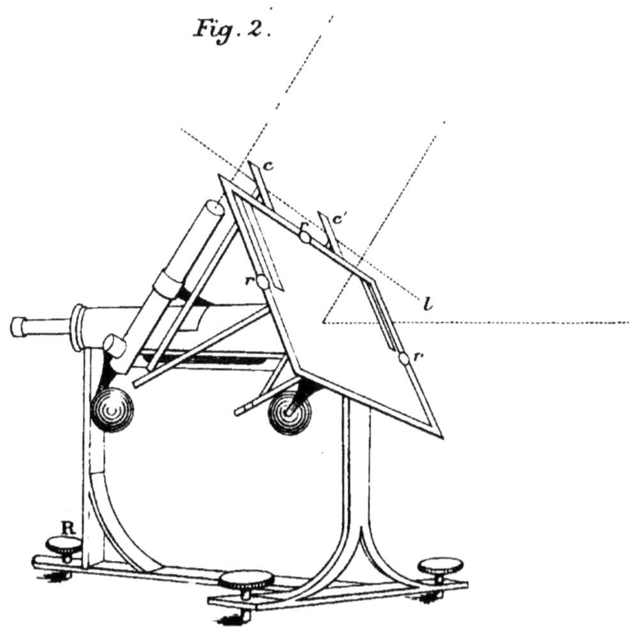

One Inch to One Foot.

those instruments is, that to Colby belongs the design, to Drummond the execution. Colby having himself used the previously existing English apparatus, and being familiar with the various instruments which had been used in the measurement of bases elsewhere, considered a new apparatus necessary. He resolved to adopt the compensation principle, and devised the form. He first satisfied himself the principle was sound, and tested the mechanical difficulties, which, he found, were all surmountable. He then devolved on Drummond the duty of superintending the construction, which Drummond, with the invaluable assistance of Troughton, successfully accomplished.

"The grounds on which I rest this statement of the relative shares of Colby and Drummond in the base apparatus are, personal knowledge and daily intercourse with all the parties concerned, having been myself one of the officers of the Tower at the time, and taking part in the early operations in the cold cellar and heated chamber, having been more than once at Troughton's with Colby, and often with Drummond in the evenings at Furnival's, where I also lived. No one at that time thought of Drummond as the inventor of the bars. He never claimed to be the inventor, and I believe, would have been the first to repudiate the idea.

"But that does not derogate from his merit. He made the bars, was the deviser and planner of the numerous and beautiful contrivances and experiments by which they were brought to perfection, and with his own hand executed most of the experiments. . . . I find among my letters from Colonel Dawson, in October 1840, when I was writing my own brief Memoir of Drummond, the following paragraph:—'Drummond's indefatigable exertions in the construction of the bars, and in the measurement of the base in Ireland, you are yourself aware of. The principle on which the compensation depends was suggested by Colonel Colby, and the means by which it should be supplied, but great credit is still due to Drummond for the ingenuity displayed by him in mastering many difficulties which were met with during the construction of the apparatus, and for the laborious experiments by which its perfection was at last established. Previous to the construction of the bars, Drummond had entertained the idea of using bands of talc for the purpose, and had made some experiments, which you may remember, at Furnival's Inn; and subsequently, on observing that the thermometers, when laid on the bars, do not immediately take and represent the actual temperature of the bars themselves, he suggested the use of thermometers instead of bars, to be made of a length suitable for the purpose. This idea, however, was, as you know, never worked out.'"

I have so far followed the course of Drummond's life to the close of his professional and scientific career. We now come to his entrance into politics, and his administration of Ireland at one of the most critical periods in the history of that country.

CHAPTER V

POLITICAL CONNECTIONS.

In 1831 Drummond met Lord Brougham, the Lord Chancellor, at the house of a mutual friend, Mr Bellenden Ker, a Chancery barrister. Brougham had heard of the Drummond light, and was anxious to see it. Ker arranged a small dinner party to meet the Chancellor, and Drummond was among the guests. After dinner he exhibited the light in the greenhouse, and he has given us a lively description of the scene.

Drummond to his Mother.

" . . By the way, I dined with the Lord Chancellor the other day, not at his own house, but at the house of an intimate friend of his, a Mr Ker, a Chancery barrister, to whom I was introduced some time ago, and with whom I have become very intimate. Mrs Ker is a pleasant woman, and their society is very agreeable. Well, the Lord Chancellor, it appears, had expressed a desire to see the brilliant light which he had heard of; and Mr Ker told him he dared say that I would show it him with pleasure. Accordingly, the Chancellor fixed a day to dine with him, and I put up the apparatus in Mr Ker's greenhouse, the lamp being directed to the drawing-room. There were only eight persons present, all intimate friends of Brougham's, so that the conversation, at and after dinner, about men and things, more especially the Reform question, was most entertaining and interesting. The

Chancellor was in great spirits, and talked the whole time. After returning to the drawing-room, I displayed the light, at which they expressed great admiration, though the Chancellor seemed greatly afraid of his eye, and could hardly be persuaded to look at it. I spied him, however, peeping at a corner, and immediately turned the reflector full upon him, but he fled *instanter*. He started immediately afterwards, at eleven o'clock, for Lord Grey's. . . ."

The acquaintance with Brougham ripened into friendship; and when, prior to the introduction of the third Reform Bill in 1832, a Boundary Commission was appointed to mark out the "rotten" boroughs for destruction and fix the new political areas, Drummond, on the suggestion of the Chancellor, was made its chairman.

How he did his work on the Commission may best be gathered from the letter addressed to him by his colleagues when the work was over.

"LONDON, *June 6th*, 1832.

"DEAR DRUMMOND,—We, who have been your fellow-labourers in the task intrusted to us by the Government, of recommending the proper limits for boroughs under the Reform Bill, entertain an anxious desire, before we separate on the completion of our labours, to express to you in some marked manner our esteem and admiration of your conduct of that work.

"We entertain no doubt that the Government will take the earliest opportunity of adequately discharging the great obligations it owes you, which can be duly appreciated only by considering the consequences if they had found in you anything short of the most perfect integrity, the most active zeal, and the most acute intelligence.

"But something would still be wanting to our own feelings, were we not to contrive some method of denoting our sense of the sound judgment and amiable manner which have marked your whole intercourse with us, making it a source of pleasure to ourselves, and contributing in no small degree to the perfection of the harassing duty in which we have been engaged.

"After much consideration on the most appropriate method of recording these feelings, we have resolved to request that you will do us the favour to sit for your portrait to one of the best artists of the day.

"We hope this will be preserved in your family as a memorial of the sense entertained of your merits by a number of gentlemen who have acted with you in the execution of a delicate and arduous duty, intimately connected with an important event in the history of our country. —We remain, dear Drummond, your attached friends,

"E. J. LITTLETON.
F. BEAUFORT, R.N.
L. B. ALLEN.
B. ANSLEY.
THOS. B. BIRCH.
H. R. BANDRETH.
J. J. CHAPMAN.
R. D. CRAIG.
ROBERT K. DAWSON.
J. ELLIOTT DRINKWATER.
J. F. ELLIS.
HENRY *G*AWLER.
H. BELLENDEN KER.
HENRY W. TANCRED.
G. B. LENNARD.
W. H. ORD.
JOHN ROMILLY.
ROBERT SAUNDERS.
RICHARD SCOTT.
R. SHEEPSHANKS.
W. EDWARD TALLENTS.
JOHN WROTTESLEY.
W. WYLDE."

Drummond sat to Mr Pickersgill for his portrait, which was finished in April 1835. In the meanwhile he began to take a keen interest in politics. His first political letters were written in 1832, when an election contest was impending in Perthshire, between Sir George Murray, Tory, and Lord Ormelie, Whig; and in Leith, between John Archibald (afterwards Lord) Murray, Whig, and Mr Aitchison of Drummore, Tory. Drummond's brother, John, threw himself with vigour into these contests in support of the Whig candidates. On July 12, 1832,

Drummond wrote to him respecting the struggle in Perthshire:—

DRUMMOND TO HIS BROTHER JOHN.

"I rejoice at any occurrence which calls forth your exertions and brings you into action. But I fairly own to you that I wish your exertions had been directed against another opponent than Sir George Murray. He is in every respect so estimable a man, and so fit to represent a county, especially in a reformed Parliament, that I regret his return being opposed. . . . Your calmness and good sense will prevent your being betrayed into any rash or unbecoming expression towards your opponents; but it is right that I should tell you that Sir George Murray is a man universally respected by all parties for his ability, moderation, and fairness, and therefore I hope you will be betrayed into nothing, either in word or deed, that is disrespectful towards him. I don't say this to damp your ardour in the cause in which you are embarked, because I am sure that it would be injured rather than promoted by any conduct which had the appearance of disrespect; I say appearance, because now that I have told you the opinion entertained of Sir George, I feel perfectly satisfied that your canvass for Lord Ormelie will never be conducted in a way offensive to Sir George or his friends."

In Leith, the Tory candidate was Drummond's old friend, Aitchison of Drummore;[1] and it pained Drummond to find himself and his family arrayed against the guide and benefactor of his youth. Reports had also reached him that Mr Aitchison had complained of the ingratitude of the Drummonds. Drummond at once wrote to his old friend:—

[1] *Ante*, p. 8.

DRUMMOND TO WILLIAM AITCHISON OF DRUMMORE.

"COUNCIL OFFICE, WHITEHALL,
"*Sept.* 14*th*, 1832.

"MY DEAR SIR,—Having, after twelve months' severe and anxious toil, brought our labours to a close, I have transmitted to Scotland a copy of our Reports on the Boundaries of the Boroughs of England and Wales, which I request you will do me the favour to accept.

"I send these volumes to you, not with any reference to their political nature, but as I have sent my former papers, as marks of respect and regard for my early friend and benefactor.

"It is but right, however, that I should take the same opportunity of adverting to a circumstance of a less agreeable nature, and one which has occasioned me considerable pain.

"I have heard that the part which my brother has taken with respect to Mr Murray's election has occasioned you much surprise, and that you have expressed much dissatisfaction, perhaps I might say indignation, at his conduct. I sincerely hope, indeed I firmly believe, that this is a very incorrect or a very exaggerated statement.

"I am well aware that any assistance which my brother can render Mr Murray must be of very small amount, and that it is to the disposition evinced by the act that your observations have been directed, if, indeed, any such have been made. In common justice to him, therefore, and in some measure to myself, I would solicit your attention to a very few observations.

"I am well aware that the political opinions either of my brother or of myself must be a matter of perfect indifference to you; nor would I allude to them at all, but that I cannot help feeling that you are disposed to attribute less influence to such opinions than they usually possess—and, as it appears to me, they ought to possess—over the mind and actions of any man who has sufficient judgment to be able to form an opinion at all, and sufficient honesty and firmness to act according to it. You will, I trust, pardon me for saying that the consequence is, you are, perhaps, apt to suppose that disrespect and ingratitude are manifested in that conduct, which is the result of very different and much more worthy motives.

"The opinions which we hold were not taken up yesterday or to-day—they were constantly avowed, so far as is possible to men who hold no public situations—that is, by discussion with their friends and associates; and they were held, too, when they were not the road either to favour or preferment. If they have brought us into connection with men who have ever been the consistent and powerful advocates of such opinions, I think we are bound, in common with every individual who entertains the same opinions, to use our utmost exertions, however feeble these may be, in favour of such men—even if, by so doing, we should have the misfortune to be brought into opposition—I do not say into collision, for I hope and trust that is not necessary—with those with whom we are connected by the dearest ties of relationship or of friendship.

"Mr Murray and myself were engaged last winter in the same political work; we met nearly every day; and, warmly attached as I am to the principles of which he has long been a strenuous supporter, I could not, without forfeiting every feeling of self-respect, hesitate to render, if required, my zealous though feeble assistance to promote his return to Parliament, in opposition to any man of contrary opinions, even if that man should unfortunately prove to be my nearest relative or my most intimate friend. The same considerations had necessarily the same influence over my brother.

"I am not ignorant that the firm adherence to opinions

may sometimes require many a painful sacrifice, and lead to many a painful separation between relatives and friends; but this, I trust, can only happen when there are any who are resolved not to discriminate between the obligations resulting from the relations of society, and those which, in the discharge of a political right, are imposed by an honourable and consistent maintenance of conscientious opinion. Fortunately, instances of such discrimination, alike honourable to both parties, are not rare; and, indeed, among my own relations, I see a complete division of a family in political subjects, without any interruption of the duties or the pleasures of family intercourse.

"Whatever my brother does, he will do openly and honourably, and I earnestly request you dispassionately to consider the circumstances which I have stated, and then I cannot doubt but you will, with your accustomed liberality and kindness, do justice to the motives which have influenced us on this occasion.

"I feel that I have trespassed on your time and indulgence by this explanation, which I have endeavoured to make, and, I trust, have made, with that deference and respect not only due from me, but which I most unfeignedly feel towards you, my old and valued friend. May I beg my best respects to Mrs Aitchison, who, I sincerely hope, is tolerably well?—And I remain, my dear sir, with great respect, very faithfully yours,

"T. DRUMMOND."

Aitchison appreciated the motives which influenced Drummond, and their friendship was not disturbed by political differences.

In April 1833 Lord Althorp, then Chancellor of the Exchequer in the Grey Ministry, asked Drummond to become his private secretary. Drummond hesitated to accept this offer, being unwilling to give up his professional career. Lord Althorp pressed, saying that his wish was also the "united wish of the cabinet," and Drummond, having taken counsel with his friend Ker, finally accepted the post. He was now fairly launched in public life; and, among public men, his greatest friend was Brougham.

In the autumn of 1833 the Chancellor invited him to Brougham Hall, Westmoreland. He was doubtful as to accepting the invitation, but Brougham would take no refusal. His secretary wrote to Drummond: "He seems determined that you *shall* go; and he adds, when you are together you can do a good stroke of work. He also says that he has written to the king, strongly adverting to your services, 'a strong panegyric on Drummond's services about the Borough Bill.'[1] You must come. I know from experience that when he once sets his heart on any thing, there is no rest till he has his way." Drummond went, and remained with the Chancellor until October, when both returned to town together.

About this time Drummond met, at Weston House, Warwickshire, the seat of Sir George Philips, his future wife, Miss Kinnaird, the attractive and accomplished ward of Richard Sharp—a man whose character Harriet Martineau has described in a few pithy sentences. "When a man of business is a man of letters, and finds himself equally at home in a London drawing-room, and in the country house, he contributes a large portion to the respectability of his country, where such a union of pursuits is not so common as it ought to be. Richard Sharp, commonly known as Conversation Sharp, was a man of this order. He was partly occupied with commercial concerns, . . . yet Sir James Mackintosh declared him the best critic he ever knew. He published letters and

[1] A Bill based on the report of the Boundary Commission.

essays which justified his position as a man of letters; he had a seat in Parliament for several years,[1] and was the associate of the most eminent literary men of his time. He died in old age in 1835."[2]

In 1834 a political crisis occurred, and the Grey Ministry went to pieces over the Irish question.[3] On May 6, 1834, Lord John Russell declared in the House of Commons, in reply to the question of an Irish member, "that, if the State should find that the revenues of the Irish Church are not appropriated justly to the purposes of religious and moral instruction, it would be the duty of Parliament to consider a different appropriation." "Johnny has upset the coach," wrote Stanley in a note to Graham. A month later Lord Althorp moved that a commission should be appointed to inquire into the state of the Church, and to consider the whole question of the Establishment. Stanley opposed the motion, which, however, was carried, whereupon he, Graham, Lord Ripon, and the Duke of Richmond left the ministry.

In July there were differences again in the Cabinet on the Irish question. Lord Grey desired to renew a Coercion Act[4]—the most stringent of its kind, perhaps, passed since the Union—which had become law in 1833. O'Connell was opposed to this measure, and announced his determination to resist it by every means in his power. Wellesley, Brougham, Althorp, and Littleton, who had now become Irish Secretary, were disposed to compromise the question by omitting the most stringent clauses of the Act. O'Connell was willing to accept

[1] He was elected for Castle Rising, in Norfolk, in 1806. He remained in Parliament until 1818.

[2] "History of the Peace," ii. 463.

[3] The chief members of the Grey Ministry were: Lord Grey, Lord Brougham, Lord Althorp, Lord John Russell, Lord Palmerston, Lord Lansdowne, the Duke of Richmond, Sir James Graham, and Mr Stanley.

[4] The Act enabled the Lord Lieutenant to proclaim districts, to prohibit public meetings, and to establish martial law.

this compromise; and negotiations were opened with him by Wellesley, Brougham, Althorp, and Littleton, without the knowledge of Lord Grey.[1] O'Connell was led to understand, that the Act would not be renewed in all its rigour, and in return for this concession, he withdrew a Repeal candidate who had been started for Wexford. But the efforts of Wellesley, Brougham, Althorp, and Littleton failed to change the determination of Lord Grey. On July 1, he proposed the renewal of the Coercion Act in the House of Lords. On July 3, O'Connell, feeling that he had been deceived by Littleton, told the whole story of the negotiations which had been opened with him to the House of Commons. Lord Grey was shocked to find that his colleagues had kept him wholly in the dark respecting these proceedings, and complained bitterly. On July 5, Littleton resigned. On July 7, Althorp resigned. On July 9, Grey retired from office, and his ministry came to an end.

On July 14-17, the first Melbourne administration was formed. Althorp returned as Chancellor of the Exchequer, Brougham remained Lord Chancellor, and Littleton was again made Irish Secretary. The other principal ministers were Lord Lansdowne, Lord Duncannon, Lord Palmerston, Lord John Russell, Sir John Hobhouse, and Mr Spring Rice and Mr Charles Grant. This ministry was short-lived. In November 1834 Lord Spencer died; Lord Althorp succeeded to the title, and left the House of Commons. The King, whose confidence was given to Althorp alone, at once dismissed the ministers, and sent for the Duke of Wellington. The Duke despatched a courier to Italy to bring back Sir Robert Peel, who was then in Rome; and in the meanwhile seized the keys of office. Drummond gives us a brief but graphic account

[1] Littleton conducted the negotiations. I have given a full account of this transaction in "Fifty Years of Concessions to Ireland." Vol. i., pp. 466, 469.

of the crisis. Writing from Downing Street on November 18, 1834, he says:—

"Great bustle at the different offices. The Duke has exhibited some promptitude in taking possession of the Home Office, but all the other appointments are yet undecided. The great seal is to be held provisionally. The seals of the different Secretaries of State are held provisionally by the Duke; and in fact everything is provisional until Peel returns. If a good spirit manifests itself in the meantime, it is possible that they may find greater difficulties than they now imagine in the way of forming a government. Peel has more sagacity, and less courage than 'His Highness,' and may not be disposed to enter upon the desperate course which the latter seems resolved to attempt. Without Peel's assistance it is over with him. Meanwhile the Duke is doing what he can: he has shown the most indecent haste to seize the seals of the Secretaries of State, and even sent for their Cabinet keys on Monday last, immediately after the Council. There is much more the appearance than the reality of vigour in this, and it simply disgusts people, even those who are against us. But it is in keeping with the political character of a man who has discovered that large Church reform is necessary, and who has found a worthy supporter in that profligate and perfidious journal, the *Times*."

On November 21, he again writes:—

"We consider the dissolution inevitable, and are preparing accordingly. The accounts from the country and from our friends are very satisfactory. They are preparing quietly, but actively and energetically, for the approaching election. The same will be done in Scotland. It is from the North, from Scotland, and Lancashire, that the spirit will come. I hope Mr Maclaren will not attack the Radicals at the present moment. It is quite true what he says; but they are sensible of their errors, and this is not the moment to exasperate, but to soothe and conciliate. If there are any district committee-rooms to which you would wish the *Chronicle* or *Globe* to be sent, let me have the names, and it will be done. The *Chronicle* advances rapidly, so does the *Globe.* The *Times* quails and wavers, as such a miserable deserves to do. . I wrote to the Lord Advocate yesterday; pray tell him that I had a long conversation to-day with Mr Abercromby, who thinks the greatest caution must be observed, to prevent its being supposed that any committee is formed for the purpose of managing the elections in Scotland. As little as possible should be said, and it should be given out, that it is merely for the purpose of distributing information. The subject to which this refers was what I wrote about to the Lord Advocate yesterday. He will understand it, and tell you."

In December Peel returned from Rome, and formed a government of which the principal members were Wellington, Lyndhurst, Aberdeen, and Goulburn. In the same month Parliament was dissolved.

The general election which ensued was unfavourable to ministers.

The numbers were :—

England.

Tories	212
Whigs and Radicals	288
	500

Scotland.

Tories	13
Whigs and Radicals	40
	53

Ireland.

Tories	39
Whigs and Repealers	66
	105

Peel, however, resolved to meet Parliament and to join issue with the Whigs on the floor of the House of Commons. The Whigs resolved to give battle on the question of the election of Speaker. The Government proposed the former Speaker, Sutton; the Whigs proposed a Scotch member, Abercrombie. Drummond had been at Brighton in ill-health since the end of 1834. In February 1835 he returned to London, and on the 15th of that month wrote to his mother:—

"On Thursday, as everybody knows, the battle begins. I think we shall beat them on the Speaker. The numbers on Saturday pledged to support Mr Abercrombie were 318."

The "battle" took place on February 19, 1835. The numbers were:—

Abercrombie, ...	316
Sutton, ...	306

Peel, however, resolved to hold on.

On February 24 the Whigs returned to the charge, and Lord Morpeth moved an amendment to the Address which was carried by 309 to 302. Still Peel cried no surrender. On March 20 Sir Henry Hardinge, Irish Secretary, brought forward a measure of tithe reform for Ireland, the essential feature of which was the conversion of tithes into a rent charge of 75 per cent. of the tithe. This was making a flank movement on the Whigs; but Lord John Russell was equal to the occasion. He out-flanked Hardinge by moving as an amendment, on March 30, "That the surplus revenues of the Established Church should be applied in some way by which the moral and religious improvement of the people of Ireland might be advanced." This amendment was carried by 322 to 289 votes. But Peel did not take the defeat as decisive. Russell, however, now resolved not to give the Government breathing time. On April 3 he moved, "That the surplus revenues of the Established Church in Ireland ought to be locally applied to the general education of all classes of Christians in Ireland," and the motion was carried against ministers by 178 to 140 votes. Nevertheless Peel refused to give way. Russell now made a final attack.

On April 7 he moved, "That it is the opinion of this House that no measure upon the subject of tithes in Ireland can lead to a satisfactory and final adjustment which does not embody the principle of the foregoing resolution."[1] Peel mustered his forces to resist this last assault, but in vain. He was beaten by 285 to 258 votes, and at length resigned.

The King, who had dismissed Melbourne in November 1834, was obliged to send for him in April 1835, and Melbourne formed his second administration—an administration famous in the history of Ireland. Its members were:

ENGLAND.

Cabinet.

Viscount MELBOURNE,	. *First Lord of the Treasury.*
Marquess of LANSDOWNE, .	. *President of the Council.*
Viscount DUNCANNON, .	. *Privy Seal.*
T. SPRING RICE, .	. *Chancellor of the Exchequer.*
Lord JOHN RUSSELL,	*Home Secretary.*
Viscount PALMERSTON,	*Foreign Secretary.*
Lord GLENELG, .	*Colonial Secretary.*
Lord HOLLAND,	*Duchy of Lancaster.*
Sir J. C. HOBHOUSE,	*President of the India Board.*
Earl of AUCKLAND,	*First Lord of the Admiralty.*
C. POULETT THOMSON,	*President of the Board of Trade.*
Viscount HOWICK,	*Secretary of War.*

[1] Of April 3.

Not in the Cabinet.

Marquess of CONYNGHAM, .	*Lord Chamberlain.*
Lord C. FITZROY, ...	*Vice-Chamberlain.*
Duke of ARGYLL, ...	*Lord Steward.*
Earl of LICHFIELD .	*Postmaster-General.*
Earl of ALBEMARLE,	*Master of the Horse.*
Mr LABOUCHERE, .	*Master of the Mint.*
Hon. *G.* S. BYNG, .	*Comptroller of the Household.*
E. S. STANLEY, . .	*Secretaries to the Treasury.*
FRANCIS BARING, .	
Sir JOHN CAMPBELL,	*Attorney General.*
Sir C. ROLFE, .	*Solicitor General.*
Earl of ERROL, ...	*Master of the Buckhounds.*
Sir H. VIVIAN, .	*Master General of Ordnance.*
Sir H. PARNELL,	*Treasurer of the Navy.*
CHARLES WOOD,	*Secretary to the Admiralty.*

Lords of the Treasury.

Lord SEYMOUR.	Mr R. MORE O'FERRALL.
Mr ORD.	Mr R. STUART.

IRELAND.

Earl of MULGRAVE,	*Lord Lieutenant.*
Lord PLUNKET, .	*Lord Chancellor.*
Viscount MORPETH,	*Chief Secretary.*
Mr PERRIN, .	*Attorney General.*
Mr O'LOGHLEN,	*Solicitor General.*

While Lord Melbourne was forming his government, Pickersgill was giving the final touches to Drummond's portrait. It was finished in April 1835, and forwarded to his mother by Littleton, with this letter.

"GROSVENOR PLACE, *April* 10, 1835.

"MADAM,—I believe you have been informed that the gentlemen associated with Mr Drummond in the late Boundary Commission resolved, at the conclusion of their labours, to offer to him some testimony of their admiration of the talents he had exhibited in directing the proceedings of that Commission, and of the great personal regard they entertained towards him.

"After much consideration, it was thought a preferable course to ask him to sit for his portrait, and when finished to present it to you. We found that such a present would be more agreeable to him than any other, and we did not doubt it would be most gratifying to you. Mr Pickersgill, the best of our artists, was accordingly employed to paint a bishop's half-length portrait of him, which he has executed with remarkable fidelity.

"It was our original intention to have had a mezzotint engraving made from it, in order that each of Mr Drummond's fellow-commissioners might have had a copy of it. Lord Althorp, Lord Brougham, Lord Lansdowne, and various others of Mr Drummond's political friends, equally desired to possess themselves of a likeness of one to whom they were attached, in common with ourselves, by a sense of obligations, and by personal regard. But your son so perseveringly insisted on the abandonment of this part of the design, that I was obliged to take upon myself to suspend the order to the engraver, who had actually commenced the work.

"It now only remains for me, in the name of all the Boundary Commissioners, to place the portrait in your hands, and to express my hope that it may long remain in your family as a record of the public and private esteem towards your son, entertained by a body who were associated with him in an honourable and highly important public trust.

"The portrait will leave town in a few days.—I have the honour to be, Madam, with great respect, &c.,

"E. J. LITTLETON."

All the posts in the Melbourne Ministry were now filled; but there was one office connected with the Government of Ireland which invited attention—the office of Under Secretary at Dublin Castle.

Sir William Gossett was Under Secretary when the Melbourne Ministry came into power. But the friends of the Administration saw that a change was necessary ; that some one, untrammelled by the traditions of the place, should be appointed. "My Lord," said Mr Perrin, the Irish Attorney General, to Lord Mulgrave, "[the Under Secretary] will be your right eye, and if we have to spend our time plucking old beams out of it, your Government will not go straight." [1]

I do not know how it came about that Drummond's name was first mentioned in connection with the office, but by degrees he was marked out for the post. Of course he was well known to the Ministry. He had received a pension of £300 for his work on the Boundary Commission; and in the report of the Select Committee on Pensions at a later date his services were referred to thus :—

"Lieutenant Drummond was a distinguished officer of the Royal Engineers, whose abilities had been shown, not only in the Trigonometrical Survey of Ireland, and the more peculiar branches of his 'profession,' but in the prosecution of various branches of science, in which he has made useful and interesting discoveries. He was employed in the Government of Lord Grey in procuring the statistical information on which the Reform Bill was founded, as well as in determining the boundaries and districts of boroughs. Those services were rendered gratuitously. He was afterwards employed in preparing a Bill for the Better Regulation of Municipal Boroughs. Finally, he was employed from April 1833 to April 1834 as private secretary to Lord Althorp, Chancellor of the Exchequer."

It is probable that Drummond himself was anxious to go to Ireland. His friends suggested other posts ; but, as his mother said, he had "a partiality for Ireland." [2]

[1] Torrens' "Melbourne."

[2] Letter, *post.*

There are few letters among the family papers that throw light on the subject, but some may be quoted :—

SIR DENIS LE MARCHANT TO DRUMMOND.

"THE VINE, BASINGSTOKE, *Thursday* [*April* 1835].

"MY DEAR DRUMMOND,—You could not find a better person than Carter to speak to on such an occasion. I have no doubt that he will influence Spring Rice, who, with all his good nature, is the person most likely to throw cold water on any generous exertions of his colleagues. By the way, I think a visit to Brougham would be no harm. You are one of the few persons he really likes, and as your interest and his do not come into collision he probably will exert himself for you. At all events he will be pleased to perceive that you continue to think him of importance. No man is more alive to such a feeling than he is. He is flattered by confidence. . . .—Always yours most truly,

"DENIS LE MARCHANT."

LORD MORPETH TO DRUMMOND.

"WAKEFIELD, *May* 7 [1835].

"MY DEAR DRUMMOND,—They must give you to me and Ireland. I have written to Lord Melbourne. I hope and believe that we are going to do better than Devon.—Ever sincerely yours,

"MORPETH."

Drummond's mother wrote to him :—

"16 SHANDWICK PLACE,
"21*st May* 1835.

"MY DEAR TOM,—This day brought us your anxiously looked for letter. You must write oftener, even though you have little to say. A person told us to-day, before your letter arrived, that they had read in a Glasgow paper of your arrival in Dublin at the Castle, so you may easily

imagine how feelingly alive and nervous we are at all these rumours. I would just like to know what are your own hopes; if you think the appointment is to take place or any other in lieu of it. . . . I daresay your going to Ireland would be much to Lord Morpeth's wish. . . . I can well believe it is no easy matter to dispose of Gossett, as he is a King's favourite. His brother is chaplain to the Royal Family at Windsor, but this is a reason for getting him to some less eligible station than where he is. Do you see that the Lords are up in arms at the brilliant entry[1] given to Lord Mulgrave. What anger has been displayed
I only wish to add, what do you think yourself as to the Irish appointment? To us it appears you are quite cut out for it, and that the sooner Government can send you there the better, as the place is ill supplied by such a Tory, and must retard public business very much by the present Under Secretary. . . .—Your affectionate mother,

"E. DRUMMOND."

"*P.S.*—I hope if you have any other place in your choice you will not reject it without weighing well all things for and against it. Your partiality for Ireland may lead you to underrate a less glaring, but perhaps better place in many respects. In saying we think you cut out for it, I fear lest we may help to mislead you, more especially as it may agree with your own wishes. This day's paper speaks of Lord Morpeth's going immediately to Ireland. Once more adieu. God bless you."

Drummond's "partiality for Ireland" prevailed, and before the end of June he was appointed Under Secretary at Dublin Castle.

In the same month he became engaged to Miss Kinnaird; and in July set out for Ireland.

[1] Into Dublin.

CHAPTER VI.

IRELAND IN 1835.

DRUMMOND found Ireland in 1835 seething with discontent. Catholic Emancipation had enraged the Orange faction, and had not satisfied the masses of the people. The measure had been grudgingly granted, and unwillingly carried out. It brought no peace. In truth, it remained practically a dead letter until Drummond came. Mr Lecky has stated the case with characteristic clearness and force. "In 1833—four years after Catholic Emancipation—there was not in Ireland a single Catholic judge, or stipendiary magistrate. All the high sheriffs with one exception, the overwhelming majority of the unpaid magistrates and of the grand jurors, the five inspectors-general, and the thirty-two sub-inspectors of police, were Protestant. The chief towns were in the hands of narrow, corrupt, and, for the most part, intensely bigotted corporations. Even in a Whig government, not a single Irishman had a seat in the Cabinet, and the Irish Secretary was Mr Stanley, whose imperious manners and unbridled temper had made him intensely hated. For many years promotion had been steadily withheld from those who advocated Catholic Emancipation, and the majority of the people thus found their bitterest enemies in the foremost places"[1] This was the case in 1833, and it continued in the main to be the case until 1835.[2]

[1] Lecky, "Leaders of Public Opinion in Ireland," p. 260.

[2] The first Melbourne Ministry (July 1834) showed a disposition to break the system of ascendency, but it was a Government without backbone, and did nothing.

In 1831 the tithe war began.[1] Six millions of Catholics refused to pay tithes to the Church of six hundred thousand Protestant Episcopalians. The Government supported the Church with all its strength. Horse, foot, police, and even artillery scoured the country to collect the tithes. The people resisted, and a struggle, to which Englishmen look back with shame, was the result.

In March 1831, a troop of the 1st Dragoon Guards, a detachment of the 21st Fusiliers, and a strong force of police were despatched to collect tithes in the parish of Graigue. The peasants offered a passive resistance; all attempts to seize their cattle failed; and, after a campaign of two months, the military and police retired, having collected only one-third of the tithes of the whole parish.

In June, some cattle seized for tithes were put up for sale at Newtownbarry. The peasantry gathered in great force, and rescued the cattle from the police. The Yeomanry were called out, and fired on the peasants, killing twelve, and fatally wounding twenty. But no sale took place. The peasants were shot down, but the law was not enforced.

During July and August vigorous efforts were made to collect tithes in the County Tipperary, but without success. As at Newtownbarry, the peasants were shot down, but the law was not enforced.

At Kilkenny and Castlepollard peasants and police again came into collision. The chief casualties were again on the side of the peasants; but the enforcement of the law was again successfully resisted. Tithes could not be collected; processes could not be served; cattle seized for tithes could not be sold.

But the fiercest of these tithe encounters took place at Carrickshock in December 1831. Peasants and police met

[1] I have dealt fully with the subject of the tithe war in "Fifty Years of Concessions to Ireland" (vol. i., book iii.), and shall but refer to it briefly here.

face to face; pitchforks and slanes were pitted against bayonets. A hand-to-hand conflict ensued. The chief of the police was killed; the leader of the peasants was killed; the police were completely routed. Eleven policemen were killed and seventeen wounded. This affair of Carrickshock brought about a truce which, however, lasted only for a few months.

In April 1832, a cow seized for tithes was put up for sale at Doon, in the County Limerick. Sixty men of the 12th Lancers, five companies of the 92d Highlanders, a strong force of police, and two pieces of artillery were in attendance. The peasants fell upon the police, and drove them out of the village. The Lancers and Highlanders charged and fired upon the peasantry, scattering them over the fields, wounding many, but killing none. The cow was "knocked down" to the owner's brother for £12.

In May, thirteen cows were put up for sale at Rathcormac, in the County Cork. Two companies of the 5th Foot and two companies of the 92nd Highlanders were present. But no sale took place. No auctioneer could be found to sell, or farmer to buy.

In September, an attempt was made to value lands in the parish of Wallstown for tithes. A detachment of the 92d Highlanders, a detachment of the 14th Foot, and a force of police, under the command of one admiral, two generals, and three magistrates, accompanied the valuers and parson. The peasants resisted the valuers, and were fired on by the military and police. Four peasants were killed, and many wounded.

In October, peasants and police again came into collision at Rathkeeran, in the County Waterford. The police, supported by a detachment of the 70th Regiment, fired upon the peasants, killing twelve, and wounding many. After this affray the Rector of Rathkeeran fled from the parish.

In April 1833, Grey's Coercion Act, suppressing the right of public meeting, and empowering the Lord-Lieutenant to proclaim martial law, and, practically, suspend *habeas corpus*, was passed. But the tithe war went on.

Towards the end of April, a force of infantry and cavalry proceeded to Kilmurry, in the County Waterford, to collect tithes. The peasants barricaded their houses and awaited attack. But the military retired without forcing a conflict. In May they returned. The peasants again barricaded their houses, but the military this time attacked, breaking into the houses, seizing the cattle, and carrying off many of the peasants to jail.

In June, a troop of dragoons, a detachment of the 29th Regiment, and a force of police were despatched to serve tithe processes in the neighbourhood of Carrigtwohill, in the County Cork. The peasants selected a point in the line of march where they should offer resistance. They fortified a large garden, surrounded by stone walls, close to the house of a farmer on whom process was to be served. Here, armed with pitchforks, scythes, slanes, and sticks, they awaited the military and police. A stubborn conflict followed. The police and soldiers tried to enter the garden, but without success. They fired upon the peasants, but without effect, the bullets passing harmlessly over the insurgents' heads. Finally, the troops retreated without serving the processes.

A few days after this affray at Carrigtwohill a party of the 70th Regiment, engaged in posting tithe notices, were set upon by a large force of peasants, and had to fly for their lives.

In September an attempt was made to value lands in the County Kilkenny for tithes; but the peasants fell upon the valuers, destroyed their measuring tapes, smashed their instruments, and drove them off the fields.

Throughout 1834 the war still went on. Boycotting was

frequently practised, and wherever military and police appeared they were met by peasants ready to die in resisting the law. The year closed with the famous affray of Rathcormac.

"On the 18th December 1834 a force of horse (4th Royal Irish Dragoons), foot (29th Regiment), and police, under the command of Major Waller (29th Regiment), Lieutenant Tait (dragoons), Captain Pepper (police), Captain Colles, J.P., and Captain Bagley, R.M., proceeded to collect the tithes of Archdeacon Ryder, J.P., in the parish of Gortroe, County Cork. The dragoons, who marched from Cork City, fell in with a small body of peasants, at a place called Barthelmy's Cross, near the village of Gortroe. The peasants were armed with their usual weapons, sticks and slanes, and some of them were mounted. Archdeacon Ryder, who accompanied the cavalcade in the double capacity of parson and magistrate, suggested to Captain Bagley, on seeing the peasants, that it might be prudent for the dragoons to draw their swords, and get ready for action; and, at the request of Captain Bagley, Lieutenant Tait ordered his men so to do. The peasants, however, made no effort to obstruct the advance of the dragoons, but retreated steadily before them through the village of Gortroe, falling back on the farmstead of one of the tithe-defaulters—the widow Ryan by name—whose indebtedness to Archdeacon Ryder amounted to the sum of forty shillings. The widow Ryan lived near the hamlet of Rathcormac. Her house (one of a cluster of houses outside the little village) stood at some distance from the high road, with which it was connected by the usual boreen entrance. In front of the house was a large yard, and in front of the yard, and on the same side of the boreen, a haggart—both yard and haggart being separated from the boreen by a mud wall about four feet high. To the rear of yard and haggart was a well planted shrubbery. The peasants, who, in their struggle against tithes, generally selected with deliberation and care the points at which from time to time they determined to 'give battle' to the authorities, had resolved on the present occasion to confront the forces of Parson Ryder at the house of the widow Ryan. With this object they 'fortified' the haggart and yard. The gate opening from the yard into the boreen they removed, and in its place wedged a cart (with the shafts resting in the yard) tightly between the piers—so tightly, in fact, that it became an immovable fixture, and could neither be pulled into the yard nor dragged back into the boreen. At the entrance from the main road to the boreen a barricade was thrown up, and behind this barricade a number of men were placed, to wait the arrival of the troops, the yard and haggart being occupied by the main body of peasants, armed with sticks, slanes, spades, pitchforks, and reaping hooks.

"While the dragoons under Tait and Bagley were marching on the widow Ryan's from Barthelmy's Cross, pushing the peasants' 'outposts' before them, the 29th and the police, under Waller, and Pepper, and Colles, were coming up from another direction to the same point. At the entrance to the boreen the peasant 'outpost' halted, and the 29th and the police joined the dragoons. Bagley addressed the men behind the barricade, requesting them to permit the troops to enter the boreen. The men answered, 'No tithes! no parson! You have no right to come in.' Bagley replied, 'We shall force an entrance if you do not give way.' The peasants again shouted, 'No tithes! no parson! no church!'

"After some further discussion between the magistrates and the peasants, and a good deal of cheering and noise on the part of the latter, Bagley at last said, 'My good people, be silent; I am going to read the Riot Act.' 'We want none of your bye-laws here!' shouted back the leader of the peasants; and then, turning to his own followers, called out as Bagley began to read the Act, 'To the haggart, boys! to the haggart! we'll defend it, or lose our lives!' and for the haggart with a rush and cries of 'No tithes! no tithes!' the peasants made. Bagley, having read the Riot Act, ordered the police to throw down the barricade; this they quickly did, whereupon the troops entered the boreen, the dragoons leading the way. On approaching the haggart the dragoons halted, and the 29th marched forward. On reaching the haggart wall the 29th halted, and Major Waller sent to Captain Bagley for further instructions.

"Bagley said: 'You must dislodge the peasants from the haggart and the yard. If they do not go quietly, you must try the bayonet. If that is not sufficient, you must fire; but do not fire except in the last resort.' Major Waller then directed Lieutenant Alves to attack the haggart with a portion of the men of the 29th, and Lieutenant Shepherd to attack the yard with another. The dragoons and the police were stationed in the boreen between the haggart and the main road, to prevent any advance of the peasants from that quarter. Hostilities were commenced by Archdeacon Ryder, who, acting upon his own responsibility, succeeded, all by himself, in clambering over the wall and entering the haggart. He was seized by the peasants, neck and crop, and literally flung back into the boreen. Alves then mounted the wall, and waving his sword, called on his men to 'follow.' Seeing Alves on the wall, the leader of the peasants shouted to his comrades, 'Don't let him in! don't let him in! don't strike him; but don't let him in!' A number of peasants quickly rushed forward and brandished their sticks close up in front of Alves. Alves parried the sticks with his sword, while his men climbed on to the wall. Many of the soldiers, having got on the top of the wall, were about to pull up some of their comrades, and to descend on the inside, when the peasant leader roared to his companions, 'Now, boys, at them!' and the peasants (sticks, slanes, and pitchforks in hand) made for the soldiers. A fierce fight ensued, the peasants striking furiously at the soldiers with their formidable weapons, and the soldiers vigorously thrusting back with their bayonets. Again and again the soldiers climbed to the top of the wall, and again and again they were driven back, maimed and bruised, with their bayonets bent and their firelocks smashed, many of the peasants having been placed *hors de combat* by bayonet wounds. After this struggle had continued for some time, Lieutenant Alves called out to Major Waller, 'We cannot, Major, take this place by the bayonet,' whereupon Archdeacon Ryder rushed up to Captain Bagley, crying out, 'What are we to do? we are so resisted!'

"Simultaneously with the struggle at the haggart, Lieutenant Shepherd was endeavouring to force his way into the yard. He had succeeded in jumping into the cart, followed by two of his men, while the rest climbed up the wall at either side, when the peasants rushed forward, and seizing the shafts and lifting them high up into the air, rolled Shepherd and his companions clean back into the boreen. However, he soon returned to the attack, and a fight, even more desperate than that being waged at the haggart, followed. The soldiers charged again with the bayonet, but to little purpose. Enter the yard they could not, either over the wall, or by mounting the cart. Then, finding it was hopeless to take either the haggart or yard by the bayonet, Major Waller gave directions to his lieutenants to fire. Alves' men fired first. After they had done so, Major Waller, who from his position in the boreen could command a better view of what was going on in the yard than in the haggart, tells us that he looked in the direction of the yard to see what effect Alves' fire had produced there. 'It produced no effect,' he says; 'the fight went on as violently as ever.' Shepherd, on hearing Alves' fire, called to Waller, saying, 'Major, must I fire?' and Waller answered, 'Yes.'

"Shepherd turning to the peasants, then said, 'Now if you do not give way, I must fire.' The leader of the peasants replied, 'We are not afraid to die; lives must be lost on either side before ye come in.' There was no alternative now left Shepherd but to give the word 'fire;' this he promptly did. 'I then,' says Major Waller, 'looked in the direction of the cart to see the effect. The crowd dispersed after the fire, but quickly closed up, and rushed back to the cart as thick as ever.' Such truly had been the case. The peasants, thrown but for a moment into confusion, quickly rallied; and as their leader called out, 'Never flinch, my boys! close up and at them again!' flung themselves once more on the soldiers, who, under the cover of the fire, had jumped into the cart, and clambered over the wall, driving them back with eminent success. But sticks, slanes, and pitchforks, though weapons which in the hands of a martial peasantry could be effectually used against bayonets, were poor instruments of defence against powder and ball. After a struggle—to the gallantry of which Lieutenant Shepherd bore testimony, asserting that he 'had never seen such determined bravery as was shown by the people on that day'—the peasantry gave way under the sustained fire of the troops, retreating steadily on the shrubbery.

"Major Waller then occupied the haggart and the yard. The peasants had not however, it seems, been completely disposed of. 'They are mustering in the shrubbery,' said Captain Colles to Waller, 'you must disperse them.' 'No,' replied Waller, who doubtless had had quite enough of work which in all probability he did not consider particularly clean; 'I'll surround the farmyard and keep what I have got, for if I leave it, the peasants will come back, and I shall have my work all over again.' At this juncture Archdeacon Ryder came up and said, 'All right, Major, I have got my tithes.' It seems that the Archdeacon—who had performed various strategical movements on his own account during the day (including the escapade in the haggart), had succeeded in taking the widow's house in the rear, while the battle was raging in front, with the result that he saw the widow, and obtained the tithes from her. It was this cheerful fact that he now announced to Waller. The parson being satisfied, all were satisfied, and Major Waller and Lieutenant Tait marched their men back to Cork. The soldiers gone, the peasants emerged from the shrubbery to take up their comrades who had fallen in the fray, and to find that the casualties had been considerable; twelve peasants were killed, and forty-two wounded.

"None of the soldiers had been killed, but many were wounded. An inquest, at which twenty-three jurors were empanelled, was, a few days later, held on the bodies of the peasants who had fallen. The inquiry lasted thirteen days, and resulted in a mixed verdict; thirteen jurors being for a verdict of 'wilful murder,' two for 'manslaughter,' and eight for 'justifiable homicide.'"[1]

This was the last "battle" of the tithe war. It was followed by a truce which lasted until Drummond's arrival; and the renewal of hostilities was prevented by his intervention.

While the tithe war raged, the eternal land war dis tracted the country, and convulsed society.

The landlords evicted without pity, and the tenants murdered without remorse. The landlord thought of little but the rent. He recognised no duties. He enforced only

[1] This account of the affray at Rathcormac is taken from "Fifty Years of Concessions to Ireland."

rights. The tenant, "scrambling for the potato,"[1] and left without any resource but the land, offered an exorbitant rent, which the landlord accepted, and exacted to the uttermost farthing.[2] Freedom of contract between landlord and tenant there was none. The tenant came into the market under circumstances which left him entirely at the mercy of the landlord. The "bit of land" meant life to him; the want of it death; for, in the absence of commercial industries, the people were thrown upon the land mainly for existence.[3]

"The treaty between landlord and tenant [in Ireland]" says Mr Nassau Senior, "is not a calm bargain in which the tenant, having offered what he thinks the land worth, cares little whether his offer be accepted or not; it is a struggle like the struggle to buy bread in a besieged town, or to buy water in an African caravan."[4] In truth, the landlord had a monopoly of the means of existence, and he used it for his own aggrandisement, regardless of the tenant's fate, and the public weal.

"The landlords in Ireland," said Lord Donoughmore in the House of Lords on February 28, 1854, "have been in

[1] Mr Bright.

[2] "Almost every proprietor in Ireland is a trader in his commodity. . . . As profit was the sole object, the proprietors had no inducement to make sacri fices, and to accept moderate rents to secure the good opinion of their tenants." —Bicheno, "Ireland and its Economy," pp. 123, 129.

"The rights of property [in Ireland] are exercised with the utmost rigour." —Lord John Russell, House of Commons, April 15, 1839.

"It strikes me that before the introduction of the poor law, the peasantry were regarded by a large proportion of the proprietors merely as individuals who paid them rent. The landlords used to get their rent from them, but otherwise took very little interest in them."—Mr Twistleton, First Report of Select Committee [Commons] on Irish Poor Law, Parliamentary Papers for 1849, vol. xv., part i., Q. 4380.

"While in most cases the relation of landlord and tenant in England is one of sympathy without dependence; in Ireland it is often one of entire dependence without a shadow of sympathy."—The Marquis of Normanby, House of Lords, November 27, 1837.

[3] There was no poor law in Ireland until 1838.

[4] Nassau Senior, "Journals Relating to Ireland," i. p. 29.

the habit of letting land, not farms." Never has a happier description of the Irish land system been given than this. The landlord let "land"—a strip of bog, barren, wild, dreary. The tenant reclaimed it; drained, fenced, built; reduced the waste to a cultivable state; made the "land" a "farm"[1] Then the landlord pounced upon him for an increased rent. The tenant could not pay: his resources had been exhausted in bringing the bog into a state of cultivation; he had not yet recouped himself for his outlay and labour. He was evicted; flung on the road-side to starve, without receiving one shilling's compensation for his outlay on the land; and the "farm," which he had made, was given to another at an enhanced rental. What did the evicted tenant do? He entered a Ribbon Lodge: told the story of his wrong, and demanded vengeance on the man whom he called a tyrant and oppressor. Only too often his story was listened to; and vengeance was wreaked on the landlord, or new tenant; and sometimes upon both. This in brief is the dismal history of the land trouble in Ireland.[2]

[1] "The landlords are unable or unwilling to expend money on their estates. They allow the tenants themselves to make the provision by building and reclaiming land from its original state of bog, or heather, or stony field. It is thus that many estates have been created and almost all have been enlarged, by generation after generation of tenants without assistance. It was the tenants who made the barony of Farney—originally worth £3000, worth £50,000 a year."—Mr Nassau Senior, quoted by Mr O'Connor Morris (the *Times*' "special commissioner") in his "Letters on the Irish Land Question," p. 117.

"The people who have thus imperfectly reclaimed bog and mountain seldom hold by lease. When they come under rent they do so as tenants from year to year, liable to be turned out at six months' notice to quit. As soon as the poor tenant has brought his farm to that degree of fertility which enables him to pay a rent and live, all further improvement is studiously avoided as a thing which the tenant believes will only increase his labour to produce a larger rent for the sole benefit of the landlord whom he regards as a vigilant spy upon every symptom of ability to pay more rent."—Master Fitzgibbon, quoted by O'Connor Morris, p. 83.

[2] "If ever crime can be excused it is when the existence of these families depends upon their retaining the land, it is their only resource for existence,

What upright and intelligent Englishmen thought of it may be judged by an extract from a letter addressed by Poulett Scrope, M.P., to Lord Melbourne, in 1834. Mr Scrope said :—

"Though God gave the land of Ireland to the people of Ireland—to the many—the law has given it unconditionally to the few. Even in the best of times, if the landlord refuses to any peasant the holding of a plot of land, if other starving wretches outbid his offers for the patch of soil, whose possession is as necessary to his existence as the air he breathes—if sickness or misfortune prevent his punctual payment of the enormous rent he has promised, and he and his family are ejected (by the cheap and summary process which landlord-made law provides) from the cabin which sheltered him from his birth, and his fathers before him—what remains? He must die! The law, at least, says so. The law allows him no other alternative. He may contrive to prolong a precarious existence on the charity of his poor neighbours (as he asks it in vain from the rich), or he may take by force or stealth what is necessary to preserve life. But the law does not recognise these means of living; on the contrary, the law forbids them. The law says if he cannot rent land or obtain work he shall starve. This is the real wrong—this is the giant grievance—this is the most crying, the most urgent of the just complaints of the Irish people. And it is against this state of the law that they combine in their Whiteboy associations—associations that will never be put down until the law extends that protection to the lives of the poor which it now lavishes almost exclusively on the property of the rich. And who will say that the peasantry ought not in such a state of the law to combine for their mutual protection?

their bread basket. The process server is as much dreaded, and as universally, as a mad dog."—Wakefield: Committee on Colonization from Ireland. Parliamentary Papers, vol. xvii., for 1847-1848, Q. 2923.

Is there no point of oppression at which resistance to the law becomes a duty? We have the recent authority of the head of the law for the principle—a principle as old as it is true—that allegiance is only due where protection is afforded, and that where the law refuses its protection it cannot claim allegiance. Does the law then protect the Irish peasant? Not from starvation. It does not protect him from being thrust out of his home and little holding, into absolute destitution, to perish on the highways of famine, or to waste away in those abodes of filth, misery, and disease in the suburbs of the towns, which Dr Doyle so faithfully describes as the ordinary refuge and dying place of the ejected cottier and his family. It does not prevent him from being visited by this fate at the command of an absentee landlord, who may desire to clear his property of some of the human encumbrances whom God has brought into being upon it. The law affords the Irish peasant no protection from so horrible a fate. Hundreds are at present exposed to it. Millions know that they are liable to it. Can the law justly require their allegiance? Can we expect them willingly to pay it? No! The peasantry of Ireland feel that the law places their lives at the mercy of the few, whom it invests with sovereign power over the land of their native country, with power to sweep them at will off its surface. They feel that the continuance of the system of clearing estates which has been for so many years in progress, is a question of life and death to them. And therefore do they combine against it. Therefore it is—however little minds may wonder at the fact—that they show no more repugnance to the shedding of blood in open day, in the presence of assenting thousands, in the execution of the sentences of self-organised tribunals, looked upon by them as the sole safeguard of their lives, than does a soldier hired to fight for his country's safety in the field of battle. It is to their own Whiteboy law that their allegiance is considered due. They look alone to the secret tribunals, of their own establishment, for the protection which the law of the Imperial Parliament denies them. And they obtain it! Let those who know Ireland deny the fact if they can. The peasantry of Ireland do more or less obtain from the Whiteboy associations that essential protection to their existence which the established law of the country refuses to afford. The Whiteboy system is the practical and efficient check upon the ejectment system. It cannot be denied that but for the salutary terror inspired by the Whiteboys the clearance of estates (which in the over-peopled districts of Ireland is considered, justly or not, to be the only mode of improving or even saving them) would proceed with a rapidity and to an extent that must occasion the most horrible sufferings to hundreds of thousands of the ejected tenantry. Some landlords have bowels of compassion and might hesitate so to employ the fearful power with which the law has unconditionally armed them for the improvement of their property. Many, the majority perhaps, would not be stayed by such scruples. It is easy to satisfy the mind of an interested party that what the law allows to be done cannot be wrong—that what appears necessary for the preservation of property must be right. May they not do as they will with their own? Yes! But for a salutary dread of the Whiteboy associations, ejectments would desolate Ireland and decimate her population, casting forth thousands of families like noxious weeds rooted out from the soil on which they have hitherto grown, perhaps too luxuriantly, and flung away to perish in the roadside ditches. Yes! the Whiteboy system is the only check on the ejectment system; and weighing one against the other, horror against horror, and crime against crime, it is perhaps the lesser evil of the two—a necessary evil in the present state of the law in Ireland—a mitigation of the otherwise intolerable slavery, which the law of the land enforces, of the Irish peasant to the Irish landlord. The Whiteboy system will never be put down until the Legislature establish a law for the end it aims at—that, namely, of protecting the lives of the Irish peasantry, and securing them the means of living by their industry." [1]

For three-quarters of a century there had been secret societies in Ireland in connection with the occupation of land. These societies possessed the sympathy of the masses of the peasantry. They were formed to keep down rents, to prevent tenants from out-bidding each other, and generally to regulate the relation of landlord and tenant in the interests of the latter. They were in fact the Trades Unions of Ireland; and like Trades Unions elsewhere, they sometimes enforced their decrees by violence, outrage, and murder. Since the Union the

[1] "In Ireland landlords never erect on their property, or expend anything in repairs; nor do leases in that country contain so many clauses as in England. The office of an agent is therefore rendered very easy, for he has nothing to do but to receive his employer's rents twice a-year, and to set out the turf-bog in lots in the spring. Six months' credit is generally given on the rents, which is called 'the hanging gale.' This is one of the great levers of oppression by which the lower classes are kept in a kind of perpetual bondage; for as every family almost holds some portion of the land, and owes half-a-year's rent, which a landlord can exact in a moment, this debt hangs over their heads like a load, and keeps them in a continual state of anxiety and terror. If the rent is not paid, the cattle are driven to the pound, and if suffered to remain there a certain number of days, they are sold. This I have frequently seen done after the occupying tenant had paid his rent to the middleman, who had failed to pay it to the head landlord. The numerous instances of distress occasioned by this severity, which everyone who has resided any time in Ireland must have witnessed, are truly deplorable; and I believe them to be one of the chief causes of those frequent risings of the people, under various denominations, which at different times have disturbed the internal tranquillity of the country, and been attended with atrocities shocking to humanity, and disgraceful to the empire."—Wakefield, "Account of Ireland," vol. i. p. 244.

"In Ireland, tenure at will is indefinite oppression; tenure by lease, oppression by lease; rents are not the proportion of, but the whole, of the produce of."—Wesley Doyle, "Ostensible Causes of the Present State of Ireland," 1822.

Referring to the facilities for evicting which the Legislature had given the Irish landlords, the *Times* said in 1835:—"It is truly alleged that such facili-

country had been overrun by these societies—Thrashers, Carders, Rockites, Terrialts, Lady Clares, Molly Maguires, Whiteboys, Whitefeet, Blackfeet. But by degrees all agrarian organisations were absorbed by the Ribbon Society, whose ramifications extended far and wide, not only in Ireland, but in parts of Great Britain. Springing out of an association formed by some Catholics of Ulster in the eighteenth century to defend themselves from the attacks of the Protestant "Peep o' Day Boys," the Ribbon confederacy had assumed the character of a Tenant's Protective League in the first quarter of the present century, and had already become a terrible power when Drummond reached Ireland. The Ribbon-man broke the law with impunity; witnesses could not be found to give evidence against him, or juries to convict. He was sheltered by the peasants of a whole country side, who regarded him as a public executioner sent forth to wreak vengeance on their enemies, and do justice to them.

I have elsewhere[1] dealt so fully with the question of landlord and tenant in Ireland, that I cannot, without danger of repetition, say more upon the subject now. But I shall conclude this reference to it, with an extract from Sir George Cornewall Lewis's work on "Irish Disturbance," which is of more value than any thing I could write. Having quoted the evidence given before various Parlia-

ties have not been afforded the English landlords whose ejected tenants are nevertheless sure of parochial support; but that against the poor Irish who, when turned off the land, have no resource but begging, robbing, or perishing in the next ditch, the severest enactments have been made, and the despotism of the landlords bolstered up to a pitch that leaves the tenant at the mercy of his caprices" (*Times*, December 29, 1835). Again, "The conduct of many Irish proprietors in the process of what they call 'clearing their estates,' is an infamous disgrace to human nature" (*Times*, December 26, 1835).

[1] "Fifty Years of Concessions to Ireland," "The Parliamentary History of the Irish Land Question," "The Irish Land Question and English Public Opinion."

mentary Committees on the causes of agrarian disturbances, Sir George says:—

"All the above witnesses[1] agree in a remarkable manner with regard to the causes of the Whiteboy disturbances; all trace them to the miserable condition of the peasantry, to their liability to certain charges (the chief of which is rent), which they are often unable to meet; and to their anxiety to retain possession of land; which, as Mr Blackburne truly states, is to them a necessary of life, the alternative being starvation. With the dread of this alternative before their eyes, it is not to be wondered that they make desperate efforts to avert it; that crime and disturbances should be the consequences of actual ejectments is still more natural. . . .

"It has already been explained how the Irish peasant, constantly living in extreme poverty, is liable, by the pressure of certain charges, or by ejectment from his holding, to be driven to utter destitution—to a state in which himself and family can only rely on a most precarious charity[2] to save them from exposure to the elements, from nakedness, and starvation. It is natural that the most improvident persons should seek to struggle against such fearful consequences; that they should try to use some means of quieting apprehensions which (even if never realised) would themselves be sufficient to embitter the life of the most thoughtless; and it is to afford this security that the Whiteboy combinations are formed. The Whiteboy association may be considered as a vast trades' union, for the protection of the Irish peasantry; the object being, not to regulate the rate of wages or the hours of work, but to keep the actual occupant in possession of h

[1] Chiefly magistrates, landowners, barristers, inspectors of police and clergymen.—Barrister engaged in administering the Insurrection Act in 1823.

[2] There was no Poor Law in Ireland until 1838.

land, and, in general, to regulate the relation of landlord and tenant, for the benefit of the latter."[1]

But of all the organisations which disturbed the peace of Ireland at this time, the most powerful was the Orange Society. This formidable confederacy was founded in the autumn of 1795. For some years previously there had been almost constant feuds between Catholics and Protestants in Ulster. Arising out of these feuds, a pitched battle was fought near the village of Diamond, in the County Armagh, on September 21, 1795. The Catholics were beaten; and the first Orange Lodge was founded on the spot.[2]

[1] Lewis, "Irish Disturbances," pp. 98-99.

[2] The opposing factions were divided into "Peep o' Day Boys" (Protestants), and "Defenders" (Catholics). It has been generally stated that the Peep o' Day Boys developed into Orangemen, and the Defenders into Ribbonmen. But the Orangemen deny that their organisation was in any way connected with the Peep o' Day Boys; and they give this reason for their opinion. The Peep o' Day Boys were Presbyterians, while the first Orange Lodge consisted exclusively of members of the Church of England. However this may be, the fact is undoubted, that on the appearance of the Orange Society, the Peep o' Days immediately disappeared. With respect to the Defenders, it has been said that originally both Peep o' Day Boys and Defenders were Presbyterians, and that the dispute which divided them was at first of a purely personal character. Two Presbyterians had fought at a fair, and the quarrel was renewed again and again. By degrees the friends of each party arranged themselves into rival factions. Finally, the Catholics joined one faction, and then the dispute assumed a sectarian hue. The original cause of quarrel was forgotten, and Catholics and Presbyterians were arrayed against each other as such.

The sectarian feuds between Peep o' Day Boys and Defenders were renewed at frequent intervals between about 1788 and 1795. A speech delivered by Lord Gosford, governor of the county of Armagh, on December 28, 1795, throws a good deal of light on these feuds. Addressing the magistrates of the county specially assembled, he said:—"Gentlemen,—Having requested your attendance here this day, it becomes my duty to state the grounds upon which I thought it advisable to propose this meeting, and at the same time to submit to your consideration a plan which occurs to me as the most likely to check the enormities that have already disgraced this country, and may soon reduce it into the greatest distress. It is no secret that a persecution, accompanied with all the circumstances of ferocious cruelty which have in all ages distinguished that dreadful calamity, is now raging in this country. Neither age, nor even acknowledged innocence as to the late disturbances, is sufficient to excite mercy, much less afford protection. The only crime which the wretched

The Society gradually increased in numbers and influence; the foremost men of Ulster soon joined its ranks. There was an Orange aristocracy, an Orange clergy, and

objects of this merciless prosecution are charged with is a crime of easy proof; it is simply a profession of the Roman Catholic Faith. A lawless banditti have constituted themselves judges of this species of delinquency, and the sentence they pronounce is equally concise and terrible; it is nothing less than a confiscation of all property and immediate banishment. It would be extremely painful and surely unnecessary, to detail the horrors that attended the execution of so wide and tremendous a proscription; that certainly exceeds, in the comparative number of those it consigns to ruin and misery, every example that ancient or modern history can afford. For where have we heard, or in what history of human cruelties have we read, of more than half the inhabitants of a populous country deprived at one blow of the means as well as of the fruits of their industry, and driven in the midst of an inclement winter to seek a shelter for themselves and their helpless families where chance may guide them. This is no exaggerated picture of the horrid scenes now acting in this country; yet surely it is sufficient to awaken sentiments of indignation and compassion in the coldest heart. Those horrors are now acting, and acting with impunity. The spirit of impartial justice (without which law is nothing better than tyranny) has for a time disappeared in this country, and the supineness of the magistracy of this county is a topic of conversation in every corner of this kingdom. It is said the Catholics are dangerous; they may be so; they may be dangerous from their numbers, still more dangerous from the unbounded views they have been encouraged to entertain; but I will venture to assert, without fear of contradiction, that upon these very grounds, those terrible proceedings are not more contrary to humanity than they are to sound policy and justice. I have the honour to hold a situation in this county which calls on me to deliver my sentiments, and I do so without fear or disguise. I am as true a Protestant as any man in this room, or in this kingdom. I inherit a property which my family derived under a Protestant title, and, with the blessing of God, I will maintain that title to the utmost of my power. I will never consent to make a surrender of Protestant ascendency to Catholic claims, with whatever menaces they may be urged, or however speciously or invidiously supported. Conscious of my sincerity in this public declaration, which I do not make unadvisedly, but as the result of mature deliberation, I defy the paltry insinuations that malice or party spirit may suggest; I know my own heart, and should despise myself if, under any intimidation, I could close my eyes against such scenes as present themselves on every side, or shut my eyes against the complaints of a persecuted people. I have now acquitted myself to my conscience and my country, and take the liberty of proposing the following resolutions:—1. That it appears to this meeting that the County Armagh is, at this time, in a state of uncommon disorder; that the Roman Catholic inhabitants are grievously oppressed by lawless persons unknown, who attack and plunder their houses by night unless they immediately abandon their lands and habitations. 2. That a committee of Magistrates be appointed to sit on Tuesdays and Saturdays in the chapter room of the cathedral church of Armagh, to receive information respecting all

an Orange yeomanry bound together by a secret oath, and working for a common object. The State patronised the organisation; the Church favoured it. In fine, before the

persons of whatever description who disturb the peace of this county. 3. That the instructions of the whole body of the magistracy to their Committee shall be, to use every legal means within their power to stop the progress of the persecution now carrying on by an ungovernable mob against the Catholics of this county. 4. That said Committee, or any three of them, be empowered to expend any sum of money for information or secret service out of the funds subscribed by the gentlemen of this county. 5. That a meeting of the whole magistracy of this county be held every second Monday, at the house of Charles M'Reynolds, to hear the reports of their Committee and to give further instructions, as the exigency of the times may require. 6. That offenders of every description in the present disturbances shall be prosecuted at the public expense, out of the funds subscribed by the gentlemen of this county; and to carry this resolution into effect, it is resolved, that Mr Arthur Irwin be appointed law agent to the magistrates."—The above resolutions being read, were unanimously agreed to, and the Committee nominated. Lord Gosford having left the chair, and Sir Capel Molyneux being requested to take it,—"Resolved, that the unanimous thanks of this meeting be presented to Lord Viscount Gosford, for his proper conduct in convening the magistrates of the county, and his impartiality in the chair."

The evidence of Mr Christie may also be quoted:—

"You are a member of the Society of Friends?—I am.

"Where do you live?—I live in the County of Down, at a place called Kircassock.

"You live on your own property?—Yes.

"Is that near the county of Armagh?—I live about two miles and three-quarters from the borders of the county of Armagh.

"What age are you?—I was born in 1771, on the 20th December.

"At what time do you first recollect having heard of Orange Societies?—I do not recollect the very period, but I recollect the Peep o' Day Boys, which began in the county of Armagh, about the latter end of 1794 and the commencement of 1795; I came to live in the place which I now occupy in 1793, and it did not occur till eighteen months or two years afterwards.

"From 1793, have you a pretty distinct recollection of public transactions?—Yes, I was nearly twenty-two years of age at that time.

"Will you state to the Committee any outrages or excesses committed by any description of people, and what description of people in the counties of Down and Armagh?—The first disturbances we had in the north of Ireland, that I recollect, were in the county of Armagh and the neighbourhood of Church-hill, where the present Colonel Verner now lives; I did not see them, for I was not in that part, but the first account we had of them was in that quarter.

"Will you state the nature of those disturbances?—'Wrecking,' as it was termed, the Roman Catholics' houses; it was termed 'wrecking' when the parties broke open the door and smashed everything that was capable of being broken in the house, looms and webs that were probably weaving; they broke

end of the century, to be an Orangeman was to be high and mighty in the land.

What was the object of the Society? In answering this question the Orange view must be given.

the webs and destroyed the yarn and everything, and sometimes they threw the furniture out of the house, smashed; and in other cases they set fire to the house and burnt it.

"Do not you distinguish between burning and wrecking?—Wrecking was applied more to the destruction of the furniture than to the burning of the houses.

"By wrecking, do you mean also the destruction of the windows and doors? —I do; we have different names for the different acts that were committed; one where the house was totally destroyed, and another where it was only wrecked.

"Will you state what you recollect of the outrages that were then committed?—It commenced in 1794, but the greatest depredation was committed in the spring of 1795. It commenced in the neighbourhood of Church-hill, between Portadown and Dungannon, and then it extended over nearly all the northern counties, commencing at where the county of Armagh and the county of Down end, at Newry, round by Antrim, Down, and Tyrone, and I believe in a very short time it extended to the county of Derry, but not to such an extent as in the other counties. Then, in the course of time, after th Catholics were, many of them, driven from the county and took refuge in different parts of Ireland, I understood they went to Connaught. Some years after, when peace and quietness was in a measure restored, some returned again, probably five or six years afterwards; they got some employment; some were weavers and other things; but they stayed out of the country while they thought their lives were in danger; but the property which they left was transferred, in most instances, to Protestants; where they had houses and gardens, and small farms of land, it was generally handed over by the landlords to Protestant tenants. That occurred within my own knowledge.

"Are you aware whether some of them had considerable interest in those houses and lands, whether they had, owing to the increased value of land and the laying out of money upon the property, a valuable interest in some instances?—I am not aware that any of them had. I think most of them were tenants at will, but there were some cases where they had life leases.

"Generally speaking, was the property transferred by the landlords from the Catholics to Protestant tenants?—I know some cases of it, but I cannot say that it was general; but I do not live in the part of the country where the greatest mischief was done.

"Were there many Catholic houses destroyed?—A great many. Sometimes I heard of twelve or fourteen houses wrecked in a night, and some destroyed. I pitied them very much in the straits they were driven to.

"This was about the spring of 1795?—The spring of 1795 was the worst, but it did not end there; it continued much longer.

"Up to what period did it continue?—For two or three years. It was not quite so bad in 1796 and 1797 as it was earlier; but after this wrecking, and the Catholics were driven out, what was called the Break of Day party merged

The Orange Society, according to the Orange view, was formed to preserve the English connection, and maintain the Protestant religion. It was a loyal and religious organisation. But its loyalty was unselfish and chivalrous; its religion enlightened and liberal. Its hero was William of Orange, the champion of civil and religious liberty. The Orange Society was the champion of civil and religious liberty too.

It was a religious organisation. A lodge always opened and closed with prayer, so said Deputy Grand Secretary Swan before the Parliamentary Committee of 1835.[1]

Opening Prayer.

"Gracious and Almighty God, who in all ages hast shown Thy Almighty power in protecting righteous Kings and States, we yield Thee hearty thanks for the merciful preservation of Thy true religion, hitherto, against the designs of its enemies, particularly in sending Thy servant, our glorious deliverer, William the Third, Prince of Orange, who freed us from tyranny and arbitrary power. We bow

into Orangemen. They passed from the one to the other, and the gentlemen in the county procured what they termed their Orange warrants, to enable them to assemble legally, as they termed it. The name dropped, and Orangeism succeeded to Break of Day men.

"From the time they were called Orangemen, did you hear afterwards of the name of Break of Day men?—I cannot say that I never heard it, but it was not a general appellation given.

"Did you hear it with regard to any body of men, subsequently in existence, after the name of Orangemen was adopted?—No; I never heard it applied to any body of people after the Orangemen had lodges, as they termed it. I think the name of Break of Day men completely subsided.

"Did the Orangemen consist of the same class of persons as those that compose the Break of Day Boys?—I suppose they did, but I cannot say, because I did not know any of them personally to identify them. The same people that made use of intemperate language towards the Catholics, whilst the Break of Day business existed, were the same people that I saw afterwards walking in the Orange processions, but I cannot say further than that."—"Select Committee (Commons) on Orange Lodges, &c., in Ireland, in 1835." See particularly the evidence of Earl Gosford, Mr Christie, and the Rev. Mortimer O'Sullivan.

[1] "Select Committee on Orange Lodges, &c., in Ireland, in 1835," Q. 1107.

with humble submission to the late dispensation of Thy Divine Wisdom, which we confess to be a righteous punishment for our sins, and for our indifference to those blessings which Thou hast bestowed upon us.

"Yet, we beseech Thee, for Thy honour, and Thy name's sake, to frustrate the further designs of wicked men against Thy holy religion, and not to suffer its enemies wholly to triumph over it; defeat their counsels, abate their pride, assuage their malice, and confound their devices. Bless, we beseech Thee, every member of the Orange Institution, with charity, brotherly love and loyalty; make us truly respectable here on earth, and eternally happy hereafter.

"These, and all other blessings, we humbly beg in the Name and through the mediation of Jesus Christ our Lord and Saviour. Amen."

Closing Prayer.

"O, Almighty God, who art a strong power of defence unto Thy servants, against the face of their enemies; we humbly beseech of Thy mercy to deliver us from those great and imminent dangers with which we are now encompassed. O, Lord, give us not up as a prey unto our enemies; but continue to protect Thy true religion against the designs of those who seek to overthrow it, so that all the world may know that Thou art our Saviour and Mighty Deliverer, through Jesus Christ our Lord. Amen."

The qualification of an Orangeman was a charitable disposition—a truly Christian heart and mind.

Qualifications.

"An Orangeman should have a sincere love and veneration for his Almighty Maker; a firm and steadfast faith in the Saviour of the World, convinced that He is the only

Mediator between a sinful creature and an offended Creator. His disposition should be humane and compassionate, his behaviour kind and courteous. He should love rational and improving society, faithfully regard the Protestant religion, and sincerely desire to propagate its doctrine and precepts. He should have a hatred to cursing and swearing, and taking the name of God in vain; and he should use all opportunities of discouraging those shameful practices. Wisdom and prudence should guide his actions; temperance and sobriety, honesty and integrity direct his conduct; and the honour and glory of his king and country should be the motives of his exertions."

But it is the ceremony by which an Orangeman is received into the fold that marks the religious character of the society more than anything else.

RITUAL OF THE ORANGE INTRODUCTION.

"*The applicant shall be introduced between his two Sponsors: namely, the brethren who proposed and seconded his admission, carrying the Bible in his hands, with the book of rules and regulations placed thereon. Two Brothers shall precede him. On his entering the room, a chaplain, if present, or in his absence a Brother appointed by the Master, shall say the whole or part of what follows:—*

"O Lord God of our fathers, art not Thou God in Heaven? and rulest not Thou over all the kingdoms of the heathen? and in Thine hand is there not power and might, so that none is able to withstand Thee?" (2 Chron. xx. 6).

"Who is like unto Thee, O Lord, among the Gods? who is like Thee, glorious in holiness, fearful in praises, doing wonders? Thou in Thy mercy hast led forth the people which Thou hast redeemed; Thou hast guided them in Thy strength unto Thy holy habitation" (Exodus xv. 11, 13).

"O Lord, Thou wilt ordain peace for us; for Thou also hast wrought all our works in us. O Lord our God, other lords beside Thee have had dominion over us; but by Thee only will we make mention of Thy Name" (Isaiah xxvi. 12, 13).

"Wherefore glorify ye the Lord in the fires, even the name of the Lord God of Israel in the isles of the sea" (Isaiah xxiv. 15).

(*During the reading of these the Candidate shall stand at the foot of the table, the brethren all standing also in their places, and strictly silent.*)

The Master shall then say—Friend, what dost thou desire in this meeting of true Orangemen?

And then Candidate shall answer—Of my own free will and accord I desire admission into your Loyal Institution.

Master—Who will vouch for this friend that he is a Protestant and loyal subject?

(*The Sponsors shall bow to the Master and signify the same, each mentioning his own name.*)

Master—What do you carry in your hand?

Candidate—The word of God.

Master—Under the assurance of these worthy Brothers, we will trust that you also carry it in your heart. What is that other book?

Candidate—The book of your rules and regulations.

Master—Under the like assurance, we will further trust that you will study them well, and that you will obey them in all lawful matters. Therefore we gladly receive you into this Order. Orangemen bring to me your friend.

(*The Candidate shall then be brought by his Sponsors before the Master; the two Brothers standing at each side of the centre of the table; during this, the Chaplain or Brother appointed shall say*)—

"Many shall be purified, and made white, and tried; but

the wicked shall do wickedly: and none of the wicked shall understand; but the wise shall understand. Blessed is he that waiteth, and cometh to the thousand three hundred and five and thirty days. But go thou thy way till the end be; for thou shalt rest, and stand in thy lot at the end of the days" (Daniel xii, 10, 12, 13.)

(*The Candidate shall then kneel on his right knee; and the Master shall invest him with the decoration of the Order—an orange sash. Then the Chaplain or Brother appointed shall say*)—

"When thus it shall be in the midst of the land among the people, there shall be as the shaking of an olive tree, and as the gleaning grapes when the vintage is done. They shall lift up their voice, they shall sing for the majesty of the Lord, they shall cry aloud from the sea" (Isaiah xxiv. 13, 14.)

"That the mountain of the house of the Lord shall be established in the top of the mountains, and it shall be exalted above the hills; and people shall flow unto it" (Micah iv. 1).

"And it shall be for a token upon thine hand, and for frontlets between thine eyes; for by strength of hand the Lord brought us forth out of Egypt. Thou shalt therefore keep this ordinance in his season from year to year" (Exodus xiii. 16, 10).

Then the Master shall say—We receive thee, dear Brother, into the religious and loyal Institution of Orangemen; trusting that thou wilt abide a devoted servant of God and true believer in His Son Jesus Christ, a faithful subject of our King and supporter of our Constitution. Keep thou firm in the Protestant Church, holding steadily her pure doctrines and observing her ordinances. Make thyself the friend of all pious and peaceable men; avoiding strife and seeking benevolence; slow to take offence and offering none, thereby so far as in thee lieth, turning the injustice of our adversaries into their own reproof and confusion. In the name of the Brotherhood I bid thee welcome; and pray that thou mayest long continue among them, a worthy Orangeman, namely, fearing God, honouring the king, and maintaining the law.

(*Then the Master shall communicate, or cause to be communicated, unto the new member the signs and passwords of the Brotherhood; and the Chaplain or Brother appointed shall say*)—

"Glory to God in the highest, and on earth peace, good will toward men" (St Luke ii. 14).

(*After which the Brother shall make obeisance to the Master, and all present shall take their seats; the certificate of the new Brother being first duly signed and registered.*)

"There appears a great deal in these [Orange] rules which is good Christian charity," said the Earl of Gosford before the Parliamentary Committee of 1835.[1]

But the Orange Society was "loyal" as well as "Christian;" and every Orangeman took an oath of allegiance.

Orange Oath.

"I, A. B., of my own free-will, and accord, in the presence of Almighty God, do hereby most solemnly and sincerely swear that I will always conceal, and never will reveal either part, or parts of this which I am now about to receive, and that I will bear true allegiance to his Majesty King George the Third, and all the heirs of the Crown, so long as they maintain the Protestant Ascendency, the laws, and constitutions of these Kingdoms."[2]

The first of the Secret Articles also provided—

"That we will bear true allegiance to his Majesty King George III., and his successors, so long as he or they

[1] "Select Committee on Orange Lodges, &c., in Ireland." Q. 3938.

[2] *Ibid.*, Q. 1382. This was the oath in 1799. The changes that have been made in the oath will appear as the narrative proceeds.

support the Protestant Ascendency; and that we will faithfully support and maintain the laws and constitution of this kingdom."

People said that the Orangemen took only a qualified oath of allegiance, that they promised to be "loyal" so long as "Protestant Ascendency" was upheld, but no longer. But the Orangemen indignantly repudiated this insinuation, without, however, giving a very satisfactory account of the use of the qualifying words.[1]

It was also said, that the religion of the Orange Society consisted in a holy hatred of Catholics. But this the Orangemen likewise denied, though admitting that Catholics, and Catholics alone, were excluded from the organization by article 9 of the "Secret Articles."

This article provided—

"No Roman Catholic can be admitted on any account."

Stewart Blacker, Esq., Assistant Grand Secretary to the Grand Lodge of Ireland, was asked by the Committee of 1835: "Would a body of Roman Catholics, united together in a similar manner as the Orange body is, be, in your opinion, dangerous to the State?" He frankly answered: "I think a Catholic body, organised as the Orange Institution, would be highly injurious and detrimental to a Protestant country as this, by the blessing of God, still is."[2]

[1] The words were finally abandoned, as we shall see, *post*.

[2] "Select Committee on Orange Lodges, &c., in Ireland." Q. 2138.

Lieutenant-Colonel Verner, M.P., Deputy Grand Master, was asked:—"Is the association exclusively a Protestant association? It is.—Can any Catholic belong to it? Not by the rules of the society.—Can any Presbyterian belong to it? Yes." Qs. 11 to 13. William Swan, Esq., Deputy Grand Secretary was asked, Q. 1204, "This purports to be the general declaration of the objects of the Orange Institution, and the Committee find in it the following words, 'we will not persecute, injure, or upbraid any person on account of his religious opinions, provided the same be not hostile to the State.'" Q. 1207. "Do you consider the Catholic religion to be hostile to the State? I do." Q. 1208. "Then out of these words, 'we will not persecute, injure, or upbraid any person on account of his original opinions, provided the same be not hostile to the State,' a man who took that declaration would consider

So much for the character and object of the Orange Institution as revealed in its rules and regulations, and explained by its witnesses.

It is doubtful if many Orange lodges were established between September 1795 and January 1796, but in 1796 the organisation spread.[1] In 1797 a lodge—destined to become the Grand Lodge of Ireland—was opened in Dublin;[2] in 1798 the Orange yeomanry took an active part in crushing the rebellion; in 1799 the first code of rules was drawn up; in 1800 the Society was divided on the question of the Union, some lodges refraining from taking any part in the controversy, while others passed strong resolutions against Mr Pitt's measure.[3]

himself authorised to 'persecute, injure, or upbraid,' the Roman Catholics? No; we do not do it." Q. 1209. "What sense do you attach to these words? I cannot attach any meaning to them till I produce my own books." —"Select Committee [Commons] on Orange Lodges in Ireland."

[1] "Committee on Orange Lodges in Ireland." Qs. 3664, 3665.

[2] *London Review*, ii. 489.

[3] These, among other resolutions, were passed against the Union:

Orange Lodge, No. 883, at Newtownbarry, 16th February 1800—

"That Orangemen ought to come forward as Orangemen and Irishmen and declare their sentiments against a legislative union which now, or at any time, would be of the most fatal and pernicious consequences to the real liberty of Ireland.

EDWARD BEALLY, *Master*.
WALLOUGHBY BUSLARD, *Deputy*.
ALEX. M'CLAUGHRY, *Secretary*."

Lodges Nos. 780 and 785. Dublin, 11th March 1800—

"That the Constitution of 1782, under which our country has advanced to greatness and prosperity with uncommon rapidity, is that which, as Orangemen, we have sworn to defend and maintain; and we are determined to co-operate with our fellow-subjects in every legal and proper method to oppose so destructive a measure.

J. CHARLES, *Secretary*."

Lodge 391, Wattlebridge, County Fermanagh, 1st March 1800—

"That, strongly attached to the Constitution of 1782, a settlement ratified in the most unequivocal manner so far as the faith of nations is binding, we should feel ourselves criminal were we to remain silent while an attempt is made to extinguish it. That, impressed with every loyal sentiment towards our gracious Sovereign, we trust that the legislative union, which is contrary to the sense of all Orangemen and of the nation at large, will be relinquished.

JOHN MOORE, *Master*."

The Society, as originally constituted, consisted of a Grand Lodge in Dublin, and of several Grand County Lodges, District Lodges, and Private Lodges scattered

Lodge 428, Newtownbutler, 18th March 1800—

"That no lover of his country could have proposed a measure fraught with such destructive consequences, and that all supporters of it should be execrated by their fellow-subjects and by posterity. JOHN CORRY, *Master.*"

Lodges 382 and 907—

"That, as Irishmen, we feel insulted by the degrading arguments held forth in favour of the Union, as if the Lords and Commons are so weak, helpless, and ignorant that they can neither support nor legislate for Ireland without British aid."

Lodge 652, Dublin, March 3rd, 1800—

"Resolved unanimously—That, as a loyal and Protestant association, attached as we are to our most gracious Sovereign and happy Constitution, we cannot, without the utmost indignation and regret, see a resolution from the Grand Lodge enjoining us to silence on the momentous question of a legislative union.

"Resolved—That, sorry as we are to differ in opinion from the Grand Lodge, we should consider our silence as being accessory to the annihilation of that Constitution which, as Orangemen and freemen, we have solemnly sworn to support.

"Resolved—That we consider the friends of that abominable measure—a union with Great Britain—as the greatest enemies to our most gracious Sovereign—a measure which would destroy our existence as a nation, and eventually involve the rights and the liberties, and even the lives, of the people of Ireland.

"Resolved—That, from the above consideration, we solemnly protest against that destructive measure, and do call upon our brother Orangemen, by every legal means, to support that Constitution for which we risked our lives and properties in the hour of danger. G. S., *Deputy-Master.*
H. F., *Secretary.*"

Lodge No. 500, Mountmellick, 4th Feb. 1800—

"*An Address to all Brother Orangemen.*

"Conscious as we are of our loyalty to His Majesty George III., and our attachment to the happy Constitution of this Kingdom as established in 1782, we have beheld with surprise and concern an address from the Grand Lodge to all Orangemen, entreating them to be silent on a question whereby the Constitution is vitally attacked, and whereby the loyalty of the most valuable part of our countrymen is shaken or endangered. We cannot think it the duty of Orangemen to submit implicitly in all cases of the utmost moment to the dircetions of a lodge, which is principally composed of persons who are under a certain person, which is exerted against the rights of Ireland, and while a lodge under such influence shall give the law to all Orangemen, we fear that our dearest interests will be betrayed. We therefore protest against its injunctions to silence, and declare, as Orangemen, as freeholders, as Irishmen, that we

throughout the country. The great functionaries of the Society belonged, of course, to the Grand Lodge in Dublin; they were the Grand Master, the Deputy Grand Masters, the Grand Chaplain, the Grand Treasurer, the Grand Secretary, the Deputy Grand Secretary, and the Grand Committee. But the country lodges had their great functionaries and grandees too.

The Grand County Lodges controlled the District Lodges, the District Lodges controlled the Private Lodges, and the Grand Lodge in Dublin controlled all. This lodge met twice a year (in May and November) for the transaction of general business, and the chief officers of the Grand County Lodges attended to represent the provincial organisations.

The leaders of the Orange Society belonged to the aristocracy of the country; the rank and file were farmers, labourers, and mechanics.

The Earl of Gosford, as we have seen,[1] said before the Committee of 1835: "There appears a great deal in

consider the extinction of our separate Legislature as the extinction of the Irish nation. We invite our brother Orangemen without delay to elect a Grand Lodge which shall be composed of men of tried integrity, who shall be unplaced, unpensioned, and unbought, and who shall avow their best qualification for such a station, that they will support the independence of Ireland and the Constitution of 1782.

HENRY DEERY, *Master.*
JOHN ROBINSON, *D.-M.*
ABRAHAM RYLAND, *Secy.*"

Lodge 651—

"Resolved—That we deeply lament the necessity which compels us to differ from the Grand Lodge, as we conceive no body of men whatsoever have so just a right to take into serious consideration the subject of Legislative Union with Great Britain as the Orangemen who have associated for the sole purpose of supporting the kingdom and Constitution. That we see with unspeakable sorrow an attempt made to deprive us of that Constitution, of our trade, our rising prosperity, and our existence as a nation, and reducing us to the degrading situation of a colony to England. That we consider this measure but an ill return to men who clung to the Constitution in the hour of danger and distress, and risked their lives and properties in its support, to have it snatched from them almost at the moment they have saved it.

GEORGE GOWNE, *Master.*
SAMUEL SMITH, *Secretary.*"

[1] *Ante*, p. 105.

[the Orange rules] which is good Christian charity;" "but," he added, "they are not always adhered to in practice."[1]

This, it must be confessed, was the case. In theory, the Orange Society was Christian and loyal; in practice, it was not always either one or the other. In truth, a hatred of Catholicism—that is to say, a hatred of the faith professed by three-fourths of their fellow-countrymen—was the basis of the religious and political creed of the Orange party.

But this was not all. Liberal Protestants were placed under ban as well as avowed Catholics. Even Protestant policemen who did their duty were denounced as Papists. "If the police do their duty in the County Down," says Sir Frederick Stoven, Inspector-General of Police, before the Committee of 1835, "they are hooted and called Papists because they do their duty."[2] "Then it is not merely that the Catholics are insulted, but any man that does his duty in the discharge of the laws, provided he is opposed to their [the Orange] processions, is exposed to insult?" Sir Frederick was asked. He answered: "I only give the instances I know; I was speaking severely to a sub-inspector in the county of Down upon the subject of some of his police that I thought were not acting quite fairly; he said, 'So far from it, that I assure you, that in some places we can hardly show ourselves, we are so hooted.' And I said, 'How hooted?' and he said, 'We are called Papists; and I have heard myself, when walking along the streets, called "Papist Duff."'" "Is Mr Duff a Catholic? No.—Then why is he called Papist Duff? Because he does his duty.—You are yourself a member of the Established Church? I am.—Do they honour you with that title? I really do not know, but I believe they

[1] "Select Committee on Orange Lodges in Ireland." Q. 3938.

[2] *Ibid.*, 1835. Q. 4520.

do. Some of them, I believe, have no great inclination towards me."[1]

In 1831 two clergymen were expelled the society for voting in favour of a Reform candidate;[2] and this resolution was passed by the Grand Lodge—"That it is the recommendation of the Grand Lodge that the lodges [in the District of Dublin] do remove from any official situations which they may occupy, such persons, being freemen of the city of Dublin, or freeholders, who voted for the Reform candidate at the late election, or who refrained from voting against them."[3]

On November 29, 1832, the Grand Lodge passed this resolution: "That the ex-Sheriff Scott be expelled the institution for entertaining Daniel O'Connell at breakfast on political principles which we do not approve."[4]

Upon one occasion an Orange yeomanry corps refused to be brigaded with another corps in which there happened to be five or six Catholics.

A Presbyterian lieutenant of Orange yeomen was forced to resign his commission because he signed a petition in

[1] "Select Committee on Orange Lodges in Ireland, 1835," 4522, 4526.

Captain Duff, chief constable of police, and private secretary to Sir F. Stoven, stated that all persons discharging their duty impartially, whether as policemen or magistrates, were called Papists in the North of Ireland. Qs. 8158, 8167. He added, "They were going to shoot the sub-inspector in the county of Down twelve months ago, of which I can produce a document. They called him 'papist Crafton.'" Q. 8160.

[2] *Ibid.*, 1939.

[3] *Ibid.*, Q. 1940.

[4] *Ibid.*, 1943.

The views of the society on the subject of Repeal were peculiar. On June 13, 1831, this resolution was passed by the Grand Lodge: "That the Orangemen of Ireland came forward at the close of last year in support of the Government when Mr O'Connell agitated the question of Repeal of the Union, in the confident expectation that they would receive that support from the Government which His Majesty's loyal subjects had a right to expect from His Majesty's Ministers; but that if the Government think proper to sacrifice the interests and endanger the existence of His Majesty's Protestant subjects in Ireland by the provisions of the Reform Bill, they must look to others to support them, should the question be again brought forward of the Repeal of the Legislative Union of the two countries."—*Ibid.*, 1940.

favour of Catholic emancipation. But perhaps the best way to illustrate the difference between Orange rule and Orange practice is to describe an Orange "drum-beating."

"Will you describe what is a drum-beating party? a Protestant witness was asked by the Committee of 1835.—There is a drum and fife playing along the road for the purpose of assembling the Orangemen, we suppose, or the boys in the neighbourhood, as they call themselves; they then proceed to their Orange Lodge, and do whatever is to be done at the lodge; I suppose the lodge is then broken up, and then they beat home again. And when one lodge goes to visit another, they all assemble with drums; very often two or three together will assemble on the roads and parade there.

"Is 'Orange Lodge' painted upon the drum?—Yes, and the number of the lodge.

"Give an account of the tunes they play, and the manner in which it tends to disturb the public peace, in your opinion?—The way in which it affects the public peace is this: if a Catholic or a Liberal Protestant, or a Presbyterian who is Liberal, has become obnoxious to any members of the lodge, the men assemble, and give him a drumming, as it is called, which is to assemble before his house and do not let him sleep all night; and if he attempts to come out, all they do is to aggravate him to the utmost extent, so as to get a legal excuse for committing some outrage upon him.

"To make him strike them?—To get the first blow struck, and then, when that is struck, it is a justification afterwards to the magistrates and to jurors, whereby the parties are dealt with according to the first blow which is struck.

"That is to say they have impunity?—Yes.

"What tunes do they play upon those occasions?—I have heard them play the 'Protestant Boys,' 'Boyne Water,'

'Colonel Vernon's March,' and 'Colonel Vernon's Dance.' I believe there are two tunes to his name.

"Have you heard the 'Prussian Drum,' or 'More Holy Water'?"—Yes.

"Are those tunes deemed offensive by the Catholics, and evidently intended to give offence to them by the party who play those tunes?—Certainly they are."[1]

A great feature in the Orange system were the annual processions held on July 12, to commemorate the Battle of the Boyne.[2]

These processions were an insult to the Catholics, and a danger to the public peace. No doubt Lieutenant-Colonel Blacker, a prominent member of the Society, said before the Committee of 1835, "I beg to say I have never seen the country so quiet, so silent, as upon these nights after the processions were over. . . . It has been a subject of general remark in my part of the world, that men whose conduct might, perhaps, have been considered loose or wild for 364 days in the year, were particular in the correctness of their conduct on that day [the 12th of July]."[3] But impartial witnesses like Mr Christie gave a flat contradiction to this statement.

"There scarcely has been a 12th of July, to the best of my recollection," said Mr Christie, "in any year from the commencement of Orangeism till the present period, when a breach of the peace has not occurred, and frequently lives have been lost in consequence of those processions."[4]

[1] Mr Handcock. Q. 7966, *et seq.*

[2] July 12 being old style for July 1, on which latter day the Battle of the Boyne was fought. Sharman Crawford. Committee on Orange Lodges. Q. 5825.

[3] "Select Committee on Orange Lodges in Ireland, 1835," Q. 8975-76.

[4] *Ibid.*, Q. 5600-5634.

The Earl of Caledon was asked, "Have you found that the public peace has been preserved, or otherwise, in consequence of the existence of Orange Societies, and the processions and demonstrations resulting from them?" He answered, "otherwise." *Ibid.*, Q. 5418-5473. See also the evidence of Mr Sharman Crawford, and Mr Sinclair; and generally.

The Government prohibited an Orange procession from being held at Crossgar on July 12, 1830. The Orangemen defied the authorities, and marched into the town, with fifes playing, drums beating, and colours flying. They were armed with pikes, and the leaders carried drawn swords. Pistol shots were fired in the air, and a determined disposition was shown to resist the law. An equally determined disposition was shown by Sharman Crawford, the magistrate in charge, to enforce it. Crawford ordered the police to pull down a triumphal arch. They did so. He then ordered them to pull down another, but the police officer said it could not be attempted without loss of life, as the Orangemen were resolved to resist. Crawford sent for reinforcements to Downpatrick. The reinforcements quickly arrived. Crawford ordered the Orangemen to disperse. They refused. He then proposed to read the Riot Act, and order the police to clear the town. But the police officer said he had not a sufficient force to do so. Crawford again sent to Downpatrick for more reinforcements, and when these arrived, the Orangemen finally gave way after several arrests had been made, and the peace was preserved.[1]

On the same date an Orange meeting was proclaimed at Dungannon. The proclamation was disregarded; the authorities were again defied. Chief Constable Duff with a party of police attempted to pull down a triumphal arch. The Orangemen gathered around and said they would defend it to the death. Armed Orangemen filled the adjoining houses. A desperate conflict seemed imminent when the magistrates ordered Duff to desist, and the Orange party were left in triumphant possession of the ground.[2]

On July 13, 1832, between 8000 and 9000 Orangemen met near Dungannon. They had sixty stands of colours,

[1] "Select Committee on Orange Lodges in Ireland, 1835." Q. 4313.
[2] *Ibid.*, Q. 7830.

and forty bands playing party tunes. Two hundred and fifty of them were armed with muskets. They were led by some of the foremost men in the county. The Hon. A. G. Stuart, D.L., whose horse was adorned with orange and purple; Mr Grier, J.P., who wore an orange ribbon around his neck; Captain Lowry of the Cameroy Yeomanry, who wore an orange and purple scarf; Captain Lloyde of the Killyman Yeomanry, the Earl of Castle-Stuart, the Hon. Charles Stuart, and several clergymen of the Established Church.[1]

On April 27, 1832, between 4000 and 5000 Orangemen marched through the town of Dungannon with colours flying, and bands playing "the Protestant Boys," "the Boyne Water," "Croppies lie Down." They were led by Colonel Verner, Mr Greer, and Captain Lloyde. A riot took place, and a Catholic had his left arm broken by a shot fired from the Orange ranks.[2]

An attempt was made to prevent an Orange meeting at Port Glenone, in the County Antrim, on July 12, 1834. A body of soldiers were drawn up to prevent the Orangemen from reaching the point of rendezvous. But the Orangemen marched onwards defiantly, forced the soldiers from their position, and reached the appointed place in triumph. The magistrates fearing bloodshed, withdrew the troops, and left the Orange party masters of the situation.[3]

In November 1834 a great Tory Orange meeting was held at Dungannon, "to address the throne in support of His Majesty's prerogative"[4] Several Tory magnates attended; among them—Lord Caledon, Lord Belmore, Lord Abercorn, Lord Claude Hamilton, Lord Corry, Lord Alexander. A scene of wild disorder took place. The Orangemen marched through the town playing party

[1] "Select Committee on Orange Lodges in Ireland, 1835." Q. 8070.
[2] *Edinburgh Review*, January 1836.
[3] "Select Committee on Orange Lodges in Ireland, 1835," 4466.
[4] The King had just dismissed the first ministry of Lord Melbourne.

tunes, waving party colours, and firing shots. One bullet whisked past the ear of Inspector-General Stoven. "I went down," says the Inspector, to "where the Orange flags and things were standing, close to the door at a public house opposite; and I went to Mr Murray, the Magistrate, and said, 'Why, Mr Murray, you may call this keeping the peace of Dungannon, but I never saw anything so bad in my life. I have just been shot at; if you do not stop this firing, I think it is the most disgraceful thing I ever saw.'" However, the firing was not stopped. The proceedings terminated by the installation of Lord Claude Hamilton as Orangeman in a public house. The Sunday after the meeting, Mrs Duff, the wife of the chief constable, on opening her prayer book at church, found this notice in it—"SIR,—As this is the last day to be in this rotten town, I send you this advice: tell Robinson that he and that d——d scout Strong will do very little on Friday at the Protestant meeting; that Duff and Sir F. Stoven had better stay in the house, or they may get an Orange ball which may cause them to stay at home on the 12th of July."[1]

A few more instances of Orange lawlessness will suffice. In November 1830 a party of Orangemen marched through the Catholic village of Maghery to hold a meeting close by. The Catholic villagers were, we are told, in "high good humour," and asked them[2] "to play tunes," which they did. When the meeting was over the Orangemen returned homewards, marching through Maghery again. The Catholic villagers again asked them to play more tunes; "play 'Patrick's Day,'"[3] said one unlucky

[1] This notice was put in the prayer book the Sunday before the meeting, but Mrs Duff did not go to church on that day. Q. 4572-4580.

[2] "Select Committee on Orange Lodges in Ireland, 1835." Mr Hancock, Q. 8018.

[3] It should be stated that "Patrick's Day" is not a party tune. It is the "Irish National air."

villager. The Orange band refused indignantly, and at once struck up "the Prussian Drum," and "the Protestant Boys." A "scrimmage" immediately occurred; the Orange drum and other musical instruments were broken, and the Orange party forced to beat a retreat. Two days afterwards an armed body of Orangemen returned to Maghery. The villagers fled before them, leaving their homes deserted.[1] The Orangemen entered the village, wrecked it, and tried to burn it. They then marched home with drums beating and colours flying.

For this outrage no Orangeman was ever punished a number were tried, but acquitted. For the attack on the Orangemen, four Catholics were tried, convicted, and sentenced to three months' imprisonment. The damage done to the Catholic village was estimated at £600; the damage done to the Orange instruments, at ten shillings.[2]

On midsummer's eve, 1830, a number of children were playing around a bonfire in a field near Tanderagee. A party of Orangemen marching through Tanderagee with fife and drum, and led by a man named Murphy, a servant of Dean Carter, J.P., saw the fire, and went towards it. They entered the field, and immediately struck up the "Protestant Boys." The owner of the field asked them to leave; they refused, and Murphy knocked the owner down. Gault, another one of the Orange party, drew a dagger, and stabbed a young fellow named M'Glade, who died of his wounds. Several others were also attacked and stabbed by the Orangemen, who then withdrew. An inquest was held on the body of M'Glade, and a verdict of "wilful

[1] "Who are more armed, the Catholics or the Orangemen? The Catholics are never armed with deadly weapons.—Are the Orangemen frequently armed? Yes; constantly."—"Select Committee on Orange Lodges in Ireland, 1835." Mr Sinclair, J.P., D.L., Q. 5055, 5056.

[2] Through the intervention of Lord Charlemont, to whom the village belonged, the Catholic rioters were released. Qs. 8014, 8732.

murder" found against four of the Orange party,—Gault, Murphy, Hagan, and Ford. Gault and Hagan escaped capture, but Murphy and Ford were arrested. They were tried by an Orange jury at the Armagh Spring Assizes in 1831. They were acquitted of the charge of murder, but found guilty of riot and assault. Each was sentenced to twelve months' imprisonment with hard labour. On the day of their discharge from prison they were escorted home by a party of Orangemen with bands and colours. Subsequently Ford was received into the police on the recommendation of Dean Carter, and Murphy was enrolled a member of Dr Patten's yeomanry corps. Dr Patten was a District Master of the Orange Society.[1]

On July 12, 1833, an Orange procession marched through Lurgan in defiance of a proclamation prohibiting it. Church bells were rung, shots fired, and Orange colours displayed. Fourteen Orangemen were arrested for this violation of the law, and committed to trial by Mr Hancock, J.P., and Mr Brownlow, J.P. They were tried at the Armagh Assizes on July 24, 1833. Eleven were acquitted on the ground of ignorance of the law, three were convicted, but discharged by the judge (Moore) with a caution.[2] On leaving the court-house they were met by a party of 2000 Orangemen, and conducted in triumph from Armagh to Lurgan. "Colonel Blacker," said Mr Hancock naïvely before the Committee of 1835, "will give you an account of the proceedings, for he stood on the steps of the inn at Portadown, and gave three cheers as the procession passed him."[3] On arriving at Lurgan the procession halted before Mr Hancock's house. Twenty-two drums were beaten, and stones thrown at the windows. "I just arrived," says Mr Hancock, "in the middle of the whole mischief. They made an attempt to shut the turnpike gates to get me

[1] "Select Committee on Orange Lodges in Ireland, 1835." Q. 6388, *et seq.*
[2] Q. 8821. [3] Q. 8825. [4] Q. 8827.

beat, but I was too quick for them"[1] Fortunately a party of the Fifty-second Regiment came up at the moment, and the procession moved away.[2] Later on, about eight P.M., a number of Orangemen assembled at Lord Mandeville's gates near Tanderagee, where Mr Hancock was hanged and burned in effigy.[3]

On November 5, 1834, a party of Orangemen met at Keady to have a sham fight in memory of the battle of the Boyne. The party was divided into two "armies." "King James" commanded one army, and "King William" the other. There was a rivulet close by. This was the "Boyne." Before the "battle" commenced, a force of military and police, acting under the directions of Lord Gosford, arrived. The Orangemen were ordered to disperse; but they showed little willingness to obey. It was the opinion of Lord Gosford, that if the police alone had been summoned, the Orangemen would have held their ground, and blood would have been shed; but the presence of the military, consisting of a troop of dragoons, and two companies of infantry, awed them into submission. Nevertheless, an order which had been given to disarm them was not carried out, as the magistrates feared that resistance would be offered, and grave consequences might follow.[4]

At the general election of 1834, 200 Orangemen armed with pistols and daggers, marched into Trim. They were led by a parson named Preston. They halted before the Tory Committee rooms, and were addressed by one of the Tory candidates, who said, "our chief reliance is on you." Subsequently they entered the court-house,[5] where a pistol was taken from one of them by the sheriff, and finally, on their way home, a Catholic, named Henry, was killed.

[1] Q. 8829.
[2] Q. 8833.
[3] Qs. 3317, 3352.
[4] Q. 3476, *et seq.*
[5] The polling was carried on in the court-house. Q. 6088.

Three Orangemen were tried for the murder; but the jury disagreed.[1]

In January 1835, a party of Orangemen entered the Catholic village of Annahagh, in noon day, and burned seven houses. They then retired to the hill of Kinnigo, close by, and took up position in military array. They were armed with yeomanry muskets. Intelligence of what happened soon reached the town of Charlemont; and a force of artillery and police proceeded to the scene of action. They found the village of Annahagh wrecked, and the armed Orangemen drawn up on the hill of Kinnigo, with fixed bayonets. The artillery and police halted at the base of the hill.

An Orange agent descended and said his party were there in self-defence; that 1000 Catholics were drawn up on a hill further on, ready to attack them. The magistrate said that the Orange party must disperse in any case. "We will," said the Orange agent, "when the Catholics disperse." The magistrate, and Inspector Stoven who commanded the police, then went in search of the Catholics; but not a Catholic was to be seen all around.

They quickly returned, but found that the Orangemen had left Kinnigo. The police were ordered to ascend the hill. On reaching the summit, they saw the Orangemen marching away "in regular order with sloped arms."

The Catholics received compensation for the burning of their houses, but no man was punished for the outrage. "To this hour is there a soul in prison," Lord Gosford was asked by the Committee of 1835, "for this attack

[1] The jury was composed of six Catholics and six Protestants; the Catholics were for a conviction, the Protestants for an acquittal.

During their stay in Trim, some of these Orangemen were lodged in the old jail; others were lodged in a house opposite the new jail, and were "supplied with bed and bedding from the new jail." The Jail Committee consisted of magistrates, all of whom, with one exception, supported the Tory candidates. "Select Committee on Orange Lodges in Ireland." Qs. 6203, 6212.

upon the houses of sixteen Catholics which were wrecked and devastated in the manner described?" He answered· "Not that I am aware of; I believe not."[1]

But perhaps the worst feature in Orangeism was its effect on the administration of justice. "Picture to yourself," said Sheil, "an Irish court of justice. An Orangeman is indicted; in the jurors' box twelve Orangemen are placed; the magistrates, if the case be tried at Quarter Sessions, are members of this fatal fraternity. Under these circumstances, what a mockery is the administration of justice. Sir Frederick Stoven spoke of it as a subject of public ridicule and contempt."[2]

"In all cases, civil and criminal," said Mr Kernan, a

[1] Q. 3474. The cause of the outrage was said to be an attack made on some Orangemen by Catholics a short time previously. With reference to this matter, Lord Gosford was examined. Q. 3613. "Terence M'Mahon [a Catholic, whose house had been attacked by Orangemen about the same time as the burning of Annahagh], the first witness examined [at an official inquiry on the subject] states that it might have been in consequence of McWhinney [an Orangeman] being beat that his house was attacked. The men charged with beating McWhinney live in Annahagh, where the houses were burned. Would it not appear from this that, in the opinion of the Protestants, the first outrage was committed by the Roman Catholics?—I can give an answer in a very few words to that. It was supposed by some that the beating of McWhinney might have been the origin of the circumstances which took place afterwards; but I do not think that was a general impression, or the general feeling at the investigation; and when that was mentioned, it was said, if you go back to what occurred at the races of Armagh [where McWhinney was beaten], you must also go back to what took place at a preceding race at a place called Clantilew; and another magistrate said, if you go to Clantilew, you must go back to the races of Blackwatertown; and another magistrate said, if you will go back to that, you may as well go back at once to the Battle of the Boyne." Q. 3613. Lord Gosford was commissioned by the Lord-Lieutenant to hold an official inquiry into the affair. He reported: "The investigation finished last Wednesday evening, after a very close and minute inquiry into the circumstances which his Excellency was pleased to submit to our consideration. The principal feature in the business was the burning of seven houses in the townland of Annahagh belonging to the Catholics; and I confess this appears to me to have been a most wanton, atrocious outrage, and any attempt to palliate or soften the offence failed in its object, and tended in no way to shake my opinion of the transaction."—"Hansard," 3rd series, vol. xxvii., p. 1074.

[2] Sheil. "Hansard," 3rd series, vol. xxx., p. 291.

Catholic barrister, before the Committee of 1835, "between Protestant and Catholic, justice is positively denied to the Catholic."[1]

In July 1811, a party fight took place between Catholics and Orange yeomen at the fair of Derrygonnelly, in the County Fermanagh. The combatants fought with sticks; the Orange yeomen were beaten. They retired for their guns, returned, and fired on the people.[2] A man named Murvounage was killed. His father went from magistrate to magistrate in the county to swear information against the supposed murderer, one Kitson. The magistrates refused to receive the information, and Kitson fled to America. At the ensuing assizes Judge Osborne was told what occurred. He reprimanded the magistrates, and directed them to take the information. Subsequently, Kitson returned, was arrested, tried, and acquitted. Several other Orange rioters were also tried; they were all acquitted. A number of Catholic rioters were then tried; they were all convicted.[3]

About 1811 a man named Hall broke into a Catholic church and stole the vestments. Moved by compunction, he subsequently caused the vestments to be returned to the parish priest. He was tried for the theft by an Orange jury at Enniskillen. He appeared in the dock with an Orange ribbon on his breast. He declined to offer any evidence or defence. The judge (Fletcher) told the jury that they had nothing to try; that the prisoner had in fact confessed his guilt. The jury found a verdict of "not guilty" without a moment's hesitation. "Thank God, gentlemen," said the judge, "that this is your verdict, not

[1] "Select Committee on Orange Lodges in Ireland." Q. 7321.

[2] "It was the constant practice on the morning of the fair for the yeomen to lodge their arms in a particular place or depôt; then, if a row took place in the evening, or a riot, they fought for some time with sticks, and after this the yeomen generally went for their arms, and fired upon the people assembled at the fair."—Mr Kernan, barrister. Q. 7316.

[3] Q. 7317.

mine; and," he added, "gentlemen, I will not treat you in this case as my highly esteemed departed friend, Judge Fox, treated a jury of this country; I will not placard your names on the session house or grand jury room door; you shall not have an opportunity of dragging me before Parliament; but I will immediately order the sheriff to discharge you from doing any further duty at these assizes." On leaving the dock the prisoner was "hoisted on the shoulders of Orangemen, and carried in triumph through the streets of Enniskillen."[1]

In December 1823, a party of Orange yeomen broke into the house of a Catholic named M'Custer, and asked for arms. M'Custer said he had none, and told the Orangemen to leave. They refused. A scuffle ensued, and M'Custer was knocked down. He jumped up quickly, seized a pitch-fork, and drove the Orangemen off. But they remained in force to the number of seventeen outside the house. M'Custer sent a messenger for his brothers who lived close by. They hastened to his rescue, but were met by the Orange party, who brutally assailed them, breaking the arm of one, and the leg of another.

The Orangemen were tried for this offence by an Orange jury, and acquitted. The case was subsequently brought before Parliament by Mr John Smith, member for London; but the M'Custers obtained no redress.[2]

In 1835 three Orangemen were tried at the Armagh Assizes for marching in procession. The judge, Baron Pennefather, suggested to them, with a view of mitigating their sentence, that they should express regret for violating the law. They replied by whistling the "Protestant Boys" in the dock. They were sentenced to three weeks' imprisonment.[3]

I have now, I think, given a sufficient number of cases to

[1] Qs. 7216, 7231. [2] Q. 7336.
[3] Sheil. "Hansard," 3rd series, vol. xxx. p. 292.

illustrate the working of the Orange system in Ireland, and shall only add an extract from a famous charge delivered by Mr Justice Fletcher in 1815.

He sums up the character of the Orange Society, thus:—

"In the next place, the country has seen a magistracy over-active in some instances, and quite supine in others. This circumstance has materially affected the administration of the laws in Ireland. In this respect I have found that those societies, called Orange Societies, have produced most mischievous effects, and particularly in the North of Ireland. They poison the very fountains of justice, and even some magistrates under their influence have, in too many instances, violated their duty and their oaths. I do not hesitate to say, that all associations, of every description, in this country, whether of Orangemen or Ribbonmen, whether distinguished by the colour of orange or of green; all combinations of persons, bound to each other by the obligation of an oath, in a league for a common purpose, endangering the peace of the country, I pronounce them to be contrary to law, and, should it ever come before me to decide upon the question, I shall not hesitate to send up bills of indictment to a grand jury against the individuals, members of such an association, wherever I can find the charge properly sustained.

Of this I am certain, that, so long as those associations are permitted to act in the lawless manner they do, there will be no tranquillity in this country, and particularly in the North of Ireland. There, those disturbers of the public peace, who assume the name of Orange yeomen, frequent the fairs and markets, with arms in their hands, under the pretence of self-defence, or of protecting the public peace, but with the lurking view of inviting the attacks from the Ribbonmen, confident that, armed as they are, they must overcome defenceless opponents, and put them down. Murders have been repeatedly perpetrated upon such occasions; and though legal prosecutions have ensued, yet such have been the baneful consequences of those factious associations, that, under their influence, petty juries have declined (upon some occasions) to do their duty. These facts have fallen under my own view. It was sufficient to say, such a man displayed such a colour, to produce an utter disbelief of his testimony, or, when another has stood with his hand at the bar, the display of his party badge has mitigated the murder into manslaughter. Gentlemen, I do repeat that these are my sentiments, not merely as an individual, but as a man discharging his judicial duty, I hope with firmness and integrity. With these Orange Associations I connect all commemorations and processions, producing embittering recollections, and inflicting wounds upon the feelings of others; and I do emphatically state it as my settled opinion, that, until those Associations are effectually put down, and the arms taken from their hands, in vain will the North of Ireland expect tranquillity or peace."

In the same charge, he says: "The ties of religion and morality being thus loosened, a frightful state of things has ensued; perjury has abounded; the sanctity of oaths has ceased to be binding, save where they administer to the passions of parties. The oaths of the Orange Associations, or of the Ribbonmen, have, indeed, continued to be obligatory. As for oaths administered in a court of justice, they have been set at nought. Gentlemen, I must further admonish you, if you are infested with any of the Orange or Green Associations in this county, to discourage them; discourage all processions and commemorations connected with them, and you will promote the peace and concord of the country; but suffer them to prevail, and how can justice be administered? 'I am a loyal man,' says a witness; that is, 'Gentlemen of the petty jury, believe me, let me swear what I will.' When he swears he is a loyal man, he means, 'Gentlemen of the jury, forget your oaths, and acquit the Orangemen.'

"A truly loyal man is one who is attached to the Constitution under which we live, and who respects and is governed by the laws, which impart more personal freedom, when properly administered, than any other code of laws in existence. If there are disturbances in the country, the truly loyal man endeavours to appease them. The truly loyal man is peaceful and quiet; he does his utmost to prevent commotion, and, if he cannot prevent it, he is at his post, ready to perform his duty in the day of peril. But what says the loyal man of another description, the mere pretender to loyalty? 'I am a loyal man in times of tranquillity; I am attached to the present order of things, as far as I can get any good by it; I malign every man of a different opinion from those whom I serve; I bring my loyalty to market.' Such loyalty has borne higher or lower prices, according to the different period of modern times; he exposes it to sale in open market at all times, seeking continually for a purchaser. Such are the pretenders to loyalty, many of whom I have seen; and incalculable mischiefs they perpetrate. It is not their interest that their country should be peaceful; their loyalty is a 'sea of troubled waters.'

"Gentlemen, I have had a long professional experience of the state of this country, travelling two circuits every year, and I have spoken the result of my professional observations and judicial knowledge. Perhaps the sincerity with which I have put forward these observations may excite some displeasure; but I hope they may do some good, and I am pretty indifferent whether they are found disagreeable or not. Living a great part of my life in the hurry of professional pursuits, I have employed the moments of my leisure in literary retirement. Attached to no party, I have never mixed with the zealots of either; I have been assailed and calumniated by both. Such is the lot of the man endeavouring to do his duty with firmness and sincerity."[1]

So far I have only dealt with Orangeism in Ireland. I shall now deal with it elsewhere.

After the Union, the Orange Society spread to England, where lodges were opened under warrants from the Grand Lodge in Dublin. But in 1808, a Grand Lodge for England was established at Manchester, under the presidency of Colonel Taylor, and thenceforth English lodges were opened under its warrants. Between 1808 and 1813, lodges were opened at Manchester, London, Birmingham, Liverpool, Norwich, Sunderland, Dover, Chelmsford, Newcastle-upon-Tyne, Sheffield, Bury, Halifax, Exeter, Plymouth, Chester, Cambridge, Oldham, and other towns.[2] In 1821, the English Grand Lodge was transferred from Manchester to London, where its first meeting was held at the house of Lord Kenyon, and under his lordship's presidency, on April 27.

The Society also spread to Scotland, Wales, and the colonies; entered the army, infected the church, and, as Orangemen boasted, stopped only on the confines of the throne itself. In 1828, the Duke of Cumberland[3] became Grand Master of the Order throughout the empire; Lord Kenyon was Deputy Grand Master of England and Wales; Lord Gordon, Deputy Grand Master of Scotland; and Lord Enniskillen, Deputy Grand Master of Ireland. The duties of Grand Chaplain were discharged by no less a personage than the Lord Bishop of Salisbury.

There was no feature of the Orange system more important than the existence of Orange lodges in the army.

"Your Committee," says the Report of the Select Com-

[1] "Select Committee on Orange Lodges in Ireland." Q. 3534.

[2] "Parliamentary Debates," vol. xxvi., p. 977. It is not quite clear whether some of those lodges were not opened before 1808.

[3] The Orangemen used proudly to allude to his Grace as "nearest to the throne."

mittee of the House of Commons, appointed in 1835 to inquire into the Orange Institution in Great Britain and the colonies, "inserts a list of military warrants issued to the following regiments to hold lodges under the loyal Orange Institution, and which was extracted from the printed register of 1830, presented by Mr Chetwoode; and, if the regiments and military corps holding warrants under the Grand Lodge of Dublin, as stated in the evidence before the House, are taken into account, it will be seen how large a portion of the army has been at different times imbued with Orangeism:—

"No. 30. 13th Light Dragoons.
" 31. Royal Sappers and Miners, 7th Comp.
" 33. 24th Regiment of Foot.
" 58. 95th or Rifle Brigade.
" 64. 35th Regiment.
" 65. Royal Artillery Drivers.
" 66. 43rd Regiment.
" 67. Royal Artillery.
" 77. Royal Horse Artillery.
" 84. 42nd Foot (Highlanders).
" 87. 59th Foot.
" 94. Rifle Brigade, 2nd Batt.
" 104. 42nd Regiment.
" 114. Rifle Brigade.
" 120. 31st Foot.
" 125. 7th Dragoon Guards.
" 131. 16th Light Dragoons.
" 165. 51st Light Infantry.
" 181. 6th Foot.
" 190. 6th Dragoon Guards.
" 204. 5th Do.
" 205. Royal Artillery, 4th Batt.
, 232. Do., 7th Batt
" 238. 67th Foot.

"No. 241. 29th Foot.
„ 243. Royal Sappers and Miners.
„ 248. Royal Artillery, 5th Batt.
, 254. Do., 6th Batt.
„ 258. 94th Foot.
„ 260. 17th Foot.
„ 269. 1st Royal Dragoons.
„ 204. 6th Dragoon Guards."[1]

Orange lodges were established among the troops in Bermuda, Malta, Corfu, New South Wales, Van Dieman's Land, and Canada, and in some cases it was sought to maintain these lodges in opposition to the military authorities. But the relations between the Orange Society and the army may best be gathered by the following extract from the Report of the Committee of 1835.

"At the first meeting of the Orange Institution of Great Britain, after the Duke of Cumberland became Grand Master, held at the house of Lord Kenyon, on the 17th of March, 1829, the Duke of Cumberland in the chair, the Report of the Grand Committee was read, received, and confirmed, and the following resolutions were unanimously adopted:—

"'That new warrants be granted—

"'No. 66. To Samuel Morris, musician, 43rd Foot, Gibraltar.
„ 94. To Hospital-Serjeant Chas. O. Haines, 2nd Batt. Rifle Brigade, Malta.
„ 104. To Private James Bain, 42nd Foot, Gibraltar.
„ 114. To Corporal John Parkinson, 2nd Batt. Rifle Brigade, Devonport.
„ 248. To R. Lawrence, 5th Batt. Royal Artillery, Gibraltar.'

[1] "Report of Select Committee [Commons] of 1835 on Orange Institution in Great Britain and the Colonies," p. xii. There were two Committees on the Orange Institution: one for Ireland, one for Great Britain and the Colonies.

"At a subsequent meeting in the same place, on the 4th of June 1832, where the Duke of Cumberland also presided, the Report of the Grand Committee and their resolutions were read before the Grand Lodge. The tenth resolution is to the effect that 'several additional letters were laid before the Grand Committee, containing complaints against Mr Chetwoode.' Among these were letters from the following non-commissioned officers and privates:—

"*Bermuda.* Serjeant Chainey, Nov. 2, 1831.
Corfu. Hospital-Serjeant Haines, 2nd Batt. Rifles, April 15, 1832.
Dublin. Brother Nichols, 50th Regiment, May 12, 1832.
Malta. Brother M'Innes, 42nd Regiment (Highlanders), May 1, 1832.
Quebec. Brother Inglis, 24th Regiment.

"By the Report of the proceedings of the Grand Lodge, held on the 16th April 1833, the Duke of Cumberland being in the chair, it appears that the proceedings of warrant 233, Woolwich (being a military warrant, Royal Artillery, 9th Battalion), were read, and Brother John Gibson (military) of the said warrant was examined; and it was resolved that Charles Nimens (a private in that battalion) should be suspended from membership, with right of appeal through the Grand Committee to the next Grand Lodge.

"There are regular entries of the names of the regiments and the corps of artillery, and to others, in the ledgers, from 1820 to 1824, the number of the warrants granted to each of them, the amount of dues owing by them to the Grand Lodge, and the amounts received from time to time from them. All these accounts are kept by the Deputy Grand Treasurer; and once a year, or oftener, the accounts of the institution were balanced and laid before the Grand Lodge; and in these printed accounts entries from lodges in the army also appear. In the accounts published and circulated within the last three years to every member of the Grand Lodge, there are many entries also of the names of the privates and non-commissioned officers from whom money was received, viz.:—

"'Dues received from the following military lodges, from the account submitted to the Grand Lodge, 4th of June, 1835:

"' *Woolwich.*	133.	13, Dues to March, 1833,	£0	15	6
	296.	1st Royal Dragoons, .	2	8	0
Gibraltar.		53rd Regiment, for new warrant, . . .	1	11	6
From Malta.		Fusiliers, granted by Commissioner Nucella, for new warrant,	3	0	0
Dover.	114.	Dues from June 1832, 1st Rifle Brigade,		0	0

"There is a register in which some thousand names are alphabetically entered, with the number of the lodge they belong to, and of these some hundreds are entered as military, and opposite to them the number of the regiments they respectively belong to.

"There exists a register, printed in 1826, and made up in manuscript by Mr Chetwoode to 1830, of all the lodges under the institution, having the names of thirty regiments or corps opposite the numbers of the warrants they held; and many of the printed circulars announced that those printed registers of the lodges were on sale at 2s. each. An extract of the registers of military lodges is given in another part of the report.

"In the printed circular reports of the proceedings of the Grand Lodge, at which his Royal Highness presided, there are entries of the warrants granted to regiments by that Grand Lodge: for instance, it appears from the minutes of proceedings of the meeting of the Grand Lodge at No. 9 Portman Square, on the 17th February 1831, the Duke of Cumberland, Grand Master of the Empire, in the chair, that the issuing of twenty-four warrants to hold new lodges was approved, and three of them are thus inserted, viz.:—

"No. 254. To Samuel Heasty, 6th Battalion Artillery.
" 258. To James Smith, 94th Foot.
" 260. To Private Wilson, 17th Foot.

"There are also entries (1947) of Serjeant William Keith having attended two meetings as proxy for the 1st Regiment of Dragoon Guards, warrant 269; and by a resolution at a meeting of the Grand Lodge on the 15th of February, 1827, 'No person can be received as proxy in the Grand Lodge, who is not of himself qualified to sit and vote therein."

"In the laws and ordinances of 1821, 1826, and 1834, there is an apparent encouragement held out for the initiation of soldiers and sailors to be Orangemen, by the remission of the fees of admission.

"On the 4th of June, 1834, there is the following entry in the printed Report of Proceedings—

"'Rule 41st.—No person can be admitted into the institution for a less fee than 15s., nor advanced into the purple order, after a reasonable probation, for less than an extra fee of 5s., except soldiers and sailors, when the fee of admission shall be at the discretion of the meeting.'"[1]

After the emancipation of the Catholics, during the

[1] "Report on Orange Lodges in Great Britain and the Colonies," pp. xx., xxi.

struggle for Parliamentary reform, and while the Grey Ministry remained in power, an important effort was made to reorganise the Orange Institution, so that it might prove a formidable barrier to further legislation in the direction of popular liberty. The Orangemen had lost confidence in the Tory chiefs, and were resolved themselves to make a stand for the "Constitution."

At this period—1829-1834—a character famous in Orange history appeared upon the scene, Lieutenant-Colonel William Blennerhasset Fairman. Fairman seems to have been a person of some energy and resource; eager for fame; and ready for the most desperate enterprises. He drew the Orange Society to the verge of treason, and was himself perhaps prepared to cross the constitutional boundary; but the Society flinched; and Fairman vanished. Writing of his plot—for the "Fairman plot" has its place in history as well as the "Cato Street Conspiracy"—Harriet Martineau says:—"The whole affair appears so unsuited to our own time, and the condition of our monarchy—so like a plunge back into a former century—that all the superiority of documentary evidence we have is needed to make the story credible to quiet people who do not dream of treason plots and civil war in England in our day."[1]

Fairman joined the Orange Society about 1815; but he was advanced to no important post until the events which have made his name notorious occurred. In 1831 he became Grand Secretary and Grand Treasurer of the Society in Great Britain.

Fairman has been charged with no less serious an offence than a plot to change the succession to the crown. It was his design, and the design of the Orange Society—so it has been said—to place the Duke of Cumberland on the throne, to the exclusion of the Princess Victoria.

[1] Martineau, "History of the Peace," ii. p. 266.

I am not prepared to assert that this charge has been proved; but it is, I think, clear that Fairman was resolved to make the Orange Society a great physical power, and to resist by arms the attempts of any Government to put it down. But the fairest way to deal with the subject is to set out the "documentary evidence" mentioned by Harriet Martineau.

This evidence consists of letters written by and to Fair man, concerning the reorganisation of the Society. These letters will speak for themselves.

FAIRMAN TO THE DUKE OF CUMBERLAND.

[*No date; but written probably in* 1829 *or* 1830.]

"SIR,—Presuming on the confidence reposed in me by the late Duke of York,[1] the result of a zealous advocacy, as also of the innumerable communications I had the honour of making to him, during a series of years, on affairs of vital importance to the safety, not alone of his august family, but to the existence of the empire, which I might be justified in affirming it was my peculiar good fortune to have been instrumental in rescuing from commotion in more instances than one—in addressing your Royal Highness, should I insensibly fall into an unreserved strain, no less indicative of a conscious integrity than of an independent mind, pregnant with patriotic loyalty, the manliness of your own character will prove my best indemnity, if through the frankness of my nature I shall happen to be guilty of an unintentional departure from State etiquette.

"Of my numerous services, both private and public, I have the amplest proofs, the most satisfactory testimonials, under the hand of the late much-lamented Commander-in-Chief, as likewise, indeed, of a much higher personage, to which I am at present only induced to allude as a medium

[1] The Duke of York had been Grand Master of the Society; he resigned the post on learning that there were some doubts respecting its legality.

of introduction and access to your Royal Highness. Unwilling to rush unnecessarily into the presence of my superiors, I may, nevertheless, be permitted to glance slightly at the danger of committing to paper that which, for the protection of all parties, might be more securely submitted in person. In evidence of this, perhaps it may be venial in me to intimate I am in suspense at this moment as to the receipt of a letter by the illustrious Prince to whom it was addressed, left at Cumberland House, in St James' Palace, so long since as January last. From my past experience of the scrupulous graciousness with which all applications were uniformly acknowledged in such quarters, I should be almost warranted in apprehending a transitive miscarriage to have occurred on one side; hence it behoves me to be somewhat more guarded on such an occasion as the present.

"At the same time, I consider it to be no less my duty than it is my inclination to add, that any command with which I may be honoured in writing upon this subject, I shall feel great cheerfulness in obeying. Here, probably, it may neither be thought superfluous nor disrespectful to premise, that all developments, as between the late Duke of York and myself, were held inviolably sacred; by whom it was understood most distinctly, that I was neither to undergo an examination, nor be questioned as to the sources through which my intelligence had been ever derived. By such conditions his Royal Highness was pleased to signify his readiness to abide, who condescended to convey to me a solemn assurance that my disclosures, to whatever they might extend, should invariably be received in strict confidence for his personal guidance, but nothing more. Long before it exploded, I detected and exposed the conspiracy against the House of Brunswick, which in 1809 assumed a tangible shape, and involved in it consequences the most painful. This, however, was only one of the many things discovered and divulged by me, the acquirement, the unravelling of which, whether the effect of apocalyptical gift, intuitive light, or of what other means, is not material to the purpose; suffice it to say, that no system of espionage was resorted to, no faith betrayed nor trust broken; but that it was done rather by a fair grapple with the enemy than by a recourse to base acts, vile agency, or unworthy aid of any kind. A spirit of enterprise, and a genius for the self-imposed task, with a moderate share of discernment, and a facility in arriving at right conclusions, were the chief auxiliaries which afforded me the happiness of preparing those, for whose preservation I had risked my life, against the storms and tempests then gathering, with the mischiefs and ills about to burst upon them.

"Should an indisposition,[1] which has agitated the whole country for a fortnight, take a favourable turn,—should the Almighty in His mercy give ear unto the supplications that to His heavenly throne are offered up daily, to prolong the existence of one deservedly dear to the kingdom at large, —the divulgement I have expressed a willingness to furnish would be deprived of no small portion of its value. Even in this case, an event, for the consummation of which, in common with all good subjects, I obtest the Deity, it might be as well your Royal Highness should be put in possession of the rash design in embryo, the better to enable you to devise measures for its frustration; at any rate, you would not then be taken by surprise, as the nation was last year, but might have an opportunity of rallying your forces and of organising your plans for the defeat of such machinations as might be hostile to your paramount claims. Hence should the experiment be made, and its expediency be established, your Royal Highness would be in a situation to contend for the exercise in your own person of that

[1] The illness of George IV.

office at which the wild ambition of another may prompt him to aspire.

"Instead of offering in the channel thus selected the revealment in question, it has been suggested to me that the . . ."

The rest of this letter has not come to light, but the "rash design in embryo" is explained in the next.

FAIRMAN TO JOHN SYDNEY TAYLOR, OF THE *Morning Herald.*

"(Private.)

"DEAR SIR,—From those who may be supposed to have opportunities of knowing 'the secrets of the castle,' the King is stated to be by no manner in so alarming a state as many folks would have it imagined. His Majesty is likewise said to dictate the bulletins of his own state of health. Some whisperings have also gone abroad, that in the event of the demise of the crown, a regency would probably be established, for reasons which occasioned the removal of the next in succession from the office of high admiral. That a maritime government might not prove consonant to the views of a military chieftian of the most unbounded ambition,[1] may admit of easy belief; and as the second heir-presumptive is not alone a female but a minor,[2] in addition to the argument which might be applied to the present, that in the ordinary course of nature it was not to be expected that his reign could be of long duration, in these disjointed times it is by no means unlikely a vicarious form of government may be attempted. The effort would be a bold one, but after the measures we have seen, what new violations should surprise us? Besides, the popular plea of economy and expedience might be

[1] The Duke of Wellington.
[2] The Princess Victoria.

urged as the pretext, while aggrandizement and usurpation might be the latent sole motive. It would only be necessary to make out a plausible case, which, from the facts on record, there could be no difficulty in doing, to the satisfaction of a pliable and obsequious set of ministers, as also to the success of such an experiment.—Most truly yours, "W. B. F."

"*Wednesday, April 16th,* 1830.

"I have scribbled this at Peel's, and if you wish it, will write a paragraph on the subject. From all that I hear, there can be little doubt the King will soon resume his rides in the Great Park now that the drawing-room is gone by.[1]

"JOHN SYDNEY TAYLOR, Esq.,
"*Morning Herald* Office."

(*Copy.*)

FAIRMAN TO SIR JAMES COCKBURN.

"THE BRITISH, *July* 14, 1831.

"MY DEAR SIR JAMES,—By private hand I lately had the pleasure of forwarding you two letters of different dates from Esher. Having, as the Metropolitan Deputy Grand Master of the Orange Institution, to preside at a district dinner on the 12th, to commemorate the glorious battle of the Boyne, Saville was kind enough to drive me up to London on Tuesday last. This has afforded me an opportunity of redeeming my promise to you, by enclosing the first of a series of essays which were addressed by me recently to a noble lord, on his own invitation, on the visionary scheme now afloat for the removal of all our political sores.

"Whenever this ill-fated branch of the empire shall

[1] The above letter was returned, as there is a post-mark dated seven at night, April 6, 1830, and addressed thus:—"To Colonel Fairman, British Coffee House, Cockspur Street."

again be involved in a civil war, against which emancipation, that balsam for its complaints, as the cathartic now in preparation is calculated to do towards the removal of the disease of England, the formidable force in review[1] will hasten with cheerfulness to the arduous scene of action. By our late returns its numerical strength now exceeds 175,000, and is fast augmenting. Though in regard to numbers we are infinitely less on this side of the water, in even that respect we are by no means despicable; and while this loyal corps is equally well affected to the constitution, its members are increasing as much in their influence as in their amount.

"My own fine fellows who compose the lodges in the capital and its environs, none of whom are Reformers, for upon this vital point I sounded them, are staunch to the backbone. Should it be required of them to muster for the protection of the lives or the property of those uncompromising men who may possess the spirit to brave hostility, by an opposition to so monstrous a plan, at my summons they would assemble, and under my command they would place themselves for putting their principles to the test. I have strong reasons to be of opinion that before long there will be some occasion.

"The unfeeling insolence of the aristocracy has attained a pitch, too, that will assuredly be the means of precipitating its tremendous downfall. Many of its wranglers, in their own council, are more than mortal, and have the daring, as worms grovelling on the earth, to vie with the omnipotence of Heaven. These vain aspirants will soon, however, be cast from their elevated seats, when we shall behold them as servile and abject in adversity as they have been overbearing and presumptuous to inferiors in prosperity, of which the arrival of the evil hour will alone

[1] The Orange Society.

make them sensible. One, moreover, of whom it might ill become me to speak but in terms of reverence, has nevertheless been weak enough to ape the coarseness of a Cromwell, thus recalling the recollection to what had been far better left in oblivion. His seizure of the diadem, with his planting it upon his brow, was a precocious sort of self-inauguration. Prior to the day fixed for the performance of the ceremony to be observed at the coronation, it is intended that the levelling scroll should have obtained the signature of H. M. For the achievement of this grand object, the most violent exertions will be made, in tenderness to the Sovereign's oath, to maintain the true principle of the constitution. Hence it should appear that his lordship entertains a more scrupulous veneration for the sacred solemnity of such a moral obligation than was. . . . by his grace.

"Lists of all the divisions in the Commons, of which I forward to you one, have been circulated most extensively, that the rabble may be apprized of those inimical to their privileges. The names of the refractory peers will be published and dispersed all over the kingdom in a like gratuitous way, that vengeance may be inflicted the more easily on those who shall have the rashness to vote against the Bill. So far from a reaction in the sentiments of the public, or at least a returning state of sanity, with a great part of it the unruffled calm that distinguishes the feelings of the Reformers is only a prelude to the gathering storm which is howling at a distance, and will draw on us anon. But under all changes I shall remain, my dear Sir, ever yours, unalterably, "W. B. F."

"*To* SIR JAMES COCKBURN."

SIR JAMES COCKBURN TO FAIRMAN.

"NEW SPRING GARDENS, *July* 27, 1831.

"MY DEAR FAIRMAN,—I am much mortified to find that you called upon me last week when I was not at my office.

"I am most sorry to have missed you, as I should have much liked to have talked over with you the subject, and thanked you for the perusal of the letters which you have so kindly favoured me with the copies of, though I cannot but regret to have given you the trouble of copying them. It is a great pleasure to me to feel that I quite agree in the view you have taken of the sentiments you have so ably expressed of the tremendous measure now agitating the country.[1]

"I scarcely know where to send this, but shall address it to the British as the surest course; and am always, dear Fairman, most sincerely yours,

"J. COCKBURN."

"LIEUT.-COL. FAIRMAN,
British Coffee-House, Cockspur Street."

FAIRMAN TO LORD KENYON.

[*No date.*]

"MY LORD,—Having acquired, in the course of a long correspondence on State affairs with the late Duke of York, and most of the Ministers of the day, a freedom from reserve which alone could render my communications of the least possible use, I now address your lordship in the same spirit, from a persuasion that one practical hint may be far better, and will prove infinitely more welcome to you, than a string of unfruitful compliments. In full exercise of such a privilege, then, I shall proceed to the discussion of some preliminary points prior to my submitting for the consideration of your lordship, and those with whom you are in the habit of acting, a few crude suggestions that ought to be calculated to open the eyes of the community to the gross

[1] The Reform Bill.

delusion which is about to be played off by the charlatans of reform."[1]

. . . . . .

LORD KENYON TO FAIRMAN.

"PORTMAN SQUARE, *August* 24, 1831.

"DEAR SIR,—From what I hear of some periodical publications, and what I collect of the state of the public mind in some parts, I certainly think a clever taking periodical should be published. If such a weekly publication, not like any paper now existing, but of a different character altogether, could be brought out, I think much good might result in enlightening and guiding the public mind. I know not where to find proper persons to direct or conduct such a work. The object, I think, should be to show the public how entirely inconsistent with their real interests is the conduct of those, whether in Parliament or out of it, whether talkers or writers, in whom they are inclined to place [confidence]. Another great object too would be to show how grievously the French and Belgians have suffered from the revolutions in which they have been engaged; a specific statement on that point would produce much effect. As to the Reform Bill, my opinion has been uniform from the beginning that that measure must be resisted by all friends to order, government, and property, because it would inevitably annihilate all three, by giving power to those who, having no property, would seek for nothing but plunder. I am at all times glad to hear from you, and shall be glad to see any specific plan.—I am, dear Sir, yours truly,

"KENYON."

"*To* W. B. FAIRMAN, Esq.,
"British Coffee-House, Cockspur Street."
("Private.")

[1] A long tirade on Reform follows, endorsed thus :—"Kenyon, Lord, letter to, on Reform."

LORD KENYON TO FAIRMAN.

"PORTMAN SQUARE, *Sept.* 22, 1831.

"MY DEAR SIR,—I have shown some of your essays, the just name for them, to H.R.H. our G. M.,[1] and he has kept them by him, and his attention is so closely given to everything of a public character, that I am convinced they will not slip from his memory or be overlooked by him. I fear we have little chance of establishing and getting into good circulation any weekly or daily publication. I know by severe experience the difficulty and expense, having expended several thousand pounds fruitlessly, and worse than so, for such purpose. Still if we could raise a public purse for the purpose, and have sufficient local and literary aid, and diffuse through its columns sound principles and useful information, I would subscribe willingly; but I am far from wishing to tempt any persons to engage in such a concern from pecuniary speculation, as I would rather hurt myself than ruin another person. My son tells me he feels convinced the House of Commons would last night have thrown out the Reform Bill by a large majority had they voted by ballot. That point seems to me worth pressing on the public in one of our sound newspapers which has circulation in the metropolis and the country. I am convinced that the former excitement now of a year ago was very much artificially created, and if we know what are the real points on which the public opinion of the mass of the population has been perverted from old English feeling, it might be well to try and set it right. These fires,[2] of which we now hear, though they are very dreadful, are still created by active insurrectionary spirit as they were last autumn and winter, but in consequence of a relaxation of all right feeling as to the extent of the crime itself, and rather from

[1] The Duke of Cumberland.

[2] Incendiary fires.

a sort of habit in indulgence of a spirit of revenge or self-will. The utter failure in London, Westminster, and Edinburgh, of the attempts to exhibit public feeling just now on the Reform Bill, though it affords no proof that a different state may be produced when the subject comes actively before our House, yet it shows conclusively, I think, that the inherent failing in the public mind is by no means deeply rooted. Short and pointed addresses to the commonalty, showing them the delusive character of the Reform Bill as framed, and pointing out the reasonableness of great public interests being permitted to have representatives to protect occupations of great national importance on which multitudes are engaged, seem to me to be what it would now be expedient to produce. I return the enclosed, as desired, but think the other letter must be in the hands of H.R.H.—Believe me, yours faithfully,

"KENYON."

" *To* COL. FAIRMAN,
" 15 Hercules Buildings."

" *P.S.*—Excuse blunders."

(*Copy*)

FAIRMAN TO KENYON.

" THE BRITISH, *Nov*, 29, 1831.

"MY LORD,—In forwarding to your lordship the enclosure of yesterday, which for itself speaks so distinctly as to leave me but little to add on the same subject, I am persuaded you will not consider me to have been importunate or obtrusive. Should those with whom your lordship is in the habit of acting see the necessity, at a crisis of danger like the present, for such an engine,[1] the sooner it shall be set in motion the better. The daily press has long been monopolised by, and is now in the sole occupa-

[1] A newspaper.

tion of, the enemy. Hence the multitude, who seldom take much trouble to reflect, who possess not the faculty of judging for themselves, are led astray by the sophistries so sedulously put forth for their misguidance. That filthy concern, the *Times*, which spares neither age nor sex, public bodies nor private individuals, which at a less degenerate era would have been burnt by the common hangman, ought to be forthwith checked in its flagitious course of unparalleled infamy. This can alone be effected by the immediate establishment of an uncompromising journal on opposite principles, for the intrepid exposure of its vile fabrications in all their deformity.

"Such a sacrilegious print is well worthy of its new friends, who are inexorable in their resentments and political animosities, as the vehicle of their rancour has ever been vindictive and diabolically mischievous in all its aims. That the King's ministers secretly connived at the dreadful menaces, at the sanguinary threats, so lavishly indulged in by the Treasury scribes, no rational person can any longer entertain the least doubt; yet these favourite papers, with the deluded whose prejudices they flatter, were the bitterest, the most vociferous in their clamourings for dropping the uplifted axe of offended justice on the devoted heads of the poor wretches whom they had been successful in stirring up to outrage by their seductive machinations. Perhaps this semblance of rigour in their denouncement of the guilty whom they had instigated to crime might be assumed at the command of their taskmasters, who, finding they had gone somewhat too far in raising a storm they were unable to direct, had recourse to that expedient for calming the turbulence of the passions thus excited by the insidiousness of their own instruments.

"With wily folks such manœuvres are not unusual, for they stick at nothing in the furtherance of their nefarious plans. Having fanned into a flame the embers of discord, when found raging with a fury which almost bids defiance to the powers of resistance, they then begin to talk of extinguishing the wide-spreading destructive conflagration. To the violated laws of their country these worthies next deliver up, without a feeling of compunction or remorse, the incendiary tribe among whom they had hurled their firebrands. As well against the persons as the property of those, who were heretofore the guardians of our dearest rights, the people have been prompted to the most atrocious deeds. In the pursuit of a mere phantom, which will neither be the means of enhancing the rate of labour nor of reducing the price of provisions, the two grand desiderata of life, they have sullied their characters as Englishmen, by betraying a disposition to become the assassins of their superiors for endeavouring to undeceive them. On the arrival, however, of the day of reckoning, the hell-hounds, who goaded on the ignorant to the perpetration of evil, will be called on to pay the full penalty of their cold-blooded tergiversations. Till to-morrow I must defer my concluding remarks on the advantages that may result from the proposal submitted.—I have the honour to be, my Lord, your Lordship's very obliged humble servant." [1]

Lord Kenyon to Fairman.

Gredington, *December* 26, 1831.

"My Dear Sir,—The *Age* newspaper seems inclined to establish a morning paper on those public principles which it has advocated before, throughout and since the memorable year 1829. Its former looseness of principle and its scurrility I cannot approve; but I do not admit, as some

[1] No signature. The letter is endorsed in Fairman's handwriting, thus:—"Kenyon, Lord, letter on the subject of Mr Porter's to me, forwarded to his Lordship."

do, that the private characters of public men ought to be considered sacred against all attack. I am very anxious we should have another sound morning paper, as well as the *Morning Post*, the steadiness of which, notwithstanding Zeta's partial obliquity, has been very praiseworthy, and some articles have been very able. I shall not now be in town sooner than January 17, if quite so soon, and I shall be glad to hear from you as any circumstances of interest occur. In my neighbourhood loyalty is predominant.—I am, dear Sir, yours truly,

"KENYON."

"Col. FAIRMAN,
"British Coffee-house, Cockspur Street."

FAIRMAN TO LORD KENYON.

(*Copy.*)

"KEW, *Monday*.

"MY DEAR LORD,—Agreeably to my letter of last Saturday, I waited on the Duke of Cumberland at the palace this morning, by whom I was received most graciously. His Royal Highness was pleased to honour me with a conference, which lasted upwards of an hour,[1] &c., &c., &c."

LORD KENYON TO FAIRMAN.

"PORTMAN SQUARE, *April* 4, 1832.

"MY DEAR SIR,—I much like the zeal of the enclosed and beg you to send an answer forthwith, for which purpose I send a frank. I was much obliged by your letter yesterday, and hope, from your consultation with Lord W——,[2] who is much pleased with them, will redound to

[1] Endorsed—"Kew, January 2, 1832. Kenyon, Lord, letter to, respecting my conference with the Duke of Cumberland."

[2] Lord Wynford.

the credit of one for whom we feel such true attachment.—Ever your sincere friend,

"KENYON."

"*To* Col. FAIRMAN,
"3 Cannon Row, Westminster."

LORD WYNFORD TO FAIRMAN.

"CHISELHURST, *May* 4, 1832.

"MY DEAR SIR,—The communication of Colonel Maxwell is highly important; and I would recommend you to give, either to Colonel Peters or to Mr Spedding, the scheme of His Royal Highness.[1]

"The letter of my friend, Sir Harcourt Lees, contains no fact that I think can be of use.

"I shall not come to town again until the second reading of the Russian Dutch Loan Bill, which probably will be Monday or Tuesday next. I will on that day take care to be in the Deputy Speaker's room at the House of Lords, at four o'clock, and shall be happy to see you.—I am, dear Sir, faithfully yours,

"WYNFORD."

"Colonel FAIRMAN,
"3 Cannon Row, Westminster."

LORD KENYON TO FAIRMAN.

"PORTMAN SQUARE, *June* 22, 1832.

"MY DEAR SIR,—I have seen Mr Wright and another gentleman this morning about the Sunderland Harbour Committee, and have promised them to attend it. I am sorry I cannot find the Rippenden papers to which you refer again, so will hope I must have returned them to you. I trust you will be able soon to settle with our illustrious G.M.[2] on the subject of your tour of inspection.[3]

[1] Cumberland.

[2] The Duke of Cumberland.

[3] Fairman proposed to make a tour of inspection among the Orange lodges in Great Britain.

He was quite willing to sanction it, if you will draw him up a form adapted to the occasion for sanctioning it.—Believe me, my dear Sir, yours most truly,

"KENYON."

"*To* Col. FAIRMAN,
"3 Cannon Row, Westminster."

FAIRMAN TO THE MARQUIS OF LONDONDERRY.

(*Copy.*)

"CANNON ROW, WESTMINSTER,
"*29th July* 1832.

"MY DEAR MARQUIS,—As a stranger to your lordship, I am to apologise for this freedom, which I am emboldened to take, from being the organ of an institution,[1] the last report of whose proceedings I have the pleasure now to enclose for you. In a conference I lately had the honour of holding with the Duke of Cumberland, His Royal Highness was graciously pleased to inform me he had written to your lordship a few days ago on the subject. As this probably might arise from a suggestion of mine to Lord Kenyon, who now happens to be at Durham, I am induced to be more explicit than perhaps I should otherwise have been. With Mr Wright of Sunderland, who was recently in London, I have had some conversation on the great advantages that might result from an extension of such a society at the conjuncture. Conceiving its principles to be strictly in unison with those entertained by your lordship, in the course of our communications your name was introduced, when that gentleman said, if the matter were taken up with spirit by you, the whole district would follow the example, and cheerfully join such an association. To urge it might be political for your lordship to do so, in a personal sense, would be to offer you a very ill compliment; but to contemplate it, as shall presently be made to appear,

[1] Orange Society.

in a patriotic view, the security of that part of the kingdom might be consolidated by such means. The pitmen would perhaps feel inclined to establish lodges among themselves, which might operate as an additional stimulus to their loyalty, and would likewise prove a partial check against their entering into cabals hereafter, no less to the preservation of private property than to that of the public peace. Knowing that your lordship has firmness to espouse the cause you approve, on this occasion I address you with the less reserve.

"When the altar and the throne are alike assailed,—when infidelity and treason are boldly avowed,—when a republic and a lord protector are confidently spoken of,—when, indeed, we have a popish cabinet and a democratical ministry, who, having given birth to a monster they can no longer control,[1] are now alarmed at their own popularity, and of the abject slaves of a ferocious, revolutionary, and subversive press, little short of miracle can work the salvation of our once happy country! It behoves us, nevertheless, to exercise our energies, and by measures at once prompt and vigorous, to stem the torrent that threatens to overwhelm us. By a rapid augmentation of our physical force, we might be able to assume a boldness of attitude which should command the respect of our Jacobinical rulers. What the Catholics and the [Trade] Unionists have achieved by agitation and clamour in a factious cause, we might then be enabled to effect in a righteous one. If we prove not too strong for such a Government as the present is, such a Government will soon prove too strong for us; some arbitrary step would be taken in this case for the suspension of our meetings. Hence the necessity of our laying aside that non-resistance, that passive obedience which has hitherto been religiously enforced, to our own discomfiture. The brave Orangemen

[1] The Reform Bill.

of Ireland rescued their country from rebellion; and their gallant brethren in England would as heroically redeem their own from such perils. On the one hand we have had minor difficulties to contend with, and less danger to surmount, though on the other hand we have not had the same encouragement, and an equal share of support from the higher orders.

"We have lodges at Newcastle, Shields, Darlington, and round about, but they are merely trunks without heads. Unless men of influence and consideration would immediately step forward as county Grand Masters (I speak advisedly), it is of no manner of use for the classes in humble life to assemble for such purposes. The field is now open to your lordship—the post of honour is exclusively your own. If then your lordship would but profit of it, you would deserve well of this country, while at such a crisis you would confer fresh confidence on your own. In a long conversation I had yesterday with Lord Longford, he intimated that the brethren of Ireland were determined to resist all attempts the Liberals might make to put them down, at the same time reproaching us for our tameness in not affording an aid commensurate with the evils by which we were menaced. In proportion to the increase in the numbers of our institution, the defeat of the Whigs will be rendered more certain. Should your lordship feel disposed to entertain views similar to my own, the Deputy Grand Master of England[1] is now in your neighbourhood to give them efficiency. Let me reiterate my apologies for the liberty thus taken, which I trust the importance of the occasion will warrant my having done.—With sentiments of respect, I have the honour to be, my Lord Marquis, your Lordship's very obedient servant,

"W. B. FAIRMAN."

"*To* THE MARQUIS OF LONDONDERRY."

[1] Lord Kenyon.

FAIRMAN TO THE MARQUIS OF LONDONDERRY.

(Copy).

"CANNON ROW, WESTMINSTER,
"*30th July*, 1832.

"MY LORD MARQUIS,—In my letter of Saturday, I omitted to mention that we have the military with us as far as they are at liberty to avow their principles and sentiments, but since the lamented death of the Duke of York, every impediment has been thrown in the way of their holding a lodge. The same observation that was applied to the colliers might be applied to the soldiery. As Orangemen, there would be an additional security for their allegiance and unalterable fidelity in times like the present, when revolutionary writers are striving to stir them up to open sedition and mutiny. In trespassing thus upon the attention of your lordship, I am not so presumptuous as to suppose that anything urged by me could influence your conduct; but, understanding the Duke of Cumberland has communicated with your lordship on this subject, I felt it my duty to put you in possession of certain facts with which you might not be acquainted.—I have the honour to be, my Lord Marquis, your Lordship's very respectful and obedient servant,

"W. B. FAIRMAN."

"*To* THE MARQUIS OF LONDONDERRY."

THE MARQUIS OF LONDONDERRY TO FAIRMAN.

"WYNYARD PARK, *Aug.* 8, 1832.

"SIR,—I am honoured with your two communications of the 29th and 30th ult.

"You do me only justice in believing that I would most willingly embrace every opportunity and do all in my power to espouse the cause and establish the institutions you allude to in this part of the kingdom; but the present state of liberal Whig feeling in this very Whig county, and the very refractory and insubordinate state of the pitmen, entirely preclude the possibility of successful efforts at this juncture. I have had a full conversation and communication with Lord Kenyon on all this matter, who has been in my house these last two days, and I have no doubt he will convince His Royal Highness,[1] as well as yourself, that the present moment is not the time when the object can be forwarded.

"I will lose no opportunity of embracing any opening that may arise; and I have the honour to be, Sir, your very obedient servant,

"VANE LONDONDERRY."

Directed—"Col. FAIRMAN,
"Cannon Row, Westminster, London."
(*Post Mark*—"Stockton.")

FAIRMAN TO THE DUKE OF GORDON.

(*Copy.*)

"CANNON ROW, WESTMINSTER,
"*Aug.* 11, 1832.

"MY LORD DUKE,—I am much flattered by your Grace's kind invitation. As I must necessarily be in Northumberland, and as my presence in Scotland may prove beneficial to our righteous cause, it is not improbable that I shall have an opportunity of offering to your Grace my respects in person, which it will be no less my pride than my duty to do, should I be able to enter North Britain. Our institution is going on prosperously; and my accounts from all quarters are of the most satisfactory kind. By our next general meeting we shall be assuming, I think, such an attitude of boldness as will strike the foe with awe; but we inculcate the doctrine of passive obedience and of non-resistance too religiously by far.

[1] Cumberland.

"A Catholic cabinet with a popish premier should be ostensibly opposed by a Protestant people. With a Government that yields to clamour what it would deny to justice, we ought to be vociferous in proportion. Had we been only a tithe as strenuous in a righteous cause as the adversary has been turbulent in an unholy one, we might have occupied the vantage-ground long ago.

"Our illustrious Grand Master was pleased to honour me with a conference a few days since, and appeared to be in excellent health. Lord Kenyon and the Marquis of Londonderry wrote me from Durham recently, as did Lord Longford and the Viscount Cole from Ireland, in the highest spirits. Our brethren in that country are determined to resist all attempts that shall be made by a Whig Ministry to interrupt their meetings or to suspend their processions; but they complain of our not affording them that support which would give vigour to their proceedings, and which would be an eternal source of terror to the enemy. Their charges are, I must admit, too well founded. However, the time is fast approaching when matters will be brought to an issue, as a conciliatory course will be laid aside, and an opposite one will be resorted to.

"But to return to our own society. What we stand chiefly in need of is men of influence to take the lead in the country, where, as we now have of districts, we should have Deputy Grand Masters of shires. To effect this object my best efforts will be directed, but I am afraid I shall find it a work of difficulty. I am about to organise a plan to render us more attractive: until this be done, and we are put upon a new footing, to expect the least practical good is out of the question. If we are to be considered as the auxiliary force of a constitutional Government, we ought to be in a state of efficiency for such a purpose; if we are to be arrayed in hostility to a Republican Ministry, we ought to be in a condition to check their subversive courses. The most that can be said of us at present is, that we are something on paper, but worse than nothing at all in the field, though in some instances we have inspirited the wavering and neutralised the bad. But these are negative points at best, and do but little good to the cause. As I shall be invested with powers the most extensive on my approaching tour, should your Grace have any friends who might feel disposed to join our fellowship, they could be initiated at once, without the trouble of attending the Grand Lodge, or even of stirring a step for that purpose. In this case, as I shall be provided with all the materials, I could open their lodges and set their warrants in full operation while on the spot.—I have the honour to be, my Lord Duke, your Grace's most devoted and respectful servant, "W. B. FAIRMAN."

"*To* HIS GRACE THE DUKE OF GORDON,
"Gordon Castle, Scotland."

VISCOUNT COLE TO FAIRMAN.

(*Copy.*)

"FLORENCE COURT, *August* 2, 1832.

"(Private.)

"MY DEAR COLONEL,—I hasten to let you know the change, it is only in the place of N—W use N—E; you understand what I mean. All is going on well. I am now going to attend a meeting, so can write no more.—I remain, ever your friend and Brother,

"COLE."

"*To* Colonel FAIRMAN,
"Cannon Row, Westminster."

LORD KENYON TO FAIRMAN.

"DURHAM, *August* 5, 1832.

"MY DEAR SIR,—I was prevented writing yesterday, but beg now to say that I really never did receive back from

H.R.H. your letter proposing your scheme of visitation. I myself gave it to H.R.H., and trust it will be found safe, and save you further trouble. It was remarkably well conceived, I thought. A much better spirit is arising, I have comfort in thinking, and I shall not desert the good cause in Denbighshire, where my son meets with much kind support. If any of the heads of the Dissenters (I mean Christian Dissenters) could be brought to assist us, we should do well almost everywhere; and I am sure ours is the cause of all friends to Christianity. I shall see Lord Londonderry on Tuesday.—Ever your faithful friend,

"KENYON.

"I quit this for Auckland on Saturday; shall then be on the move till the 18th, when I am to be for eight days at Peel Hall, Bolton, and then I trust we shall reassemble at Gredington in health and peace."

"Colonel FAIRMAN,
"3 Cannon Row, Westminster."
"R. Bristol."

THE DUKE OF CUMBERLAND TO FAIRMAN.

"KEW, *Sunday night.*

"The Duke of Cumberland is very sorry that he cannot receive Mr Fairman to-morrow at twelve o'clock, as he has an engagement at twelve o'clock in London, which he cannot put off; but if Mr F. would come here on Tuesday morning at ten o'clock, he will receive him with pleasure. The Duke of Cumberland is not aware of having any warrants to sign, unless Mr Fairman has brought them with him; if so, they will be signed."

"*To* —— FAIRMAN, Esq.,
"Castle Inn, Brentford."
"Er."

Fairman to an Unknown Friend.

"*Friday night.*

"Dear M——,—I am almost fagged to death. I was closeted three hours the other day with our illustrious chief at Kew, and since have had the honour of a conference with him at St James's. I was again at Kew yesterday, and this day, and was at Lord Kenyon's on Tuesday and Wednesday. I have been, too, with Lord Cole, who will leave town in a few days. Enclosed are the letters as you desire, with one likewise from my friend Stanhope. I have left it unsealed for Condell to read, but I think he should not deliver it in an open state. I am afraid it will not be in my power to attend his lodge on Monday, and Losack will not, unless I am present. Inconvenient as it will be to me, I shall have to go again to Chiselhurst, I am afraid.—Most truly yours,

"W. B. F."

The Duke of Cumberland to Fairman.

"The Duke of Cumberland only perceived late last night that there were two notes of Mr Fairman's, and is exceedingly sorry for the inconvenience this must have occasioned Mr F.; but the truth is, that there being no post on a Sunday, he never went to his writing-table till the evening, when first he found these notes. He immediately inquired after the Rolls, and after some trouble has been fortunate enough to get them; they are sealed and signed."

"*To* —— Fairman, Esq."
"Castle Inn, Brentford."

On August 13 the Duke of Cumberland, as Grand Master, gave Fairman a warrant to proceed on his tour of inspection throughout Great Britain.

WARRANT TO FAIRMAN TO MAKE TOUR OF INSPECTION.

. . . .

"Be it known, therefore, that from a knowledge of his experience, and confidence in his integrity, our trusty, well-loved, and Right Worshipful Brother, Lieutenant-Colonel Fairman, Master of the Metropolitan Warrant, Member of the Grand Committee, Deputy Grand Master of London, Acting Deputy Grand Treasurer, and Deputy Grand Secretary of the Institution, is hereby nominated, constituted, delegated, and appointed to undertake the said visitation or tour of inspection, in order to examine the accounts, and ascertain the actual state and condition of the respective warrants, to conciliate and arrange all controversies and misunderstandings, and to perform, settle, and terminate every matter of business in anywise connected with the Society or its affairs, or tending to promote its prosperity and welfare; and, in short, to do, execute, and transact all such things appertaining thereto, as in the exercise of a prudent and sound discretion he shall deem to be judicious, expedient, and fitting.

"For these objects and general purposes, by virtue of the authority vested in me, as Grand Master of the empire, by the code of laws and ordinances of the 30th day of March 1826, I have hereby granted this my special commission, with a dispensation to empower and enable the dignitary and officer hereinbefore named to admit and initiate members into the Institution, to communicate to the brotherhood the signs and passwords of the new system, to teach the lectures in both orders, to open new lodges, and to set them in full operation on the payment of such dues and fees to the Grand Lodges, through the medium of the said dignitary and officer, as have been already agreed on by the Grand Committee; and finally, to suspend or expel contumacious or refractory members, subject to a ratification of his proceedings, and adjudications by the Grand Lodge, at its next meeting, in the event of any appeals being made thereunto, but whose orders and decisions are in the meantime to be obeyed and held conclusive.

"Given under my seal, at St James's, this 13th day of August, 1832.

"ERNEST, *G. M.*"

"[Under this warrant] Lieutenant-Colonel Fairman made two visitations or tours of inspection of the kingdom, at the expense of the Grand Lodge, assembling and visiting the lodges at Birmingham, Wolverhampton, Manchester, Sheffield, Bolton, Wigan, Chowbent, Burnley, Bolton-le-Moors, Preston, Blackburn, Bury, Middleton, and other places. He visited the established Orange lodges at those places, and in their neighbourhood, and exerted himself also to form new lodges wherever there was a prospect of success. At Edinburgh and in other places in the West of Scotland, as stated elsewhere, he visited the old, and established some new lodges, thereby giving life and activity to Orangeism in that country. Lieutenant-Colonel Fairman had the power and authority of initiating any person, when travelling in the country, or under certain circumstances, by virtue of the special commission; and he often initiated persons at his own house." [1]

But to resume the correspondence.

SIR HARCOURT LEES TO FAIRMAN.

"GLASGOW, *Sept.* 16*th*.

"MY DEAR COLONEL,—Leaving this for Belfast to-morrow, I resign now all hope of seeing you, so draw

[1] Report of Committee on Orange Lodges in Great Britain and Ireland, p. ix. Amongst the letters delivered in by Colonel Fairman, we find one from James Graham, private soldier, No. 1 company, 53rd Regiment, Gibraltar, *applying* for a warrant, with the following *indorsement*:—"Graham, John, 53rd; send this warrant with circulars, &c. Apply at the agent's for the amount. Applied; amount received by D.G.S." App., page 215, No. 22.

enclosed from post-office, and send it through our noble and revered friend Lord Kenyon; and I have only to hope that as you appear not to have been in Dublin for more than a couple of days, that you may not have completed altogether the business that brought you over, and may intend to return from Scotland by Dublin; if so, I need not say my house is to be your hotel the entire time you remain here.—With fervent esteem and regard, ever yours,

"H. LEES."

LORD WYNFORD TO FAIRMAN.

"LONDON, *Oct.* 22, 1832.

"MY DEAR SIR,—On my return from Hastings I found your letter. I have heard from several quarters accounts confirmatory of those you have sent me. As His Majesty's Secretary of State is already informed of these proceedings, I am not aware of anything that I can do until the meeting of Parliament. I have long been convinced that if Parliament does not put these persons down, they will supersede Parliament. If His Majesty's ministers were to attack them they would destroy their only support, for they cannot hope for much assistance from the superior classes. If anything more comes to your knowledge that can be proved, and you do me the favour to communicate it to me, I shall, as I am bound by my oath as a Privy Councillor, communicate it to the Secretary of State. I shall be happy to receive any communication from your friend that he may be kind enough to make to me; of course I shall lay that communication also before Government. Collect all the information you can; when Parliament meets some use may be made of it.—Faithfully yours,

"WYNFORD."

"Colonel B. FAIRMAN,
"P.O., Birmingham."

LORD WYNFORD TO FAIRMAN.

"CHISELHURST, *Oct.* 24, 1832.

"MY DEAR SIR,—I am much obliged to you for thinking of my son. When you return to London I will talk to you on the subject. I am very glad to see by the paper that you did me the favour of sending me, that the health of my illustrious friend was so well received. He (the Duke of Cumberland) is one of the best, and most ill-used men I know; but the Whigs will never forgive his using the influence which his excellent understanding, and his steady adherence to his principles, gave him with his brother to unseat them when last in office. The Tories have not been sufficiently grateful to him. The country, as it becomes better acquainted with Whig misrule, will learn to appreciate his merits. As you are so obliging in your last letter as to ask my advice as to whether you should pursue the course you have so ably begun, I can only say that you must exercise your discretion as to the company in which you make such appeals as that which I have seen reported. When you meet only sure Tories you may well make them feel what they owe to one who is the constant, unflinching champion of the party, and who, by his steady course, has brought on himself all the obloquy that a base malignant faction can invent.—In great haste, faithfully yours,

"WYNFORD."

"COLONEL FAIRMAN,
"Post Office, Birmingham."

LORD WYNFORD TO FAIRMAN.

"MY DEAR SIR,—I received a letter from Miss Kenyon this morning, enclosing one from you. The reason that you have not heard from Lord Kenyon is, that he has been dangerously ill, and although (I hope) getting better, is still confined to his bed, and unable to write. Miss K. has forwarded your letter to me safe. She says that although she has not thought it right to mention this or any other business to his lordship, she is certain that if it be thought proper to hold a meeting his house is at your service for that purpose. I ought not to presume to give an opinion on Orange affairs, for, although I am sincerely attached to Orange principles, from my repugnance to belong to any club, I have not yet proposed myself to become a member of that club. The reasons that you gave, in your letter to Lord Kenyon, appear to me most satisfactory to show that the meeting should at present be holden. But of that the Duke will judge. What the Radicals proposed to do in Parliament can only be met in Parliament. We ought, however, to be on the alert, and I am therefore obliged to you for the information. From what I hear of the elections, I think we should defeat the Radicals in the next Parliament. The thing to be considered is, how to check the spirit of Radicalism, which will gain a frightful ascendency if the Conservatives do show that, whilst they are resolved to bury themselves under the institutions of the country, they are zealous to correct real abuses, and that they will, above all things, attend to the correction of the vices and improving the condition of the poor.—In haste, faithfully yours,

"WYNFORD."

"The first part of your letter is not arrived, which prevents me from understanding the whole of the latter part.

"WYNFORD."

"CHISELHURST, *November* 6, 1832."

"COLONEL FAIRMAN, Birmingham."

LORD WYNFORD TO FAIRMAN.

"CHISELHURST, *29th November*, 1832.

"DEAR SIR,—I received your letter this morning, with the division (Note) enclosed. Some one has sent me this a week ago, and I have read it with great pleasure. I have some friends coming to me the early part of next week; as soon as they leave me I shall go to Bath for a month, if Parliament will permit me. I am sorry to hear of your account of Birmingham. I had hoped that there would have been considerable reaction. I am ready to do my duty whenever Parliament shall meet. Mr Horsley Palmer's retiring from Birmingham greatly surprises me. I understood at the Carlton Club that his return was certain. Had a requisition been sent to my son when it was sent to Mr Palmer, he would have stood if there had been a fair chance of success; and he had, I believe, nerves to abide the pelting of any storm. But I think it is now too late, and I have no opportunity of conferring with him, as he is not with me. If I do, I think at this late hour I should advise him to reserve his money for another opportunity, when he can meet his adversary on more equal terms.—I am, my dear Sir, very faithfully yours.

"WYNFORD."

"You speak of coming in on a petition. Any person who comes before a Committee of the House, as a party on an election contest under the Bill, will be ruined, be the case what it may.

"*To* Colonel FAIRMAN, Birmingham."

LORD WYNFORD TO FAIRMAN.

"CHISELHURST, *December* 2, 1832.

"DEAR SIR,—Your letter only reached me this morning, which is the last of the three days, and the post leaves us to-night. I have received letters of this sort, and never took any notice of them; your letter has something about it which induces me to think that it does not come from one who meditates mischief. Men bite before they bark. I would recommend you to be on your guard; and as brethren days are over, if there is nothing that requires your remaining at Birmingham, I would leave it. I would not recommend any application to a magistrate, or any advertisement of reward, nor any letter to the Secretary of State; neither of these ways can do any good. If it is the letter of a person who means mischief, you will not find him out; if it is only an attempt to frighten you, an advertisement or application to a magistrate will flatter the writer that he has succeeded. There may be expressions to frighten, but I cannot think they have as yet gone the length of forming combinations to execute their horrible purposes.—Faithfully yours.

"W."

"Lord Kenyon is much better. I have had a letter from him."

"Colonel FAIRMAN, Birmingham."

LORD KENYON TO FAIRMAN.

"PEEL HALL, 28*th December* 1832.

"MY DEAR COLONEL AND BROTHER,—I am here again with my venerable aunt, eighty-nine years of age, on a Christmas visit, but return to Gredington next Thursday. Anxiously do I wish that the Cock of the North may think it right to come to Glasgow. The warm feeling of Lord John Campbell, who was a little my junior at Christ Church, Oxford, is very gratifying, and promises (please God we may be blessed with better times) much good in the North hereafter. His old relation, John Campbell, accountant-general, was always proud of him as a Campbell, and I heartily wish he may live and in due time enjoy the family honours. I will send our Grand Treasurer your circular. His Royal Highness promises being in England a fortnight before Parliament reassembles, and I hope will come well. To him, privately, you had better address yourself about your military proposition, which to me, appears very judicious. I wish such as His Royal Highness would, without neglecting the prime consideration, namely, the fitness of anything proposed, attend in addition to what is popular. Our enemies attend to that alone, which is base; we seem to disregard it too much, which is foolish.—Ever yours, faithfully,

"KENYON."

LORD KENYON TO FAIRMAN.

"GREDINGTON, *January* 7, 1833.

"MY DEAR SIR,—The enclosed from J. Clarke I forward to you, as it is fit you should see his statement. It was the fourth application for money I received on the day on which it arrived, and reminded me of Terence, In se res redit Phormio; for such applications go little elsewhere. I hope to be in town the very beginning of next month at latest, and hope to hear a good report of your visitations. The good cause is worth all the help that men can give it, but our only trust must be in God. In the last two years and a half I shall have spent, I suspect, in its behalf, nearer £20,000 than £10,000. If you are with an honoured brother the Duke of Gordon, please to tender my best respects to him and the Duchess.—Ever your sincere friend,

"KENYON."

"Ellesmere, January 7, 1833.
"*To* Colonel FAIRMAN,
"The Duke of Gordon's, N.B."
"Kenyon." (Free.)

LORD KENYON TO FAIRMAN.

"PORTMAN SQUARE, *8th February* 1833.

"MY DEAR SIR,—I called at 3 Cannon Row, yesterday, having attended His Royal Highness, our Grand Master, to the House of Lords, to sign Lord Aberdeen's proxy, and gave Clarke a frank to write to you, to say that His Royal Highness and I agreed that we were bound by our rules to have a meeting there on the 15th, and to notify to you, therefore, the necessity for your immediate return. You can easily return to the north, and continue your initiation, but we must not run the risk of disappointing our brethren if they come up to attend our meeting.—Ever yours, most faithfully,

"KENYON."

"*To* Lieutenant-Colonel FAIRMAN."

FAIRMAN TO LORD KENYON.

(*Copy.*)

"DONCASTER, *Tuesday, Feb. 12th*, 1833.

"MY DEAR LORD,—. . . Lord Wynford, the soundness of whose judgment few persons would be so hardy as to call in question, was kind enough to write me word he had read with much pleasure the report of my proceedings at Birmingham. I believe I mentioned that I had consulted his Lordship on the propriety of my continuing to introduce the Duke's[1] name in the prominent shape I had previously done, and with the policy of which he seemed to agree. There is one strong point which induces me to cherish a hope that I have worked a change in the sentiments of the press, which is that the foulest part of it, I fancy, has not attacked me, nor attempted to gainsay my comments in refutation of the calumnies so lavishly put forth against our illustrious Grand Master. If he would but make a tour into these parts, for which I have prepared the way, he would be idolized.—I am, with sincere respect, my dear Lord, ever most devotedly your Lordship's,

"W. BLENNERHASSETT FAIRMAN."

"*To* Lord KENYON."

[1] Cumberland.

FAIRMAN TO LORD KENYON.

(*Copy.*)

"REINDEER, DONCASTER, *Tuesday.*

"MY DEAR LORD,—As I once mentioned to Lord Wynford, I really write such a number of letters, that I scarcely know to whom or where. I think, however, that I not only addressed one or two to your Lordship from Leeds as well as from this place (before I received yours yesterday), but that I also sent you some documents in a parcel to Gredington, which I hope have been forwarded to you in London, as it might be very desirable to lay them before the Grand Lodge. The keeping a memorandum is wholly out of the question, from the constant state of turmoil and interruption I have endured, though I am frequently not in bed till two in the morning, labouring to get my business under, which in spite of all my industry still gains upon me. In the midst of my bustle yesterday, in consequence of my recall, and which, by the way, I consider to be highly complimental, a party of gentlemen came over to me from Barnsley, to aid my endeavours for the establishment of a new lodge in this town, of the first respectability, for which I hope the way is paved. It was impossible that I could do otherwise than invite my new brothers, by whom I had been treated most princely, to take their dinner with me. About a week ago I opened for them their warrant, and by way of beginning I initiated ten members, and, could I have stayed another day, might as many more, who have since joined it; but the subsequent fees cannot be claimed by the Grand Lodge. These brethren are all men of fortune, of high spirit, to whom money is no object. In proof of this, Mr Jadison, the Master, who dined with me yesterday, said that a subscription of £50 each had already been talked of, to get up an entertainment for our illustrious Grand Master, if they might be permitted to look forward to so distinguished an honour as a visit from him in the autumn of the year.

All the ladies are with us, and 'the *blue* belles of Yorkshire' are noble dames. So sensible were they of the injuries that have been heaped on our much-injured prince, that at a dinner party at Mr Jadison's, when His Royal Highness's[1] health was proposed (and in every party which I have attended it has been drank with enthusiasm), they actually shed tears. By excess of toil my own nerves are so unstrung too, that in making to your Lordship this report, I am playing the woman; though I am proof against persecution, I am not against kindness. While the one kindles my indignation, the other at once subdues me. I find, however, I must not pursue such a subject at this moment. The enclosure goes to the corroboration of what might probably have been effected could I have stayed longer in a place since the elections.

I have many more letters of a similar kind, upon which I cannot lay my finger at present, but doubtless shall speedily be able to do so. I have notified to most, if not the whole of the districts in this county, in Lancaster, and in Cheshire, as well as in Derbyshire, the assembling of the Grand Lodge on Friday next. I have written to the Duke of Gordon, to Glasgow, and elsewhere, to intimate that in all probability I should be directed to renew my circuit of the country so soon as the circular should be published. My inefficiency at the ensuing meeting will be excused, I hope, as I really stand in need of rest, and cannot promise to be more than a mere cipher. Towards its termination I will rally all my spirits, to give some account of my mission, but the very thought now unmans me.

"The new lodge at Barnsley is named 'The Royal

[1] Cumberland.

Cumberland Lodge.'—In great haste, my dear Lord, ever most devotedly your Lordship's,

"W. BLENNERHASSET FAIRMAN."

"*To* Lord KENYON."

LORD KENYON TO FAIRMAN.

"PORTMAN SQUARE, *May* 2, 1833.

"MY DEAR SIR,—I will try to keep all right to-morrow at the meeting of the Grand Committee. I truly grieve you are so poorly, and beg you to take care of yourself. I will see if anything can be done to-morrow on the subject of fees; but though character ought doubtless to be our first object, numbers attached to the cause must be a necessary ingredient as to strength. I don't know whereabouts Hercules Buildings are, or some fine morning I might try to beat up your quarters. When we consider who our Grand Master is, we ought to feel—

"'Nil desperandum,
Teucro duce et auspice Teucro.'

—Ever your faithful friend,

"KENYON."

"*To* Colonel FAIRMAN."

LORD KENYON TO FAIRMAN.

"PORTMAN SQUARE, *May* 25, 1833.

"MY DEAR SIR,—I return the gallant Duke's warm-hearted letter. Would to God we had hundreds of such men! The wretch in *The Satirist* would be best corrected, if it might be, by an opposite paper ruining his scandalous one. He well deserves, however, the severest punishment, and ought to be prosecuted in all cases where conviction seems absolutely certain. The difficulty of obtaining honest juries, to which Peel's Bill has subjected us, is very fearful. —Ever your faithful friend,

(Signed) "KENYON."

"*To* Colonel FAIRMAN."

Lord Kenyon to Fairman.

"Portman Square, *May* 30, 1833.

"My Dear Sir,—With respect to the composition of the Grand Committee, the pleasure of His Royal Highness, the Grand Master, is the only rule by which its formation can properly be regulated. Its being so framed as to produce harmony in the institution will no doubt be the principle by which His Royal Highness will be guided; and I am confident that, feeling, as he must do, the essential importance (especially with reference to your undertaking a new tour to consummate the zeal and harmony of which you have laid the foundation in North Britain and the northern and trading districts of England) that you and the Grand Committee should be in entire harmony and mutual confidence; that, therefore, neither brother South nor brother Morris should continue a member of it.

The will of the Grand Master is conclusive, and no names ought to be submitted to His Royal Highness in Grand Lodge but such as will be satisfactory to him. The suggestion at the meeting of the Grand Lodge is not for the purpose of election otherwise than in accordance with the pleasure of the head of the institution, whose authority is justly declared to be supreme. You may communicate this to the Grand Committee, for we must not let our high and zealous friends who meet at the Grand Lodge be disgusted any more by discussions at those meetings. Should any such be apprehended, His Royal Highness should be informed that he may, previous to the anniversary of June, interdict the attendance of any brethren who would so forget themselves.—Believe me, my dear Sir, your faithful brother and friend,

"Kenyon."

" *To* Colonel Fairman," &c., &c.

LORD KENYON TO FAIRMAN.

"*June* 1.

"MY DEAR SIR,—Lord Wynford has fixed Monday, at half-past twelve, at the House of Lords, to be initiated an Orangeman. He has a private room of his own there, as Deputy Speaker. . . .—Believe, my dear Sir, yours truly,

"KENYON."

LORD KENYON TO FAIRMAN.

"PORTMAN SQUARE, *June* 13, 1833.

"MY DEAR SIR,—I am grieved that *our valued brother Cumberland* should suppose for one moment he could have given me the slightest offence. It may happen sometimes to me, as applied by Shakespeare to *Brutus*:—

"'Poor *Brutus* with himself at war,
Forgets to show his love to other men;'

but I never can forget to feel it for so zealous a friend to every cause most dear to me, as our brother Cumberland has always proved himself to be. The statements you made to me before, and respecting which I have now before me particulars from Portsmouth, are out of my sphere, and should be referred, toties quoties, to His Royal Highness as military matters of great delicacy. At the same time, private intimations, I submit, should be made to the military correspondents, letting them know how highly we esteem them as brethren. I hope the circular will soon be out.—Your faithful friend and brother,

"KENYON."

"*To* Colonel FAIRMAN."

LORD KENYON TO FAIRMAN.

"PORTMAN SQUARE, *June* 28, 1833.

"DEAR SIR,—I will lay your letter, proposing various important suggestions, before His Royal Highness our illustrious Grand Master. There is weight in every one of the suggestions; and the zeal shown by Brother Craigie is very refreshing in these days of mawkish apathy. I had the delight of expressing to our royal Grand Master, on the evening of the day of the honest verdict of the twelve loyal jurymen, my gratification at the tardy justice which had been done him. I have replied to the enclosed in such manner as to enable our brethren to show my letter to any magistrate with whom they may think my sentiments and feelings can have any influence.—Ever your faithful friend and brother,

"KENYON."

"*To* Colonel FAIRMAN."

LORD KENYON TO FAIRMAN.

"PORTMAN SQUARE, *July* 2, 1833.

"MY DEAR SIR,—I wrote yesterday to Mr Plunkett concerning your tour and other matters. If H.R.H. pleases to start you, I see no need for any delay. The statements of these accounts might be issued after you have agreed on the facts to be stated by Eedes or any other steady brother you please to authorise to do so. You must, however, arrange your course generally with H.R.H.,[1] and let him or me know from time to time where for a certain indefinite [period] you may be sure to be found. H.R.H., I think, judges well in thinking it undesirable to have any meeting, now that the Irish Church Spoliation Bill hangs over our heads. If we go only quietly in and out of Parliament till that comes forward, I am confident we shall, by God's mercy, throw it out on the second reading. Excuse more, but early any morning if you like to call I shall be glad to see you, but I am very early.—Ever your faithful friend and brother,

"KENYON."

"Colonel FAIRMAN,
"Hercules Buildings, Lambeth."

[1] Cumberland.

LORD KENYON TO FAIRMAN.

"PORTMAN SQUARE, *July* 3, 1833.

"MY DEAR SIR,—There is so much relating to myself in the enclosed, that I cannot presume to give any opinion as to its publication. H.R.H., the G.M., I dare say, will consult with Lord Wynford on the subject, on account of the legal sentiments expressed by him, and you will act according to H.R.H.'s order, and whether in giving he is pleased that the publication should be considered official or volunteer on your part.—Ever your faithful friend and brother,"

(Signed) "KENYON."

"Colonel FAIRMAN,
"Hercules Buildings, Lambeth."

LORD KENYON TO FAIRMAN.

"PORTMAN SQUARE, *July* 10, 1833.

"MY DEAR SIR,—I send you some anti-Roman Catholic books, which you may distribute among the following Peers:—Manvers, Stradbroke, Liverpool, Harrowby, Northampton, Carnarvon, the Bishops of Llandaff, Lincoln (Warren's Hotel), &c., &c. I can say nothing as to Mr Staveley's publication, but if done it should be forthwith and I would take a few copies. You know much better how to manage our brethren than I do, and they must be kept together as well as they can be. If you hear anything further from the Military Districts, let His Royal Highness know all particulars fit to be communicated. The times, I really trust, are improving quietly and gradually. Let us act firmly, and maintain all that is sacred, and provoke no one more than can be avoided.—Believe me, my dear Sir, yours faithfully,

"KENYON."

Lord Kenyon to Fairman.

"Eastwell Park, *August* 13, 1833.

"My Dear Sir,—Be so good as to send the Earl of Winchelsea, in a day or two (but not over-weight, as yours of this morning is to me), the circular of June 4th, and any other circular which will contain good names and matter in it. You can say you did it by my desire, and in hopes that he, as one of the staunchest of Protestants, would join us. I am glad to hear that several persons of judgment think we might have a Government with which the House of Commons would act. If so, it is a sad pity the Hero of Waterloo and others would not act so as to have obtained such a Ministry during the existing session. When Parliament is prorogued, it is well known nothing can be done, unless some death of importance occurs. I hope to be in town on Thursday morning, for two nights.—Ever your faithful friend and brother,

"Kenyon."

Lord Wynford to Fairman.

"Dear Colonel,—I returned here yesterday, and found your letter. I fear by this time that you are started on your tour. To whom am I to pay my debt to the Orange Lodge in your absence? Wishing you a pleasant and prosperous journey, faithfully yours.

"Wynford."

" *Tuesday, August* 29."

"Chiselhurst, *August* 30, 1883.

"Colonel Fairman,

"Cannon Row, Westminster."

"Wynford."

Lord Wynford to Fairman.

"My Dear Sir,—On the other side is a check for the eighteen guineas that I owe the Orange Lodge. I am sorry to hear of your illness. I am waiting for a letter from Dover (which I hope my servant, who delivers you this, may bring me) to set off to London, and from thence to Dover, where my daughter has been expecting me for this week past. On my return, should you be near London, I shall be happy to see you.—Faithfully yours,

"WYNFORD."

"Colonel FAIRMAN,
"Cannon Row, Westminster."

LORD KENYON TO FAIRMAN.

"GREDINGTON, *September* 10.

"MY DEAR SIR AND BROTHER,—It certainly is desirable that our enemies should be informed, through such sources of information as they will read, in what respects the Orange institution has been injuriously misrepresented. Great care, however, must be taken as to statement of facts, that we may not be accused of inaccuracy. I *think* His Royal Highness the Grand Master did not take any oath on admission; for, I think, every oath was discontinued previous to the admission of His Royal Highness. It was otherwise with myself and our late illustrious Grand Master.[1] What is the present rule, however, is the only question worth considering, and now we decidedly take no oath.[2] I expect my good friend Lord Wynford here on the 15th, to stay a few weeks, I hope. We have sad wet weather, and yet have much barley out. One of our most saleable productions, cheese, is advancing, which will be some relief, I hope, to our distressed farmers.—Ever your faithful friend,

"KENYON."

"Colonel FAIRMAN, &c., &c."

[1] The Duke of York.

[2] See *post*.

LORD RODEN TO FAIRMAN.

"Lord Roden presents his compliments to Colonel Fairman, and has received his obliging letter; in reply to which, Lord R. would say that he does not think this by any means a favourable time for visiting the Orange brethren of Ireland. There is just now such strong feeling amongst them, and, Lord Roden is sorry to say, so much difference of opinion as to the processions, that he thinks it would be better to let that subside before the deputation of our English brethren went round. Lord Roden hopes that the Conservative meeting about to be held in Glasgow may strengthen our cause."

"TOLLYMERE PARK, *September* 24, 1833."

THE MARQUIS OF LONDONDERRY TO FAIRMAN.

"EGLINTON CASTLE, *October* 4, 1833.

"SIR,—I have the honour to acknowledge the receipt of your letter. It would give me great pleasure to attend any great Conservative meeting in Scotland, if the Stewards or Secretary honoured me with an invitation; and that I could accomplish, being in Glasgow on the day of the meeting. At present, I am going on the 8th to Dalkeith, and on the 16th or 17th to Scone, after which I am not certain of my movements, or whether I shall not be obliged to return to Durham.—I remain, Sir, your very obedient servant,

"VANE LONDONDERRY."

"Colonel FAIRMAN,
"His Grace the Duke of Gordon's,
"Gordon Castle."

LORD KENYON TO FAIRMAN.

"GREDINGTON, ELLESMERE, *Oct.* 20, 1833.

"MY DEAR SIR,—I will forward our zealous friend Craigie's letter to Eedes, to whom I wrote the other day, expressing my readiness forthwith to suspend, and, if necessary, to expel, some disorderly men in or near Bolton, who have shown something like a radical spirit. Watkins went among them gallantly, and we shall set them to rights, I trust. Sawney takes some time to be well roused, but when he imbibes the heat of Orangeism he will not lose again. I am every way grieved that our gallant northern duke is not in health to attend the Orange Conservative meeting. It is a great pity, too, that the amiable Duke of Buccleugh does not see the immense importance of his sanctioning such a cause as the Orange cause, identified as it is with the high Conservative principles.

"His Grace does not yet see the difference between what may be, perhaps, expedient in respect to political leaders and placemen, as to temporizing, and what is the high station, as to abiding by principles and promoting them, which becomes men of rank and influence; nor how much more such a course would benefit the cause of party as well as that of truth, by principles. In Pitt's time, and in the Duke's grandfather's, much was done by high principles and zeal, which would not in many cases have emanated from Pitt himself. Their Graces of Gordon and Buccleugh are the two men of Scotland to whom alone Orangemen and Conservatives look up with hope. The young Marquis Douglas will, I hope, from his high connection with the high-minded Duke of Newcastle, train on well in time. My dear son and his bride seem as happy here as I could wish, and possess the kindest wishes of all around them. My kindest remembrance to the gallant duke, and believe me, your faithful friend and brother,

"KENYON."

"*To* Colonel FAIRMAN,
"Gordon Castle, Fochabers, N.B."
"(Free) Kenyon."

LORD THOMOND TO FAIRMAN.

"*March* 29, 1834.

"Lord Thomond's compliments to Col. Fairman; he encloses him the subscription book and £20.

"Lord Thomond begs to say that he pays an annual subscription to the Grand Lodge in Dublin."

LORD WYNFORD TO FAIRMAN.

"DEAR SIR,—I returned from London too late to write to you by last night's post. I have lately had so many things on my hands that I forgot to tell you that H.R.H., Lord Kenyon, and myself, discussed the propriety of purchasing the newspaper you mention, and were of opinion that there [are] many reasons [why] we should not make such purchase.

"If we cannot get *The Despatch* more favourably supported, it will be necessary that a Conservative paper should be published. But this must be undertaken, not by three persons, but by the Carlton Club.

"I think it highly probable that something will soon be done by the Club.

"In the meantime I must decline putting myself forward. I am just returning from Seven Oaks, and the letters are going to the post.—I am in great haste, faithfully yours,

"WYNFORD."

"CHISELHURST, *April* 11, 1834.

"Colonel B. FAIRMAN,

"P.O., Birmingham."

"Wynford."

THE DUKE OF GORDON TO FAIRMAN.

"GORDON CASTLE, *July* 27, 1834.

"MY DEAR SIR,—I return our most excellent friend's letter; it pleases me to find that he thinks I did my duty at Glasgow. The exertion was great, but the dinner did good to the true cause. I am glad that the unprincipled ministers remain to do more mischief, as yet we are not ready for a change; in six months I think a Conservative cabinet will be able to stand their ground against Whig and Radical united, for the tide is turning. May we live to see better times. I am getting ready for the hills.—Believe me, yours very sincerely,

"GORDON."

"*To* Colonel FAIRMAN."

THE DUKE OF GORDON TO FAIRMAN.

"GORDON CASTLE, *Oct.* 21, 1834.

"MY DEAR SIR,—Many thanks for your polite attention, the communication gives me real concern, and causes serious reflection. These sad events should open people's eyes, and one in particular; but the Lord Chancellor is a very dangerous man, and at last the world will find him out. His tour in this part of the country has done us good. Sir George Murray's dinner at Perth has brought good men together, and on the 29th I am to preside at a dinner at Aberdeen, given to Captain Gordon; seven hundred are expected; and every man must do his duty.

"Winter has come upon us, and we feel it the more after the fine weather we enjoyed. I trust your health is good.—Ever, my dear Sir, yours very truly,

"GORDON."

Addressed—"Fochabers, Oct. 1834.
"Col. FAIRMAN,
"Falkland Cottage, Lambeth, London."
"Gordon."

LORD KENYON TO FAIRMAN.

"GREDINGTON, *Sept.* 3, 1834.

"MY DEAR SIR AND BROTHER,—I have not received back from Encombe your letter suggesting an alteration in the rules. If you have to suggest anything special, or supplementary, which would probably be better, as consequently temporary instead of permanent, let me know again. I am now fixed here I hope, with little variation, till February next; and you will be glad to hear a good account of all most dear to me, and that my neighbours here seem very glad to see us returned.—Believe me yours truly,

"KENYON."

"*P.S.*—I shall always direct Cannon Row; I always presume there is no alteration from my corrected copy, if you don't point any out to me."

"*To* Colonel FAIRMAN."

LORD KENYON TO FAIRMAN.

"GREDINGTON, *September* 13, 1834.

"MY DEAR SIR AND BROTHER,—I wish you would be so good as to send me the ipsissima verba which you wish to introduce to prevent disloyalty among our brethren; but be so good as to send it under weight, as to-day's letter has cost me 3s. 8d. What you propose to insert I presume you mean to do as required at the present moment. Be so good, therefore, as to state also the grounds on which you consider it necessary. I think the castigation, if given, had better be given as an hypothesis, so as to let those apply it who feel it to be due to them. A reprimand to a whole body constituted like our O. I.,[1] would do anything but good; certainly if the whole body were rotten it had better be dissolved and renewed; but that could only, perhaps, be after communication with the sound heads or sound members of the different lodges. I am very sorry to hear of your taking up money from the money-lenders. I think our lodges should be called upon,

[1] Orange Institution.

on pain of suspension, to pay up all that is due on the *old* rules forthwith, and be urged to pay as required by the revised rules of the O. I. Before very long I shall probably be in Lancashire, and will endeavour to see Major Watkins. I expect my excellent zealous friend, Lord Wynford, here in two or three days.—Ever your faithful friend and brother,

"KENYON."

Addressed—"Ellesmere, September 14, 1834.
"*To* Col. FAIRMAN,
"3 Cannon Row, Westminster."
"Free—Kenyon."

LORD KENYON TO FAIRMAN.

"PEEL HALL, *September* 19, 1834.

"MY DEAR SIR AND BROTHER,—In this, by another cover, I return your papers. I have paid my best atten tion to all your suggestions as I did before to those heretofore proposed to be admitted. Let enough be printed for present distribution, and on economical principle as to the number, which you understand, and I don't; and pray let it, after the lapse of above three months, be finished. I have been too busy to see Major Watkins, and return on Tuesday to Gredington.—Ever yours faithfully,

"KENYON."

"About circulars.—Bolton, September 20, 1834.
"*To* Col. FAIRMAN,
"3 Cannon Row, Westminster."
"Free—Kenyon."

LORD KENYON TO FAIRMAN.

"PORTMAN SQUARE, *April* 27.

"DEAR SIR,—I heartily wish I could hope to be of any use in applying at Chelsea in behalf of the writer of the enclosed. I think we had better communicate it to His

Royal Highness, as he is the only person, except yourself, who can judiciously interfere in military matters connected with the Orange institutions. I hope your attack is going off, and that we shall have a thoroughly amicable meeting next Friday. Brother Mair seems very frank, and well-meaning. If you could get Mr Knipe, who is a favourite, I think, with His Royal Highness, to attend, it would be well.—Ever, my dear Sir, faithfully yours,

"KENYON."

FAIRMAN TO A FRIEND UNKNOWN.

"23 KING STREET, WESTMINSTER,
"*Tuesday Evening.*

"MY DEAR SIR,—By returning the Palladiums, with a small packet of letters from kings and princes I left for your perusal, you will oblige me very much. As circumstances will at length compel me to seek a compensation from royalty, for my services and surrenders in their service, should not an appeal to their justice, made confidentially and respectfully, in the first instance, be productive of the desired end, I shall enforce my claims through the medium of the press, both in pamphlets and papers, when a dread of exposure may prompt them to do that which ought to have emanated from a sense of gratitude.—Most faithfully yours, my dear Sir,

"WILLIAM BLENNERHASSETT FAIRMAN.

"*P.S.*—Mr Aburrow will do me the favour to take charge of the above, when it shall suit your own convenience to hand them over to that gentleman."[1]

"*To* D—— C——, Esq."

While the Orangemen were thus engaged in the work of reorganisation, the Irish members resolved to strike a blow

[1] This correspondence was obtained by Hume, and published in the *London Review. post.*

at the Society. On March 23, 1835, Mr Finn, member for Kilkenny, moved for a Select Committee to inquire into the Orange system in Ireland. The Orangemen accepted the challenge readily, and a Committee was at once appointed. Twenty-two years previously a similar motion had been made by an English member, Mr Wynn, but it was not pressed.[1] Ten years previously, when Mr Canning suppressed the Catholic Association, he also suppressed the Orange Society. But it was reorganised in 1828, and at the time of Finn's motion, was stronger than ever.[2] It now had to withstand a more serious attack than any hitherto made.

[1] "Parliamentary Debates," vol. xxvi., p. 974. The motion ran: "That a Committee be appointed to inquire into the existence of certain illegal societies under the denomination of Orangemen."

[2] It should be stated that between 1799 and 1826 a change had been made in the Orange oath.

Oath in 1799:—

"I A. B. do solemnly and sincerely swear, of my own free will and accord, that I will, to the utmost of my power, support and defend the present king, George III., and all the heirs of the Crown, so long as he or they support the Protestant ascendency," &c.

Oath in 1814:—

"I A. B. do voluntarily and sincerely swear that I will, to the utmost of my power, support and defend the present king, George III., his heirs and successors, being Protestants," &c.

Oath of 1824:—

"I A. B. do sincerely promise and swear that I will be faithful, and bear true allegiance to His Majesty King George."

It will be seen that in 1824 a simple oath of allegiance was substituted for the former conditional oath. But it was necessary, by the rules of 1824, to take the oath of supremacy and the oath of abjuration. In 1828 the same oaths (of allegiance, supremacy, and abjuration) were taken, and no reference was made to "Protestant ascendency," or to the "king," or "his heirs," being Protestant.

In 1834 oaths were abolished, and this declaration was used instead:— "I A. B. do solemnly and voluntarily declare that I will be faithful, and bear true allegiance to His Majesty the King; and that I will, to the utmost of my power, support and maintain the laws and constitution of the United Kingdom of Great Britain and Ireland, as established by William III. of glorious memory, and the succession to the throne on His Majesty's illustrious house being Protestant; I do declare that I am not, nor ever was, a Roman Catholic or Papist; that I am not, was not, or ever will be a member of the society called 'United Irishmen,' or any other society or body of men who are enemies

Finn's Committee sat on April 7, and continued to hear evidence until August 5. On August 4, Hume, without waiting for the final report of the Committee,[1] made a fresh attack upon the Society. Quoting the evidence given before the Committee, he called the attention of the House to the existence of Orange lodges in the army, and finally demanded the appointment of a Select Committee to inquire into Orangeism in Great Britain and the Colonies, as well as in Ireland.[2] But the Orangemen were no longer eager for the fray. They had had quite enough of inquiry, and they resisted Hume's motion with vigour and persistency; but it was carried by a decisive majority.[3]

The Committee began their sittings on August 13, and the inquiry closed on August 31. The Duke of Cumberland refused point blank to give evidence, and Fairman refused to produce all the books and papers relating to the Society. He appeared before the Committee on August 13, and handed in some papers, but the Committee asked for

to His Majesty or the glorious constitution of these realms; and that I never took the oath to that or any other treasonable society.

"I declare that I will, as far as in my power lies, assist the magistrates and civil authorities of these kingdoms in the lawful execution of their official duties when called upon. That I will be true and faithful to every brother Orangeman in all just actions; that I will not wrong, or know him to be wronged or injured, without giving due notice thereof, if in my power.

"And I solemnly declare that I will always conceal and never will reveal either part or parts of what is now to be privately communicated to me unless to a brother Orangeman, knowing him to be so by strict trial and due examination, or from the word of a brother Orangemen, or until I shall be authorised so to do by the proper authorities of the Orange institution. That I will not write it, indite it, cut, carve, stain, stamp, or engrave it, or cause it to be done, lest any part thereof might be known. And lastly, I do declare that I have not, to my knowledge or belief, been proposed or rejected in, or expelled from, any other Orange lodge."

[1] The Committee presented three reports; the final report on August 6.

[2] Finn's motion limited the inquiry to Ireland.

[3] Hansard, 3rd series, vol. xxx., pp. 58, 239. Hume first moved a series of resolutions practically condemning the Society; but, finally, on August 10, asked for a Committee. The motion was carried by 39 to 25 votes. There were three divisions on the subject, but Hume succeeded in all by about the same majority—14.

more, and more Fairman was resolved they should not have. Hume determined to push Fairmain to extremes, and on August 19 moved that he should be called to the bar of the House and examined. Fairman appeared, amid a scene of much excitement, and was examined by the Speaker.

Speaker—" . . . Have you produced any documents in your possession which were demanded of you?"

Fairman—" I have produced a variety of documents."

Speaker—" Have you produced all the documents that were asked of you?"

Fairman—" All that I considered public documents I have produced—or rather, they were extorted from me."

Speaker—" Have you produced all that were required of you, or have you refused to produce any particular document?"

Fairman—" I do not know that I have. Everything in my possession I have given up with the greatest pleasure—no, not with the greatest pleasure, but with the greatest readiness."

Speaker—" Have you any book that you have refused to produce?"

Fairman—" No; not any that I considered the Committee had any right to call for."

Speaker—" Is there any book that you have refused to produce, and which was required of you?"

Fairman—" Yes; there is one. A private book which I have at home."

Speaker—" For what reason have you refused to produce this book?"

Fairman—" Because I considered it a private book—a book which never was laid either before the Grand Lodge or the Grand Master, and for which consequently the Committee had no right to ask. I conceive I had a right to refuse its production."

Speaker—"Does that book contain any information respecting the proceedings of Orange lodges?"

Fairman—"It contains my answers to letters I received; those letters more particularly relate to private matters unconnected with Orange lodges in the army."

Speaker—"Does it contain any official answers to communications—official communications—made by you connected with the business of Orange lodges?"

Fairman—"A great many."

Colonel Perceval—"Has any proposition been made to you to extract such letters as related exclusively to Orange institutions?"

Fairman—"Yes."

Col. Perceval—"I wish to know what was the answer of the witness to such a proposition?"

Fairman—"Being disposed to meet the wishes of the Committee, I wanted to come to a distinct understanding that nothing else should be required. I refused the production of the book more upon public than private principles, and least of all upon Orange grounds."

Col. Perceval—"Did you offer to produce all matters relating to military lodges—that being the principal object of the inquiry?"

O'Connell—"I rise to order." [Fairman was ordered to withdraw.] "No distinction was made by the Committee between the military and civil part of the inquiry."

Col. Perceval—"I contend that the Committee were bound to confine themselves to the army alone."

O'Connell—"I must suggest to the House whether the line of examination which the hon. and gallant officer is pursuing, is the proper one under the circumstances. The witness has been asked, not whether he has refused to give up all letters relating to Orange lodges in the army, but whether he has refused to give up all letters whether relating to the Orange lodges in the army or not?"

Hume supported O'Connell.

Col. Perceval—"Notwithstanding the lecture on evidence which I have received from the hon. and learned member for Dublin (O'Connell), I must say that I can conduct the examination of the witness in as fair, manly, overboard and impartial a manner as if I had taken the lesson that has been read to me. I will not, however, take the hon. and learned gentleman's lesson."

O'Connell—"That is no proof that the hon. and gallant officer does not want it."

(Fairman was recalled.)

Col. Perceval—"Now, sir, I wish to know whether the book which you have called a private book, and which you have refused to furnish the Committee, is a continuation of the letter book of which the Committee is already in possession?"

Fairman—"It certainly is not a continuation."

O'Connell—"That book contains letters subsequent to those which are to be found in the book which you have produced?"

Fairman—"Decidedly."

O'Connell—"Is there in that book other correspondence respecting Orange institutions, addressed to members not in the army?"

Fairman—"Decidedly. The correspondence contained in it is principally with persons not in the army. The exceptions do not amount to more than three or four."

O'Connell—"And those others you refuse to produce?"

Fairman—"Yes, I refuse to produce them on public principles, and not on Orange grounds. . . ."

Sergeant Jackson—"Does the book already produced to the Committee belong to you or the Orange Society?"

Fairman—"That book I found in the office when I

entered it. I never had any control over it. But my own book I consider as my own private document."

Sergeant Jackson—"Does it contain private correspondence?"

Fairman—"Yes it does in many instances."

Sergeant Jackson—"Did you make any offer respecting it to the Committee on Orange affairs?"

Fairman—"I did; but I was afterwards obliged to withdraw that offer, because they would not accede to the proposition which I made to them. I think no honourable man could do otherwise under the circumstances."

Sergeant Jackson—"Have you then a decided objection to produce the book?"

Fairman—"I have."

O'Connell—"Do the private letters you speak of refer chiefly to Orange matters?"

Fairman—"Chiefly."

Mr Shaw—"Were you directed to keep the other book which you refuse to produce by any person connected with the Orange institution, or was it merely a proceeding of your own?"

Fairman—"I kept that book on my own and sole authority."

Mr Shaw—"Were the letters in that book official, or written in your own private capacity?"

Fairman—"They were written in my own private capacity."

Mr Shaw—"Was it, or was it not, a continuation of the other book?"

Fairman—"It certainly was not."

Mr Shaw—"Was that book which you refuse to give up official, or was it kept for your own private purposes?"

Fairman—"I kept it for my own private purposes, and merely as a remembrance."

Mr Shaw—"Did you not consent to give up such portions of it as related to military lodges?"

Fairman—"Such a proposition was made to me, and I did express my readiness to consent to it, but with a condition, namely, that I should not be brought to the bar of this House."

Mr Shaw—"Have you any objection to give up those portions which relate to other lodges?"

Fairman—"Certainly."

Mr Shaw—"Do you now object to give up that portion which relates to the military lodges?"

Fairman—"Now, after what has occurred, I do."

Mr Shaw—"Are you desirous of concealing the information which that book contains?"

Fairman—"No, I would not care a halfpenny if the contents were known from Whitechapel Bars to Hyde Park Corner."

Mr Shaw—"Then your refusal now to produce it is on a point of honour?"

Fairman—"Exactly so."

Mr Shaw—"Then, it is upon no Orange principle that you now refuse to produce the book."

Fairman—"It is not."

Mr Shaw—"If you had not been brought up, is it likely you would have produced the book?"

Fairman—"The probability is that I should not have produced it."

Mr Warburton—"Do you still persevere in your refusal to produce the book?"

Fairman—"Yes."

Mr Warburton—"Where is the book?"

Fairman—"It is in my own possession."

Mr Warburton—"Is the book under lock and key."

Fairman—"Yes."

Mr Warburton—"Have you given any orders for the removal of that book since you have been in the presence of this House—in the course of the last quarter of an hour?"[1]

Fairman—"No."

Mr Harvey—"Were the letters you received addressed to you in the character of secretary to the Orange lodges?"

Fairman—"Certainly."

Mr Harvey—"Does the book in question, which you refuse to produce, contain any answer from you, as secretary of the Orange Society, to letters written on Orange subjects?"

Fairman—"Many."

Mr Scarlett—"Is the book in question your property?"

Fairman—"I consider it my property."

Mr Scarlett—"Are the entries in that book for your own satisfaction, or for the use and benefit of this Society?"

Fairman—"For my own satisfaction."

Mr Sheil—"I beg to ask the witness whether part of that book is not in the handwriting of the Deputy Secretary of the Orange lodge?"

Fairman—"No doubt about it."

Mr Scarlett—"You say the book contains copies of answers which you made to the Orange institutions. Did you sign your name simply, or did you add your title?"

Fairman—"Generally speaking, I signed but my own name. It is universally known what office I hold, and I do not think it necessary to sign D.G.S."

Mr Harvey—"Do you consider the letters addressed to

[1] Fairman had been ordered to withdraw from time to time during his examination, and the suggestion was that in one of these intervals he had given the order.

you in your capacity of Secretary your own private property, or the property of the Society?"

Fairman—"The property of the Society."

Mr Harvey—"Do you consider the official answers which you give to those communications to you, in your capacity of secretary, to belong to the Society?"

Fairman—"I do; because if I am called on to do so by the Grand Lodge, or by the Committee, I must produce them."

O'Connell—"Have you any other books containing correspondence between the Orange lodges and the Grand Secretary?"

Fairman—"None."

Fairman was ordered to withdraw, and the Chancellor of the Exchequer (Spring Rice) then moved that he should produce the book. The motion was resisted by Inglis, Shaw, Jackson, and the Orange party in the House, but carried by 71 to 26 votes.

Fairman was recalled, and addressed by the Speaker thus:—

"It is my duty to inform you that this House is of opinion that you should produce the book which has been alluded to in your evidence, and which you declined to produce before the Committee. Without adverting to the foundations for that which you considered as a point of honour obligatory on yourself, I am confident that you will feel, that when the House has come to the resolution that you are bound to produce that book, you will forthwith comply with the opinion of this House, because you must be aware that your first duty, and one which supersedes all private and personal feelings of your own, is to yield prompt obedience to the pleasure of this House. You may now withdraw."

Fairman did withdraw, and never appeared again either before the Committee or the House. On August 21 the Sergeant-at-Arms, who had been ordered to apprehend him, reported that the Grand Secretary had left his residence, and could not be found. Fairman kept out of the way until the end of the session, and no further steps were taken to arrest him.

In September the Select Committee reported. They condemned the Orange Society, root and branch.

"It is notorious," says the Report, "that the Orange lodges exist, under the patronage of men high in rank, in England, Ireland, and in Scotland; and the countenance given, in consequence of all the orders of the Orange institution being issued by and under the authority of such men as His Royal Highness the Duke of Cumberland, as Imperial Grand Master, and of His Grace the Duke of Gordon, as Deputy Grand Master for Scotland, will be found to have a greater effect on the poor and the ignorant—of which the Orangemen there chiefly consist—than might be expected. When we see an emissary despatched for two successive years to extend Orangeism in that country, under the special and extraordinary commission of the Duke of Cumberland, bearing his sign and seal, with powers to propagate Orangeism, to form lodges, to dismiss members, or to pardon offences of Orangemen how and when he pleases, it appears time for Government to interfere. When that emissary is entertained and countenanced for weeks as an inmate of Gordon Castle, the influence of the peer may be by the ignorant transferred to the emissary in everything respecting Orange lodges in that country.

"There are various ways of enlisting men in a cause; and when it is seen by the reports of the proceedings of Grand Lodges that such men as the Duke of Cumberland, the Duke of Gordon, Lord Kenyon, Lord Wynford, peers and Members of Parliament, are united by the same secret signs and passwords, and seated in the same room with a poor pensioner of one shilling a-day, or any Orangeman, whatever his state in society may be, allowance must be made for the sacrifices that may be made by such persons to be able to call the Duke, or any other Orangeman, his brother—with permission to apply, whenever in difficulty or distress, for the assistance of such wealthy and influential men.

"As a proof of the baneful effects of the existence of Orangeism in Scotland, Mr Innes states one example where a lodge of pitmen lately expelled from their body all the Catholics, who had previously lived and worked together with them in peace and harmony.

"Your Committee will only add, that the mischievous effects of Orange lodges, shown, though on a small scale, in Scotland, may be expected wherever such a system is upheld and promoted by men of high rank and by influential members of society; a reference to the evidence before the House of the working of Orangeism in Ireland, on the broadest scale, and after many years' continuance, will completely bear out that opinion.

"Your Committee, in looking for a corrective to those evils which disturb both civil and military society so much, and which threaten the most serious consequences to the community of the United Kingdom, if allowed to continue, do not contemplate that any new legislative enactment is necessary; the power of the law being at present, in the opinion of your Committee, sufficient to protect the country from all such associations, bound together, as the Orange lodges are, by religious sanction, with secret signs and passwords, by which the fraternity may be known to each other in every part of the world. It appears only to be necessary to enforce the existing laws against all such offenders, whether belonging to Orange lodges, to Ribbon lodges, or to any other Society having secret signs and bonds of union. . . .

"Your Committee think it right to place before the

House the words of the statute 39 Geo. III., c. 79, regarding corresponding societies. Section 9: 'Any society composed of different divisions or branches, or of different parts, acting in any manner separately, or distinct from each other, or of which any part shall have any distinct president, secretary, treasurer, delegate, or other officer, elected or appointed by, or for such part, or to act in any office for such part,' &c.; and, in conclusion, your Committee submit, that it will be for the House to consider whether the present organisation of Orange lodges, in connection with the Imperial Grand Lodge, comes within the words of that statute; and if so, whether the law officers of the Crown should not be directed to institute legal proceedings, without any delay, against the Grand Officers of Orange lodges."[1]

A month after the publication of this Report an Orangeman named Haywood stated that Fairman had been hatching a plot to place the Duke of Cumberland upon the throne, and had actually sounded the Orangemen of the provinces on the subject. Fairman denied the charge indignantly, and filed a criminal information against Haywood for libel.[2] Hume and the English Radicals met

[1] "Report of Select Committee on Orange Lodges in Great Britain and the Colonies," pp. xxv., xxvii.

[2] "Haywood, after being dismissed from a lodge, had addressed a letter to Lord Kenyon, in October 1835, and in which he asked: 'Did not His Royal Highness, as Grand Master, and Lord Kenyon, as Deputy Grand Master, know what their missionary, Colonel Fairman, had done in 1832; or rather, did he not act under the directions of His Royal Highness, or Lord Kenyon; and was he not, under their directions, instructed to sound the brethren how they would be disposed, in the event of King William IV. being deposed, which was not improbable, on account of his sanctioning reform in Parliament; and that, if so, it would become the duty of every Orangeman to support His Royal Highness, who would then, in all probability, be called to the throne?' There was something very suspicious in this revelation of supposed designs entertained by a body to which the maker of the revelation had, nevertheless, continued to belong for three years. Colonel Fairman immediately published a letter, declaring the whole statement to be a falsehood, and adopted judicial proceedings against Haywood, which dropped, however, in consequence of the death of the latter."—"Annual Register, 1836," p. 12, Speech of Mr Hume.

this move by a counter move. They demanded the prosecution of the Duke of Cumberland, Lord Kenyon, the Bishop of Salisbury, and Fairman, as members of an illegal society. Preliminary steps were taken in both cases. Evidence was collected, counsel were engaged, the pleadings were ready, when the sudden death of Haywood stopped the proceedings; not, however, until the evidence which had been amassed enabled Hume, in the next session of Parliament, to strike a serious blow at the Orange Society.[1]

In the midst of all this excitement, and while Ireland was in a state of general disorder, Drummond took up his post at Dublin Castle.

[1] The counsel engaged for Haywood were Sergeant Wilde, Charles Austin, and Charles Buller. The Radicals said the case of the Orange Society was analogous to the case of the Dorsetshire labourers. "In the commencement of 1834 it occurred to some people that an organization similar to a Trades Union might be extended with advantage to agricultural labour. Dorsetshire was a purely agricultural county, in which labour was paid at a miserably low rate. A union was formed, and in the formation of the union no law was broken. It was, however, customary in these unions to administer an oath to the unionists. An old Act of George III., passed amidst the terror which the Mutiny of the Nore had caused, had made it an offence, punishable by transportation, to administer illegal oaths. The statute had been rarely enforced; practically, it had been disregarded by every Trades Union in the kingdom. It was suddenly resuscitated to punish the men who had formed the first agricultural union. Six wretched labourers, wholly ignorant of the law, were prosecuted at Dorchester for administering illegal oaths. The jury found them guilty; the judge, after two days' consideration, thought himself bound to inflict the punishment set out in the law, and sentenced them to seven years' transportation."—Walpole's "History of England," iii., p. 229. But a storm was raised in and out of Parliament, and finally, after two years' transportation, the convicts were granted a free pardon, and allowed to return home.

CHAPTER VII.

DRUMMOND AT DUBLIN CASTLE.

TRIFLES best show character. For this reason I give a letter, unimportant in other respects, written by Drummond shortly after his arrival at Dublin Castle. It illustrates his kindly nature and strong sense of justice.

"MY DEAR STEWART,—Pray look into this case of great hardship and distress, and do what you can for this poor creature. The facts are correctly stated. Would any man in a better situation be turned off after twenty years' service without a penny?—Faithfully,

"T. DRUMMOND."

"*July* 29, 1835."

I have not been able to ascertain fully the facts of this case; but I gather that an official named Toole had been superannuated "without a penny," and died soon afterwards. His widow, who was left in straitened circumstances, applied to the Castle for help. While it was doubtful how her application would be received, Drummond arrived, and supported her claims with energy and success.

On the day that Drummond wrote this letter, Lord Morpeth wrote to him from London:—

LORD MORPETH TO DRUMMOND.

"*July* 29, 1835.

"MY DEAR DRUMMOND,—I have missed your predecessor every time he has called, but I hear he says, and

Lord Mulgrave writes, that you have begun swimmingly. I must try to bother you as little as possible till you are quite afloat in the main stream. It is represented to me that Orange outbreaks go on at Belfast, and that a stipendiary magistrate is much needed there. If so, I should like to send Mr Hancock of Lurgan; he is now in London. I shall wish at all times to hear what reaches you relative to distress. I think we are doing well here, though I cannot wish the Lords joy on their prospects of a speech from Wetherall, on every branch and bearing of the Corporation Bill.—Ever most sincerely,

"MORPETH."

This was among the first of a series of bright, cheery letters written from time to time by Lord Morpeth to Drummond, which show that nobleman in the light of an extremely pleasant and agreeable correspondent and companion. His Lordship does not seem to have held the House of Lords in great reverence, for we find him writing to Drummond on August 4:—

". . . The House of Lords! we take no heed of them, but it may delay my getting to you. Lord Spencer did not look very happy there at three this morning."

One of the subjects to which the new Under-Secretary turned his immediate attention was the organisation of an efficient police force.

Practically the first Irish Police Act was passed in 1787. It empowered the Lord Lieutenant to appoint a Chief Constable for each barony: sub-constables were appointed by the Grand Juries. No Catholic could enter this force.[1] In 1792 another Act was passed, enabling Grand Juries to increase the number of sub-constables fixed by the first

[1] 24 Geo. III., c. 40 (Irish Statutes). It was entitled, "An Act for the better execution of the law, and the preservation of the peace within counties at large."

Act.[1] The next Act was passed in 1814. It empowered the Lord Lieutenant to appoint a resident magistrate, a chief constable, and fifty sub-constables in any disturbed district. The Lord Lieutenant decided (by proclamation) what was a disturbed district. This force was wholly independent of the local authorities. It was under the control of the resident magistrates, who acted on instructions from Dublin Castle.[2]

In 1822 a fourth Act was passed. This was practically an amendment of the Act of 1787. Leaving to the Lord Lieutenant the power to appoint chief constables, it transferred the power of appointing sub-constables from Grand Juries to local magistrates. But its most important feature was the appointment (by the Lord Lieutenant) of four Inspectors-General—an inspector for each province.

These were the statutes in force when Drummond came to Ireland. None of them worked well;[3] and prior to Drummond's time the Government contemplated a change in the organisation and management of the police. That change was now made.[4] On August 10 Lord Morpeth introduced a Bill "to consolidate the laws relating to the constabulary in Ireland."

This measure deprived the local magistrates of the power

[1] Sixteen for each district. 32 Geo. III., c. 16. This Act was entitled, "An Act for regulating the office of constable, and for the better enforcing the process of criminal law in certain parts of the kingdom."

[2] 54 Geo. III., c. 131. It was entitled, "An Act to provide for the better execution of the laws in Ireland by appointing superintending magistrates, and additional constables in certain cases." The resident magistrates received a salary of £700 a year, *see* secs. 2 and 4. For "a list of stipendiary magistrates in Ireland between 1817 and 1831," *see* "Parliamentary Papers," vol. xiii. for 1831-32.

[3] 3 Geo. IV., c. 103.

[4] A Constabulary Bill, the same substantially as that now introduced, had been drafted by Littleton.—Hansard, 3rd ser., vol. xxx., p. 1189. In fact, the Earl of Haddington said in the House of Lords, on August 26, 1835, that the Constabulary Bill then under discussion had been "ready prepared for the last three or four years." Lord Hatherton said, on Sept. 1, 1835, that the Bill had been in his office "all last year."—Hansard, 3rd ser., vol. xxx., p. 1189.

to appoint constables, and placed the whole force under the control of an Inspector-General at Dublin Castle. The Lord Lieutenant appointed the Inspector-General, and, in fact, all the officers and men. Under the Inspector-General were two deputy inspectors-general, four county inspectors, thirty-two sub-inspectors, chief constables, and head constables. Prior to this Bill the police had been under the control of a divided authority: the Executive Government appointed the officers of the force, the local magistrates the men. By this Bill the Lord Lieutenant was empowered to appoint both officers and men. The contentious part of the measure was the proposal to transfer the power of appointing constables from the local magistrates to the Lord Lieutenant. The Ascendancy were strongly opposed to this change. The Bill, however, was read a first and second time in the Commons without discussion.

On August 11 Lord Morpeth wrote to Drummond :—

LORD MORPETH TO DRUMMOND.

"MY DEAR DRUMMOND,—I got leave last night to introduce the Constabulary Bill without discussion. It cannot expect such good luck throughout. . . . No effort of mine shall be wanting. But passing contested Bills in August is not quite so easily done as said, my good collaborator. . . .—Ever yours,

"MORPETH.

"*P.S.*—More than all the rest, am I, as I hear, to wish you joy? Its great cordiality will only be damped by my just vindictiveness at the suppression of such a topic in our daily interchange of less interesting news."

In Committee, on August 18, the first note of dissent to the Constabulary Bill was struck by the Ascendancy. Colonel Perceval led the way, and Shaw followed. The clause empowering the Lord Lieutenant to appoint the constables was, they said, a slur on the magistracy. Morpeth denied this, and declared that in many instances the magistrates had already abdicated their functions, and allowed the Government to appoint constables. The Bill in reality was only giving effect to the wishes of the magistrates themselves. The discussion was not pushed to a division. On August 19, Morpeth wrote to Drummond:—

"The Constabulary Bill went through Committee yesterday with a labour of five hours, and was delivered with less disfigurement on the whole than could have been expected, but with some slight curtailments of salary, &c."[1]

But the real fight was reserved for the House of Lords. On August 25 Morpeth wrote to Drummond:—

"Duncannon says the Lords mean to throw out the Constabulary Bill, for which I shall be very sorry on all accounts, but chiefly because I think you will not be able to refrain from butchering every member of the aristocracy. . . . The Duchess of Sutherland, who is with me now, desires me to say, with what great interest she heard of what must so deeply affect your happiness."[2]

The Lords did throw out the Constabulary Bill on August 26 by 51 to 39 votes. Foremost among the opponents of the measure were the Marquis of Londonderry, the Earl of Roden, the Earl of Wicklow, the Marquis of Westmeath, Lords Fitzgerald and Vesey. They all protested against the proposal to transfer the power of appointing the constables from the magistrates—"a most excellent and fearless body of men"[3]—to the Lord Lieutenant. The effect of the Bill, the Marquis of London-

[1] On August 13 Morpeth had written to Drummond:—"We have murmurs from friends against the Constabulary Bill, chiefly against the number and expense of the police staff. I believe, to do you justice, these parts were principally added to the Bill on this side of the water."

[2] Drummond's engagement to Miss Kinnaird.

[3] Roden.

derry said, would really be to hand over the control of the police to Daniel O'Connell. "I would be ashamed," said the Marquis of Westmeath, "to show my face among my brother magistrates in Ireland if I consented to take from them that control which they had so long and so faithfully exercised."

On August 27 Morpeth wrote to Drummond:—

LORD MORPETH TO DRUMMOND.

"MY DEAR DRUMMOND,—Well, the Lords have done it. I allay my disgust by thinking how much more keen yours must be. But it is thought that nearly everything is in our favour without an Act of Parliament. I am ready for any degree of vigour, so turn in your mind whether we might not issue a general order announcing that everyone who, by a certain day, would not give his solemn assurance that he was not a Ribbonman or Orangeman should be instantly dismissed from the force.[1]

"I have sent up the Dublin Police[2] to-day to this grave of all the Capulets, where, I suppose, it will not have a longer living existence than Juliet.[3] I suppose you would still wish it [the Constabulary Bill] passed if we are able. It seems still uncertain when we shall rise. It will turn on Monday in the House of Commons.—Ever yours,

"MORPETH."

The rejection of the Constabulary Bill was the beginning of active hostilities between the Ascendancy and Drummond; and, for nearly five years, that is to say, until Drummond's death, the conflict continued. It was the policy of Drummond to govern Ireland by the vigorous

[1] Under the existing system, Ribbonmen and Orangemen sometimes got into the police.

[2] A Bill for the reorganisation of the Dublin police had also been introduced.

[3] It had not. It was rejected without a division on September 4. The Duke of Wellington opposed it.

enforcement of the ordinary law, and a generous regard to the grievances of the people. It was the policy of the Ascendancy to govern by coercion, so that all agitators might be put down, and all grievances kept out of sight. "Law and order" was the cry of the Orange faction. "Law, order, and justice" were the watchwords of the Under Secretary.

Before Drummond's arrival it had been the practice, as we have seen, to employ police and military in the collection of tithes.[1] The Ascendancy wished the practice to continue; Drummond was resolved it should end. In October 1835, he wrote this letter in reply to one of the usual applications for police aid to collect tithes :—

"DUBLIN CASTLE, *Oct.* 14, 1835.

"SIR,—Referring to your letter relative to granting police aid in the recovery of your tithes, I am now directed by the Lord Lieutenant to acquaint you that he cannot comply with your application.

"His Excellency does not deem it expedient in this, or in any other case of the enforcement of civil rights by distress, that either the military or the police should be called out unless their presence shall be rendered necessary by actual riot, or breach of the peace. In such cases, I am desired by his Excellency to add, that, the military and the police will be directed to attend on the requisition, and under the control of the local authorities; and distinct orders will be issued to provide as far as possible for the repression and punishment of all violations of the public peace.—I am, faithfully,"

(Signed) "MORPETH."

"The Rev. B. COTTER."

The position here taken up was never abandoned. The

[1] "Was not the Government forced to employ horse, foot, and artillery for the collection of tithes?" Sharman Crawford was asked by the Committee on Orange Lodges. He answered, "The Government did so."—"Select Committee on Orange Lodges, &c., in Ireland." Q. 6039.

ground on which Drummond took his stand—that the police should be used, not to collect tithes or rents, but to keep the peace—was held firmly to the end.

To understand Drummond's position, it must be borne in mind, that there was at this time a land war as well as a tithe war. The tenants complained of excessive rents and general oppression. The landlords opposed all suggestions of reform. Drummond stood aloof from the contending parties. He refused to collect either tithes or rents at the point of the bayonet. He sent both parson and landlord to the ordinary legal tribunals for "redress." It was for the courts to enforce legal process; it was for him to keep the peace. The Sheriff, not the Lord Lieutenant, was the functionary to conduct distraints and carry out evictions. The Executive was responsible for the public tranquillity, not for the enforcement of personal claims, just or unjust. This was Drummond's position. He was never driven from it.

The Rev. W. Beresford applied for police to attend a tithe sale. Drummond replied that no police should be sent to aid Beresford in carrying out the sale; but that the peace would be kept. The sale took place, the police were stationed out of view; and everything went off quietly. The Chief Constable reported to Drummond:—

"I beg to report that the sale of distress made by the Rev. W. Beresford at Ballincally went off quietly yesterday. The police were not in view. Major Gallway went to the place and spoke to the people, who seemed to pay attention to what he said to them."

Upon another occasion Major Gallway said to a clergyman who was anxious that the police should take an active part in levying a distress for tithes, "The duty of the police will be confined to patrolling the neighbourhood without at all assisting in levying the distress."

Lord Mountcashel applied for a police force to execute writs of ejectment for non-payment of rent. Drummond replied, "Police shall be sent on affidavit being made that there is reasonable ground to apprehend a breach of the peace." Major Sykes, a Tipperary landlord, applied for a police force to attend a sale of goods which he had distrained for rent from Thomas Burke, "a very bad character, and connected with a lawless faction in the neighbourhood. Acting on their motto, 'who dare,' he refuses to pay rent, and disregards the usual course of the law." Sykes feared the "effusion of blood" if the police were not present. Drummond endorsed the letter, "Inform that his Excellency regrets that he cannot afford police aid under the circumstances stated by Mr Sykes."

To another application of a like kind he replied, "This being an application for aid in removing goods distrained, his Excellency has not the power to order the police to interfere." These refusals brought the denunciations of the Ascendancy on Drummond's head. But the Under Secretary kept on the even tenor of his way. He preserved the peace. But he did not place the police at the beck and call of either parson or landlord.

While Drummond was thus dealing with these applications, Lord Morpeth received the following letter from Poulett Scrope, M.P.

Poulett Scrope was then member for Stroud. He was an able and moderate politician. For many years he had taken a keen interest in the question of landlord and tenant in Ireland. It was his opinion that the miseries and crimes of the Irish peasantry were due to landlord oppression, and he constantly strove to bring the fact before the English public. A Royal Commission had been appointed to inquire into the condition of the poorer classes in Ireland. Scrope felt that the work of this Commission would be incomplete, if the causes of agrarian crime were not investigated, and accordingly he wrote to Lord Morpeth :—

Poulett Scrope to Lord Morpeth.

"Castlecombe, Chippenham, *October* 1835.

"My Lord,—I write at your Lordship's request to remind you of a promise made to me before you quitted London, that an immediate examination should be made of the reports of the provincial constabulary officers for some years back, for the purpose of obtaining, and laying before Parliament, a view of the state of crime in Ireland—and especially of the nature and extent of those agrarian offences which are so peculiar to that country, as to demonstrate the existence of some corresponding peculiarly exciting cause.

"I cannot but think that the inquiry now in progress under a Royal Commission, into the condition of the poorer classes in Ireland, will be exceedingly imperfect if so important a branch of the subject is omitted, as that which relates to their remarkable proneness to the commission of a class of offences almost unheard of in other countries—which are, however, not only of frequent occurrence in Ireland, but seem to meet with the general approbation and countenance of the bulk of the population; it being notorious that, while the apprehension of a thief will be aided by the peasantry assembled at a fair or market in Ireland, a person accused of a criminal outrage—nay, even of a murder—of an agrarian character, will be generally aided to escape from justice, and probably supported and befriended by the people of the country.

"The tacit and occasionally active participation of crowds of bystanders in assassinations, and violent outrages of this nature, and the general existence of secret societies in execution of whose formal sentences these deeds of blood and violence are usually perpetrated, form symptoms of a disordered state of moral feeling among the mass of the peasantry, which in any honest inquiry into their condition, it would betray the grossest blindness to neglect. .

"Knowing that reports are regularly made to the Lord Lieutenant of the state of crime in the different provinces, accompanied by comments both of a general and particular nature fitting to throw light on this important subject, I venture to make the suggestion to your Lordship which has been the cause of my present application; and I would now only remind your Lordship of your engagement to institute the inquiry, and at the same time express a hope that your Lordship will take the necessary pains to prevent a party or partial bias being given to it, either by the method adopted, or the persons engaged in it.

"It must be obvious to all who know the heated state of party feeling in Ireland, that, unless the entire documents as sent up by the constabulary are produced and printed (which their bulk may render impossible or difficult without a selection, which opens another door to partiality), it will be in the power, and, without great care taken in his choice, may be the object, of the person employed, to make the result of the inquiry tell for or against the credit or interest of the political, or religious, party to which he is attached.

"My own impression is that such an inquiry should form a branch of that now making into the state of the poorer classes, and that no fitter person could be employed to prosecute or direct it than Mr Revans, the Secretary to that Commission.

"But I feel sure your Lordship's discernment and impartiality may be depended on for securing an unprejudiced, and, at the same time, a thorough inquiry. The facts and their bearings, I am aware, will be such as must, if fully disclosed, necessarily excite feelings of a very strong character. Still, I cannot think that your Lordship will allow any veil on this account to be thrown over them.

The moral and physical state of the Irish people has reached a crisis of disease in which any concealment would be criminal, since nothing but such strong remedies as the extremity of the case calls for can be of any avail. The English, and even the Irish themselves of the upper classes, are in almost complete ignorance of the real condition of the Irish people—a condition more frightful in its deformity than can be conceived except it be witnessed—and the truth must be told, or they will not be prepared for the application of the real remedies.

"The volume just printed—Appendix A to the first Report of the Commission of Inquiry—offers such a picture of a professedly civilised community as the world never yet saw. But the picture must be completed, and for this purpose the inquiry on which I write is essentially necessary.

"I trust your Lordship will institute it in time to produce the result before the next meeting of Parliament, and contemporaneously at least with the final Report of the Commission. In this hope, and apologising for anything that may appear presuming in the way in which I have taken the liberty to communicate my views,—I have the honour to remain, your Lordship's very obedient servant,

"G. POULETT SCROPE."

Morpeth sent this letter to Drummond with the following note:—

"Please to look over this letter, and then return it. Before its arrival I received an application from Mr Revans to be allowed to look over the constabulary reports with the same view. I think the request reasonable, and may turn to use, but I wish first to submit it to you. "MORPETH."

This letter may be followed by one from an Irish tenant to Lord Althorp. The original was found among Drummond's papers.

AN IRISH TENANT TO LORD ALTHORP.

"MY LORD,—It is reported that you are about to charge the tenantry of Ireland a Land Tax instead of tithe. We, the peasantry (for the peasantry are almost the tenantry of this poor country), are not objects fit at all for any taxation, however small. You do not know the kind of creatures you are going to tax—creatures that are reduced to the necessity of subsisting on the same food with their pig, and lying on a bed of the same quality with her. The Irish are reduced to the necessity of entirely subsisting on the lumper potato—a kind that grows something better in the poor man's impoverished land than the potatoes of good quality. The lumper is not indeed human food at all. Mix them with any other kind of potatoes and lay them before a pig, and she will not eat one of them until all the good kind are devoured, even if her hunger be not at all abated. There is a demand on us for two or three years' tithe; you might as well try to get back the snow of last year as to try to get that or any part of it from nineteen out of twenty of us; to get anything from us you should have a police on the spot to snap it from us whilst it is on its way from our hand to our mouth. That is the way the tithe was always wrung from creatures like us. If we were to be shot for it we could not keep it on hands for one week, such is the pressing nature of our wants. And you will have as much difficulty in tearing it from us under the name of a Land Tax as under its proper name. And all for this best of all reasons, because we have it not nor can afford it.

"God knows if we could pay it, we would do so, and it would be better and easier for us to do so (however unjust), than to be at the trouble and danger we are in refusing it. It would be better for us to pay it if we could, than to have our heart's blood shed instead of it. We dread, you may believe it, the ugly deaths we meet at the hands of the bloody tithe ministers, but certainly we dread the death of ourselves and our poor children by starvation much more. We have daily in our view death staring us in the face, in the shape of poverty, hunger, and starvation. We have also daily in our view and our dreams the not much less horrid and revolting figure of the tithe clergyman with the police, the instruments of death, at his back. Under these circumstances, and surrounded by Martial Law, there is no alternative left but to choose the easiest way to die.

"People like you cannot have the least idea of our misery. The great governors of nations ought to go in disguise through the country, and enter the hovels of the peasantry, to make themselves acquainted with the kind of food they live on, and how they must labour for that food. If they did so, even though they may be without a heart, brute instinct would make them see that they are not fit objects even of the most necessary taxation, not to say a tax so unjust in its nature and so unnecessary, as to be pampering the teacher of piety and humility with three or four thousand a year. If such an enormous sum be necessary to induce these saints to impart a share of their piety and humility to their fellow-creatures, levy it off the rich for them. Tax not for them eaters of the lumper potato and the grain of salt. Tax only such as have for themselves at least the necessaries of life. Tax no one for them that has not more than an interest of one hundred a year in their land. Tax but that description, and it will be paid; from one hundred a year upwards to sixty and eighty thousand, the scale should rise rapidly.

"These are the description of persons that ought to be taxed, because they can pay unknown to their bellies, and because it will be less trouble to them to do so than resist, even should they think it unjust. But if you tax the lumper potato eater, the tithe owner who receives it will often have his head dish sweetened with the blood of the victim from whom it is torn. But that is sauce that the saints are well accustomed to, and therefore will have no objection to. But, my Lord, that the Almighty may put it in your heart to rescue the poor people of Ireland from these voracious vultures, and that God Almighty may reward you, shall be the prayer of me, a poor tiller of land, and who subscribes himself,—Your Lordship's humble servant,

"PADDY CAHILL."

"*17th June* 1833."

In November Drummond left Ireland to be married; and on the 19th of that month he became the husband of Miss Kinnaird.[1] They were married from Weston House, Warwickshire, the seat of Sir George Philips, where, two years previously, they had met.

In December, Drummond and his wife were settled down at the Under Secretary's lodge in the Phœnix Park, Dublin; thenceforth, it is no exaggeration to say, the thoughts of both were given up to the well-being of the country where their lot was cast.

Drummond's life in Ireland was one of constant anxiety and trial; but the burdens of a cheerless office were lightened by the comforts of a happy home. In Miss Kinnaird he had found a lady whose intellectual gifts did not fall short of her personal attractions; who was a sympathetic helpmate, a bright companion, a tender, thought-

[1] Hearing of the approaching marriage, the poet Wordsworth wrote to Samuel Rogers: "Miss Kinnaird, I am told, is about to be married to Lieut. Drummond, of calculating celebrity. Is he an amiable man? I should like to know, for she is a great favourite with me and mine."—Clayden: "Rogers and his Contemporaries."

ful wife. She entered into the spirit of her husband's work, held his views, shared his counsels, cheered his labours. The murmurs of the political storm which raged round Dublin Castle were not heard in the Phœnix Park. The gloom of public care was lost in the brightness of domestic joy.

We get a glimpse of Drummond at the Phœnix Park in a letter from Mrs Sharp, Richard Sharp's widowed sister-in-law, to whose care Miss Kinnaird had been confided from a very early age, and whose home now was the Under Secretary's Lodge. Writing to Drummond's mother, in December, she says:—

"My Dear Madam,—As I am the person whose time is the least occupied, it would indeed be most unkind of me to withhold from you the daily occurrences and details which I well know must be most interesting to a mother. I only regret that the pen is not held by one of your dear children, either of whom would send you a much better letter than myself. Maria is a good deal engaged at present in making her domestic arrangements, and dear Mr Drummond's laborious duties (for truly his situation is no sinecure) leave him no time for writing letters to those with whom it would be a delight to him to correspond.

"In my last hastily-written letter I promised to give you some description of this lovely place. To begin with the house, which you enter by a handsome stone porch, which leads through a glass door into a very pretty hall. On the right hand is the drawing-room, two windows of which open into a very pretty green-house looking nearly south; on the east side is a handsome bow with three French windows opening on the lawn, which is beautifully diversified with shrubs and flower beds. Communicating with the drawing-room by a double door, is a spacious dining-room with a large bow window, commanding the same view as the bow in the drawing-room. Another door in the dining-room opens into a passage which leads to the housekeeper's room and other offices. A very pretty staircase conducts to the second floor; the first room on the landing is Mr Drummond's study fitted up as a library; but if his business continues as laborious as it is at present, I regret to say that it should rather be called his office.

"The next room is a noble bedroom over the dining-room, occupied by him and his dear wife, with a nice dressing-room for him. Then follows my room, which is truly comfortable, and commanding the same view as theirs. The next is a larger room, which was kindly offered to me, but I much prefer the one I have chosen, and, even if I had not, it would have been most selfish of me to have taken it, as there is a dressing-room attached to it, which would have been to me quite useless. There are a great many other rooms all very comfortable, but those I have described are what may be termed the principal apartments. The house abounds with every convenience, hot and cold baths, &c. Mr Drummond's domain contains, I believe, about forty-two acres, three of which are laid out as pleasure grounds. The situation is beautifully retired, not a house being visible from any part of it, but not in the remotest degree dull. I can assure you that Maria and I, and, I think I may add, your son, will be very, very sorry to leave it for the Castle, but we understand that it is the etiquette for the Under Secretary to remove there when the Lord Lieutenant takes possession of the Castle, which it is usual to do in the month of February. Our hope is, that as Lady Mulgrave is said to be very fond of the Phœnix Park, she will have the good taste to return here early in the spring.

"And now, my dear Madam, it remains for me to give you some insight into the manner in which we pass our time. We rise at eight o'clock, and at a quarter after nine all the servants who are not Catholics assemble in the dining-room for family prayer, preceded by reading a portion of Scripture. At present, Maria alone conducts the worship, but Mr Drummond has promised occasionally to assist her, but, with the feelings of a doting husband, he thinks no one can do it with so much effect as she. I am sure you will be gratified to hear that he is always present. Then follows breakfast, at which we are joined by two gentlemen, who are his assistants, but who do not reside in the house. Immediately after breakfast, Mr Drummond returns to the library, and we do not see him until about two o'clock, when he rides to the Castle, from whence he never returns until just in time to dress for a seven-o'clock dinner.

"You would then suppose his labours were ended, but not so—an hour, at least, is devoted to business; but in order not to lose a moment of each other's society, Maria sits in his study with him, and there we generally take our tea. My poor Maria is not a little annoyed to find that even the little time they have to enjoy each other's society is likely to be broken in upon by stupid dinner parties, which, as a man in office, he and his wife will be obliged to attend. I earnestly hope that some means will be devised for abridging them, for I am sure they will be injurious to the health of both.

"Our first visitor here was Lord Morpeth, who called the day after our arrival, invited us to a dinner on the Saturday, and only let us off on condition of our going to his ball on the following Tuesday—on which day Mr Drummond and Maria dined at the Viceregal Lodge, where they met a very small party, consisting of the Rev. Dr Murray, Mr and Mrs Grattan, Mr Sheil, together with many military men, attendants on the household. I called for them at half-past ten, and accompanied them to Lord

Morpeth's, where there was a large assembly, looking very gay from the number of military men.

"Lord Morpeth received Maria in the most flattering manner, taking her on his arm, and introducing her to many of the company. Indeed, throughout the evening the introductions were so numerous, that I think she must have been weary of hearing her new name.

"Her husband was very much pleased with her dress, which was white satin trimmed with blond lace; her hair dressed in the Grecian style, with some very pretty ornaments of beads, intermixed with green and silver leaves, a beautiful gold chain, brooch, earrings, and bracelet gold-studded with emeralds.

"The whole of my amusement was in watching the admiring looks of her happy husband, and the scrutiny with which he seemed to look into the faces of those to whom she was introduced, to see if they approved her. During Mr Sharp's life we went a great deal more into society than I liked, but I felt I was more in my duty in going with Maria than suffering her to go alone. Now that she is married, the case is altered, and I no longer feel it necessary. I shall therefore indulge my own inclinations, and keep much at home.

"On Sunday (the only Sabbath we have spent here) we set out in the car to go to the Hibernian Chapel, but the horse being a little unruly we took fright, and Mr Drummond went alone. I am at present quite at a loss to know where to attend, but am hoping to be furnished with some information on the subject from a friend in England. I suppose it will be expedient for Maria to appear at church at the morning service, but unless their pulpits are better filled here than they are in the generality of churches in England, she will have a very different fare to what she has been accustomed. I therefore anxiously hope that she will attend afternoon or evening service (whichever it may be) with me, should I meet with a preacher whose religious opinions coincide with my own.

"Mr Drummond went this morning directly after breakfast to the Lord Lieutenant, I have therefore not had an opportunity of reading him that part of your letter which you wished me to communicate. I shall be silent as to the slowness of the amendment of his dear sister's health, about which I know he is most anxious; indeed, I may truly say that we all are. At present the weather here is unusually mild. If that be the weather that suits Miss Drummond, I hope it is so in Scotland; for my own feelings, I rather prefer a more bracing air.

"I am just told it is my duty to take a walk while the sun is shining so beautifully, and if I do not seal my letter before I go I shall lose this day's post. I therefore must conclude this very short epistle, and only add the united kind regards of our two to your trio.—Believe me, my dear Madam, your sincere friend,

"A. M. SHARP.

"Your son and daughter are quite well. I can say the same of myself."

CHAPTER VIII.

1836.

IMMEDIATELY on the meeting of Parliament in 1836, the Irish members renewed their attacks on the Orange Society. They were supported by Hume, who revealed the whole story of the "Fairman plot," and wound up a vigorous speech with a strong resolution demanding an address to the Crown for the removal of every judge, privy councillor, lord lieutenant, magistrate, militia officer, police inspector, or constable who belonged to the organization. Lord John Russell interposed with a moderate speech, and moved as an amendment to Hume's resolution, that His Majesty should be prayed to take such steps as he deemed "advisable for the effectual discouragement of Orange lodges, and generally of all political societies." The Orange members, wincing under Hume's onslaught, and possibly fearful of further revelations, offered but a faint-hearted resistance to Russell's amendment. They proposed the omission of the words "Orange lodges." Russell insisted on retaining the words. Verner said he would take the opinion of the House on the point. Shaw urged his friends not to press the question to a division. Shaw's advice was taken, and Russell's amendment agreed to unanimously.[1]

On February 25, the King's answer to the address was received—

[1] Hansard, 3rd ser., vol. xxxi, pp. 332, 345, and 779, 859.
It was stated during the debate, that of 27,000 men in the Irish yeomanry corps, 25,000 were Orangemen; that of 7000 policemen, 5000 were Orangemen. *Ibid.*, p. 333.

"WILLIAM REX—I willingly assent to the prayer of the address of my faithful Commons that I would be pleased to take such measures as may seem to me advisable for the effectual discouragement of Orange lodges, and generally of all political societies, excluding persons of a different religious faith, using secret signs and symbols, and, acting by means of associated branches. It is my firm intention to discourage all such societies in my dominions, and I rely with confidence on the fidelity of my loyal subjects to support me in this determination."

The Orangemen bowed to this mandate. Cumberland flung up the Grand Mastership. The Orange Society of Great Britain and the Colonies was dissolved. But the Orange Society of Ireland remained to threaten the public peace and thwart the policy of conciliation.[1]

[1] The Orange Society was dissolved as a system of affiliated lodges under the Grand Lodge; but it remained in Ireland as a system of unaffiliated lodges.—McLennan.

The Orange Society of Great Britain was, so far as I can make out, reformed in 1845.

By the new "Laws and Ordinances," the Orangeman's declaration ran as follows :—

". . . And I further declare that I will, to the utmost of my power, support Her Majesty Queen Victoria the First, the laws of the country, and the succession to the throne in Her Majesty's illustrious house being Protestant." "Laws and Ordinances of the Grand Orange Society of Great Britain," p. 19. (Published at Bolton in 1848.) By law 1, Catholics were excluded from the Society.

By the "Laws and Ordinances of the Orange Institution of Ireland," published at Belfast in 1872, we learn :

"THE BASIS OF THE INSTITUTION.

"The Institution is composed of Protestants united and resolved to the utmost of their power to support and defend the rightful sovereign, the Protestant religion, the laws of the realm, the Legislative Union, and the succession to the throne in the House of Brunswick, BEING PROTESTANT; and united further for the defence of their own Persons and Properties, and the Maintenance of the Public Peace. It is exclusively an Association of those who are attached to the religion of the Reformation, and will not admit into its Brotherhood persons whom an intolerant spirit leads to persecute, injure, or upbraid any man on account of his religious opinons. They associate also

Morpeth lost no time in bringing forward the Constabulary Bill again. He introduced the measure on February 18. Meeting the main objection of the Orange party—the nomination of constables by the Executive Government instead of by the local authorities—he declared, in effect, that the Irish magistracy could not be trusted to make good appointments. "Within the last three months, not fewer than ninety-six constables and sub-constables had been dismissed from the force for belonging to secret societies."[1]

in honour of King William III., Prince of Orange, whose name they bear as supporters of his glorious memory.

"PARTICULAR QUALIFICATIONS OF CANDIDATES.

"It is also to be ascertained—

"That the Candidate will be faithful, and bear true allegiance to Her Majesty Queen Victoria, and to her Protestant successors; that he will, to the utmost of his power, support and maintain the Laws and Constitution of the United Kingdom, and the succession to the Throne in Her Majesty's illustrious House, BEING PROTESTANT. That he is not and never was a Roman Catholic or Papist, or married to one (unless in cases under the 3rd Law); that he is not, and never was, and will not become, a member of any society, or body of men who are enemies to the lawful sovereign, or the glorious constitution of the realm, as established in 1688, and that he never took, and never will take, any oath of secrecy, or any other oath of obedience, to any treasonable society. . .

"[Law] 3—

"No person, who at any time has been a Roman Catholic, or married to one, shall be admitted into the Institution, except by a unanimous vote of the Grand Lodge, and of the District and County Grand Lodges, founded on testimonials of good character, and a Certificate of his having been duly elected (pursuant to 2nd Law), in the lodge in which he is proposed.

"[Law] 2—

"The admission of Members shall be by Ballot or otherwise, at the option of each lodge; and when by ballot, one black bean in seven to exclude, and no Candidate shall be admitted or balloted for without having been regularly proposed and seconded, at least one month previous to such admission of ballot."

[1] Orangemen got into the force in the North, and Ribbonmen in the South. Though the magistrates had the power of appointing the constables, the Government had the power of dismissing them. This power Drummond used freely, and was clearing the force of Orangemen and Ribbonmen while Parliament was discussing the Constabulary Bill. It would seem that the magistrates in the North exercised their power in a partizan spirit, and made Orange appointments; while the magistrates in the South were lax in the discharge of their duties and failed to keep the force free from objectionable members.

O'Connell supported Morpeth. "Two constables," he said, "had lately been broken. One of them had exclaimed to a crowd of persons in a public-house, 'Now for a bumper,' and having filled his glass he gave as a toast, 'The Pope in the pillory, the pillory in hell, and the devil pelting him with priests.' The other gave as a toast, 'May the ears of all the papists be nailed to the chapel doors, and the chapel transplanted into hell.'" The question was whether the police should be appointed by the Grand Orange Lodge or the Government. He was in favour of the Government.

The Orange members showed a disposition to make a stand against the Bill. But, to their dismay, Peel rose, flung them overboard, and sided with the ministers.

Morpeth wrote to Drummond:—

"*February* 19, 1836.

"I have written to Lord Mulgrave about the House last night, where we had a most prosperous evening. The reception of the Constabulary Bill will secure its passing. Colonel Shaw's name[1] did the business of itself. Peel entirely threw over the Orangemen to their much displeasure."

The Bill passed the Commons on March 23. The second reading was moved in the Lords on April 12. No real opposition was now offered to the measure. Lord Haddington criticised its details in a feeble speech, marking out for special objection "clause 10," which, he said, violated the common law. By the common law the police were bound to serve tithe processes; but by this clause the Lord Lieutenant was given power to overrule the law, and control the customary proceeding. The police were forbidden to afford any aid in the collection of tithes, except where forcible resistance was proved. Lord Haddington thought this an unjustifiable provision.

[1] Colonel Shaw Kennedy was named as Inspector-General.

In Committee on May 2, Lord Roden protested against the increase of stipendiary magistrates contemplated by the Bill. Under former Acts, he said, stipendiary magistrates could only be appointed in the disturbed districts of the South; but now they might be appointed "in the peaceable province of Ulster." Lord Melbourne met all objections by showing that the Bill really gave no powers which the Executive did not already possess.[1] It was a consolidation Bill, nothing more nor less. Lord Hatherton, in a short but effective speech, again told the House that a Bill of this nature had long been in contemplation. Such a measure had been approved of by Lord Anglesey, Lord Stanley, Lord Wellesley, and even Lord Haddington himself.

Before the Bill left the Lords, Morpeth wrote to Drummond:—

"How the Lords do lie about the constabulary, and our men will never tell them so. However, I think, Hatherton's presence is being of use among all sides."

Finally the Bill, with some amendments added by their Lordships, became law before the end of May. When it was safely landed, Morpeth wrote to Drummond:—

"*May* 21, 1836.

"MY DEAR DRUMMOND,—The Constabulary Bill has received the Royal assent, and whatever is in it, if this effect was to incarcerate us both for life, still at that consummation I must rejoice. . . . Now wish me joy. I am off to Eastbourne for six days.—Ever yours,

"MORPETH."[2]

[1] This was proved by the fact that Drummond, without the Bill, had forbidden the police to aid in collecting tithes; which, according to Lord Haddington, he could not do by law except under the Bill.

[2] 6 and 7 Wm. IV., cap. 13. In the same year the Bill for regulating the Dublin Police also passed (6 and 7 Wm. IV., cap. 29). The Acts by which the force had previously been regulated were, 48 Geo. III., cap. 140, and 5 Geo. IV., cap. 102.

48 Geo. III., cap. 140. This Act placed the police under the control of

Fortified by this enactment, Drummond organised a police force which, it is scarcely an exaggeration to say, has been the admiration of the world. But it was his desire to make the police popular as well as capable.

Some members of the Government doubted the wisdom of admitting Catholics to the force. But Drummond said, "if you do not admit Catholics, you will not gain the confidence of the people," and his opinion prevailed.[1] He left the Irish Constabulary an efficient, a remarkable, and a popular body of men. They are still efficient and remarkable, but no longer popular. In Drummond's time they were looked upon as the protectors of the people, the guardians of the public peace. Since his time they have been looked upon as a body of mercenaries paid to keep their country in servitude.[2] Perhaps nothing illustrates the genius of this extraordinary man more than the fact that respect for the law and for the officers of the law, begun and ended with his government. Why? Because he impressed the people powerfully with his strong sense of justice. At the present day stipendiary magistrates are disliked and distrusted. But in Drummond's time the people used to say, "Oh, we can get justice now, we have a

eighteen justices, twelve of whom were appointed by the Lord Lieutenant, and six by the Corporation. All were removable by the Lord Lieutenant. (Secs. 4, 8.)

5 Geo. IV., cap. 102. By this measure the Lord Lieutenant was empowered to divide the police district into four divisions, and to appoint twelve justices, consisting of four barristers, four aldermen, four sheriff-peers. These magistrates, taken from each set, were attached to each of the police divisions. (Sec. 2.)

6 and 7 Vic., cap. 29. One central police office was established under the control of the Chief Secretary or Under Secretary; and two divisional police magistrates were appointed.

[1] He threatened to resign if Catholics were excluded.

[2] I express no opinion. I state a fact. An Irish gentleman well versed in the history of his country once said to me, "How do you account for the fact that when I was a youth [1843] the police were very popular; but they are not so now?"

stipendiary come."[1] Every thing that came from Drummond's hand was accepted with confidence, because he was known to be just. "You do everything well," Lord Morpeth wrote him in April 1836.

This was a true commentary upon his government.

While Parliament was dealing with the Orange Society and the Constabulary Bill, an exciting debate took place in the Commons respecting Drummond's refusal to employ police in the collection of tithes. Towards the end of 1835 the Ascendancy had formed a "Lay Association," practically for the purpose of overawing the Executive. This association hit on the expedient of obtaining writs of rebellion from the Court of Exchequer, by virtue of which it was believed Drummond would be bound to send police to arrest tithe defaulters. But the writs produced no effect on him. He said they did not change the situation in the least. A writ of rebellion was a document addressed to a "Commissioner of rebellion." It was for the "Commissioner" to execute the writ as best he could. It was for the Executive to take care that he sustained no injury in carrying out the law. The duty of the police, he again insisted, was to keep the peace, to arrest public offenders, but not to aid in civil process.

Acting on Drummond's directions, several police officers refused to aid in executing the writs. These officers were

[1] "Select Committee on Orange Lodges in Ireland," Q. 4649 (evidence of Sharman Crawford). Drummond used the stipendiary magistrate freely. It is a fact which ought to be stated, that, before Drummond's time, the stipendiary magistrates were more or less popular; always more popular than the local magistrates. But they were not used by previous administrators so much as by Drummond. The local magistrates were too strong for the previous administrators. "Grossly," wrote Drummond to his mother in July 1836, "have the local magistrates abused their power in many—in very many instances; but their wings are clipped, and I hope and believe that there is some chance of justice being better administered soon, and ultimately of being well administered. The confidence of the people will be regained; though given to the Government now, it is withheld from their local courts, and no wonder."

brought before the Court of Exchequer, and committed or reprimanded. They appealed from the Exchequer to the House of Lords, and while the cases were pending, the Irish members called the attention of the Commons[1] to the whole question. They said the action of the Exchequer was illegal, and O'Connell denounced the judgment of the court as a "political decision." O'Loghlen, in a powerful speech, showed that Drummond was only acting in accordance with the law, as laid down by no less a personage than the Chief Baron of the Exchequer himself (Joy) when Attorney-General. Amid cheers and laughter O'Loghlen read Joy's opinion, in which, using almost the very words employed by Drummond, he said the police were to act "in cases only where a breach of the peace is committed."[2]

Again in 1825, the Chief Secretary of the day, writing under Joy's advice in reply to a demand by the Sheriff of Clare for police aid, said: "I am commanded to acquaint you that constables cannot legally be employed by the sheriff or his deputy in the execution of civil process. In the execution of criminal process, or for the maintenance of the public peace, the sheriff has a legal power of requiring the service of the constable." As this was the exact position taken up by Drummond, the reading of these extracts fairly brought down the House. Morpeth followed O'Loghlen, and amid great laughter, read a letter from Drummond's predecessor Gosset—who was now Sergeant-at-arms—written in March 1835 (under the Viceroyalty of the Tory Lord Haddington), refusing police aid on the grounds that the police could only interfere "to preserve the public peace." This debate strengthened Drummond's hands, and was a victory for the Government. Morpeth described the scene in a lively letter to the Under Secretary.

[1] Hansard, 3rd ser., vol. xxxi., pp. 566, 611.
[2] Joy's words. Opinion written in 1824. *Ibid.*, 591.

MORPETH TO DRUMMOND.

"*Feb.* 1836.

"MY DEAR DRUMMOND,—. . . The Exchequer case was glorious, and the Haddington precedent invaluable: it brought down the House in shrieks, and it was great sport reading Gosset's letter in his presence. It is all vilely reported, especially in the *Chronicle.* I think you had better just warn our Dublin press friends of this. O'Loghlen's speech was excellent.—Ever yours, "MORPETH."

But the appeal cases were not to come before the House of Lords until August; meanwhile Drummond held his ground resolutely.

In February Parson Anderson of Ballinarobe applied for a "small force of police" to protect his "driver," stating that there was a combination against tithes in the neighbourhood, which "was generally quiet." Drummond endorsed the letter: "Request cannot be complied with."

In February and March the famous correspondence with Talbot Glascock took place. Glascock was a "red hot" Orange attorney. He belonged to the firm of Glascock & Cradock, solicitors to the Dean of St Patrick's. He had more than once—though in a somewhat grotesque way—"stood up" to O'Connell, and now resolved to break a lance with the Under Secretary.

GLASCOCK TO DRUMMOND.

"*Feb.* 27, 1836.

"SIR,—The state of the country, and particularly the county of Kilkenny, touching the recovery of tithe rents, renders it absolutely necessary to have the *aid*[1] of the civil and military powers to effect the *service* of the *process of the Court of Exchequer* for the *recovery of the tithe composition rent* due to the Dean of St Patrick's there. In confirmation of the obvious fact, we beg leave to enclose

[1] The italics are Drummond's.

you the joint affidavits of two authorised bailiffs in the parish of Castlecomer. We therefore have to request that directions may be given for that end.—Faithfully yours,

"T. GLASCOCK (Cradock)."

DRUMMOND TO GLASCOCK.

"*March* 2, 1836.

"GENTLEMEN,—As the proceedings have been taken in the superior courts, through which Messrs Glascock & Cradock may either obtain an order to substitute service of process, or may procure the assistance of the sheriff in serving the processes in question, and as the sheriff, the recognised and responsible officer of the law, is invested with full power to call upon the military and police to protect him in the execution of his duty, His Excellency cannot consent to any direct interference on the part of the Government, when the object may be obtained through the ordinary tribunals in a manner provided for by law.—Faithfully yours, "T. DRUMMOND."

GLASCOCK TO DRUMMOND.

"*March* 4, 1836.

"SIR,—We have the honour to acknowledge the receipt of your letter, dated the 2nd instant, but not the affidavit [1] which accompanied ours of the 27th ult., to which your letter received yesterday purported to be a reply.

"If you will please refer to that affidavit, which you still hold, you will see that the deponents who swore it, stated facts of outrage which happened to them when distraining tithe composition rent due to our client, the Dean of St Patrick's, and further swore that it would be useless to make any attempt to effect service of any law process for tithe in the said parish unless the protection of the police be afforded, and that they believe that their lives would be in danger without such protection.

[1] The affidavit of the "authorised bailiffs."

"We beg leave to state that, having considered it prudent, with a view to avoid collision with the peasantry, to abandon our proceedings by distress, we have issued subpœnas, at the suit of the Dean of St Patrick's, from the Law and Equity side of the Court of Exchequer, which are directed to the parties' defendants, and not to the sheriff; and as it would be impracticable to obtain orders from the court to substitute service of such subpœnas until next term, the right of our client will be greatly prejudiced by the delay if we cannot procure services to be effected during the present vacation.

"We also beg leave to submit that we cannot procure the assistance of the sheriff in serving the process in question. Though the 'recognised and responsible officer of the law is invested with full power to call upon the military and police to protect him in the execution of his duty,' yet we respectfully submit that it is no part of his duty to assist in effecting service of law or equity subpœnas which are not directed to himself (as in the present case).

"We, therefore, request that you will be pleased to lay this and our former letter before the Lord Lieutenant, for the reconsideration of His Excellency, or his legal adviser, in the hope that His Excellency may yet consent to a direct interference on the part of the Government to prevent, probably, the loss of life in an attempt to recover, in a manner provided for by law, the rights of the Dean of St Patrick's, which have been so long and so unjustifiably withheld.—Faithfully yours,

"GLASCOCK & CRADOCK."

DRUMMOND TO GLASCOCK.

"*March* 12, 1836.

"GENTLEMEN,—Your further letter of the 4th inst., in reply to mine of the 2nd inst., has been received and laid before the Lord Lieutenant.

"His Excellency has to observe that there is not the slightest reason stated by you which would justify him in departing from the course taken in this and similar cases. His Excellency refers you to the practice of the Court of Exchequer in general, more especially to the proceedings of the court last term, in proof that the court will direct a writ of assistance to the sheriff though the subpœnas are not directed to that officer, and will make an order to substitute service of the process on sufficient grounds being shown. These are facts which His Excellency supposed had come within the knowledge of professional men.

"But you apply for assistance on another ground, viz., that the order to substitute service of process cannot be procured till next term. His Excellency would certainly not consider this a sufficient ground for departing from the rule, which, after mature consideration, has been laid down in cases where Government aid is applied for. But on reference to the affidavits, it appears that the facts sworn to occurred in August last, and if any injurious consequences have resulted to the Dean of St Patrick's by your neglecting to apply to the court last term, you are yourselves to blame, and are certainly not entitled, on the ground of delay which must ensue, to claim the special and direct interference of Government.—Faithfully yours,

"T. DRUMMOND."

Glascock replied in a furious letter, evading all Drummond's points, but abusing the Government in the most scurrilous manner. Drummond endorsed the letter: "to be put with former papers"; and there the matter ended.

Many other applications were made throughout the year, but they were all met in a like spirit. Drummond's invariable answer was in effect: "Police shall be sent if there is danger of a breach of the peace, but not otherwise."

In August the Rev. W. Beresford wrote to Lord Mulgrave :—

"INNISCARA, *August* 10, 1836.

"MY LORD,—Under the conviction that a portion of the police were bound to assist in executing Writs of Rebellion, I made the reasonable request of the police officer at Ballincollig to protect the Commissioners after sunrise, and received for reply that he had instructions not to leave his barrack until after six o'clock in the summer, and daylight in winter. As this order if persevered in must materially injure me in the recovery of my debts, I shall, however reluctantly, be obliged to take proceedings against the officer in question, unless it be so modified as to meet the request I have made for attendance after sunrise.—Your Lordship's obedient servant,

"W. BERESFORD."

Drummond endorsed this letter:—

"His Excellency gave the order on mature consideration, and cannot comply with Mr W. Beresford's request,

"T. D., August 15."

In October the Rev. P. B. Maxwell wrote :—

"SIR,—In consequence of the outrage mentioned by Captain Roberts,[1] in addition to the peremptory refusal of my tenants to pay tithes, I must reluctantly feel myself called upon, in the critical state of the barony of Ennishowen, to apply to the Government for the assistance of the police. I beg to observe that, though a clergyman, I have no church preferment, and that I apply as a landlord obliged to pay tithes for tenants at will.—Truly yours,

"P. B. MAXWELL."

Drummond endorsed the letter :

"Enclose copy of the letter of the 14th October, by which Mr Maxwell will perceive that in conformity with

[1] A band of men went around to tenants warning them not to pay tithe.

the decision of His Excellency in similar applications, his request cannot be complied with,

"T. D."

Drummond's action in dealing with these tithe applications sometimes puzzled Lord Morpeth. He once wrote to the Under Secretary during 1836:—

"MY DEAR DRUMMOND,—I arrived in Babylon this afternoon. Let me have all my tithe cramming as soon as possible. What am I to say when it is objected thus: 'You tell applicants that the sheriff or the court may order out assistance for them, but you tell the police never to budge, without a reference to, and the direction of Government.' You will never quarrel with my letters for being laconic. I hope sincerely Mrs Drummond mends.—Most sincerely,

"MORPETH."[1]

Unfortunately I have not been able to procure Drummond's reply to this letter. But I can from other papers conceive what his answer might have been. He would probably have said: "The sheriff or court may order assistance if the peace is likely to be broken. But it is for the Government to judge whether the peace is in danger or not."

Passing from the subject of tithes, we shall take a glance generally at Drummond's work and life in Dublin during 1836. We can, perhaps, see him best through his letters, and the letters of his colleagues and friends. This chapter will therefore conclude with a selection from such correspondence—official and private.

In January there was a lively interchange of letters between Baring, one of the Lords of the Treasury, Spring Rice, and Drummond respecting the resignation of an

[1] This letter was written in January 1836. It will be observed that the Constabulary Bill had not passed at this time. So it would seem that without that measure the Government controlled the police.

official named Burrowes. I have not been able to collect all the facts of the case, but it would seem that the Treasury was anxious to get Burrowes' resignation before making him an allowance, while he was anxious to know what the allowance might be before resigning.

BARING TO DRUMMOND.

"LONDON, *January* 15, 1836.

"MY DEAR DRUMMOND,—Will you have the kindness to let us have official intimation of Burrowes' resignation, and the particulars—namely, age, length of service, which may enable us to fix his entire allowance?

"We are bothered to death about it, and we cannot get anything we want from your side of the water.—Ever yours,

"J. BARING."

SPRING RICE TO DRUMMOND.

"DOWNING STREET, *January* 15, 1836.

"MY DEAR DRUMMOND,—Mr Burrowes seems determined to put the cart before the horse. How the devil can there be an official notification of his retiring allowance before the Treasury have received his resignation? The Chancellor of the Exchequer has written to Lord Plunket, letting him know that everything has been settled in the most satisfactory way, and that the only thing wanted is Mr B.'s resignation.—Yours always,

"T. SPRING RICE."

DRUMMOND TO BARING.

"DUBLIN CASTLE, *January* 17, 1836.

"MY DEAR BARING,—We are bothered too, and I think your remark is somewhat unfair as to getting nothing from this side of the water. We were told through Lord Plunket, and on the authority of a letter from the Chancellor of the Exchequer, that Burrowes' letter, already sent, was a sufficient announcement of his intention to resign, to enable the Treasury to act; that it would, in fact, be considered a resignation, and that a Departmental minute had been prepared accordingly. We were not told that anything more was required. We were not told what the amount of the retiring allowance was to be, but we were told that everything was arranged in the most satisfactory manner.

"We were not told to send Burrowes's official resignation. We have no such resignation, nor do I believe that we shall be able to get it till we are able to tell Burrowes what his retiring allowance is to be. He will not trust to the assurance that everything is arranged in the most satisfactory manner. The particulars as to age, length of service, &c., asked for two days ago, will be forwarded immediately; but as to the resignation, I do not think we shall get it officially unless we can tell him what the Treasury are prepared to give as retiring allowance.—Always yours,

"T. DRUMMOND."

I have not been able to learn how this matter was finally settled, as the correspondence is incomplete.

In June Drummond received this letter from the poet Moore:—

THOMAS MOORE TO DRUMMOND.

"SLOPERTON, DEVIZES, *June* 1, 1836.

"MY DEAR MR DRUMMOND,—I wish very much that Lord Mulgrave should see the enclosed letter, and shall feel greatly obliged by your sending or giving it to him. I should have sent it direct to him myself, but that I feared to transgress some of those forms which I know 'hedge' a Lord Lieutenant as well as a King; and though he, I am well aware, would readily forgive me such slips, others would not be so tolerant. The poor fellow who pleads so pitifully for himself in this letter is really deserving of what he asks, and I should rejoice to be, however remotely, the means of serving him.

"Lord Brougham, to whom I recommended him, is little aware of one obligation which he owes to me, and that is preventing this person from publishing a long pamphlet which he had written in his (Lord B.'s) *defence*. It was almost all that B. wanted at the time to ruin him.—Ever yours,

"THOMAS MOORE."

In July Drummond wrote to his mother on the subject of Orangeism :—

DRUMMOND TO HIS MOTHER.

July 10, 1836.

"MY DEAR MOTHER,—. . . I am very busy with the arrangements for the 12th of July—the day on which the Orange demons walk. It is very difficult to allay their fiendish spirit; but we are improving. There will be so large a force of military and police, with nearly thirty stipendiary magistrates, stationed at the different points at which processions are apprehended, that no great mischief can be done by them, and we shall be enabled to lay hold of and prosecute a pretty considerable number of them. . —Your affectionate son,

"T. DRUMMOND."

"No great mischief was done." Twelve troops and a half of cavalry and thirty-four companies of infantry, under the direction of thirty-three stipendiary magistrates, kept the peace, and many of the "demons" were arrested and prosecuted.

On August 28, Drummond again wrote to his mother:—

"What is to happen before this time next year in the political world no man can, I think, foresee. I shall regret very much any change that moves me from this. I think another year of such tranquillity in Ireland would produce results which, a few years ago, no one could have hoped to see realised."

On the subject of the "tranquillity" of the country, the following letter to Drummond from an Irish lady, belonging to the landlord class, may be quoted:—

August [1836].

"SIR,—I am very much obliged to you for your prompt attention to my communication.

"The chief constable has brought me the threatening letter addressed to 'Miss Osborne,' and I am now sending it into Clonmel in hopes of being able to discover the writer. I suppose the *Evening Mail* will be too happy to copy an attack made upon me in our provincial Tory paper. If you happen to see it, I hope you will be so good as to assure His Excellency, that the charge made against Miss Osborne's tenantry of being concerned in the murder of Keefe, I consider to be wholly without foundation, as I never heard a word of it before.

"We are going abroad to see Rome and Naples; but we are so far from being driven out of the country by fear, that we have been sleeping for many months in this house while some alterations are making, which leaves the house completely exposed. There is a ladder and scaffolding before a window next to our room; the ladder is never removed at night; and the door of the exposed room is not even locked. Could this be ventured upon in England?

"When I first came to this country, houses were constantly broken open for firearms. This house was broken open. On one occasion armed men kept possession of the lodge for half the night, waiting to murder the gamekeeper. A house was burned down, and a woman in it, on the borders of this domain. Now, no real outrage ever occurs in this neighbourhood. The depredations are singularly few.

"The barn, at a great distance from the house, was entered by a ratcatcher. The sheep stealing was an old story which occurred eight years ago; but nothing like disturbance occurs now. This neighbourhood of Two Mile Bridge, which used to be notoriously bad, is now equal in good conduct to the very best part of England.—I have the honour to be, Sir, your obedient servant,

"CATHERINE OSBORNE."

In August Drummond's eldest child[1]—a daughter—was born. On this occasion Drummond wrote to his mother:—

DRUMMOND TO HIS MOTHER.

"DUBLIN, *September* 4, 1836.

"MY DEAREST MOTHER,—I send you a lock of your little grand-daughter's hair; where it has got the colour I cannot tell, for it is neither like its father's nor its mother's. Poor little thing; it looks so gentle and innocent. Both mother and child go on admirably, and, as to Mrs Sharp, she is always peeping at baby. Dr Johnson said to her, when sitting by its little cot, 'You seem to be watching as if you were afraid somebody would run away with it.' . . .

"Have you any fancy about the child being called after you? I have always considered my own name such an abomination that I should certainly never have a child called after me. My notion is to give them pretty sweetly sounding names. Maria feels in regard to this as I do; and as we both agree with Walter Scott in thinking Mary the prettiest name on the list of female names, we are disposed

[1] Mrs Kay.

to call it Mary Elizabeth; the latter of course after you. Now tell us honestly whether you have any feeling on the subject, any desire that it should have your name alone, or that it should be Elizabeth Mary. I like the sound Mary Elizabeth rather better, so does Maria; but we shall be delighted to do what is agreeable to you if you have any wish on the subject.

"I am glad, very glad, that you give a favourable account of Eliza, and that you look forward to a better winter this year than last. Kindest regards to my aunt, kindest love to my dearest Eliza and to John, and believe me,—Ever, my dearest mother, your truly affectionate son,

"T. DRUMMOND."

I find among Drummond's papers one letter from O'Connell. There was a rumour that Mr Sergeant Greene would be raised to the bench. O'Connell regarded the appointment as objectionable, and wrote to Drummond on the subject.

DANIEL O'CONNELL TO DRUMMOND.

"DARRYNANE ABBEY, *Oct.* 13, 1836.

"MY DEAR SIR,—Nothing but the overwhelming sense of the importance of the subject on which I write could move me to do so. It is said that there is a question of Mr Sergeant Greene being promoted to the vacant place on the bench. I, however, firmly believe, that Lord Mulgrave would resign first, and, for his honour, I hope so.

"I could wish he should know—if you can convey to him respectfully—that the leading object of the Irish Reform members in supporting the present Government is to purify the administration of justice. The Tories have filled the bench with men who distort justice on every occasion—and they are multitudinous when their party can be served by injustice.

Partiality on the bench—judicial as well as magisterial—is the great curse of the country. The country actually pants with impatience to have the place of Baron Smith filled by an honest, intelligent, and impartial man. If the ministry place Mr Greene there, they take away the mainspring of my attachment to them. Why should I suffer the obloquy of a moment in supporting a Government treading in the most vital points in the foul footsteps of our, and their, enemies. I speak of myself, of course, as one of many—and supposing Greene a judge.

"Lord Plunket is, I am quite convinced, the 'calamity' of the Irish Government. His conduct in having all the filth of the magistracy introduced is most melancholy, and—if it be he who suggests Greene—he should himself be separated from this administration.

"This is the very touchstone of the ministerial wishes for Ireland.

"Pardon me, but it drives me almost mad to think of the cruelty to your friends of even hesitating about Greene, who is in heart and conduct Orange, and who, besides, is not of that competence in knowledge to entitle him by any means to the bench.

"I write this, of course, in confidence to you as indeed a duty I owe to the first and only honest Lord Lieutenant I have ever seen.

"I sincerely congratulate *you* upon escaping the calamity of calamities.—I have the honour to be, Sir, your obedient servant,

"DANIEL O'CONNELL."

Drummond endorsed this letter ·

"I have not heard Sergeant Greene mentioned for this or any other appointment."

Drummond sent O'Connell's letter to Lord Mulgrave, who was then in London; Lord Mulgrave replied :—

LORD MULGRAVE TO DRUMMOND.

"*Oct.* 1836.

"MY DEAR DRUMMOND,—

"I hope you will express to O'Connell as strongly as possible that I think he might have known me enough now, from everything I have done since I have been in Ireland, to feel very sure that nothing would have induced me to make a doubtful or fadical appointment upon this vacancy. I am too well aware of the importance of using every opportunity to make my government, to the utmost of my power, particularly beneficial to the Irish people, ever to have contemplated the possibility of making such a mistake.

—Ever yours, "MULGRAVE."[1]

In November Drummond's attention was turned to an incident in the ever-disturbing career of Orangeism. An Orangeman had died, and his brethren, always anxious for occasions of display, marched in solemn procession at the funeral with fife, flag, and drum. The procession passed close to a police barrack, where two constables were on duty. Drummond, who was determined to put down all Orange processions, no matter on what pretence they might have been got up, wrote to the chief constable of the district for the names of the men who had marched on this particular occasion. The chief constable reported:—

"Sub-constables Ker and Keenan, who were in charge of the station at this time, could not recognise any of the party, *although they walked very close to the barrack.*"

Drummond underlined the words in italics with red ink, and wrote:—

[1] The vacant judgeship was given to Mr (afterwards Sir Michael) O'Loghlen. He was the first Irish Catholic judge since the Revolution; and one of the best judges and men that ever sat on the Irish bench.

"As the party walked very close to the barrack, sub-constables Ker and Keenan must be very inefficient persons if they were not able to recognise any of them. His Excellency desires that these sub-constables be forthwith removed to another station.

"T. DRUMMOND."

"*Nov.* 25, 1836."

As an instance of the sharp and decisive way in which Drummond managed the police, I may quote a minute made by him on a report, stating that a faction fight had taken place, that some hundreds of men, "armed with blunderbusses, guns, and pistols," had taken part in it, and that the police were unable to stop the riot until several people were seriously wounded.

"This occurrence is discreditable to the police. The constable will state:—Why he was on the alert several days previously? What force he assembled at the fair? What force he might, without difficulty, have assembled at the fair? How near is the nearest military station to the village? And he will further state whether forty men, armed with blunderbusses, guns, and pistols could have entered the village unknown to the police, if the police had been doing their duty? When did this riot begin? When did the party proceed to the grave? How long did they remain there? Was there time to have sent for a reinforcement of constabulary or military? Was their intention of returning unknown to the police? Were any steps taken with a view to identifying any of them? Have any since been taken? The police appear to have been utterly useless on this occasion. Let the chief constable give £10 for such information as will enable him to bring any one of these rioters to justice (£10 per head); and let him well and fully understand, that he is expected to use more diligence and show more intelligence in bringing these offenders to justice, than he has done to prevent the exhibition, so disgraceful to the police, of a village being in the possession of a band of armed ruffians. Why is the number of persons injured not reported, and the injuries which they received not stated?"

I shall conclude this correspondence with a bright and humorous letter written by Drummond on a subject in which he and his wife felt deeply interested. In 1836 it was proposed to run a line of railway through their property at Fredley, in the charming valley of Mickleham, Surrey. Drummond was strongly opposed to the scheme. With characteristic frankness, he said that his interest was chiefly personal; but on public grounds he urged, that the line might with more advantage be brought another way.

DRUMMOND TO MR VIZARD.

"DUBLIN CASTLE, *March 11th*, 1836.

"MY DEAR SIR,—When you proposed to me to become the purchaser of Mrs Smith's property, I did not expect that your Railway Co. were to be the sellers.

"I do not deny that your power of annoying me has become much greater by your having acquired this ground, if it be in the position which we suppose it to be, but of which your description does not enable us to judge very accurately. My course is therefore clear. I must either redouble my efforts in opposing,—sticking close to you through the Commons, if you should unhappily ever get through, and making common cause with all sufferers, and fighting you by every means in our power in the Lords. I must either do this, or come to terms of neutrality with you.

"I most sincerely wish your destructive Railway and its

[1] Mr Vizard was solicitor to the promoters of the railway.

energetic solicitor at the bottom of the sea, with Mrs Smith's thirty acres on the top of you, to keep both down. I mean I wish you this watery grave in your capacity of solicitor to the Railway, for I have no desire to part with my friend.

"Your railway under any circumstances, even the most favourable, will be to us a serious inconvenience; but if, in the event of success, you choose to build on the land which you have got possession of, undoubtedly you could drive us from the county, and destroy what I had hoped would some day have been one of the prettiest things in that part of the country; therefore, with respect to continued and increased opposition or neutrality, I must be guided by circumstances. I do not love you; but I hate and fear you.

"You will oblige me much by allowing a friend of mine, Mr Dawson, to look at the plan of Mrs Smith's ground, and to take a sketch of it, that I may understand how it lies with respect to Fredley.

"To prevent any misunderstanding, I must state at once that I cannot under any circumstances take any steps to withdraw either the letters or the arguments which I have used against you. The treaty must only be as to my further non-interference.

"This you will of course consider a confidential communication.—Always, my dear Sir, very truly yours,

"T. DRUMMOND."

" I have been applied to, to come over and oppose you."

"W. VIZARD, Esq."

Drummond's objections, and the objections of others, prevailed for the time being, and the bill was thrown out. But a line of rail to Brighton now runs through the valley of Mickleham, and Mrs Drummond's charming residence at Fredley is none the worse.

CHAPTER IX.

1837.

THE question raised by Drummond, that the police were not bound to aid in executing writs of rebellion, still remained open. The subject was to have come before the House of Lords in August 1836,[1] but it was postponed on the motion of Lord Lyndhurst.[2] It remained postponed until May 1838. In the meanwhile Drummond continued to hold his ground firmly. He allowed no departure from the rule that police aid could only be given when the public peace was in danger. He was overwhelmed with abuse, but he never flinched. He was denounced as a partisan, but his resolution stood unchanged.

How little there was of partisan feeling in the calm and thoughtful judgment of Drummond may be gathered from an incident which occurred at this time. A hot-headed Catholic named Balfe posted this placard in the County Meath :—

"The Orangemen—once more the base, bloody, and brutal Orangemen—are endeavouring to usurp the reins of government and to make Ireland weep tears of blood, and unless every man in Ireland lends the present Government his most strenuous support, we will have to curse the hour that gave us birth. Let every man who is not an Orange man attend the meeting on Thursday at Drumcoura to petition the King and House of Commons not to allow

[1] *Ante*, p. 224.

[2] Morpeth to Drummond, Aug. 11, 1836. "Lyndhurst," Morpeth said, "feared an adverse decision."

the bloody miscreants to pollute the constitution by the imposition of their hands."

Balfe was caught in the act of posting the placard by a policeman named Hogg.

Hogg—"You must take down that notice."

Balfe—"Why?"

Hogg—"Because there is no name to it."

Balfe—"I'll put my name to it."

Hogg—"No. I won't let you."

Balfe—"I don't care about you, you brat of an Orangeman."

Hogg—"Yes, I am an Orangeman, I won't deny it."

Drummond had made it an inflexible rule that no Orangeman should be allowed in the police. Hogg, therefore, by his confession laid himself open to instant dismissal. But he had only done his duty in pulling down Mr Balfe's violent rigmarole. In such circumstances how ought he to have been treated? He was reported to the Inspector-General for having declared himself an Orange man, and his dismissal was demanded. The Inspector-General wrote to Drummond:—

"I find great difficulty in coming to any decision in this case; and there seems to me so much of a political feeling in it, that I submit it."

Drummond asked for a copy of the placard. It was sent him. He then replied:—

"Mr Balfe seems a very hot-headed man, and the notices which he posted are of a very reprehensible character. All that seems necessary in this case is to remove the policeman at such a time and in such manner as the Inspector-General may think fit, taking care that such removal will not be looked on as a punishment."

Drummond's action in this matter may be contrasted with the action of an Orange grandee in another. Mr Handcock, J.P., wrote to Drummond in March 1837:—

HANDCOCK TO DRUMMOND.

"LURGAN, *March* 29, 1837.

"MY DEAR SIR,—At the last Armagh Assizes, David M'Murray, Thomas Larken, George Gibson, jun., John Best, William Wilson, John M'Murray, Robert Fitzsimons, Samuel M'Gladdery, James Menzies, and James Gray, were found guilty of a riot at Miggravaly on the 8th of August last, and were sentenced to two months' imprisonment each.

"The prosecutors in this case were Patrick Rowley and his brother. The whole transaction arose out of a party row at a public house—the convicted men being of the Orange party and the prosecutors being Catholics. Since the assizes, the Catholics have been turned out of possession of their houses and lands by Mr John Overend, the agent of the property, upon the grounds that the Catholics attempted to prosecute the Orangemen for this riot. Mr Overend is the District Master of Orangemen, and it is really a pity for the unfortunate prosecutors, who have lived in the present houses and lands for four generations.

"I should be the last person to interfere in the slightest degree with the prerogative of mercy so wisely and properly exercised upon many occasions by His Excellency the Lord Lieutenant. I understand a memorial is about to be presented in this case. I wish His Excellency should be fully acquainted with all the circumstances of the case which occurred in the petty sessions district of Lurgan, and at the very spot where a sham battle was to have been fought on the 13th of July last, and which was only prevented by the attendance of Colonel Osborne and myself, with the police and military there placed at our disposal, and upon which occasion several persons were convicted summarily of a breach of the Procession Act, and sent to Armagh for one month by Colonel Osborne and myself.

"What will become of the Rowleys and their families I really do not know; but persecution such as they have suffered should be met in a decided manner. I hope you will excuse my troubling you on this occasion.—I am, my dear Sir, "WM. JOHN HANDCOCK."

Drummond endorsed this letter:

"If such a memorial should be presented to His Excellency, Mr Handcock may rely upon careful inquiry being made with respect to the facts stated in it.

"T. D."

Between March and June affairs went smoothly in Ireland. Drummond had established a government which was at once strong, just, and rational.

His predecessors had ruled for a faction and by a faction. Drummond ruled for the people and by the people. They had coerced. He conciliated. They feared. He trusted. They relied on bayonets and gibbets; he on a just administration of the law, and the removal of grievances. They failed. He succeeded.

It has been said of O'Connell that he was "the incarnation of a whole people." He said of himself in the House of Commons: "I am not the representative of any particular borough, or of any particular county; I am the representative of a nation." Yet this man, throughout his career, had been the bugbear of English parties and Irish Ascendancy men. He was the friend of Drummond. Even Lord Melbourne had once said: "We cannot govern with O'Connell, and we cannot govern without him." Drummond governed with O'Connell, and the verdict of history has justified the experiment. "I have never," said Lord Plunket, in 1836, "known Ireland in such a state of tranquillity as at this moment."[1]

Indeed, it is scarcely an exaggeration to say that Drummond was the first ruler who really introduced constitutional authority into Ireland; who insisted on governing by the

[1] "Hansard," 3rd series, vol. xxxi. p. 1296.

ordinary law, and who, from the beginning to the end of his administrative life, consulted and considered the representatives of the people.

The three great elements of disturbance in Ireland during Drummond's administration were, as we have seen, Orangeism, Ribbonism, and the Factions.

To suppress Orangeism, Drummond relied on the stipendiary magistrates. The local justices could not be trusted; they were almost all Orangemen. No one could depend on such functionaries to stop Orange processions, or punish those who walked in them; to prevent Orange outrages, or make those who committed them amenable to the law. We have seen how, in July 1836, Drummond sent twelve troops and a half of cavalry and thirty-four companies of infantry, under the directions of thirty-three stipendiary magistrates, to preserve the peace in Ulster. This system—the system of striking at Orangeism whenever and wherever it showed its head—the Under Secretary kept up to the end. The system proved successful, and Orange rowdyism was held in check in Drummond's day. The police, the shrievalty, the magisterial bench, the jury box, were weeded of Orange partizans, and Catholics no longer saw an enemy in every official from the highest to the lowest in the land.

Orangemen grew careful of violating the law, when they were forced to face impartial tribunals. Catholics respected the law when they found that it was honestly administered. In the general result, Orange Ascendancy steadily declined; Catholic loyalty steadily increased.

The Factions, which consisted of local parties among the peasantry, and whose quarrels arose out of domestic feuds, were easily dealt with.[1] Faction fights generally

[1] Major Willcocks was examined on the subject of Factions before a Committee of the House of Commons in 1824.

"Q. You spoke of parties or factions; are the Committee right in supposing that all the peasantry have a particular name, suppose the Delaneys, the

took place at markets or fairs. On these occasions Drummond massed a strong force of police, with orders to interfere on the slightest sign of disturbance; to disperse rioters, and arrest all disorderly persons. Formerly, the Factions had been allowed to fight it out among themselves, and Drummond was warned by Castle officials, that if the police were allowed to interfere, bloodshed would ensue; a most extraordinary, and, indeed, almost incredible representation. But we have the fact on Drummond's word. "I ought to mention," he says before a Committee of the House of Lords:[1] "that it was a practice at one time not uncommon, to draw the police from fairs with a view to prevent collision with the people; and when the order that they should attend was given, I received a representation from Sir John Harvey, the provincial inspector of Leinster, begging that the subject might be well considered before the order was sent out, for he felt that very serious consequences might result from it—the policy having been to withdraw the men out of sight, and leave the people to fight among themselves unrestrained, rather than risk the loss of life by collision with the constabulary."

What a light does this simple statement throw upon the administration of Ireland. There was no hesitation in allowing the police to shoot down peasants who refused to pay tithes; but drunken brawlers at markets and fairs were not to be interfered with! Sir George Cornewall Lewis sup-

O'Briens. the O'Ryans, or whatever particular name it may, belong to one faction in a particular district of country, and that two or three other particular names may belong to another district of country?

"A. Yes; if one of the Delaneys was beaten at a fair, he would recruit all his own friends to avenge it at the next fair.

"Q. Will you state a little of the original cause of war on these occasions? What may have excited, for instance, the Delaneys, the O'Briens, and the O'Ryans to take up arms against each other in the way you have described?

"A. It arises very often out of some family dispute or quarrel, as I have stated before, from intoxication."—Lewis, "Irish Disturbances," p. 282.

[1] *Post.*

plies the explanation. "At one time the local authorities encouraged faction fighting; it seemed to them that the people must necessarily raise their hands against some one; and they thought that factions would serve the same purpose as the stone thrown by Cadmus among the earth-born warriors of Thebes—that of turning the violence of the combatants from themselves upon one another."[1]

[1] "Irish Disturbances," p. 289.

"The following statement furnishes the details respecting the factions in the northern part of Tipperary at the end of 1834.

"Factions frequenting fairs and markets to fight, in the following baronies of the county of Tipperary.

"Barony of Owney and Arra [Iffa and Offa ?]—Ruskavallas and Caffees, Dingens and Dawsons.

"Upper Ormond, in the vicinity of Nenagh—Bootashees, Bog Boys, and the Tubbers.

"Toomavara, five miles from Nenagh—Cumminses and Darrigs.

"Lower Ormond, from Burrisakane to the Shannon and Brusna River. —There are no particular designations for rioters in this district. The parishioners of Kilbarron are most celebrated for their turbulent disposition.

"EXPLANATION.

"Ruskavalla is a district near Newport; people named *Murnanes* reside there, and have a long-standing quarrel without any rational foundation with the Caffees. The Dingens have taken their name from a hill near their different dwellings; they consisted of 'Kennedys,' 'Ryans,' and 'Gleesans,' of Kilmore, Ballinaclough, and Beneathen. The cause of the quarrel between those parties cannot be at present ascertained. The Dawsons are composed of 'Breens and Seymours,' all of Duharrow, assisted by the mob of Nenagh, and have taken that name in opposition to the party calling themselves Dingen. The cause of the quarrel between these parties is: a woman named Seymour died; she was married to a man named Gleesan; the Seymours wanted to have her buried in their native churchyard, this the Gleesans opposed, then a serious battle ensued in which two men were killed and others severely wounded at different periods up to the present. The Bootashees are the O'Briens. A leader of their party appeared in boots, and all his followers had pieces of leather or other material wrapped around their legs, tied with thongs, from which they obtained the name of Bootashees. The Bootashees mostly reside in Ballywilliam and Carrigatsher; the Tubbers and Bogboys opposed to them are 'Kennedys and Hogans;' they reside in the parishes of Kilmore, Youghal, and Ballywilliam. The original cause of the quarrel was, that two small boys, one named Hogan and the other O'Brien, had been playing marbles; the boys quarrelled and one knocked down the other, when men, relatives of both, interfered and struck each other. This happened about thirty years ago, and from that period to the present, the factions have continued fighting at fairs and markets, and other public meetings.

"The Bogboys were those living in and near the lands of Cappaghrue and bogs of Tulla, about four miles from Nenagh.

But Drummond did not confine his efforts to the employment of force; he was not satisfied in dealing only with symptoms. He conciliated; he struck at causes. The causes of faction fights were, in a great measure, fairs and markets at which fighting was the principal business. He broke up many of those markets and fairs, and appealed to the good feeling of the peasantry.

An Irish Secretary reasoning with an Irish peasant was a strange sight. But Drummond's whole administration was a strange sight. His sister tells us :—

"On the Sunday afternoons and evenings crowds used to assemble in the Phœnix Park. Drinking booths were opened, and few Sundays passed without riot and mischief ensuing. My brother talked over the matter with some friends, who told him he must not dream of interfering, because it was a very old custom, and it would not do to attempt to put it down. He resolved, however, that he would make the attempt; so one Sunday afternoon, the people having assembled as usual, he rode out unattended among the crowd. To the keeper of the nearest booth he represented the consequences of the meetings—drunkenness, brawls, fighting, and then punishment; he said these things were to him very painful, and that it would give him great satisfaction could the meetings be altogether given up. The man immediately, without a word of remonstrance, complaint, or even a show of sullenness, set about packing up. He quickly left the grounds, and never returned again. The same result occurred at other booths, and in a short time the park was cleared, and the 'old custom' given up for ever."

"The Cumminses are a numerous body of men residing in the mountains, between Toomavara and Borrisaleigh. The Darrigs are Kellys and Kilmartins, who mostly reside in the line of road between Kilcommon and Borrisaleigh; they took that name from a man named Kelly, a leader, who had red hair and a florid complexion; Darig signifies red."—Lewis, "Irish Disturbances," pp. 288, 289.

Thus in putting down the Factions, as in dealing with all Irish disorders, Drummond adhered to the principles on which his government was based: faith in the people; strength in the Executive. "There is no doubt," said a police inspector, who at first disbelieved in the possibility of preventing faction fights, "there is no doubt, if the business be well followed up for a sufficient time, those disgraceful riots will presently be put a stop to." The business was "followed up;" the "disgraceful riots were put a stop to;" and the Under Secretary lost none of his popularity for abolishing the "old custom."

But Drummond's greatest trouble was the Ribbon Society. Orangeism and the Factions could be put down by administrative skill; but the suppression of Ribbonism required legislative enactments. Ribbon outrages were the result of landlord oppression. Rackrenting and evictions drove the peasantry into crime. The remedy lay in curbing the landlords' power; but the Legislature was not prepared to do this in Drummond's time, nor for more than a quarter of a century afterwards. Nevertheless Drummond struck vigorously at the Ribbon Society. He brought more Ribbon offenders to justice without coercion than his predecessors had done with it. Why? Because by showing the peasantry that the Government sympathised with their grievances, he drew them to the side of law. Witnesses were forthcoming to prosecute; juries ready to convict. He made the law popular, and sympathy with lawlessness decreased. In Tipperary, the centre of agrarian disturbances, a society of peasants was formed to put down Ribbonism. Its members pledged themselves "to discourage bad characters; to refuse to employ or keep such persons in their houses; to report to some one of the committee the appearance of any bad character, or any person accused, or suspected of crime in their neighbourhood; to communicate to a magistrate, or to any one of the committee, any facts likely to lead to the prevention of outrage; and to use every exertion to prevent fighting between factions at fairs." The reasons for its formation were publicly given. "They (the members) have associated thus at this time (1836), because they are convinced that a spirit and temper have fast grown up among the people, inclining them to aid the efforts of a vigorous and enlightened Government in extending to all parts of this island the protection of equal law; and in order to answer the reasonable expectation of such a Government that the exertion thus made for the people's benefit shall be seconded by the people's co-operation."[1]

This society died with Drummond; no similar society has ever been established since. The fact is a significant commentary upon his government, and upon the government of those who came after him. His successors tried to force the people to the side of law; he to win them. His name alone is associated with the successful administration of Ireland.

In June 1837 William IV. died, and a general election ensued. The Government of Lord Melbourne came back triumphantly from the polls, and Drummond continued at his post in Dublin.

On June 23rd he wrote to his mother:—

DRUMMOND TO HIS MOTHER.

"MY DEAREST MOTHER,—Every day brings its own work, and often something more to that. I have not been able to write my scrap till this morning. The death of the king being expected for the last two or three days has not caused much sensation; but there are certain acts and ceremonies to be performed in consequence, and the

[1] *Edinburgh Review*, vol. lxvi. p. 242.

arrangements for them occupied much of my time yesterday. We are all well; my eyes are better; I save them as much as possible; Maria quite well. Mrs Sharp and the little pet better—indeed, quite well; she is sitting at my feet while I write, pulling a basket to pieces, turning it, and examining it, and talking to it, and wondering at it. She is a delightful little plaything.

"What alterations may occur in the Government in consequence of the death of the King I cannot foresee. But I do foresee much embarrassment from new claims and fresh arrivals. There must be some persons admitted to office who have hitherto been excluded; perhaps O'Connell; Sheil certainly should be; and Dr Droiken is fit for nothing but to embroil—considerable ability, but totally destitute of temper, and disliked, without exception, by every man who has been his colleague. . . —Your affectionate son,

"T. DRUMMOND."

O'Connell, as we know, did not enter the Government, but Sheil accepted office as Commissioner of Greenwich Hospital. Later on he became Vice-President of the Board of Trade.

About this time a remarkable man visited Ireland—Gustave de Beaumont. It is allowed by competent critics that one of the best books ever written on Irish subjects is De Beaumont's 'L'Irlande.'[1] And it will be interesting to the students of Irish history to learn that De Beaumont, during his stay in Ireland, was in close communication with Drummond, and that his admirable work was in no small degree inspired by the Under Secretary.[2] De Beaumont brought letters of introduction to Drummond from Mr Drinkwater Bethune and Lord Morpeth.

[1] "L'Irlande Sociale, Politique, Religieuse." The work was translated by Dr Cooke Taylor of Dublin University, *post*.

[2] *post*.

DRINKWATER BETHUNE TO DRUMMOND.

"HOME OFFICE CHAMBERS,
"*June* 19, 1837.

"DEAR DRUMMOND,—I wish to make known to you my friend Mons. de Beaumont, who will introduce himself to you with this letter. He is probably well known to you already by name as the fellow-traveller of De Tocqueville in America, and the author of "Marié, ou L'esclavage." He has recently married a grand-daughter of Lafayette, and is now on the point of passing over to Ireland with Madame de Beaumont for the purpose of informing himself on the condition of the country and its inhabitants, on which subject he has been occupying himself for some years. He was in Ireland two or three years back, and is acquainted with Lord Mulgrave; but he says that he does not know you, and I know that I am doing you both a kindness in making you acquainted. I ask you to receive him, in the first instance, for my sake; I am sure you will cultivate his acquaintance for his own. . . .—Yours very truly,

"J. E. DRINKWATER BETHUNE."

LORD MORPETH TO DRUMMOND.

"*June* 23, 1837.

"MY DEAR DRUMMOND,—This is brought by Mons. de Beaumont, who accompanied Tocqueville to America, and wrote an admired book, 'Sur L'esclavage aux États-Unis.' He is now engaged in a work upon Ireland; he seems an intelligent and truth-loving man, and though I have told him you are very busy, any little attention or assistance you could render him would be well bestowed.—Ever yours,

"MORPETH."

We have a letter from Mrs Sharp to Drummond's mother, saying how the De Beaumonts fared in Dublin.

"*June* 1837.

"MY DEAR MADAM,—I will begin by answering your inquiry about Mons. and Madame de Beaumont, the foreigners, for whom the O'Connell party was made. Madame de Beaumont is a grand-daughter of the late Marquis Lafayette, and her husband is a private gentleman, I believe, in no profession, but very fond of literature, and himself an author. He is now writing a statistical account of Ireland.

"Mons. de Beaumont is a lively talking man, a thorough Frenchman; his wife, to whom he has been only married a year, a pleasing, sensible, lady-like young woman, who has evidently lived in good society. They brought a letter of introduction to Mr Drummond from a friend in England, and as His Excellency was absent from Dublin on their arrival, Mr D. was the first person who showed them any attention, and being quite strangers here, they appeared grateful for it. Finding that they had a vehement desire to be in company with O'Connell, whom Mons. de Beaumont had heard deliver the speech when he pulled off his wig, Mr Drummond good-naturedly made a dinner for the express purpose of their meeting; and as Dublin was very empty at that time, poor Maria had some difficulty in getting a party together who could speak the French language fluently, as Madame de Beaumont does not speak English. Well pleased at having succeeded, you may imagine her great disappointment on hearing, on the very morning of the day, that Lord Mulgrave had sent them an invitation, which invitation, according to etiquette, is a command.

"The De Beaumonts returned from the Viceroy's party

about half-past nine, and seemed like birds let out of a cage; the dulness of the Viceregal Lodge dinner giving an increased zest to the party they met here. O'Connell talked a great deal with the foreigners. He speaks French beautifully. In case the *Register* should not name the party, I will tell you who they were as far as I can recollect: the Baron and Baroness de Robeck, Mr and Mrs Tighe Hamilton (a niece of Lord Duncannon), the Hon. Mr and Mrs Vaughan, Dr Stock, Mr Curran, Mr Kennedy, O'Connell, and Mr Hutton, his colleague.

—Yours affectionately,

"A. M. SHARP."

We have another letter about the same date from Mrs Sharp, giving a picture of Drummond's home life. It was also written to Drummond's mother.

[*June* 1837.]

"MY DEAR MADAM,—I yesterday at breakfast inquired of dear Mr Drummond if it was his intention to write to you; and knowing how he was torn to pieces with business, I was surprised at his saying 'yes.' On his return from Dublin at half-past seven o'clock, he told me that he had found it impossible, and begged I would tell you to-day how very much he regretted it. We shall rejoice when the elections are all over, for until then there will, I fear, be no cessation of his labours. For the last fortnight we have never sat down to dinner until eight o'clock, and last night at eleven o'clock, as we were taking ourselves off to bed, poor Mr Drummond, quite tired out with the fatigues of the day, was summoned to the Viceregal Lodge, and did not return home until a quarter before one o'clock this morning. I am happy to say that he stands all his fatigue better than might be expected, and that his eyes are not worse. When I see the delight he takes in playing with his dear little girl, and receiving her little caresses, it quite grieves me to think how little he sees of her. She is exceedingly fond of him, and her animated countenance always lights up at the sight of him. When she is in her mamma's chamber, and I ask her which is papa's door, she always points to the door that leads to his study, and her little legs begin kicking as soon as she finds me approaching the door to take her in to him. She seems to consider my tapping, and waiting for him to say 'Come in,' as a very good joke. . . .—Your attached friend,

"A. M. SHARP."

A few days afterwards Mrs Drummond wrote to her mother-in-law.

[*June* 1837.]

"My husband's eyes are better. . I am exceedingly anxious he should have the best advice, as no one can tell what it may come to. At present there seems little to apprehend. After a day's hard writing they are always much worse. It does not seem as if it were the mental work that hurts, for often when some very puzzling and hard case has engrossed him to the exclusion of all other thoughts, when his brow has been knit, and eyes fixed, as it were, with intense thought, his eyes have not suffered. When, after a hard day's mere routine business, when he has had to scramble off a parcel of stupid, uninteresting letters, his eyes have been so much injured, that I have been quite uneasy. I do not suffer him to read or write a single line by candle light. If there is any business which must be got through, I sometimes read the necessary documents to him, particularly the railway investigations;[1] but even when he begs and prays to be allowed to write a little at night, I am peremptory, and exert the authority of a nurse.

[1] *post.*

The merely bodily fag of this situation is tremendous, and, unfortunately, he cannot be more assisted than he is. So much is purely and strictly confidential, that the answers must be in his own handwriting, or the writers would think themselves betrayed, so that even I cannot assist him there "

In July there was keen distress among the peasants of Donegal, and Drummond sought to obtain help from the Treasury for the sufferers. "How patient they are under their sufferings," he had written to his mother; "but poverty depresses before famine destroys." A correspondence on the subject passed between him and Spring Rice, the Chancellor of the Exchequer:—

SPRING RICE TO DRUMMOND.

"TRIN. COLL., CAMBRIDGE, *July* 24, 1837.[1]

"MY DEAR DRUMMOND,—The letter which you enclose to me is no doubt a deplorable one, but, at the same time, it is in itself so general, and contains so very slender a recital of facts, that I am perfectly sure that there has been scarcely any one season or district in Ireland relating to which similar statements might not have been made.

"To tell you the truth, I have not had much confidence in Mr Dombrain's representations, and this letter seems to be written after his most approved fashion. Consider the application of your own principle. The landlords, you think, oppress the people, and export the produce. Your remedy is to import food for the people, and this affords additional facilities for the game which you attribute to the landlords.

"Had we followed the suggestions of Colonel Shaw Kennedy, we should have had half the districts of Ireland

[1] This letter was written in reply to one from Drummond, which has not been preserved.

in a state of misery and dependence; and £100,000 of public money would have been unprofitably expended. If, however, with the more perfect local information which you have means of acquiring, but subject to the caution which my experience compels me to give, you judge additional sum of £500 to be required, it shall be provided. An official letter shall be written to you on my return to London. Remember we are now approaching the month of August, and with the prospect, as I believe, of a favourable season. This sum should be expended like the former, in sales at a reduced price, restricting all gratuitous assistance to the sick, the old, and the infirm.—Yours in great haste,

"T. SPRING RICE."

DRUMMOND TO SPRING RICE.

"DUBLIN, *August* 1, 1837.

"MY DEAR MR RICE,—We rejoice at your victory.[1] We are just beginning our battle, and it will be well fought everywhere. In the way of preparation, everything has been done that can be done.

"As to Donegal—I hope that the extra £500 will enable us, with this fine season, to struggle through the distress. I have as little confidence in Dombrain as you have; but it is impossible to resist the evidence of Major Jones, Dr Stephens, &c., &c., sent expressly to report on the condition of the poor, and warned to be on their guard against exaggerated statements. As you have furnished us with the means of meeting the present evil, and as I earnestly hope some general measure of relief will have passed before the next season of distress, I shall say no more on this subject, the more so as I am pressed to death with election correspondence.

[1] At the General Election.

"I must, however, protest against what you impute to me as my remedy. I stated a fact—that the landlords are exporting food, while the Government is importing it for the relief of the tenants of those very landlords; and I did so in answer to your having expressed some surprise at such a report having reached you last year. But it was to counteract such a monstrous state of things that I urged over and over again that there should be a power to enforce a compulsory assessment on the proprietors of those districts in which extreme distress prevailed—such assessment to be expended in the employment of the distressed poor on public works. You objected to this; and substituted certain clauses in the Public Works Bill. These are useful, and valuable; but the benefit of them will be felt more in improving districts suffering from temporary and unusual distress, than in such districts as the western coast of Donegal presents.

"As regards these and others under similar circumstances, namely, extensive tracts with a population miserably poor, and with almost no resident proprietors, I foretold Lord Morpeth that the Bill would be inoperative—that the proprietors would not take the initiative—that they would as heretofore suffer the people to perish without extending the smallest particle of relief—that they would witness unmoved a degree of suffering and privation which the Government of a civilised country would not be justified in refusing to relieve—and hence that we would again be compelled to import food for the sustenance of those whose labour, in the shape of provisions, is exported without deduction by rapacious and unfeeling landlords.

"It was of this that I earnestly, but ineffectually, complained. I urged that when it was proved that a district was in a state of extreme distress, that there should be a compulsory assessment put in force; but I ventured to foretell, that if the proprietors were to be the judges of that state, nothing could be done; and that, as heretofore—for it now becomes an annual tax of the worst kind, and expended on the worst principle—the Government would be compelled to pay the poor-rates of the west coast of Donegal.

"I am really sorry to trouble you with this; but I am anxious to exonerate myself from advocating a principle or a remedy against which I have uniformly protested, and which we are only compelled most reluctantly to resort to, because the Government will not heed our appeal, or give us the means of putting an end to a state of things which is a disgrace to a civilised community.—Always, my dear Mr Rice, very truly yours,

"T. DRUMMOND."

While Drummond was thus engaged in fighting the battle of the starving peasantry of Donegal, he came suddenly into conflict with the Orange faction. Colonel Verner, Deputy-Lieutenant of the county of Tyrone, and an Orange Deputy Grand Master, gave as a toast at an election dinner, "The Battle of the Diamond."[1] On August 22, Drummond wrote him.

DRUMMOND TO COL. VERNER.

DUBLIN CASTLE, *August* 22, 1837.

"SIR,—It appearing in *The Newry Telegraph* of the 10th instant, that, at an election dinner given by you on the 7th, one of the toasts was, 'The Battle of the Diamond,' I am desired by His Excellency, now that the elections are all terminated, to desire that you will inform him whether it can be possible that you were thus a party to the commemoration of a lawless and most disgraceful conflict, in which much of the blood of your fellow-subjects was spilt, and the immediate consequences of which was, as testified at the time by all the leading men and magistrates of your

[1] *Ante*, p. 96.

county, to place that part of the country at the mercy of an ungovernable mob.—I have the honour to be, your most obedient servant,

"T. DRUMMOND."

COL. VERNER TO DRUMMOND.

"CARLTON CLUB, *Aug.* 29, 1837.

"SIR,—I have received a letter, dated August 22, bearing your signature, and inquiring of me, by the direction of His Excellency, 'whether it can be possible that I was a party to the commemoration of a lawless and most disgraceful conflict, in which much of the blood of my fellow-subjects was spilt, and the immediate consequence of which was, as testified at the time by all the leading men and magistrates of the county, to place that part of the country at the mercy of an ungovernable mob?'

"I am disposed to think that when you put a question in a form like this, you can hardly expect, on cool reflection, that I should condescend to answer it—at least, I would imagine you could expect no other answer than one which I hold superfluous—namely, that I am not capable of being a party to the commemoration of anything 'lawless or disgraceful!' I would request, if I am ever again to be favoured by a question which you are directed to propose, that it may be expressed in terms better calculated to invite an answer, and more likely, also, to be understood. I must say your letter does not appear to me very intelligible.

"His Excellency seems to assume that the appearance of a statement in a public newspaper authorises a call upon me to contradict or confirm it. I had the honour to entertain several of my friends at dinner on the day to which your letter refers. I am bold to affirm that at that entertainment nothing took place which loyal and honourable men would hesitate to own most frankly. But I speak, I am confident, the sentiments of my friends, and of every gentleman whose freedom is not restrained by official station, when I say that a question like this in your letter ought not to be proposed to me, and that I am bound to decline replying to it. . . .

"Upon the various misrepresentations, unintentional, I have no doubt, which your letter contains, I have no desire to comment. I feel it necessary only to assure you that, of all the conflicts which took place at any of the various places called by the name of 'Diamond,' in the county of Armagh, there is none to which your description is, in the least degree, applicable."

LORD MORPETH TO COL. VERNER.

DUBLIN CASTLE, *September* 5, 1837.

"SIR,—I have had the honour of submitting to the Lord Lieutenant your letter of the 29th ultimo.

"His Excellency regrets that you should have had any difficulty in understanding the letter addressed to you on the 22nd August. But for such an assurance, His Excellency would not have supposed that the unsatisfactory nature of your answer could, in any degree, have been ascribed to that cause.

"As a magistrate, appointed to administer justice between Her Majesty's Protestant and Roman Catholic subjects, His Excellency desired that you should be called upon to state whether, at an election dinner, of which an account appeared at length in a public paper, you had proposed, or been a party to the proposal of, a toast commemorative of a sanguinary feud between the Protestants and Roman Catholics of Armagh. By whom, or to whom, that dinner was given—on what occasion, or in what place, His Excellency considers a matter of comparative indifference; but, as head of the Executive Government in Ireland, it concerns him to know whether you and other gentlemen in the commission held up such an event as that known by the name of 'The Battle of the Diamond,' as one deserving of being commemorated.

"You profess yourself unable to recognise the conflict alluded to under the above title, by reason of the many such conflicts which have unhappily occurred in the county of Armagh, at places called by the name of the Diamond. If His Excellency could have anticipated that you would have experienced, from this cause, any difficulty in replying to the question addressed to you, he would have referred you to your own evidence, published in the Report of the Committee on Orange Lodges in Ireland, and more especially to the following question and answer, No. 92:—

"*Question.* 'The Battle of Diamond Hill took place the 21st of September 1795—did it not?' *Answer.* 'It did.'

"His Excellency need scarcely observe, that the number of such conflicts does not render the commemoration of one or more of them less objectionable, or make it less imperative on him to ascertain the fact of magistrates having joined in such a proceeding.

"On account of the long-continued and bitter animosities springing from religious differences, which have disturbed the good order of society, and led to the most lamentable consequences, especially in the county of Armagh, the Legislature has declared certain acts to be penal in Ireland, which, in other parts of the empire, are not only not punishable, but not blameable, because perfectly harmless. If an assemblage of persons, even less in number than those who were present at the election dinner in question, should walk in procession through the streets, bearing party emblems or playing party tunes, they should thereby subject themselves to the punishment of the law; and it may be known to you, that many have suffered imprisonment, and many are at this moment amenable to the law for no greater offence.

"The peasant thus offending is, in His Excellency's opinion, less culpable than the man of station and education who, on an occasion to which publicity is given through the public press, celebrates a lawless action arising out of the civil discords of his country, in which the lives of many of his countrymen were lost, as an event the remembrance of which it is desirable to perpetuate with honour.

"The former offends against a positive enactment; the latter, keeping within the letter, violates the spirit of the law, counteracts the object and intention of the Legislature, and thwarts the exertions of the Government to carry them into effect.

"If you and other gentlemen had not seemed to question the proposition, His Excellency would have considered it too obvious and incontrovertible to require to be stated, that, if any meeting of persons is held—no matter under what circumstances of apparent privacy,—and if such persons take such steps to permit, or do not take steps to prevent, publicity being given to their opinions and proceedings, they are as fully and justly answerable for whatever effect these may have, or may be calculated to have, on the well-being of society, as if such meeting had been held with open doors, or in the open air.

"But that is a question which does not arise in the present case. The meeting to which His Excellency drew your attention was in every respect public, and not private. It was attended by every circumstance which distinguishes a public from a private meeting. It was a dinner given at a public hotel, on the occasion of a public election, to celebrate a public event; public toasts were given and political speeches made, as usual at public dinners; the entire proceedings were reported in detail, in a public newspaper, as public intelligence. The newspaper which first reported the proceedings was one not likely to misrepresent what had happened to your prejudice.

"Conceiving the occurrence reported to be such that a

participation in it would disqualify you and others invested with the powers of a magistrate from beneficially exercising your authority, and would naturally and deservedly cause your fellow-subjects of the Roman Catholic creed to withdraw their confidence in your administration of justice, His Excellency, in the exercise of his bounden duty, called on you and them to state whether the report was correct.

"It is the invariable practice, when any representation is made to Government affecting the character and usefulness of a magistrate or other public officer, for whose appointment or continuance the Executive Government is responsible, to communicate such representation to him before any proceedings are taken thereon, that he may have an opportunity of explaining or disavowing the statements made to his prejudice. That course was followed in the present instance, and His Excellency conceives that he had a right to expect a distinct and unequivocal avowal or disavowal of your having been a party to the proceedings in question, or a satisfactory explanation that the nature and tendency of the proceeding did not deserve the character imputed to it.

"His Excellency deems the public considerations dependent upon this transaction to be of such importance, that he is less inclined to remark upon the extraordinary tone in which your whole letter is written, considering that it is an answer to an official communication, addressed by direction of Her Majesty's Representative, to a gentleman holding a commission of the peace, and requiring an explanation of his conduct.

"Upon a full consideration of the case, His Excellency will deem it expedient to recommend to the Lord Chancellor that you should not be included in the new commission of the peace about to be issued, and will also direct your name to be omitted from the revised list of Deputy Lieutenants for the county of Tyrone.—I have, etc.,

(Signed) "MORPETH."

The subject was subsequently brought before the House of Commons, and an animated debate took place on the "Battle of the Diamond."[1] Drummond was denounced by the Ascendency and their allies as a partial and partisan ruler. He had, said Colquhoun, a Scotch member, censured Colonel Verner for proposing the toast, "The Battle of the Diamond;" but what notice had he taken of the bloodthirsty speech delivered by O'Connell at Carlow? 'Men of Carlow,' said the agitator, 'are you ready? I am the last man to recommend the shedding of one drop of blood, but we have tried every means of obtaining our just rights, and they have failed; we have no means left but what I have hitherto deprecated—the shedding of blood, and blood must be shed.' What had Mr Under-Secretary Drummond said of this speech? Had he written to O'Connell? Had he made any inquiries in the matter? Had he not let the agitator go scot free while condemning the Tory gentleman?

These remarks brought O'Connell to his feet. He said · "The hon. member says Mr Drummond did not write to me respecting that [the Carlow] speech. Now I tell him that the first intimation I ever had of that speech having been made for me was by a letter which I received from Mr Drummond. I was in Dublin when I received that letter. I got it at my house, and the moment I read it I asked for liberty to see Mr Drummond. I did see him, and I then said to him: 'Good heavens! who told you that I ever made such a speech?' 'Oh,' he replied, 'it was stated in the *Evening Mail* of last night.' I said to him I was then going to a public meeting, and I would, if he wished it, contradict that speech. Now, I never said a word in contradiction of that speech, but others did. The High Sheriff of the County, who was present at the dinner where the speech was said to be delivered, contradicted it.

[1] Hansard, 3rd series, vol. xxxix. pp. 634, 687.

The late Roman Catholic bishop, Dr Nolan, who is since dead, contradicted it. Mr Houghton, and one or two other magistrates who were present, contradicted it. Their statement was published in the newspapers, and by their signatures they attested the utter falsehood that I ever made such a speech. There happened, too, to be the reporters of the Dublin morning papers present. There was, too, a reporter from the *Morning Advertiser* at the dinner, and the moment he saw such a statement attributed to me, that gentleman came forward and stated distinctly, upon referring to his report, that there never was a grosser falsehood than the imputation of such words to me. I really never should have contradicted the speech, nor paid any attention to its contradiction, if my attention had not been called to it by Mr Drummond."

O'Connell's speech drew the attack from Drummond to himself. Litton, an Ulster member, denounced him as the instigator of tithe outrages. In 1836 O'Connell had said: "I have not advised the people against the payment of tithes, but I would rather permit the bed to be dragged from under me and my body thrown into jail than pay one farthing of tithe." "Such, sir," said Litton, "was the language used by the learned member for Dublin. Thus did he talk to the country of the 'blood-stained tithes'; 'blood-stained,' I say, by himself."

Mr O'Connell—"I submit, Mr Speaker, that the hon. member is out of order in imputing to me a share in tithe conflicts."

The Speaker—"I think the hon. and learned member [Mr Litton] is out of order."

Mr Litton—"Oh, there is no gentleman in this House who will, I am sure, imagine that I meant to say the learned gentleman was ever present at a tithe conflict; he takes too good care of himself for that."

Mr O'Connell—"The hon. member knows he is safe in

insulting me; but I submit, Mr Speaker, that he is out of order in accusing me of having instigated tithe conflicts."

Mr Litton—"And I repeat the charge. Can any man assert that the learned member has not instigated tithe resistance?"

The Speaker again interposed, and Litton "bowed with cheerfulness and respect to the opinion of the Chair," adding, nevertheless, that "the country had been deluged with blood" in consequence of the speeches of O'Connell.

Morpeth ably defended the action of the Irish Administration, quoting, with much effect, this extract from Col. Blacker's evidence before the Committee on Orange Lodges, referring to the "battle" of the Diamond:—

"What did you see at the Diamond?

"When I got up I saw the Defenders making off in one direction, and the firing had nearly ceased; I may say had ceased, excepting a dropping shot or two, and I saw a number of dead bodies.

"Can you state about the number?

"No; they were conveying them away on cars in different directions, so that I could not make an exact calculation.

"Were there fifty?

"No; if there were thirty killed, that was the outside.

"Were there any Protestants killed?

"Not that I could hear of."

To commemorate such a conflict, the Chief Secretary urged, was an indefensible and disgraceful proceeding.

The debate ended in a complete victory for Drummond. No man attempted to defend Verner; no man could show that Drummond was wrong in the particular transaction in question. Even Colonel Perceval said, "he was sorry that the 'Battle of the Diamond' should be added to the list of party toasts current in Ireland." The Ascendancy were in fact driven to the favourite expedient of denouncing O'Connell, and railing generally against the Government.

The discussion bore testimony to the strength of Drummond · to the discomfiture and feebleness of the Orange faction.

In November Parliament met after the General Election; and this paragraph, in the speech from the throne, was seized by the Ascendancy as a point of attack on ministers :—"The external peace and domestic tranquillity which at present happily prevail, are very favourable for the consideration of such measures of reformation and amendment as may be necessary or expedient, and your attention will naturally be directed to that course of legislation which was interrupted by the necessary dissolution of the last Parliament."[1]

Lord Roden led the way. He denied that there was "tranquillity" in Ireland. The Government had basely surrendered the country into the hands of O'Connell, and disorder and tumult were the result. The Protestant religion was in danger, the constitution was undermined, the throne was imperilled. He appealed to the Prime Minister to save the State, and preserve the faith of their fathers.

Lord Mulgrave replied in an able speech.

"My Lords," he said, "the fair meaning of the paragraph in the speech is that the general domestic tranquillity of Ireland, founded on the absence of all insurrectionary movements, and of political agitation, renders the public mind exceedingly favourable for the consideration of measures of a more permanent nature than if, as in other times, it were necessary to act on the odious necessity of passing a coercion bill. Three years ago the whole country rang with the cry of repeal. Where is that cry now? From one end of Ireland to another the people are mute upon the subject of that once popular demand; not a murmur is heard in any part of the kingdom. The people are perfectly satisfied, perfectly content with the English Government." There were, unfortunately, social disturbances. "But those dis-

[1] Hansard, 3rd series, vol. xxxix. p. 212 *et seq.*

turbances might be expected to continue so long as the grievances which gave rise to them remained unredressed. There has always been in Ireland combination in connection with the tenure of land," and "to the neglect of their duties by landlords, has at all times been attributed many of the worst evils of Ireland."

Referring to the charge that the Government of Ireland had been placed in the hands of O'Connell, Lord Mulgrave said—"It has been stated by persons who must know better, that Mr O'Connell has all the patronage of the Government in Ireland. I utterly and indignantly deny the truth of that statement. Mr O'Connell, like any other member of Parliament requiring information from the Government, has, I admit, had several communications with it, but I can confidently state, that the applications of Mr O'Connell have been fewer than those of any other member of Parliament. Neither has Mr O'Connell been consulted more than any other member of Parliament in any one appointment made by the Irish Government. Mr O'Connell holds no Government patronage in Ireland, nor does he exercise any of the patronage that belongs to the Government. Mr O'Connell does not bind or control me in the exercise of my judgment, or in the distribution of my patronage. I bow to no man. But whilst I bow to no man, like Lord Chesterfield, I will 'proscribe' no man. The taunt against me is, that I have treated Mr O'Connell in the same way as I would treat any other member of Parliament. So I have, my Lords, and so I will always continue to do. But I fearlessly and utterly deny that the Government has been controlled by Mr O'Connell, or has consulted with Mr O'Connell as to any of the appointments that have been made; and as to the charge of the Government having the steady support of Mr O'Connell, I honestly confess that that is a circumstance, considering how much he carries with him the hearts and affections of the Irish people, that I can regard only as a great advantage, and as one that ought not to be made a matter of reproach."[1]

Lord Melbourne followed with an able speech, in which he vindicated the Irish policy of the Government. Verner did not divide the House. He asked for papers, and he got them; there the matter ended. In truth, his attack failed all along the line; and the year 1837 closed, leaving Drummond's position, as an Irish ruler, unassailable.

In December Drummond received a letter from Thomas Moore, which may fittingly conclude this chapter.

THOMAS MOORE TO DRUMMOND.

"SLOPERTON DEVIZES, *Dec.* 19, 1837.

"MY DEAR MR DRUMMOND,—I want you to do me a little favour in the historical line, and as you have so much business on your hands at the present time, a little airing into the past will perhaps be wholesome for you.

[1] The Drummond papers—those placed in my hands by the family, and those I have read at the Record Tower, Dublin Castle—bear out this statement. The Irish patronage was, so far as I can make out, controlled chiefly by Lord Morpeth and Drummond. O'Connell was, no doubt, considered; but I rather infer not consulted. There is nothing in any of Lord Morpeth's, Drummond's, or Lord Mulgrave's letters from which the contrary can be gathered. No doubt if a bad appointment were contemplated, the Government must have felt that O'Connell would have promptly interfered. But, it is scarcely too much to say, that there was no chance of a bad appointment by a Government which had Drummond as Under Secretary, and Perron and O'Loghlen as Law Advisers. O'Connell had confidence in these men; and, I am disposed to think, did not interfere with them. He was certainly resolved to oust all Orangemen from official posts, and would have attacked any Government that gave them places; but this, I believe, was in the main the beginning and the end of his "control of the Government patronage." The notion that O'Connell interfered constantly, or frequently, in the patronage is without authority, so far as these papers are concerned.

Upon one occasion Drummond wrote to O'Connell:—

"In the performance of a difficult and responsible, but generally disagreeable duty—the distribution of patronage—it has been the anxious wish of both Lord Mulgrave and Lord Morpeth to give due weight to the merits, the services, and the recommendations of all." . . .

"If there are persons who have represented to you that your recommendations do not receive that fair consideration to which they are justly entitled, I shall

The Record Commission here have, as in duty bound, sent me all their massive volumes—but there is one work which, from my not finding it among them, must belong, I take for granted, to a Dublin publication—its title being, as well as I can recollect, 'Inquisitorium in officio rotulorum Cancellario Hibernio asservatorium Repertorium." The copy I saw of it is in the British Museum. Would you kindly make some inquiries for me on the subject, and by your official interposition procure me a copy of the work, pleading, if necessary, the example of the Record Commission here.

"My best remembrances to Mrs Drummond, and tell her that one of her many admirers (Rogers) was here with us in the autumn, as gay and blooming as ever.—Yours very truly, "THOMAS MOORE."

Drummond endorsed this letter. "The book sent 25th and 26th December. Ans. 17th January 1838." '

only say that I hope they have done so in ignorance of the facts, and not from a desire to promote their own selfish and more important objects."—*Letter penès me.*

Drummond once dismissed a stipendiary magistrate—Captain Gleeson. Dr MacHale asked O'Connell to interfere, with the view of having Gleeson reinstated. O'Connell wrote to the Archbishop :—"The day after I arrived in town I had communicated to the Lord Lieutenant that my conviction was that Captain Gleeson was treated with great injustice. In consequence, the documents in the matter were handed over to Mr Drummond to be prepared to meet me, and to justify the conduct of the Government." O'Connell met Drummond. He then wrote to the Archbishop :—"Mr Drummond admitted to me that Captain Gleeson had prevented much bloodshed [at the Carlow Election]. As far as Carlow is concerned, his case cannot be made much stronger. . . . [But] there is one decisive fact to warrant the dismissal of this unfortunate gentleman, which is admitted most distinctly by himself, and, indeed, cannot possibly be denied, namely, his publication in the newspapers of the most peremptory contradiction of O'Malley—a species of publication most emphatically prohibited by the printed rules of the service. How, then, can I talk of investigation when I am met by this plain proposition? Suppose every other charge disproved, here is one of the gravest admitted, and only palliated by showing the truth of the matter published; but the publication itself, not its truth or falsehood, is the offence. It seems to me that there is no reply."—Fitzpatrick, "Correspondence of Daniel O'Connell."

I desire to thank Mr Fitzpatrick for sending me the letter from Drummond to O'Connell, from which I quote above.

CHAPTER X.

1838.

IN April 1835 the Government of Lord Melbourne came into office, pledged to pass remedial measures for Ireland. It was now January 1838, and not a single remedial measure had yet been placed on the statute book. Ministers, however, were not to blame. In 1835, 1836, and 1837, measures for the settlement of tithes, and the reform of municipal corporations, had been carried through the Commons; they were all rejected by the Lords. Nothing can testify more strongly to the efficient administration of Drummond, than the fact that he kept the peace in Ireland, and even made the Government popular, while the English Parliament failed to do justice to the people. He certainly showed that there is some force in the lines:

> "For forms of government let fools contest,
> Whate'er is best administer'd is best."

In May 1838 the fourth Tithe Bill of the Government was introduced. It fell far short of its predecessors. In 1835 it had been proposed to convert tithes into a rent charge at £65 per cent. of the tithe, and to apply the surplus revenues of the Church to "purposes of general education in Ireland." The bill of 1838 simply provided for the conversion of tithes into a rent charge at £75 per cent. of the tithe; the clause appropriating the surplus revenues of the Church to educational purposes was abandoned altogether. This bill became law in August. It was a feeble measure, showing the incompetence of Parliament to deal effectually with the question.[1]

Three months before the passing of the "Tithe Commu-

[1] An account of the struggle over the various tithe bills is given in "Fifty Years of Concessions to Ireland," vol. i. book iii.

tation Act" the House of Lords gave judgment on the subject of Writs of Rebellion. Their Lordships held that a Commissioner of Rebellion was in the same position as a sheriff, and could, in cases of emergency and at his own discretion, call out the *posse comitatus*, when the police, as citizens, would be bound to attend.[1] This decision was, practically, in Drummond's favour, for he had only contended that the police had no special duty in the premises; that they were not bound, as police, to aid the commissioner in serving the writs; that their sole duty was to interfere only when the public peace was in danger.

The very day—May 22—on which this judgment was given, Drummond wrote his famous letter to the Tipperary magistrates. On April 5, Mr Austin Cooper, a Tipperary landowner, had been killed. The magistrates of the county seized the opportunity to urge upon the Government the necessity of adopting coercive measures for the suppression of agrarian outrages. On April 7, they addressed a memorial to the Lord Lieutenant:—

THE TIPPERARY MAGISTRATES TO THE LORD LIEUTENANT.

"*To His Excellency the Lord Lieutenant and Governor-General of Ireland, &c., &c., &c.*

"CASHEL, *7th April* 1838.

"We, the undersigned magistrates of the county of Tipperary, this day assembled at Cashel, at a very short notice, beg leave respectfully to state to your Excellency, that it is with feelings of the deepest horror we communicate to your Excellency the dreadful and atrocious attack made by some villains upon the lives of Samuel Cooper,

[1] *Miller* v. *Knox*, 4 Bingham, N. C., p. 574. The Court differed on the point as to whether an attachment would lie against "a stranger to the cause" who refused to assist in executing the writ. The effect of the decision altogether was, that the police, as citizens, were bound to assist the commissioner in cases of emergency; but it was left in doubt whether any measures could be taken against them if they refused.

Esq., J.P., Austin Cooper, Esq., and Francis Wayland,[1] Esq., on the 5th day of April.

"It appears that these gentlemen were proceeding to the fair of Tipperary on that day, the two Mr Coopers in a gig, and Mr Wayland on horseback, when they were fired upon by four men. Mr Samuel Cooper and Mr Wayland returned the fire, but it is horrifying to relate that Mr Austin Cooper was shot dead by a ball passing through his head, and Mr Wayland was severely wounded in the hip.

"There are circumstances connected with these horrible facts illustrative of the state of society in this county which we, the undersigned, deem it our duty to represent to your Excellency.

"It appears that it was known for some time previous to this attack that it was the intention of the miscreants of the country to assassinate these two gentlemen; that a committee of villains had met and determined on the death of Mr Austin Cooper; that his friends had warned him repeatedly of his danger; yet, notwithstanding the precautions he took, he was unable to avoid the fate to which he had been doomed. Mr Wayland's house was attacked a few days previous with the intention of shooting him.

"Comment upon these events we feel to be unnecessary. We beg leave to state to your Excellency that the large additional force of police and military ordered into these districts, in consequence of the memorial addressed to your Excellency by the magistrates assembled at Tipperary last November, has not been productive of those effects which your Excellency then calculated upon.

"This scene of slaughter occurred in the barony of Kilnemanagh, on the borders of the barony of Clanwilliam. The magistrates at that meeting declared that neither life nor property was safe in that part of the country. We, the

[1] Mr Wayland, who accompanied Mr Cooper, was wounded. He died subsequently of his wounds.

undersigned, declare that in that district neither life nor property is safe. We therefore respectfully trust that your Excellency will put in force the strongest powers which the laws of the land permit in those districts.

"We consider it our duty to state to your Excellency that we believe the result of the late assizes for this county has proved how terrible is the state of intimidation which exists, or seems to exist, among the juries of this county, an effect which the Crown can at all times prevent, by again resorting to the old and wholesome practice of challenging, which, properly acted on, would be productive of the best effects.

"We beg leave respectfully to hope that Her Majesty's Government will bring in a Bill to Parliament for the purpose of inflicting a heavier penalty than that now in force on persons, for having unregistered arms or ammunition in their possession. We also recommend that licenses granted for keeping arms be renewed annually, and that additional powers for searching for arms be given to magistrates "[1]

DRUMMOND TO THE TIPPERARY MAGISTRATES.

"DUBLIN CASTLE, 18*th April* 1838.

"MY LORD,[2]—I am commanded by the Lord Lieutenant to acknowledge the memorial of several magistrates of the county of Tipperary, assembled at Cashel on the 7th inst.

"His Excellency heard with the deepest concern of the lamentable occurrence to which the magistrates have called his attention, and has not failed to direct the most prompt and vigorous measures to be adopted with a view to bring to justice the perpetrators of so atrocious an act. His Excellency has reason to hope that these measures will be speedily attended with success.

[1] This letter was signed by Lord Glengall, Lord Lismore, and thirty other magistrates.

[2] The letter was addressed to Lord Donoughmore, the Lord Lieutenant of the county.

"His Excellency will not now notice the other topics contained in the memorial, further than to observe, that he deems them deserving the most serious attention. They are so much at variance with the official information which has come to his knowledge, that he considers it necessary to institute an immediate and careful inquiry, with a view to ascertain, in the clearest manner, the actual extent of the evils which the magistrates represent to exist, and, so far as may be possible, the immediate causes to which they may be attributed.

"When His Excellency has received the information which he expects to derive from such inquiry, he will communicate fully to the magistrates his opinion as to any steps which he may in consequence deem it his duty to adopt or recommend.—I have, &c.,

"T. DRUMMOND."

"THE EARL OF DONOUGHMORE."

THE SAME TO THE SAME.

"DUBLIN CASTLE, *22nd May* 1838.

"MY LORD,—In the communication of the 18th of April, which I had the honour to make to your Lordship by command of the Lord Lieutenant, in reference to the memorial of several magistrates of the county of Tipperary, your Lordship was informed that His Excellency considered it necessary to institute an immediate and careful inquiry, with a view to ascertain, in the clearest manner, the actual extent of the evils which the magistrates represented to exist, and, so far as might be possible, the immediate causes to which such evils might be attributed; and that when His Excellency had received the information which he expected to derive from such inquiry, he would communicate fully to the magistrates his opinion as to any steps which he might in consequence deem it his duty to adopt or recommend.

"Before proceeding to state to your Lordship the nature

and result of that inquiry, I am directed by His Excellency to observe that he certainly read with great surprise the statement put forth by the memorialists, in which they declare that the juries of their county act under a feeling of terrible intimidation, and refer to the proceedings at the last assizes for proof of that assertion. For the first time since the government of Ireland was entrusted to His Excellency had such a statement been made to him, and His Excellency found great difficulty in believing that, if such a state of things had existence, no report of it should have reached him from any of the numerous public officers engaged in the administration of justice, under whose cognisance it must necessarily have come in the perform ance of their duties ; nor could His Excellency suppose that a matter of so much moment, so vitally affecting the administration of the law, and the consequent security of life and property, should not have become known to the judges in their intercourse on their respective circuits, not only with grand jurors and magistrates, but with sheriffs and other ministerial officers, or indeed could have escaped the discernment of those learned persons themselves while presiding at the trials of offenders.

"His Excellency could not for a moment doubt that, if any of the officers of the executive, or any of the learned persons to whom he has alluded, had witnessed, or even heard on credible authority, that juries had ceased to be capable of discharging their important functions, from the apprehension of danger, he would at once have brought so serious a matter under the immediate notice of the Government.

"Though no such statement had been made to the executive, His Excellency, nevertheless, in deference to the representation made by the memorialists, and with a desire that a matter so serious should not rest in vague conjecture, or on opinion not sustained by facts, deemed it his duty to direct, among other inquiries, letters to be addressed to the several stipendiary magistrates of the county, calling upon them to state whether any and what instances of injury to the persons or property of jurors had come under their observation which could be distinctly attributed to verdicts given by such jurors. In the answers received from all these gentlemen, they uniformly declare that not a single instance of the kind has ever occurred to their knowledge.

"Major Carter says: 'There are no records of such events in this district; and occurrences of that nature could not have passed my observation, or that of the sub-inspector, formerly chief constable for twenty-seven years, with whom I have conversed on this subject.'

"Mr Willcocks—'I am not aware of any instances of injury to the person or property of any juror distinctly attributable to any verdicts which he may have given.'

"Mr Vokes—'I do not remember an instance in any county where a juror was injured on account of any verdict he may have given.'

"Mr Singleton—'No instance of the sort at any time came under my observation.'

"Mr Tabuteau—'No instance of the kind has come under my observation, nor has any complaint been made or information given to me of any juror having in any way suffered for any act done by him in the execution of his duty as a juror.'

"Captain Duff—'None such has come under my observation; and I may safely add that none could have occurred in this district without coming to my knowledge or to that of the chief constable, whom I have questioned on the subject.'

"Captain Nangle—'In no instance that has ever come under my observation has any juror suffered injury attributable to any verdict he may have given.'

"His Excellency also directed a similar communication

to be made to the Crown Solicitor of the circuit, and has received from that officer the answer that—

"'No case of the kind has come within the knowledge of the Crown Solicitor.'

"In reply to a similar communication to Mr Barrington, Crown Solicitor of the Munster circuit, three out of the four counties which adjoin Tipperary, he states—

"'No instance has occurred on the Munster circuit while I have been Crown Solicitor (now nearly twenty-five years), of injury suffered by any person in consequence of having found a verdict of conviction in any case.'

"As the magistrates referred to the result of the last assizes, His Excellency deemed it proper to inquire particularly into what occurred on that occasion in reference to that class of cases with respect to which intimidation, if it had at all existed, would have been most likely to operate, and His Excellency called for such information as would enable him to compare the result of the trials which then took place with those for similar offences at former assizes in the same county. The following table shows the result:—

	Number of Cases of Homicide prosecuted and tried.	RESULTS OF THE TRIALS.		
		Number of Cases in which the Jury convicted.	Number of Cases in which the Jury acquitted.	Number of Cases in which the Jury disagreed.
1834—Spring......	18	11	7	...
" Summer....	20	10	10	...
1835—Spring......	22	12	10	...
" Summer....	15	11	4	...
1836—Spring......	25	18	7	...
" Summer....	20	10	10	...
1837—Spring......	30	16	14	...
" Summer....	17	8	7	
1838—Spring......	25	12	12	

"It thus appears that at the last assizes the proportion of convictions to acquittals was precisely the same as at the summer assizes of 1834 and 1836, the convictions and acquittals being exactly equal in number, and that the result was nearly similar at the spring assizes of 1836 and at the spring and summer assizes of 1837. It further appears that, while at the spring assizes of 1834 the proportion of convictions to acquittals was as eleven to seven, the proportion was diminished to an equality at the summer assizes of the same year; and that, while at the spring assizes of 1836 the proportion of convictions to acquittals was as eighteen to seven, they were at the next assizes again exactly equal.

"It appears also that, while at the last summer assizes the juries disagreed in two cases of homicide, one instance only of such disagreement occurred at the spring assizes of this year.

"Results varying so considerably within very short intervals of time, lead naturally to the conclusion that in Tipperary as in other places, the issue of trials in convictions and acquittals is produced, not by the increased or diminished virtue or infirmity of jurors, but by those varying, complex, and often accidental causes, against which no vigilance can guard, and which operate in every country and in every condition of society.

"His Excellency finds, on referring to the two northern circuits, that the proportion of acquittals to convictions in cases of homicide has been considerably greater within the same period.

"His Excellency has also obtained a return of the several juries at the last assizes of Tipperary, and he finds that the great majority of the jurors resided in towns, chiefly in Clonmel, and therefore were not likely to be influenced by apprehensions of danger to person or property; and further, on examining the list, it has been found that, of the 100 jurors who constituted the juries in the several cases of homicide, fifty-two served both on convicting and acquitting juries, thirty on convicting juries only, and eighteen only on acquitting juries.

"His Excellency also felt it his duty to refer the statement of the memorialists to the judge who presided at the last assizes, and His Excellency has received a reply from that learned person, of which the following is an extract:—

"'It did not appear to me there existed any grounds, either of facts or inference, for apprehending that the juries were intimidated; on the contrary, I considered they discharged their duties free from any bias arising from personal apprehension, or any other cause; and with regard to their verdicts, they uniformly received and acted upon the legal character of the crime as laid down by the Court, at the same time exercising their own judgments, as in their exclusive province, upon the credit to which they considered the witnesses were entitled.'

"With such facts and evidence before him, His Excellency is wholly at a loss to understand on what grounds the memorialists have asserted that the juries at the late assizes acted under 'terrible intimidation.' His Excellency cannot but think that, in putting forth a statement, unsustained by proof, so deeply affecting the administration of justice, and so seriously impugning the acts of men who appear to have faithfully and fearlessly discharged their responsible duties, according to their oaths, the memorialists have been influenced rather by the excitement prevailing at the time of their meeting, and naturally produced by horror at the atrocious crime just then perpetrated, than by that due and calm consideration which such a subject requires, and which, under other circumstances, they would doubtless have given to it.

"The magistrates suggest a remedy for the supposed intimidation, in a recurrence to what they term 'the old and wholesome practice of challenging.' As the evil appears to have no existence, His Excellency might have deemed it unnecessary to advert to that part of the memorial; but as it would seem that the present course of proceeding with regard to challenging on the part of the Crown is not perfectly understood by the memorialists, and as it is important that it should be generally known, His Excellency thinks it right to explain to them what the actual directions are, by which the Crown prosecutors are governed in this respect.

"The privilege of setting aside jurors has not been abandoned, as the memorialists seem to think; but the exercise of it is strictly confined to cases in which those concerned in the conducting of Crown prosecutions can, upon their responsibility, say that just grounds of objection exist to any individual called on the jury; the direction of the law officers of the Crown being express, that no man shall be objected to merely on the ground of his religion or his politics. His Excellency entirely concurs in the wisdom and justice of that course, and he has not heard of a single fact that would lead him to conclude that the ends of justice would be advanced by the adoption of any other practice.

"His Excellency has no reason for believing that the recurrence from time to time of serious outrages in the county of Tipperary is justly to be ascribed to the existing state of the law, or the manner in which it is administered.

"The Government has been at all times ready to afford the utmost aid in its power to suppress disturbance and crime; and its efforts have been successful, so far as regards open violations of the law. Faction fights and riots at fairs, which were generally of a very ferocious character and the fruitful source of much subsequent crime, have been to a very great degree suppressed, though heretofore most commonly suffered to pass unchecked and unpunished; but there are certain classes of crime, originating in other causes, which are much more difficult of repression. The utmost exertion of vigilance and precaution cannot always effectually guard against them; and it becomes of importance to consider the causes which have led to a state of society so much to be deplored, with a view to ascertain whether any corrective means are in the immediate power of the Government or the Legislature. When the character of the great majority of serious outrages occurring in many parts of Ireland, though unhappily most frequent in Tipperary, is considered, it is impossible to doubt that the causes from which they mainly spring are connected with the tenure and occupation of land. But His Excellency feels that it would be quite beyond the limits, and not consistent with the character of a communication of this nature, either to enter into an examination of the lamentably destitute condition of a cottier tenantry, possessing no adequate means of continuous support, or to advert in detail to the objects for which the formation of such a class was originally either permitted or directly encouraged. If from political changes, or the improvements in modern husbandry, these objects are not any longer to be attained by the continuance of such a state of things, His Excellency conceives that it may become matter of serious question whether the proprietors of the soil are not in many instances attempting too rapidly to retrace their steps, when he finds the fact to be, from returns furnished by the Clerk of the Peace for Tipperary, that the number of ejectments in 1837 is not less than double the number in 1833. The deficiency of a demand for labour, and the want, as yet, of any legal provision against utter destitution, leave this humble class, when ejected, without any certain protection against actual starvation. Hence the wholesale expulsion of cottier tenants is unfortunately found with the great body of the people to enlist the strongest feelings—those of self-preservation—on the side even of guilt, in vindication of what they falsely assume to be their rights; and hence a sympathy for persons charged with crimes supposed to have arisen from those causes, is still found a lamentable exception to that increased general respect for the laws which has of late years been remarked with satisfaction by those concerned in the administration of justice.

"Property has its duties as well as its rights; to the neglect of those duties in times past is mainly to be ascribed that diseased state of society in which such crimes take their rise; and it is not in the enactment or enforcement of statutes of extraordinary severity, but chiefly in the better and more faithful performance of those duties, and the more enlightened and humane exercise of those rights, that a permanent remedy for such disorders is to be sought.

"Whatever a Government can do to protect the rights which the law has conferred, and to suppress violence and crime, from whatever cause arising, His Excellency, as head of the Executive, will direct and enforce; but His Excellency firmly believes that the end so earnestly to be desired will be more speedily and effectually attained by the vigorous administration of the ordinary laws than by the adoption of any more vigorous measures. The experience of the past confirms and justifies that belief. When it was reported last November that a spirit of intimidation and violence had manifested itself in the barony of Clanwilliam and certain portions of the adjoining baronies, His Excellency, after duly weighing the representations of the magistrates, who on that occasion urged that the country should be proclaimed, came to the conclusion that the ordinary powers of the law would be found sufficient to meet the exigency.

"He directed the constabulary to be strengthened,

military detachments to patrol the district, and stipendiary magistrates to superintend their proceedings. Several persons were arrested, and have been either brought to trial at the last assizes, or are now awaiting their trial at the next.

"In the course of a short time it was reported that the symptoms of disturbance had disappeared. The cavalry which had been sent into the district were withdrawn upon the favourable reports of the military authorities, confirmed by the magistrates, the detachments of infantry and extra force of constabulary being, by way of precaution, still retained. It was therefore with some surprise that His Excellency read in the memorial of the magistrates the following statement in reference to these measures and their results:—

"'We beg leave to state to your Excellency, that the large additional force of police and military ordered into these districts, in consequence of the memorial addressed to your Excellency by the magistrates assembled at Tipperary last November, has not been productive of those effects which your Excellency then calculated upon.'

"In contrast to that statement, it appears by a report of Mr Wilcocks, on the barony of Clanwilliam, the district to which the special attention of the Government was directed in consequence of the memorial alluded to, that in the only case of serious outrage—the homicide of James Hayes, which occurred between the 8th of January and the 16th April, the date of the report—the perpetrators were arrested and made amenable on the same day. Reports of the state of the adjacent districts, of an equally favourable character, were also received from Captain Nangle and Mr Singleton; and the latter, who had been sent to Cappawhite in December, having reported that his services were no longer required in that district, was directed to return to his station on the 21st of February.

"His Excellency has also been informed by Judge Moore that applications were made to him when on the bench at the last assizes, by persons acting on behalf of three very extensive proprietors of the county, whose tenants were under charges of opposing the law and disturbing the peace, viz., Lords Glengall, Hawarden, and Lismore, the substance of which applications was, to pray him not to permit the proceedings against those persons to be brought forward, and to have the charges against them abandoned; and that the grounds on which those gentlemen mainly urged the judge to comply with their respective applications were, the tranquil state of the several parts of the county in which those criminal occurrences had taken place, and the good effect which his compliance would have in the country. The judge added, that those applications which regarded the tenants of the two first-named lords were made by letters addressed to him in court, and that in the other instance the application was personal, but strongly pressed.

"With such facts before him, His Excellency, with all the respect for the opinion of the memorialists, must still believe that the proceedings which he then directed were in the main effectual, and that the adoption of those measures of severity which are at variance with the generous spirit of our laws, and are only intended to meet extraordinary emergencies, was not called for on that occasion.

"His Excellency has given, and will continue to give, to the improvement of the administration of the laws, his most anxious consideration, and will willingly receive and carefully examine any suggestions offered to him with that view.

"His Excellency is encouraged to hope by what has been effected under circumstances of much difficulty, that more may be accomplished. The rest must be left to time, to the faithful and diligent performance of their duties by the local magistracy, to the beneficial exercise of their rights as landlords, and to the operation of such measures of general policy as the Legislature in its wisdom may adopt.—I have, &c.,

"T. DRUMMOND."[1]

"The EARL OF DONOUGHMORE,
"&c., &c., &c."

The way the Tipperary magistrates dealt with this letter is one of the most extraordinary things in the history of Irish landlordism. They suppressed it. They feared that the publication of the aphorism, "property has its duties as well as its rights," would demoralise the peasantry and drive them into crime and outrage. This may seem incredible, but the fact rests upon the authority of Lord Donoughmore himself. Examined before the Lords Committee on the state of Ireland in 1839, he told the whole story with great frankness.

Committee—"With regard to the reply signed by Mr Drummond to the memorial of the magistrates respecting the murder of Mr Cooper and Mr Wayland, what steps did your Lordship take upon the receipt of that reply?"

Lord Donoughmore—"I considered the reply of such a nature I was very unwilling to make it public, and I sent for Lord Glengall and Lord Hawarden and Lord Lismore, and read the reply over to them three or four times; and although I do not conceive the document, though directed to me as Lord Lieutenant of the county, to be my document, for Lord Glengall was the chairman of the meeting, I said, 'Though this is your document, I shall not give it up under the state of excitement in which the country is; I shall not allow it to be published at present, inasmuch as I

[1] Three men were arrested for the murder of Mr Cooper. One of them turned informer; the other two were hanged.

am the party to whom it is addressed.' It was so worded that it threw the blame upon the landlords of having been the authors of the outrages. That was the impression upon my mind, and I did not wish it published."

Committee—"Did your Lordship express that opinion to any gentlemen of the county, except the gentlemen you have named?"

Lord Donoughmore—"Yes; when I went over they asked me what the reply was, and my answer to the magistrates individually was, that I considered it of such a nature that I would not publish it."

Committee—"Your Lordship considered it a dangerous thing with regard to the landowners of the country?"

Lord Donoughmore—"I considered it of that nature. I may be wrong."

Committee—"Will your Lordship have the goodness to point out the passages which appear to you to have that tendency?"

Lord Donoughmore—"The part of this answer to which I particularly objected was this: 'Property has its duties as well as its rights; to the neglect of these duties in times past is mainly to be ascribed that diseased state of society in which such crimes take their rise.'"[1]

The Ascendancy never forgave Drummond for the letter to the Tipperary magistrates. They denounced him as the instigator of outrage, and vilified him as the defamer of the landed gentry of the country.

It is a strange commentary on Irish landlordism, that fifty years ago Irish landlords should have shrunk from telling their tenants that property had its duties as well as its rights; should have assailed the man who announced this simple truth.

[1] "Parliamentary Papers for 1839," vol. xii. Q. 12,038, *et seq.*

Moore wrote to Drummond anent the letter to the Tipperary magistrates: "How I envy that pregnant sentence about duties and rights, *teterrima belli causa*, or, as I would suggest reading, *tetorymi*."

While the storm caused by the enunciation of the potent aphorism, "Property has its duties as well as its rights," still raged, Drummond finished his labours on a special work undertaken at his instance for promoting the national welfare. In 1836, a Royal Commission was appointed to consider the means of establishing railway communications throughout Ireland.[1] Drummond was the life and soul of this Commission, and the chief interest which now attaches to it centres in those parts of the Report written by him. He was resolved that the Commission should not only consider the question of railways, but should also inquire generally into the social and economical condition of the people. The result of these inquiries he has with his own hand set forth in the final Report which appeared on July 11, 1838. The document is of historical importance, and must be fully given :—

"REPORT OF THE RAILWAY COMMISSION.

* * * *

"*Amount of the Population.*—The population of Ireland was in the year—

1731,	2,010,221
1791,	4,206,602
1821,	6,801,827
1831,	7,767,401
1834,	7,943,960

"Estimating the increase going on for each of these periods, we find it during the first period of sixty years to be at the rate of $1\frac{1}{4}$ per cent. per annum; during the next period of thirty years, $1\frac{3}{5}$ per cent. per annum; during the next ten years, $1\frac{1}{3}$ per cent. per annum; and for the last period, only $\frac{3}{4}$ths per cent. per annum. But this interval is perhaps too short for a very exact result. Taking for our guide the rate of increase between 1821 and 1831, the popu-

[1] Drummond's brother commissioners were General Burgoyne, Mr Barlow, and Sir Richard Griffith.

lation at the present time, 1838, would amount to 8,523,750. The population of England, Wales, and Scotland, computed in the same manner, from the census of 1821 and 1831, would amount at present to 18,226,725; whence it appears that the population of Ireland is at this time within 600,000, of being equal to one-third of the population of the United Kingdom.

"*Distribution of the Population.*—To give a distinct view of the manner in which this immense mass of the people is distributed over the surface of the country, a map has been prepared, which indicates, by various degrees of shade, the relative densities of the population—the figures denoting the number of inhabitants, per square mile, within the respective boundaries. A glance at this map will show that the population is most crowded and numerous in the counties of Armagh, Monaghan, and in part of the counties of Antrim and Down. Diminishing in density, but still furnishing a large proportion to the square mile, the population extends over the counties of Longford, Westmeath, King's, Queen's, Kilkenny, Carlow, and Wexford; and thence a large mass, second only to the northern portion, spreads over the southern counties of Tipperary, Limerick, and parts of Cork and Waterford.

"Beyond the Shannon lies a district very thickly peopled; and the parts of Roscommon, Leitrim, &c., adjacent to the river, have nearly the same proportion of inhabitants.

"These four divisions of the population differ in social condition, in habits, character, and even in personal appearance, more than the narrow limits of their location within the same country would lead us to expect. The northern portion are better lodged, clothed, and fed than the others; the wages of labour are higher, being, on an average, about one shilling per day, and their food consists chiefly of meal, potatoes, and milk. They are a frugal, industrious, and intelligent race, inhabiting a district for the most part inferior in natural fertility to the southern portion of Ireland, but cultivating it better, and paying higher rents in proportion to the quality of the land, notwithstanding the higher rate of wages.

"In the southern districts we find a population whose condition is, in every respect, inferior to that of the northern; their habitations are worse; their food inferior, consisting at best of potatoes and milk, without meal; the wages of labour are found reduced from one shilling to eightpence per day; yet the peasantry are a robust, active, and athletic race, capable of great exertion; often exposed to great privations; ignorant, but eager for instruction, and readily trained, under judicious management, to habits of order and steady industry.

"The population of the midland districts does not differ materially in condition from those of the south; but the inhabitants of the western district are decidedly inferior to both in condition and appearance; their food consists of the potato alone, without meal, and in most cases without milk; their cabins are wretched hovels, their beds straw; the wages of labour are reduced to the lowest point, upon an average of not more than sixpence per day. Poverty and misery have deprived them of all energy; labour brings no adequate return, and every motive to exertion is destroyed. Agriculture is in the rudest and lowest state. The substantial farmer, employing labourers and cultivating his land according to the improved modes of modern husbandry, is rarely to be found amongst them. The country is covered with small occupiers, and swarms with an indigent and wretched population. It is true that some landed proprietors have made great exertions to introduce a better system of agriculture and to improve the condition of their immediate tenants, and a few of the lesser proprietors have made humble attempts to imitate them; but the great mass of the population exhibits a state of poverty bordering on destitution.

"The distinctions we have drawn as to the usual diet of agricultural labourers in the different parts of Ireland, are strictly applicable to those only who have regular employment. When they are out of work, which is the case in many places during three or four months of the year, the line is not so easily perceived. Then a reduction in the quantity as well as in the quality of their food takes place, but still, though on a diminished scale, their relative local degrees of comfort or of penury are maintained nearly according to the above classification. In no extremity of privation or distress have the peasantry of the northern counties approached to a level with those of the west; whilst Leinster and the greater part of the south, though sometimes reduced to the lowest condition, retain, generally, even in the most calamitous periods, a shade of superiority. There are districts, indeed, in every quarter of the land, where, through peculiarities of the situation, or other causes, distress falls with an equal pressure upon all; but such exceptions are rare, and so limited in extent, as scarcely to qualify the foregoing observations.

"We may here observe, that in proportion as wages fall below a fair standard of compensation, the work received in return will be dear. This striking and interesting fact, sufficiently attested by experience as a general truth, has been confirmed to us, with regard to the districts of which we are now speaking, by the authority of a practical engineer, who has had most extensive professional experience in every quarter of Ireland.

"No vigilance of superintendence can be an effective substitute for the motive which adequate remuneration supplies; and for want of such a stimulus, a sauntering, dilatory, apathetic mode of working becomes, in progress of time, the confirmed habit of the district—an evil for which an increase of wages will not prove an immediate remedy.

"*Employment of the Population.*—With respect to the employment of the people, it is essentially agricultural; but in the northern district, besides their rural occupa tions, numbers of the peasantry are engaged in the linen trade. The culture of flax, its preparation and manufacture, occupy a considerable portion of the time and labour of the population of the counties of Armagh, Antrim, Down, Tyrone, Londonderry, and part of Monaghan.

"If agriculture were more perfect in these districts, the farms larger, and the distinction between the farmer and the labourer more marked, such a combination of trades would probably be found neither convenient nor conducive to profit; but the farmers being also, for the most part, labourers, and the labourers small land-holders, the spare time not required for the cultivation of their land, and which in other districts is so often given up to idleness, intemperance, or crime, is here devoted to a profitable and useful employment, which rewards industry with a fair return, and promotes habits of peace and order. The variety of occupation afforded by this system of domestic manufacture to the different members of the family, is its chief recommendation. While the men are engaged in weaving the yarn, the task of preparing it for the loom by breaking, hackling, and spinning, is performed by the females, who find such a mode of industry congenial to the habits of their sex, and compatible with their household duties. . . .

"Besides these (trades), it can scarcely be said that there is any other manufacture in Ireland conducted on so great a scale as to be of much national importance. Under the now exploded system of bounties and protecting duties, several manufactories sprang up; but not being the natural growth of circumstances favourable to their establishment, most of them gradually disappeared as soon as the undue encouragement, which had created and stimulated them, was withdrawn. Still there are to be found in every district, establishments of various kinds, conducted in the most creditable manner; but they do not exist to such an extent as to claim especial notice in a general view of the employment of the people. If it were necessary to show that there is no inaptitude among the population for manufactures, for such even as require the greatest ingenuity, neatness, and skill, we would select the damask of Lisburn and the tabinets of Dublin. Worked muslins produced in many parts of Ireland, and very often from the poorest cabins, rival those of France, and are sold at half the price; embroidery on silks and satins is also carried to great perfection, and schools have been established in many places for the instruction of the female peasantry in this beautiful art.

"But while the manufactures which were formed under the system of bounties have been sinking into decay, the various processes to which agricultural produce is subjected, have been gradually extended and improved. Grinding, malting, brewing, and distilling, have made great progress within these few years. Until lately, the mills of Bristol and Liverpool enjoyed almost the exclusive advantage of converting the Irish wheat into flour. That process is now performed in Ireland. The construction of water-wheels and other machinery has been much improved, and the use of them, under favourable circumstances has greatly increased; but there are few large mills in which steam is not united with water power, in order that supply may be constant and regular during the summer as well as the winter months—a proof of a better system of trading and of more enlarged means.

"From north to south indications of progressive improvement are everywhere visible, and most so in places which are accessible to the immediate influence of steam navigation; but these signs of growing prosperity are, unhappily, not so discernible in the condition of the labouring people as in the amount of the produce of their labour. The proportion of the latter reserved for their use is too small to be consistent with a healthy state of society. The pressure of a superabundant and excessive population (at least, with respect to the resources as yet developed for their maintenance and occupation) is perpetually and powerfully acting to depress them.

"*Circumstances peculiar to the condition of the population of Ireland.*—The present social aspect and condition of Ireland is an anomaly in itself. Whilst the country is making a visible and steady progress in improvement, and signs of increasing wealth present themselves on all sides, the labouring population, constituting a large majority of the community, derive no proportionate benefit from the growing prosperity around them. In many places their condition is even worse than it has been. This apparent incongruity is, however, easily understood and explained by a reference to the peculiar state of property, and to the complex relations which subsist between the proprietors and the several parties deriving interests under them, from the immediate tenant down to the actual occupier of the soil.

"The division of the land into small farms, and their subdivision into portions, continually decreasing in extent with each succeeding generation of claimants, until, on some estates, literally every rood of ground maintained, or rather was charged with the maintenance of 'its man,' was the immediate cause of the rapid increase of the population, which, within a period of fifty years, has risen from four millions to upwards of eight.

"The defective state of the law, which, for a long time,

afforded the landlord no adequate security against the partition of his estates—and the long term of years or lives for which it was customary to grant leases, without any valid limitations being set upon the power of the tenant to underlet—contributed without doubt to this result. But there were other causes in which the proprietors had a more direct and personal participation, and which justly imposed upon them a full share of responsibility for the consequences. Not only did they not discourage the multiplication of small tenures (which they might have done effectually by their influence, even in cases where, by former demises, the management of their estates had been placed in the power, and depended upon the will, of others), but they were themselves active promoters of that system, and that from two obvious and intelligible motives—a desire to swell the amount of their rent-rolls, which were at first considerably increased by the operation of this principle, and a wish to possess themselves of political influence and power at the elections. The local operation of the latter cause is manifest, and admits of distinct proofs in almost every populous district in Ireland; and its general effect may be inferred from the remarkable and accelerated increase of the population which took place from the year 1793, the date of the Act for conferring the Elective Franchise on that class of voters known as the Forty Shilling Freeholders. In 1791 the numbers were 4,206,602; in 1821 they were found to have increased to 6,801,827; in 1831 to 7,767,401; and now they amount to more than eight and a-half millions. It is due to the proprietors and intermediate landlords who took no measures to repress this astonishing increase, while it might have been beneficially checked without inconvenience or injury to any individual, to admit, that few persons during its early stages foresaw its rapid extension, or suspected the evils it would bring in its train.

But this consideration, while it exonerates them from the imputation of culpable design or indifference, does not exempt them from the necessary consequeuces of their improvidence, or from the first obligations and duties inseparable from the possession of property.

"The misery and destitution which prevail so extensively, together with all the demoralisation incident to the peculiar condition of the Irish peasantry, may be traced to this source. The country, particularly in the west and south-western counties, is overspread with small but exceedingly crowded communities, sometimes located in villages, but more frequently in isolated tenements, exclusively composed of the poorest class of labourers, who, removed from the presence and social or moral influence of a better and more enlightened class, are left generally to the coercive power of the law alone to hold them within the bounds of peace and order. No system of constant or remunerative industry is established amongst them. The cultivation of their patches of land and the labour of providing fuel are their sole employment, which, occupying but a comparatively small portion of their time, leaves them exposed to all the temptations of an idle, reckless, and needy existence.

"In such a community there is no demand for hired labourers. Every occupier, with such assistance as his own family can furnish, manages to raise the scanty supply of food which he may need for their support, and as much grain, or other produce, as may be required to pay his rent; but beyond this there is no solicitude about cultivating the land, nor the least taste for improving or making it more valuable. At the periods of active labour, when additional hands are absolutely necessary, every expedient is resorted to in order to avoid the employment of a single paid labourer. Children of tender years are then forced to do the work of men in the fields, to a degree far beyond their strength, and all the females who are capable of rendering assistance are tasked in many ways utterly unsuited to their sex, and incompatible with the slightest attention to their proper cares and duties. At all times, indeed, of the year, whether the case be urgent or not, the share of labour, out of doors, imposed upon women and young girls, who might in every respect be so much better occupied, is as injurious to the moral condition as it must be to the personal and domestic comfort of the peasantry.

"There is a class of landholders superior to these, holding from eight to twelve or fifteen acres, who are equally slovenly and careless in the management of their land; but necessarily obliged, on account of its greater extent, to procure assistance out of their own families. Sometimes, but rarely, these persons hire daily labourers among the neighbouring poor; and in such cases they are usually guided in their choice, not by the character or capability of the man they employ, but by the lowest rate of wages at which they can possibly obtain his service. More commonly, however, they engage as farm servants, young men between sixteen and twenty-five years of age, who reside in the family of their employer, and hire themselves out at remarkably low wages, seldom exceeding £1 per quarter, and, in numerous instances, scarcely more than half that sum.

"The litigation which occupies a great portion of the time of the several Courts of Petty Sessions, arises out of the disputes of this class of servants with their employers; the former being usually impatient to break off their engagements at the busy and more profitable season of the year, and the latter anxious, of course, to reap the full benefit of the contract. Another common subject of angry contention before the same tribunals, is furnished by ill-defined boundaries, neglected fences, and consequent trespass between the neighbouring tenants of the small divisions of land above described. More time and money are commonly wasted in such contests than would suffice to repair all the damage which forms the ground of quarrel; and animosities are engendered which often lead to feuds of a lasting duration, and the most deadly consequences.

"It is plain that, under such a distribution of property, no rational hope can be entertained of the general introduction of an improved system of husbandry, or the employment of the labouring poor, to the extent and in the manner which would be beneficial to them, and conducive to the prosperity and good order of the community.

"It is therefore much to be wished that such a system should no longer continue. For the preservation of property—for the interests of the public peace—for the progress of civilization and improvement—and for the permanent good of the rural population, it is desirable that a speedy alteration should take place. The evil cannot remain stationary; it must either be met with effective opposition, or it will, by its own accumulative force, proceed to the last point at which the process of subdivision is practicable; and what may be the consequences of suffering it to go so far, it is painful to contemplate. How rapidly it is in some places approaching to that point, may be gathered from the Population Returns of the Board of Trade, which represent an increase to have taken place between the years 1821 and 1831, amounting, in certain western counties, to one in five, and in others nearly to one in four, of the whole number of inhabitants, viz.:—

"In Donegal, . . .	increase,	20	per cent.
In Mayo, . . .	"	24	"
In Galway, . . .	"	23	"
In Clare, . . .	"	24	"

"Among the effects of this rapid increase of population,

without a corresponding increase of remunerative employment, the most alarming, though perhaps the most obviously to be expected, is a deterioration of the food of the peasantry. It could scarcely be thought, indeed, that their customary diet would admit of any reduction, save in quantity alone; yet it has been reduced as to quality also, in such a way as sensibly to diminish their comfort, if not to impair their health. Bread was never an article of common use amongst the labouring poor; but it is now less known by them than it was at the time when a sum exceeding £50,000 per annum was paid in 'bounties,' to induce the landholders to grow a sufficiency of grain for the supply of the city of Dublin. Milk is become almost a luxury to many of them; and the quality of their potato diet is generally much inferior to what it was at the commencement of the present century. A species of potato called the 'lumper' has been brought into general cultivation, on account of its great productiveness, and the facility with which it can be raised from an inferior soil and with a comparatively small portion of manure. This root, at its first introduction, was scarcely considered food good enough for swine; it neither possesses the farinaceous qualities of the better varieties of the plant, nor is it as palatable as any other, being wet and tasteless, and, in point of substantial nutriment, little better, as an article of human food, than a Swedish turnip. In many counties of Leinster, and throughout the provinces of Munster and Connaught, the lumper now constitutes the principal food of the labouring peasantry — a fact which is the more striking when we consider the great increase of produce, together with its manifest improvement in quality, which is annually raised in Ireland for exportation, and for consumption by the superior classes.

"For years the proprietors of land have endeavoured to counteract the evils arising from the increase of a pauper and unemployed population, and to prevent its extension. Their eyes have long been opened to the mischief partly created, and, in a great measure, countenanced by themselves; and they are quite willing to retrace their steps, and reduce their estates, if possible, to a condition more favourable to a judicious mode of cultivation, and to the regular and profitable occupation of the poor. The habit of letting their grounds in small allotments has altogether ceased in the agricultural districts, though it still prevails in parts of the manufacturing counties of Armagh and Down, where the skill of the artisan is rendered in some degree subsidiary to the toil of the labourer. Generally, however, as often as opportunities occur, they are gladly embraced to enlarge the divisions of land to farms of dimensions better adapted to the development of agricultural science, and the beneficial employment of capital and labour. In some cases these changes have been conducted with judicious humanity; in many, it is to be feared, without much regard either to humanity or justice; but where they can be effected without injury to individual happiness or equitable rights, without doubt they must, in all cases, tend to the ultimate advantage of society, as a means of checking a great and growing evil, of increasing the wealth of the country, and, consequently, laying a firm and sure foundation of prosperity for the Irish people.

"Already considerable progress has been made towards the establishment of a better system of agriculture, and the altered and much improved appearance of the country in many places is owing to the success which has attended those endeavours. But although the land has thus been rendered more valuable, and its produce more abundant, the condition of the labouring poor has not advanced, even in those improved localities.

"The fair inference to be drawn from this fact is, that the labourer is not allowed a just proportion of the product of his own toil and industry; but the cause of that inadequate remuneration will be found in the increased number of persons forced into the market-place in quest of daily employment, in consequence of their being deprived of the resource of the potato garden and the mud hovel, in order to make room for the improvement of the land. The number of hands absolutely unemployed being thus increased, the price of labour will, of course, be kept down. Nor should it be omitted or disguised, that in proportion as these improvements shall become more general, the multitude of applicants for employment will still farther exceed the demand for their labour; and consequently their condition, if left entirely dependent upon the aid of the mere agriculturist, will be still more depressed, while the country is advancing in wealth and abundance.

"Such appear to be the inseparable concomitants of that transition which a considerable portion of the Irish peasantry are actually undergoing at present, and through which it is necessary, for the general good, that they shall all pass —a transition from the state of pauper tenants to that of independent labourers, maintained, as the same class are in England, by their daily labour. This change cannot much longer be delayed with safety. It is not possible to avoid it by any other alternative than that of permitting a state of society, pregnant with all the elements of disorder and confusion, to go on unchecked, until it forces the whole population down to the lowest depths of misery and degradation.

"The proprietors of estates claim public support in their endeavours to bring the country to a sound and secure condition, by opposing and counteracting the further progress of so ruinous a system; and if they would proceed in all cases with discretion, and a just consideration of those whose interests are as nearly concerned as their own, they are entitled to it. Of course we do not palliate the injustice and cruelty of turning families adrift helpless and unprotected upon the world. There is a compact, implied at least, between the landlord and the peasantry who have been brought up on his estate, by which the latter have as good a right to protection as the lord of the soil has to make arbitrary dispositions for the future management of his property. Nor do we think that it makes much difference as to the force of this obligation whether the injurious subdivision of lands was made by the direct sanction and for the immediate benefit of the tenant in fee, or by others to whom the power of a landlord over the property had been delegated by lease. It is not denied that those subdivisions were lawful at the time they were made. They were a part of the system then recognised and in operation for the management of property; for their effects, therefore, upon the general welfare and security, the property itself is justly to be held accountable. Nor is this responsibility to be shuffled aside, or laid at the door of persons who, having ceased to possess an interest in the lands, are no longer in a state to repair the error that has been committed; but the country will look to those who now hold the property, having received it charged with all its moral as well as its legal engagements.

"Still, however, as the landholders and owners of estates are really unable to sustain the whole of this liability, and to proceed at the same time with that work of improvement which is so essential for the interests of all classes of the community, and, eventually, of none more than of the labouring poor, it is much to be desired, as an object of public importance, that means may be speedily taken to distribute a part of the burden through other channels. If there were no other public ground for doing so it would be motive sufficient, that the suffering and privation which seem inevitable, during the transition of so vast a number of people from one state of living to another, would be thereby alleviated, and its period considerably abridged.

"Among the measures proposed for this purpose, that which appears to have obtained the most favourable share of the popular attention is the reclaiming of waste lands, such as bogs and mountains, of which there are millions of acres in Ireland very capable of improvement. No doubt a great deal of most useful improvements might be effected in this way; and what is more to our present purpose, a wide door might be thereby opened for the profitable employment of numbers of the peasantry; but much will depend on the regulating principle and the object of such undertakings, whether the people shall be set to work as daily labourers to divide and cultivate large tracts for the agricultural capitalist, or as colonists to reclaim and make rude settlements for themselves. If the latter be contemplated, it would, in effect, but spread and magnify the evil which it is proposed to remedy, only removing its pressure partially, and for a short period. As a measure of immediate relief, the change would be scarcely attended with any increase of comfort to the peasantry, while their position would be rendered far more hopeless than it is even now, and the ultimate consequences to society in its moral as well as in its political results would be most disastrous. An extensive reclamation of the waste lands, however, by the application of capital and intelligence, and upon a well-ordered system, would add most materially to the resources of the country, and besides affording the means of present employment to great numbers, assist in providing permanently and beneficially for them as paid labourers, on the land reclaimed through their exertions.

"Emigration is another project to which there can be no objection, except that of its insufficiency as a remedy for so wide-spread and multitudinous evils. It is impossible that emigration could be effected on so large a scale were the people themselves ever so anxious to embrace it, as wholly to remove the pressure of distress arising from the excess of the population over the means now available for their support. It can only be resorted to as a secondary relief, effectual as far as it goes, and therefore deserving of attention and encouragement; but it must always leave behind it so many destitute and unemployed, that the cares of the Legislature or the burdens of the country can experience no very sensible alleviation from its aid.

"The measure now before Parliament for the relief of the Irish poor,[1] is also relied on as a means of enabling the peasantry to buffet and overcome the difficulties of their present and impending position. It is not for us to canvass the merits or probable effects of that Bill. But we may observe, that an effective Poor Law must greatly assist the object we are considering; and it is therefore most desirable that its provisions should be carried into effect promptly and fully. It should be recollected, however, that the landed interest will be taxed heavily for the support of the poor under that Act; and it would therefore be a most auspicious introduction of so great a change in the social state of the country, if the pressure of that measure were lightened by the commencement of some works of great magnitude, which should last for a considerable time, and afford employment to large numbers of the people in various parts of Ireland. And if such undertakings were of a nature evidently calculated to open new avenues to laborious industry, and thus hold out a reasonable prospect of constant occupation, even after the period of their completion, the anxiety which, both on grounds of humanity and of policy, must attend the adoption of so great a change, would be allayed, and the most formidable of its immediate inconveniences be effectually obviated.

[1] The Irish Poor Law was passed in 1838.

"The works necessary for completing such a system of railways as our report contemplates, would serve both these purposes, by affording present employment to vast numbers of the people, and by throwing open resources and means of profitable occupation, which are now inaccessible and almost unknown. The immediate effect would be to afford extensive relief to the most indigent portion of the population, and that in a manner the most acceptable to their feelings, and the most conducive to their moral improvement. 'In all the views of Ireland placed before the Empire,' as Mr Stanley in a letter to Mr Nicholls well observes, 'there is a remarkable concurrence in attributing the poverty which exists to the want of continuous employment of the population.' To that want of continuous employment and of adequate remuneration when employed, may be traced the cause, not only of the poverty of the Irish people, but, in a great measure, also of that heedless improvidence, and of those habits of lassitude and indolence, which it may possibly require years of a better system to eradicate wholly from their character.

"The effect of these depressing circumstances, aggravated, of course, in a very high degree, by the backward state of agricultural knowledge and improvement, is strikingly illustrated in the deficiency of the produce of work performed by Irish labourers to that of the same class in England. The Irish Poor Law Commissioners state that the average produce of the soil in Ireland is not much above one half the average produce in England, whilst the number of labourers employed in agriculture is, in proportion to the quantity of land under cultivation, more than double, namely, as five to two; thus, ten labourers in Ireland raise only the same quantity of produce that two labourers raise in England, and this produce, too, is generally of an inferior quality. So striking a disproportion, though certainly admitting of very considerable qualification with reference to the different nature and degree of aid and facilities afforded to the labourers in the two countries, still shows a decided advantage in favour of the English workman, and fully confirms an observation which we have elsewhere made, as to the dearness of ill-requited labour.

"But the spirit of the Irish peasant is by no means so sunk by the adverse circumstances of his lot, as to be insensible to the stimulus which a due measure of encouragement to laborious industry supplies. Where employment is to be obtained without difficulty, and at a fair rate of compensation, his character and habits rise in an incredibly short space of time with the alteration of his circumstances. In a state of destitution no race of people are more patient and resigned. Their uncomplaining endurance seems almost to border on despondency. They make no effort to help themselves, probably because they despair of being able to do so effectually; and it ought to be mentioned to their honour that in such emergencies they have scarcely ever been known to extort by violence that relief which cannot be obtained from their own lawful exertions, or the benevolence of others. Their fortitude during the unparalleled sufferings of 1822 was regarded with the greatest admiration and respect; feelings which have not failed to be renewed by their conduct on every subsequent trial of a similar kind. Within the last two years, namely, in the summer of 1836, a populous district on the coast of Donegal was exposed to all the miseries of famine, rendered tenfold more agonising by the knowledge that there was food enough and to spare within a few miles; yet the poor people bore their hard lot with exemplary patience, and throughout the entire period, though numbers were actually without food, and reduced to eat sea-weed, there was no plundering of stores, no theft, nor secret pillage. Such forbearance, almost approaching to insensibility, might be deemed to belong to a character incapable of being roused to exertion in any circumstances; yet the same race, who endure the last extremes of want without a murmur, are no sooner placed in a condition of supporting themselves by independent industry, than they cast aside the torpor which distinguishes them in a depressed state, and become active, diligent, and laborious. The unsparing exertions and obliging disposition of the poor, half-starved harvestmen who periodically visit the west of England, are well known, and will, we are sure, be cheerfully acknowledged by all who have had occasion to employ them.

"The moral effect upon a people of a system of steady and remunerative employment is an object of public importance, not inferior to its influence upon their physical condition; for it is invariably found that where industry prevails, order and respect for the laws accompany it. Ireland forms no exception to this rule. The vice and the bane of its people is idleness. They have little to do; no useful or profitable occupation to devote their time and thoughts to; and hence those habits of intemperance, and that proneness to outrage and contention, which unhappily distinguish them. But those amongst them who have been for any considerable time engaged in pursuits which afford encouragement to industry, rarely trouble themselves about angry local differences, or frequent the resorts of low profligacy and dissipation. The hand of the thrifty and diligent is not often raised in fierce and clamorous dispute, or seen amid scenes of sectarian strife and rancour. These are vices which proceed from idleness and the habits engendered by it; nor can there be any reasonable ground to doubt that they would speedily disappear before the civilising power of occupation and successful industry.

"To afford the means of present employment to such a people, and, at the same time, lay the foundation of their future prosperity and improvement, is surely an object worthy of a wise and great nation, and will not be opposed from any narrow and short-sighted views of economy. The interests of these countries are so inseparably interwoven, that nothing which concerns one part of the United Kingdom can be alien from the rest. But it is the direct interest of Great Britain that Ireland should be raised, and that as speedily as possible, from its present condition. Mr Stanley shows, by a very moderate calculation, that if the Irish peasantry were placed, in point of comfort, on a par with those of Great Britain, the result to the public revenue would be an annual increase of six millions in the article of Excise. This consideration alone ought to silence any objections, on the ground of expense, against affording public aid, such as may be required for these works; for it gives assurance of an enormous profit on the greatest contemplated outlay.

"On prudential considerations alone, then, we should not hesitate to recommend an immediate and liberal attention to the claims of Ireland for assistance, which cannot be conferred in any shape more likely to prove beneficial than by encouraging public works of extensive and permanent utility. It is a waste of the public available resources to suffer so large a portion of the empire to lie fallow, or leave it to struggle, by slow advances and with defective means, towards its own improvement, when the judicious aid of the State might quickly make it a source of common strength and advantage.

"The policy of rendering such assistance is unquestionable. It is acknowledged to be necessary towards a colony, and must be considered more so in the case of a part of the United Kingdom, comprehended within its domestic boundaries, where neither the land nor the population can continue to be useless without being hurtful at the same time, and nearly in the same degree. Looking, therefore, at the proposition as a mere account or estimate of profit and loss, the balance is clearly in favour of a prompt and liberal encouragement on the part of the Legislature, to whatsoever tends manifestly to call into action the great powers and capabilities of this fine country. In every instance where such encouragement has been afforded, even in the construction of a common road, the returns to the State in improved revenue have hitherto more than repaid the public outlay; and, viewed in this light, public assistance, well directed and applied with judgment and economy, is in effect a beneficial expenditure of capital, similar in kind to that which a provident landlord makes for the improvement of his estate. The only measure of both should be the assurance of an adequate remuneration.

"It were easy to show, from the actual state of Ireland, that the moral results which may reasonably be expected to flow from an improvement of its social condition, should suffice, even in the low ground of concomitant financial advantages, to fix the attention of the Legislature to this subject. We need but refer to the burdensome and costly establishments of soldiery and police, which are necessarily maintained for the preservation of peace and order, and which, in a really wholesome state of society, might be greatly reduced.

"But there are other considerations equally important to the general welfare, and which it is more pleasing to dwell upon, as being more worthy of a great and enlightened nation—considerations of justice, of generosity—of a liberal concern for the improvement and civilisation of our countrymen. In attending to such considerations, no nation was ever faithless or blind to its own best and dearest interests; and were there no commercial advantages for England in the projects which we submit for adoption, nor any promise of actual benefit to the public treasury, or of relief from the heavy contributions which the unsettled state of society in Ireland annually extracts from it, yet the certainty of rendering this country prosperous, and diffusing the blessings of peace and industry, with their attendant fruits of knowledge and moral culture amongst its people, ought, as we have no doubt it would, be considered an ample recompence."

Generally, the Commission recommended the construction of railways by the State, and a motion was made by ministers to give effect to this recommendation.[1] But it was defeated by party and trade combinations. The Tories opposed the measure because it was introduced by the Whigs, and private speculators and projectors joined in the opposition, because they believed that a system of State railways would destroy their market. On the subject of Irish railways, as upon other subjects relating to Ireland, Drummond was before his time. The purchase of Irish railways by the State would now be hailed with delight by all classes of the community. But the proposal for State interference in 1838-39, raised as great a storm as the letter to the Tipperary magistrates.

The work on the Railway Commission taxed Drummond's strength severely, and his friends urged him to give up these extra duties; but he stood at his post to the end. Mrs Drummond saw how this labour told on her husband, and watched eagerly for the time when rest and change might be possible.

In June she wrote to her mother-in-law:—

[1] Lord Morpeth moved, on March 1, 1839: "That Her Majesty be enabled to authorise Exchequer Bills, to an amount not exceeding £2,500,000, to be made out by direction of the Lords Commissioners of the Treasury, and to be by them advanced for the construction of a railway or railways in Ireland, the sum so advanced being secured, and the interest and sinking fund to be secured on the profits of the works; the deficiency, if any, being provided for by an assessment on the several districts through which such railway or railways may be carried, or which may be benefited thereby."—Hansard, 3rd ser., vol. xlv., p. 1080.

"[KINGSTOWN], *June* 17, 1838.

"My husband is in Dublin railroadising, so I know not whether he will be able to write a scrap to-day. . . . The sea air has certainly done him good; but he is very thin and very much older in appearance than when you last saw him. The railroad business will, I trust, soon be over; but even his every-day official business occupies him from nine in the morning till a quarter to eight (our dinner hour); so that any extra work brought on by any investigation must either be done before nine in the morning, or in the evening after dinner. I often say that I might as well have no husband, for day after day often passes without more than a few words passing between us. Now, Dr Johnson has forbidden his working after dinner; but then he must read the newspapers. Our dinner is not over till half-past eight, and half-past ten or eleven is quite late enough for a man who is up before six. From last Monday until this morning—a week all but a day—he never even saw his baby, although in the same house with her. . . . He manages to get a peep at Mary for about five minutes every day almost, but he is on thorns even for these five minutes.

"MARIA DRUMMOND."

THE SAME TO THE SAME.

"[KINGSTOWN], *July* 1838.

"MY DEAR MOTHER,—You will be delighted to hear that the horrid railroad report is finished. I suppose that the Commissioners will be assailed with all sorts of abuse, as they bear rather hard on the private railroad companies.

"My husband has now only the usual routine of the office business, which is quite enough to wear anybody down; but he says that he shall try and take it more quietly. He still goes into Dublin at a quarter before nine in the morning; he gets to town by the railroad. Now and then I hope we may be able to get a walk on the pier together in the evening. By your letter I imagine you take rather too serious a view of my husband's illness. A little excitement does him a great deal of good: and when by some chance he gets a few minutes' romping with that little wild gipsy Mary, he is always better. When Lord Morpeth comes we talk of taking a fortnight or three weeks' excursion to Killarney, but of course my husband cannot stir till he comes. What seems to tire and harass him most is the constant wearying petty details of office business. It is certainly the most laborious situation under Government.

"He is decidedly better. His digestion seems stronger, and he sleeps better. Whenever he comes home I take care to prevent, as much as possible, any allusion to public matters, and I try to interest him in any other subject. . . . With kind love from all to all, believe me, ever yours affectionately,

"MARIA DRUMMOND."

It was Drummond's lot always to have his hands full. Duties succeeded duties in rapid succession, and with ever-changing variety. Before the railway report had been completely disposed of, the Under Secretary's attention was turned to Ulster. The July celebrations of the Orange party were at hand, and had to be dealt with.

We have seen how, in July 1836, Drummond had sent a force of twelve and a-half troops of cavalry and thirty-four companies of infantry, under the direction of thirty-three stipendiary magistrates, to keep the peace in Ulster. A lesser force was now sufficient; nine troops of cavalry and five companies of infantry, under sixteen magistrates, were enough. An order sent by Drummond at this time deserves to be quoted as illustrating the vigour and directness with which he always acted. It was supposed that an Orange procession would take place at Kingscourt on July 12. Captain Despard, a magistrate, was stationed there with a force of cavalry and infantry to prevent disturbance in the vicinity. But suddenly intelligence reached the head constable of police to the effect that the Orangemen had changed their plans, and were resolved to march through Bailieborough instead of Kingscourt. The head constable immediately asked Captain Despard to move his forces to Bailieborough, but Despard refused, saying his instructions were to remain at Kingscourt—a stupid interpretation of his orders. The head constable at once wrote to Drummond:—

"KINGSCOURT, *July* 9, 1838.

"Mr Despard informs me that by his instructions he cannot leave this town on the 12th, and that I must look to Mr Little at Cavan, a distance, I believe, of 18 miles, which will place me in a very awkward position."

Drummond replied promptly:—

"DUBLIN CASTLE, *July* 10, 1838.

"*Immediate.*

"*Send Copy to Capt. Despard.*

"Captain Despard's instructions by no means confine him to the town in which he is stationed; on the contrary, his attention must always be given to the neighbourhood, and if he finds that his services are more required in any other part than at his station, he is to proceed to it. This is one of the principal objects in sending cavalry, and in authorising the employment of cars for the rapid transportation of constabulary. If Captain Despard should learn that Bailieborough, or Ballyjamesduff, or any place in the vicinity is more likely to be disturbed by processions than Kingscourt, he will take his measures accordingly."

"T. DRUMMOND."

"Let this be posted to-day."

This letter woke up Despard; it was quickly acted upon; and the Orangemen found themselves confronted by cavalry and infantry wherever they went. In the result the peace was kept.

In September Drummond at length yielded to the entreaties of his friends, and, pressed by his medical adviser, went abroad with his wife for a short holiday. But even then he was not allowed, nor apparently willing to free himself from Irish affairs.

De Beaumont, who was finishing his book on Ireland, kept up constant communication with the ever obliging and ever ready secretary. Drummond wrote him a helpful letter from Mannheim; and on September 19 De Beaumont replied.

De Beaumont to Drummond.

"Chateau de la Grange,
"*September* 19, 1838.

"My Dear Sir,—I hasten to answer your letter, dated Mannheim, which has arrived this very moment. First, I wish to tell you at once that I have received the important document which you sent me through the English Embassy, which has been more obliging than the French Embassy.

"Among the precious collection of documents which you send me, I find your pleasant and interesting letter from which I gained so many good ideas and useful information, for which I thank you greatly. . . .

"We can hardly imagine how, in the middle of your work and when starting on your journey, it was possible for you to give me so much time. I admire sincerely your faculty of doing so many things at once, and am profoundly grateful for so much kindness.

"Now, then, thanks to the light you have given me, and to your extreme kindness, which I shall never forget, I am in possession of documents sufficient to explain the complicated mechanism of your Government. If I do not succeed it will be my fault and not that of my enlightened friends, who have so generously lent me their assistance.

"I much fear that I may fail in my enterprise, for the task is singularly difficult; but I can say that at least I neglect no effort to do well, and I ardently desire to present a faithful and sincere view of the social and political state of Ireland, as well as of the political question to which that situation gives rise both in Ireland and in England.

"Certainly, if I can succeed, I shall be thoroughly repaid for my labours, and if I obtain your approval as well as that of some men whom in my journey to Ireland I have learnt both to love and to esteem, I shall receive the pleasantest recompence at which I can aim.

"My work goes on apace. In the last month I have finished several important chapters, among which are those entitled, 'The Association,' 'O'Connell,' 'The Catholic Clergy,' 'The Middle Classes,' and 'The Parties;' and I have now arrived at the 'Conclusion,' that is, the examination of the two final questions—What ought to be done? and (2) What ought and can England do?

"The private information which you give me on the spirit and progress of the Central Executive in Ireland have been a great help to me in appreciating the true character of the Whig Administration. I have, however, taken great care to make no ill use of what is confidential, and I have availed myself of the answer to the magistrates of Tipperary without making it public. I still hope that in two months I may approach the end. You may guess, my dear Sir, with what eagerness I shall send you my work as soon as it is printed—you to whom I owe so much.

"But enough of Ireland. You have been away a month—happy in escaping the burden of public affairs for a few moments, and here I am writing two pages to bring you back to it.—Your grateful and affectionate

"GUSTAVE DE BEAUMONT."

THE SAME TO THE SAME.

"CHATEAU DE LA GRANGE,
"*October* 14, 1838.

"MY DEAR SIR,—I profit by the occasion which offers itself to recall myself to your kind memory.

"Mr Daniel O'Connor, my friend and neighbour in the country, son of General Arthur O'Connor, whom you must certainly know by reputation, has been passing two days with us at the Grange, and tells me that he is just about to go to Ireland, whither he is called by private business. I will therefore beg him to take these few words for you.

"I duly received your letter from Mannheim, and I trust that that which I wrote to you to Munich reached you. In it I gave you a thousand thanks for all the kindnesses you have showered on me, and the immense services you have rendered me. . . .

"Thanks to all your good introductions, I work, if not well, at least much, and I see that my work is getting on pretty well, so that I am sure of finishing it this year. At this moment I am engaged on a chapter in which I undertake to explain what the Whigs are doing and can do for Ireland, and I arrive at the conclusion that the Whigs are carrying out, and have carried out, considerable reforms in Ireland, although they seem to me placed by English passion and English interests, under the impossibility of doing all that the interests of Ireland require. I assure you that it is very pleasant to be able, in my modest sphere of an obscure writer, to render justice to all that is genuine and elevated in the administration of Lord Mulgrave, whose right arm you have been for three years.

Moreover, disinterested as I am in the questions of policy, I bring to it views which are quite free from a spirit of party. My judgment is, as much as possible, that of a philosopher, and I try to put aside passions of the moment to look at the future. I wish, above all, not to make a book for the present occasion only.

"I shall wait your judgment with much impatience and anxiety, but we have not got to that point, and, unfortunately for me, I have great difficulties to get over before I finish.

"Mr Daniel O'Connor takes charge all the more willingly of my letter to you, because he is anxious to make your acquaintance and that of Mrs Drummond. He will be some time in Dublin this winter, and though he is half Irish, he knows fewer people in Ireland than in France. His mother is the daughter of the celebrated French philosopher Condorcet. His relations are people of very good society in Paris, and I venture, dear Sir, to recommend him to you.

"Pray give my best compliments and those of Madame de Beaumont to Mrs Drummond, and, believe me, your grateful and affectionate

"GUSTAVE DE BEAUMONT."

"*P.S.*—I saw in the *Dublin Evening Post* the publication of your famous answer to the magistrates of Tipperary. . . . This letter does you great honour."

In November Drummond was again at Dublin Castle. But his holiday had done little to restore him to health. Prior to his return from the Continent, his mother had urged him to fling up the Irish office altogether, and seek prolonged rest. He replied: "If on my return I feel the work oppressive, I shall give the office up. But I do not anticipate anything like the labour I have had. Things are now better organised." Things were indeed "better organised," but Drummond's "labour" was not ended. He had yet to pass through the most trying year of his whole administration. At the beginning of 1839, the Tory Orange party opened fire on the Government, and the attack was sustained to the day of Drummond's death. When the battle had once commenced it was hopeless to expect that Drummond would leave the field. He stood his ground manfully, repelling assault after assault with a vigour and success that astonished his friends; but the constant strain exhausted him. He died at his post.

CHAPTER XI.

1839.

ON the first of January 1839, Lord Norbury, the son of the notorious judge, was shot while speaking to his steward in his own demesne. The bullet pierced the left breast, and the unfortunate nobleman died on January 3. The assassin escaped, and was never brought to justice. To this day the affair is shrouded in mystery. Lord Norbury was not an unpopular man. He took no part in politics. He does not seem to have had any quarrels with his tenantry; and there is no proof that the murder was agrarian.[1] Yet the landlord party seized the opportunity given by this tragical affair to denounce Drummond, and assail the Government. The murder of Lord Norbury, they declared, was the direct result of the letter to the Tipperary magistrates. On January 10 a meeting of landlords was held at Tullamore, and these resolutions were passed :—

"1. That it appears to this meeting that the answer conveyed to the magistrates of Tipperary by Mr Under Secretary Drummond, has had the unfortunate effect of increasing the animosities entertained against the owners of the soil, and has emboldened the disturbers of the public peace.

"2. That finding from the circumstances mentioned in the former resolution, that there is little room to hope for a

[1] Lord Normanby said in the House of Lords on March 21, 1839, "I must say as yet there is no evidence that the crime was the result of any extensive conspiracy. Like the murder of Mr Wayland and others, I believe it arose out of a local conspiracy connected with the possession of land." But evidence was never given to prove this.

successful appeal to the Irish Executive, we feel it a duty to appeal to the people of England, the Legislature, and the throne for protection."

The *Times* denounced Drummond with even more directness. Writing on January 15, it said:—

"A meeting of the Lord Lieutenant and magistrates of the King's County has been held to pass resolutions expressive of the sense entertained by the magistracy of the horrible crime which has been committed [the murder of Lord Norbury],—declaratory of their anxious willingness to co-operate with the Executive Government in whatever efforts it might be induced to make for detecting the murderers, and bring them to condign punishment—acknowledging, however, their strong reprobation of the insolence displayed by Mr Drummond, Under Secretary, at the Castle, in his treatment on a former occasion of the Tipperary magistrates, when, instead of heartily assisting them to discover and punish the authors of murderous atrocities perpetrated within their county, and to preserve the peace thereof, this Jack-in-office had taken upon himself to lecture the vast body of its landed proprietors in the discharge of their duties as landlords, and to more than insinuate that all the evils they complained of had been caused by their own misconduct."

Writing again on January 25, it added:—

"Mr Drummond's famous letter to the magistrates of the county Tipperary had the merit of holding up [the landlords] to the popish multitude as offenders against the most important obligations of society, and as justly amenable to whatever punishment or persecution the vengeance of that multitude might dictate. Whatever acts of violence or outrage—whatever attacks on life or dwelling—whatever robberies or ferocious murders have been perpetrated since the publication of that letter, it is not too much to say, have been abetted, encouraged, and stimulated by its abuse of the country gentlemen, under the eyes of the peasantry, who were thus vindicated *ex cathedrâ* in their lawless conduct, as being no more than a righteous retaliation for the wrongs inflicted on them. It remains to be seen whether Mr Drummond's letter may not have had its influence in the propagation throughout the Queen's County of that diabolical spirit out of which arose Lord Norbury's lamentable murder."

The campaign thus opened was carried on with vigour. On March 7, Shaw (Dublin University) attacked the Government in the Commons. He moved for a return of the crimes and outrages committed in Ireland since the beginning of the administration. His speech was pitched in the ever familiar Ascendancy key. Popery and agitation were the curse of Ireland. Both were encouraged by the Government. Papists were appointed to the foremost places, and the arch-agitator O'Connell was the confidant of ministers. The Under Secretary instead of putting down crime, lectured the landlords, and showed sympathy with the disturbers of the public peace. Of course crime and outrage increased; disloyalty was rampant; Protestantism insulted and betrayed. It was time for the English people to end this condition of things, to save their loyal and Christian brethren in Ireland. The work could only be done by hurling the ministry of Lord Melbourne from power.

Emerson Tennent, Colonel Conolly, and Mr Litton, all good and true Ascendancy men, supported Shaw. The Pope, O'Connell, and Drummond formed the staple of their speeches. If all three could be got rid of, Ireland would be a happy land.

Morpeth led the defence, and was followed by O'Connell in one of those stirring speeches which threw the House into a ferment. Morpeth produced statistics proving that, far from increasing, crime and outrage had steadily diminished. Political agitation had ceased; and at no time had the people shown such a loyal feeling towards England. He ridiculed the notion that Drummond's letter to the Tipperary magistrates had encouraged outrages. Landlords were shot in Ireland before Drummond had ever put a foot in the country; and it was notorious that "disputes as to the tenure of land were at the bottom of almost all the graver forms of outrage which infest the soil, and blight the social system in Ireland." Drummond had given the landlords some wholesome advice. Would it be contended that they did not need it? Let the House listen to this return.

"Gross number of ejectments brought in the Superior Courts, Dublin, in the following years in the counties named:—

"Tipperary—In 1833, 117; in 1834, 195; in 1835, 175; in 1836, 205; in 1837, 100; in 1838, 90—total, 882.

"Carlow—In 1833, 33; in 1834, 40; in 1835, 61; in 1836, 17; in 1837, 18; in 1838, 12—total, 191.

"Longford—In 1833, 30; in 1834, 23; in 1835, 36; in 1836, 48; in 1837, 24; in 1838, 11—total, 172; besides 330 from Quarter Sessions Court.

"Queen's County—In 1833, 45; in 1834, 37; in 1835, 32; in 1836, 42; in 1837, 37; in 1838, 20—total, 213.

"King's County—In 1833, 28; in 1834, 22; in 1835, 42; in 1836, 31; in 1837, 17; in 1838, 16—total, 156.

"Sligo—In 1833, 33; in 1834, 36; in 1835, 34; in 1836, 43; in 1837, 21; in 1838, 13—total, 180.

"Westmeath—In 1833, 42; in 1834, 37; in 1835, 47; in 1836, 44; in 1837, 18; in 1838, 12—total, 200.

"In this return the House might take the average of families at four in each case, and the average individuals in each family at five. That was about twenty persons turned out in each case of ejectment. . There were proceedings which, while the condition of Ireland continued to be what it long had been—nay, more, while human nature was what it was—would beget resistance. There were sufferings which would defy endurance. 'The flesh will quiver where the pincers tear.'"

No amount of denunciation, Morpeth urged, would make the Government swerve from the course on which they had entered. They would do justice to the Irish people, they would uphold the law, they would put down crime, but they would not "withdraw their deliberate opinion that 'property had its duties as well as its rights.' Nay more, I feel constrained from a knowledge of the past history, as well as of the present circumstances of Ireland, to impress it more and more, with even a more deliberate warning on all without exception."

O'Connell, who sat calmly under the denunciations showered upon him by the Orange faction, at length rose. He said :—

"There is a feature in this debate which ought to be remembered. Speeches have been made by four gentlemen,[1] natives of Ireland, who, it would appear, came here for the sole purpose of vilifying their native land. (Oh! oh!) Yes, of vilifying their native land, and endeavouring to prove that it is the worst and most criminal country on the face of the earth. (Oh! oh!) Yes, you came here to calumniate the country that gave you birth. It is said that there are some soils which produce venomous and crawling creatures—things odious and disgusting. (Ironical Orange cheers.) Yes, you who cheer—that you are—can you deny it? are you not calumniators? (Oh! oh!) Oh! you hiss, but you cannot sting. I rejoice in my native land. I rejoice that I was born in it. I rejoice that I belong to it. Your calumnies cannot diminish my regard for it; your malevolence cannot blacken it in my esteem; and although your vices and crimes have driven its people to

[1] Shaw, Tennent, Conolly, Litton.

outrage and murder. (Order, order.) Yes, I say your vices and crimes. (Order, order, chair, chair.) Well, then, the crimes of men like you have produced these results. (Oh! oh!)

"The learned Recorder (Shaw) has told us the number of murders which have lately taken place in Ireland, but the number given by the learned Recorder is fourteen since the 16th of November; but if the learned gentleman had called our attention to England, he will find that there have been twenty-five since the same date, leaving no less than eleven to the credit of Ireland; and yet no English member has risen and said, 'What an abominable country mine is, what shocking people are the people of England.' Besides these murders, however, there have been two cases of supposed murder, that is, where bodies have been found in a mutilated state. There have been thirteen distinct attempts to commit great personal violence, and there have been twenty incendiary fires, one of which, by the way, was at Shaw, in Berkshire. (Laughter.) The learned Recorder in his list cannot enumerate a single incendiary fire. I have calculated the number of crimes in England of the greatest enormity,—those which have been punished with imprisonment above six months,—and I find that the number in Great Britain is 6259, while the total number in Ireland is only 2577, though the population in Ireland is within a third as much as the population in England. Notwithstanding these facts Ireland is to receive abuse, and above all, the abuse of her own children.

"The Government had been attacked because it had been weak enough, unjust enough, forsooth, to show some sympathy and pity for the wretched multitudes who had been subjected to the horrors of summary ejectments; because they had betrayed some feeling towards the decrepit father, the aged mother, and the helpless children who, driven from the warmth of their homes, were left to perish in ditches. Yes, the Government had dared to pity them; had dared to say, that the Irish landlords had duties to perform as well as rights to enforce. That was the whole ground of complaint. A matter of this kind marks distinctly the character of the people who complained. They said, 'we will not be told that we have duties to perform, we have nothing but rights.' Did any man ever hear such a complaint made gravely? Yet it had been made repeatedly. The hon. and learned gentleman (Litton) made it the chief topic of his speech, he insisted upon it with emphasis, he advanced it with all the powers of his oratory, and claimed the attention of the House to it with many a blow upon the box. (Laughter.) I trembled for the box, as with uplifted hand and indignant voice the hon. and learned member exclaimed, 'Behold the wrongs of Ireland! an excited multitude is told by the Government that the landlords have duties to perform as well as rights to enforce.'

"It was said that the Government had distinguished none but agitators, had given to none but agitators the emoluments of place, nay, it was said that they had abused the seat of justice, and placed none but agitators on the bench. Was Sergeant Ball an agitator? Was Mr Woulfe an agitator? Was Sir Michael O'Loghlen an agitator? These were the last appointments made by the Government,—appointments which the hon. and learned member for Bandon (Sergeant Jackson), had done everything in his power to prevent, as if he were not an agitator himself. It was also said that the system of abolishing peremptory challenges adopted by the Government has led to miscarriages of justice. Was this true? The Government had followed the English practice, and no man was now set aside on a jury panel on account of his religion, or on account of his political opinions. What has been the result? Has a single case failed? On the trials of the late Special Commission there were seven Catholics and five Protestants on each jury, and yet there had been convictions.

"This motion was a trick, a party trick to prejudice England in favour of that faction which had so long oppressed and trampled upon Ireland—foul and malignant murderers—stained by blood and dishonoured by the breach of treaties; for three hundred years making religion the pretext for their crimes, and now again enlisting the sacred name of religion against right and justice."

After O'Connell's speech, all interest in the debate flagged, and an attempt to prolong the discussion for a second night ended in a "count out" on March 11.

After the debate, Drummond wrote to his mother:—

"The debate on Shaw's motion will show you the cause of my having been so much occupied of late. . . . Lord Morpeth made an admirable speech, . . . and you will perceive that he was well supplied with ammunition. It takes no small time, and gives no small trouble, however, to collect it. Lord Roden has just given notice of a similar attack in the Lords, and now a fresh demand comes from Lord Normanby. These men, Roden and Shaw, &c., keep us busy enough; but I am in hopes we shall sail more quietly after these squalls."

On March 21, Lord Roden moved for a Select Committee "to inquire into the state of Ireland since 1835, in respect of crime and outrage, which have rendered life and property insecure in that part of the empire." His Lordship's speech was a feeble echo of the Ascendancy orations in the Commons. Indeed, it consisted chiefly of phrases and catchwords, with which the students of Irish history are familiar. "Life and property were insecure;" "civil and religious liberty" was imperilled; "the country was governed under the tyranny [of agitators];" "crime [existed] in the most frightful and repulsive forms;" "the laws of England were paralysed, the laws of Rome" alone obeyed; "the great object" of the agitators and demagogues who were corrupting the people was "the annihilation of the Protestant faith." He "entreated their Lordships" to interpose "in the interests of the empire." "It was impossible to separate the interests of England from those of Ireland, so closely were they united; and even while he was addressing their Lordships, Ireland was the battlefield of the empire for the Protestant establishment."

Mulgrave, now Marquis of Normanby, replied. He had ceased to be Lord Lieutenant, and was succeeded in the office by Lord Ebrington, afterwards Earl Fortescue. However, he now took upon himself the defence of the Irish administration. He was responsible for it; he was ready to vindicate it. Roden had said that the country was in a state of "unparalleled" disorder. Normanby proved that it was in a state of "unparalleled" tranquillity. Reviewing the social history of Ireland for twenty years previous to his administration, and showing the disorder and anarchy which prevailed during that period, he continued:—

"Let me now contrast with this picture the state of some of the counties to which I have adverted in the years 1836 and 1837, and see what the same class of testimony proves with regard to them.

"1836—In Down, the Chief Justice congratulated the Grand Jury on the extreme lightness of the calendar. In Louth, Chief Baron Joy said it gave him great satisfaction to observe that the calendar at the present assizes was very small when compared with former years. In Waterford, Chief Justice Bushe remarked on the extreme lightness of the calendar. In Kilkenny, Baron Pennefather congratulated the county on the lightness of the calendar, which contrasted happily with the former ones. In the Queen's County, Judge Johnson congratulated the county on the extreme lightness of the calendar, and said some of the principal cases were adjourned from the last assizes. In Wexford, Judge Johnson congratulated the county on the state of the calendar—very few cases. At Fermanagh, Baron Pennefather congratulated the county on the pleasing appearance of the calendar. In Limerick, Judge Perrin congratulated the Grand Jury on the reduced state of the calendar, which was evidence of the peaceable state of the county. In Kildare, Judge Johnson complimented the Grand Jury on the lightness of the calendar. In Sligo, Judge Burton remarked on the lightness of the calendar; and in Clare, Baron Foster said he was happy to congratulate them upon the great diminution of crime that had taken place in the county, compared with former years. In Carlow, Baron Smith remarked on the lightness of the calendar. In Wexford, Baron Pennefather said he was happy to inform them that there was little to be done; he was really surprised to see a county of such extent so free from crime.

"1837—In Fermanagh, Chief Justice Bushe said the calendar was only of ordinary description. In the Queen's County, Baron Pennefather said, there is nothing on the face of the calendar which requires observation. In Cork, Sergeant Greene said, there is nothing in the calendar requiring observation. In Roscommon, Judge Burton said he saw nothing in the calendar that could make him think that the county did not enjoy the utmost tranquillity. In Leitrim, Judge Perrin remarked on the lightness of the calendar. In Kerry, Baron Richards said, the calendar was swelled with minor offences that should be tried at sessions. In Down, Judge Torrens said, the offences on the calendar are of such a nature as must occur from the extent of the county. In Louth, Chief Baron Joy told the Grand Jury that the criminal business would be very light. . . In Limerick, Sergeant Greene said the calendar was unusually light, containing no crime worthy of comment. In Wexford, King's County, and Kilkenny, Judges Johnson and Foster severally remarked on the lightness of the calendar. In Armagh, Chief Baron Joy said the calendar contained the smallest number of cases he ever saw. In Kerry, there were only thirty-four persons for trial. In Donegal, Baron Pennefather congratulated them on the lightness of the calendar; and in Monaghan, Judge Burton did the same.

"1838—*Spring Assizes.*—In Meath, there was but little civil or criminal business. In Wexford, there were but twenty-two prisoners for trial, and all were minor offences except two; and Baron Foster, in addressing the Grand Jury, said there were no cases that required any observation from him. In Louth, Judge Burton, in addressing the jury, said he was happy to state, from the appearance of the cases on the calendar, it would not be necessary for him to make any lengthened observations, and give them any particular directions. The number of cases was not large: the crimes were not of a serious character; they were such as might be expected in a densely-populated county such as Louth. At Limerick, Sergeant Greene said he was happy to have it in his power to repeat the congratulation which at the last assizes he offered upon the state of the calendar; the offences were neither numerous nor of a serious character. At Cavan, Judge Torrens congratulated the jury on the state of the calendar. In Kilkenny, the number of prisoners for trial amounted only to twenty-eight: eleven of the number were bailable offences; and this the quantum of crime in a population amounting to 200,000: in the county the calendar used to exceed considerably 100. In Kilkenny County, Baron Foster congratulated the jury on the lightness of the calendar, and said it formed a great contrast with former calendars in the county. In Waterford County and City, Baron Foster and Judge Moore congratulated the juries on the lightness of the calendars.

"1838—*Summer Assizes.*—In Wicklow there were but eighteen prisoners on the calendar, and Judge Moore said the extremely peaceful state of the county spoke so well both for the higher and lower classes in the county. In Louth, Judge Burton said the state of the calendar rendered any observations unnecessary. In Kilkenny, Judge Crampton said he was happy to find that his labour would be light. In Clare, Baron Richards congratulated the jury on the lightness of the calendar. In Roscommon, Judge Perrin said, 'It is with great satisfaction I feel myself called upon to congratulate you on the peaceable and tranquil state of your great and populous county;' and in Leitrim, Sergeant Greene said he took occasion to express his great pleasure at witnessing the very light state of the calendar. In the county of Cork, Baron Richards observed that he had great pleasure in offering his congratulations on the unprecedentedly light state of the calendar; it ought to give the county great pride. In May, Sergeant Greene said, that although there were many cases on the calendar, still, with a few exceptions, they were not of a heinous character; and at Enniskillen, County Fermanagh, Baron Pennefather said, 'I have to congratulate you on the appearance which your county presents; not only by the calendar, which is light, but by its general tranquillity.' While in Galway, Judge Perrin said, with the exception of two or three heavy cases, standing over from last assizes, there was nothing to call for any particular observation, and nothing that might not be expected in so extensive and populous a county. Sergeant Greene addressed similar observations to the Grand Jury of the town. At Armagh, Judge Burton said, from an examination of the calendar, the business would not be heavy or protracted. In Londonderry, Mr Justice Torrens said, 'I have pleasure in again congratulating you, and communicating that the calendar is excessively light. In fact, at every successive assizes I find crime decreasing, and tranquillity becoming established in your county.'

"These, my Lords, were the opinions of the judges, giving the impression on their minds at the time, by a recent examination of all the commitments; and if your Lordships are to go into a Committee, what further evidence can you produce to set against this testimony to the improvement of the country within the last three years?

"On another point, I have been frequently accused of a disposition to appoint exclusively Catholics, to the prejudice of Protestants. Mind, in the list I read in answer, I do not claim any merit in the proportions in which they appear, any further than as it is an answer to an unjust charge. Of judges and assistant barristers, I have appointed 8 Protestants, 6 Catholics; of the higher appointments of the constabulary, 69 Protestants, 37 Catholics; of promotions in that force, 27 Protestants, 8 Roman Catholics. The disproportion here is greater from there having been fewer officers of long standing Catholics. Of legal and other appointments in the courts and offices in Dublin—Protestants 40, Catholics 37

"The noble Earl (Roden) has alluded to certain phrases used by Mr O'Connell at some meetings of the Precursors' Society. Now, the noble Earl has not always been very guarded in his own language, or very cautious as to his companions. In the year 1831, at a meeting in the county of Down, the noble Earl in the chair, a Mr Cromelin talked of the time being come to drive the Papists from the land. Again, in 1834, in a letter to the Protestants of Ulster, the noble Earl said that he knew their strength, their moral courage, and their numbers, and that the time might come when these might be important.

"My Lords, it has been my lot to live on terms of intimacy and friendship with many of your Lordships to whom I am politically opposed. I will not affect to be indifferent to your good opinion. It is more than probable I may have often erred. No one can be more sincerely aware of his manifold personal deficiencies. But even to secure your Lordships' approbation, or to avert your sentence, I would not change or modify the intention and tendency of any one act during my administration in Ireland. My conduct of affairs in that country is now the question at issue. Whatever this night's result may be, your Lordship's decision cannot deprive me of the affections of a long-suffering, warm-hearted people, nor of that which I alone value more —the approval of my own conscience."

All attempts to answer Normanby's speech failed hopelessly. Nevertheless Roden's motion was carried, though by a narrow majority.

Content, .	63
Non-content,	58
Majority,	5

Defeated in the Lords, Lord John Russell resolved to give battle to the Tory-Orange party in the Commons. On April 15 he moved—"That it is expedient to persevere in those principles which have guided the Executive Government of Ireland of late years, and which have tended to the effectual administration of the law, and the general improvement of that part of the United Kingdom."

Apropos of this motion, Drummond wrote to his mother on March 24:—

"The debate in the Lords, and the subsequent notice by Lord John Russell, will show you that the existence of the Irish Government is in peril, and that it is to be fairly and fully tried in the House of Commons immediately after the Easter holidays. I am glad of this. It will either confirm our friends, or put an end to an Administration which cannot be conducted usefully subject to the control of the Lords."

The day before Russell's motion came on—April 14—Drummond wrote again to his mother:—

"Our meeting[1] has gone off admirably, and has produced a strong sensation. It will have its effect on the other side. There has not been such a reunion of all classes of reformers—nobles, gentry, merchants, and shopkeepers here for years.

"The Orangemen attempted some little interruption, but they were crushed, and their presence gave vivacity to the meeting and energy to the speakers. . . . We now wait the result of Monday's discussion, having done our part well. It was no small matter getting the Duke of Leinster to preside. He had declared that he would never meet O'Connell at a public meeting for political purposes. I had some share in getting all this managed. I got Charlemont to go down and dine with the Duke, and then propose to him to take the chair. This succeeded. The next consideration was where to get a room large enough, and I proposed the Theatre. The objection was, not having sufficient daylight, but this was met by proposing to have the usual gaslight. . . . My new master [Lord Ebrington] goes on very well. He is an excellent man, very different in manner from Lord Normanby, of a much graver cast, and the ladies will miss the gaiety of the Normanby Court; but the course of policy will be as firmly and inflexibly followed as before."

On April 15 Russell brought forward his motion. The House of Lords, he said, had practically passed a vote of censure on the Government. He would ask the House of Commons to reverse that vote. The Government had been charged with "favouring outrage, and almost encouraging murder." Would the House of Commons find them

[1] A public meeting in Dublin convened to support the Government.

guilty? That was the issue which he raised. Let them try it. He was there to defend the Irish policy of the Government in principle and detail. He was there to avow the determination of Ministers to persevere in that policy whatever might befall. It was said that crime and outrage had increased, but no man had attempted to disprove the statistics which demonstrated the fact that crime and outrage had enormously diminished. Ireland was not wholly free from crime and outrage. Nobody said that. Was England? But the crimes of the Irish people sprang from their miseries. Men were shocked, forsooth, because the Under Secretary had said, "Property has its duties as well as its rights." Was the warning unnecessary? Did they not know that the eviction system was the disgrace of Ireland? "I am not referring to what was done in former days; I am not referring to the year 1775, but to that of 1837, up to the April of which these ejectments have been continued. At that time persons were driven from their homes by means of a large military force, by means of infantry, cavalry, police, although no resistance of any kind was offered. Any Government that exists in Ireland has to deal with the outrages that may be produced by persons of this kind being left to starve, the landlords merely providing for them for a few weeks, or at most for two or three months, after which period their existence is left wholly uncared for. Tell me not, then, that in 1839, or in any period that has elapsed from 1835 to 1839, or at any period of those four years, we could remedy the evils that were so deeply rooted." Constant misgovernment had produced the evils from which Ireland suffered. England had oppressed Ireland when she was able; she conciliated when she could not help it. That had been the case in the past. Her Majesty's Government had sought to establish a new order of things in the future. For this they were assailed. But they would not flinch.

They had come into office to do justice to Ireland. They might fail, but they would not change their policy. They might be driven from the positions they had taken up; but they would defend those positions to the last.

"At present I have only to consider, that although a majority of this House may approve of our Irish policy, yet that the present Government may have run its course, and that another Government may succeed it. Sir, I may think the consequences to Ireland will be dangerous; I may think the consequences to the empire very doubtful; but, personally, as regards ourselves, I think we shall have no reason to regret that result. We repent not of the measures that we have proposed; we have no inclination to give way to the measures which we thought it our duty to resist. It will be a consolation to us on the dissolution of the Ministry that, with regard to the affairs which I have this night brought under your consideration, that, with regard to these affairs of Ireland, we have endeavoured to introduce a friendly relation between this country and that part of the United Kingdom; and that in so doing we have been ready to encounter any opposition, to incur the loss of much strength, and of some popularity in this part of the United Kingom; that we have been ready to endeavour to unite by affection, to unite by feelings of good-will and love, the people of this country and the people of Ireland; to make the whole United Kingdom stronger against all its enemies; to found the Government of Ireland, as the Government of England has long been founded, upon opinion, upon affection, upon good-will; and that if the Ministry should fall, it will fall in an attempt to knit together the hearts of Her Majesty's subjects."

Peel replied in a moderate, but singularly ineffective, speech. He would not, he said, censure the Government, but he would not approve of all they had done. The House of Lords was quite within its right in appointing a

Select Committee to inquire into the state of Ireland. How would the Government be injured by the work of this Committee? If crime had decreased, the fact would be proved before the Committee, and the position of the Government strengthened. He hoped the noble Lord (Russell) would not persevere in his motion. It could lead to no practical result. He (Peel) was perfectly ready to give the Government every fair play in the administration of Ireland. He had the interests of that country as much at heart as any man in the House.

Stanley took the same line, but rather shocked the Orange members by approving of some of the recent Government appointments. In fact, he took credit to himself for having, when in office, promoted certain barristers whom the Ministry had since placed on the bench. He ridiculed the notion that the present Government was the first that had made Catholic appointments. Why, he himself was constantly in favour of Catholic appointments. He had made O'Loghlen a sergeant, and given Woulfe a silk gown. He was as much in favour of justice to Ireland as any man.

Sir R. Bateson said agitation was the bane of Ireland; and "the authors of this agitation were responsible for the violence and bloodshed which they had caused."

Smith O'Brien defended the Government, and censured the landlords. "I will say in justice to my countrymen, that when they were kindly treated there was not a more grateful or attached people on the face of the earth. Certainly they suffer from various oppressions. The manner in which high rents are exacted, and ejectments enforced, is particularly exasperating. Many wretched people were annually expelled from their holdings, and then having no place to go to, and no means to subsist on, they lived for a while on the charity of their neighbours, and erected huts by the ditch sides, where they in many cases perished by fever or famine." He approved of the policy of the Government in every particular. The Government were seeking to make a real union between England and Ireland; and the "time is now come to decide whether the people of Ireland will be admitted to a perfect union, or whether there shall be no union at all."

Morpeth demolished the position taken up by Peel and Stanley in a rattling speech—one of the best delivered during the debate. Peel urged Russell to withdraw his motion; Morpeth emphatically said "No." Ministers had been attacked again and again in desultory warfare. But they now had their enemies in the open field, and would fight the battle to the bitter end.

"Whatever be the aim or object of the recent demonstration on the part of the House of Lords—whether it be, according to the turn which it now seems it is more convenient to give it, and which is described in the lines already applied by the hon. member for Belfast,

> "Willing to wound and yet afraid to strike,
> Just hint fault, and hesitate dislike,"

or whether it be according to what I suspect to be the more accurate conception of the matter, only an attempt to supersede us in the due conduct and control of the Executive Government of Ireland, and to substitute another system utterly at variance with it—but whether it be this as I say, or the other as said by the hon. member, at all events we are now determined to have this point cleared up. We will not accept your commentaries, nor your gloss, nor your palliations. We will leave no room for ambiguity. We have had enough of partial attacks, and isolated charges, innuendos, and abuse, of motions for papers here, and for committees there. We now come for a direct and unequivocal opinion at your hands. We will take no low ground. We will exist no longer on sufferance. We tell you that we shall not put up with passive acquiescence or base endurance. We will not even be contented with acquittal. My noble friend asks you this night for a direct, downright vote of approbation. In the name of the Irish Government, and of the whole Government, as implicated in its Irish policy, I assert fearlessly that we have deserved well of our country. Upon this issue I call you representatives of the empire to come this night to the vote."

The debate dragged on for five nights. It closed on April 19. The motion was carried by 318 to 296 votes.

But the Lords appointed their Committee. It sat on April 22, and continued to sit until July 19. Drummond said he would appear before this Committee. His friends tried to dissuade him. What was the good of it? Who cared about the Lords' Committee? His health was bad. It would tax his strength to give evidence. He would be worried, and harassed, and to no beneficial purpose. The game was not worth the candle. Such were the arguments they urged. But Drummond held to his resolve. He said in effect: "These men are our accusers. I shall go before them. I shall hear what they have to say, and tell them what I have to say."

He appeared before the Committee on June 14. Mrs Drummond was very anxious about him. He left Ireland ill. Physically, he was not at all equal for the work he volunteered. But he was sustained by intellectual vigour and a strong sense of duty. Mrs Drummond placed him under the care of the Irish Solicitor General, Pigot.[1]

THE SOLICITOR GENERAL PIGOT TO MRS DRUMMOND.

"LONDON, *18th June* 1839.

"MY DEAR MRS DRUMMOND,—I know—from some experience of that anxious creature called a spouse—that a line about Drummond will be acceptable to you. He has

[1] Afterwards Chief Baron Pigot.

been under examination two days, and has got, happily, a day's interval between. He was examined on Saturday and yesterday, and he will be examined again to-morrow.

"His evidence has been, according to the concurring accounts of all parties, admirable; clear, frank, able, firm, given in perfect temper. I was against producing him,—not for his sake, because I knew it would redound to his honour for all time,—but upon general grounds. Since these men got ready, it is, of course, most fortunate that an opportunity is given of unfolding such a tale as he is telling. He is admirably prepared. If anything can lift him as a public man, this evidence will. Happy for Ireland—unfortunate for our party—that his official lot is not cast here. They want half a Drummond to manage these matters, which, even in the particular position he held while in employment in London, he showed so much capacity to guide. He is very well, only complaining that he gets vastly hungry while under examination, and craves for a lunch. He took the precaution the second day of laying in a few slices of food belonging to the Committee.

"We won't let him back to you till he rests, and has some amusement, after the fag of this wearisome duty.—Believe me to be most faithfully yours,

"D. R. PIGOT."

Drummond was seven days under examination—June 14, 17, 19, 20, 24, 25, 27. A fire of cross questions was opened on him from almost all sides of the Committee. But, as Pigot said, he remained cool and firm. He gave his evidence with calmness, fulness, frankness. Indeed, he appeared more like a friendly than a hostile witness. But now and then some member of the Committee more rash than the rest asked a question directly impugning his conduct, then the Under Secretary took the offensive and soon silenced his opponents.

One of the first topics taken up was the employment of stipendiary magistrates. This was an offence against their dignity which the Ascendancy never forgot and never forgave. Why were stipendiary magistrates employed instead of local justices? This was a question which had been constantly asked. The Committee asked it again now. Drummond, in reply, reminded them that there had been stipendiary magistrates in Ireland before he ever set foot in the country. When he arrived in Ireland in 1835 there were twenty-nine stipendiary magistrates; he had certainly increased the number to fifty-four; but he was ready to justify his conduct. Stipendiary magistrates were employed because the local justices could not be trusted.

Committee—"Why did you send stipendiary magistrates to the north? Were not the local magistracy adequate to suppressing those [Orange] processions?"

Drummond—"It was the opinion of the Government that the local magistracy did not exert themselves generally as much as they might have done for the suppression of such processions. There were several distinguished exceptions, but, generally speaking, it was felt that there had not been that decided interference on the part of the local magistracy which their duty required. . . ."

Committee—"What proof can you give to the Committee that the local magistracy did not exert themselves?"

Drummond—"Notwithstanding the great number of processions which took place, those processions were met chiefly by the stipendiary magistrates. There were few cases in which they had the co-operation from the local magistracy which might have been expected."

Committee—"Was not the appointment of stipendiary magistrates itself a sufficient reason for the local magistrates to withdraw?"

Drummond—"I think not. The stipendiary magistrates

were directed in every case to endeavour to secure the co-operation of the local magistracy."

Committee — "Was the appointment of stipendiary magistrates because the local magistrates refused to do their duty?"

Drummond—"It was because it was apprehended that the local magistracy would not attend; and, if they neglected to do so, the time would not have admitted of other precautionary measures being taken."

Committee—"What grounds had the Government to apprehend that the local magistracy of that part of Ireland would not do their duty?"

Drummond—"From those processions having been for many years suffered with impunity, and from their having taken no steps to check them in the years 1835 and 1836."

Committee—"When you state that they were suffered with impunity, were there any processions contrary to law previous to the years 1835 and 1836?"

Drummond—"I confine my attention to 1835 and 1836, the period with which I am acquainted."

Committee—"When did the Act rendering processions illegal come into force?"

Drummond—"The Act was for five years, and expired, I think, in 1837. It was renewed again in 1838."

Committee—"Do you believe that the illegal processions could have been suppressed without the attendance of stipendiary magistrates in those counties?"

Drummond—"I do not; I believe they would have been at this moment in as active operation as ever."

Drummond was essentially a serious, practical, downright man. But he was not devoid of humour. There was occasionally a playful archness in some of his answers to the Committee, when the questions struck him as too absurd. For instance, he was asked if it were not the object of the Ribbon Society to overthrow the English power in Ireland, and to establish an Irish monarchy. He laughed at the question, because he well knew that the Ribbon Society was an agrarian organisation, wholly unconnected with political movements.

Committee—"Have you not read the evidence of Mr Rowan, Mr Warburton, Mr Tracy, Captain Despard, and others, and do you not know that such is their opinion?"

Drummond—"So they have been informed."

Committee—"Are you aware that the witnesses who have been named have stated that the objects of the Ribbon Society are those referred to?"

Drummond—"I think those objects have been more or less distinctly stated in the evidence of several of them, not as the opinion of the witnesses, but as the information given to them. According to Mr Rowan's[1] informant, for example, it is stated, that the object is to make Mr O'Connell king, and to appoint Mr Maurice O'Connell head of the Ribbonmen."

This sally had the desired effect, and the subject was dropped. Elsewhere Drummond told the Committee that he had received constant assistance from O'Connell in coping with Ribbonism. Upon one occasion O'Connell sent an informer to the Castle who promised to give most valuable evidence about the society. Drummond examined the man, and found him to be a boundless liar. But the fact proved O'Connell's anxiety to stamp out Ribbonism.

Committee—"What is your opinion of the general character of the informers whose information you have read?"

Drummond—"The character of informers, as far as it has come to my knowledge, is very bad. I have got a list of them. The person who has given the most detailed information respecting the Ribbonmen is a person of the name of ——, who was made known to the Govern-

[1] Rowan was a great finder of mares' nests.

ment by Mr O'Connell himself. I sent him to the Police Commissioners, by whom he was transferred to Mr Rowan. I had a good deal of intercourse with this man. After repeated assurances that he would give information of outrages, which were then of daily occurrence, and still receiving no information from him, whilst he was constantly in receipt of money, I came to the conclusion that he had not those means of information which he pretended to have. He then desired to be established in a public-house, stating that he should thus have better opportunities of learning the designs of those secret associations. He kept a very disorderly house, and became bankrupt. He is now living in a very disreputable house in Dublin. Another man, of whom we had certainly a better opinion, because he declared that he should ask no money until he should have given important information, has commenced the usual course, by begging that he may be put into some way of business, by which means he should be able to get a great deal more information. We find on inquiry respecting that person that he has been three times convicted of felony, and three times in Newgate. Then with regard to the informer on whom Chief Constable Hatton and Captain Despard relied, he is a man of the name of ——. The expression which Mr Hatton used to me in speaking of him was that he was an 'infernal blackguard.' He brought him to Dublin just before I came away, that I might see him, and that the Attorney-General might examine him; but he disappeared."

"[About another informer, Mr Barnes, a magistrate, wrote]:—I have the honour of stating for the information of His Excellency the Lord Lieutenant, that being perfectly aware of the character of Mr Warburton's correspondent, I considered it unnecessary to proceed to Ballinasloe without first laying the following statements before Mr Drummond. The man in question is now in Longford

Jail, as will appear from the annexed letter which I received from him on Saturday last, undergoing his sentence for an assault. This man has been known to me since the month of October last; and from my knowledge of him, I have no hesitation in designating him one of the most consummate and specious villains in all Ireland. He was formerly a policeman, and discharged for misconduct; a Protestant, and turned to mass for the purpose, as he stated to me, of becoming a Ribbonman and betraying their secrets; was in my employment for four or five months as a secret agent to get me information, received in that time upwards of £15 from me, and ended our connection by stating, and offering to swear to his statement, that he himself was one of the party who murdered Morrison, Lord Norton's bailiff —tendering himself to me as an approver, and claiming the reward and pardon offered by the proclamation. Knowing this statement to be false, I determined to have nothing more to do with the fellow, and accordingly ceased all communication with him; when in a little time after I was told by my orderly constable, Armstrong, that he had met —— when tipsy, who bragged to him that although his master had turned him off he had soon got employment from Captain Warburton of Ballinasloe, and that he was then in correspondence with him on Sligo business."

Drummond's information about these informers came as an unpleasant surprise to the Committee. The Ascendancy asserted that the Ribbon Society was a political organisation. But Drummond proved, step by step, that the men on whose information this statement was based, were a gang of "consummate and specious villains," able to impose on the Rowans, and the Despards, whose political sympathies made them easy victims; but not able to impose on the cool-headed Scotchman at the Castle, who desired only to get at the truth.

Of course Drummond was asked about Irish sympathy

with crime, but he rather astonished the Committee by his answer.

Committee—"A good deal has been said respecting the sympathy of the population of Ireland with the perpetrators of crime. Do you consider that that sympathy extends only to agrarian outrage, or to all cases universally?"

Drummond—"I think it is mainly confined to cases which are called agrarian outrages, and political cases probably. But of this [political cases] I have no experience, unless the opposition to tithe be so considered. The term agrarian, with reference to crime, is, I believe, sufficiently understood to apply to offences connected with regulating the occupation of land. There is a remarkable instance which occurred lately of a dreadful murder in Queen's County; the murderer was pursued from Queen's County into Kilkenny by the police, who were close upon him during the whole pursuit. He was arrested at Ballyragget in Kilkenny, by the aid of the villagers, and was conveyed to Maryborough. The people, when the party came into the Queen's County, turned out to cheer the police as they returned with the prisoner. The murdered man was a pensioner from the police, and a Protestant. The criminal was brought to trial and executed for murder."

He was examined respecting O'Connell's Carlow speech,[1] and the Lord Lieutenant's action in allowing the agitator to dine at the Castle after making that speech. O'Connell, as we have seen, was reported to have said:—

"Men of Carlow, are you ready? I am the last man to recommend the shedding of one drop of blood, but we have tried every means of obtaining our just rights, and they have failed. We have no course left us but that which I have hitherto deprecated, the shedding of blood."

Drummond said he did not believe that O'Connell ever used the words. He said he never used them. Moreover,

[1] *Ante*, p. 265.

"the expressions were contrary to the general tenor of Mr O'Connell's speeches."

Committee—"When you state that the expressions alluded to were contrary to the general tenor of Mr O'Connell's speeches, have you ever read in any speech,

> "'Hereditary bondsmen! know ye not,
> Who would be free, themselves must strike the blow?'"

Drummond—"I have read these words, but I have no hesitation whatever in saying that I never regarded those lines as an incitement to the shedding of blood, or violence; and I think if so strict a rule of construction were laid down, that the quoting of these lines should be interpreted as a recommendation of bloodshed, other honourable gentlemen and chairmen who have spoken at public meetings would find it very difficult to escape the inferences which may be drawn from their own expressions. I have heard of other chairmen who, on more than one occasion, have addressed public meetings, and expressed their exultation at the display of 'Protestant bone and sinew.'"

"This was a shot fired straight at Roden and the Orange faction, and it told. The subject was dropped. But Drummond enlightened the Committee further upon Orange doings. He read this letter from Police Inspector Cramer Roberts, written on June 29, 1837:—

"I was about to recommence the proceedings[1] when I was informed by Chief Constable Mansfield that a most atrocious murder had been committed within four miles of Castleblayney. I immediately adjourned the investigation, and proceeded in company with W. Hamilton, J.P. of the county of Monaghan, and resident in this town, to the spot, where we were shortly afterwards joined by Captain MacLeod, stipendiary magistrate. It appears a party of about twelve persons, principally boys and children, were assembled on the night of the 28th instant, between the

[1] An inquiry into the conduct of some of the constabulary.

hours of eleven and twelve o'clock, around a small fire on the hill of Mollyash, Parish of Muckno, distant about five miles from Castleblayney, on the old Newry Road, leading to Newtown Hamilton, in celebration of St Peter's Eve. While seated round this bonfire laughing and talking, a party of persons unknown appeared distant about one hundred yards above them on the hill. Shortly afterwards three shots were fired in the direction of this party, by which two persons, Michael Devine, twenty years, and Peter Devine, ten years of age, were shot dead; and two others, Patrick Devine, fifteen years, and Francis Devine, fourteen years of age, were wounded, the former dangerously, the latter slightly. These four sufferers were brothers, and sons of Francis Devine, a small farmer, holding thirty acres of land on Mollyash. This family of Devines are Roman Catholics, extremely well spoken of by all, even by their Protestant neighbours. They are, by all accounts, a most industrious, well-conducted, quiet, inoffensive, and peaceable family, highly respected, and free from all party spirit, as universally admitted by persons of all persuasions and parties. A more wanton, unprovoked, premeditated, cold-blooded, and cruel murder has never fallen under my observation, and is clearly characteristic of strong party feeling. I attended at the scene of these diabolical murders until evening, making, conjointly with Mr Hamilton and Captain MacLeod, every exertion to trace out the perpetrators. We examined several witnesses, but I regret much to say that nothing material was elicited, which could lead to a discovery. Two persons, George Donaldson and Patrick M'Cullogh, master and labouring man, both Protestants, have been detained in custody for further examination, but only on slight suspicion. In searching the house of the former, two stands of arms unregistered, together with the stock and lock of another, and a dagger, were found. George Donaldson is, I understand, the Master of an Orange Lodge."

Drummond also read the following report of Inspector Cramer Roberts, dated Feb. 23, 1837:—

" It appears that on the fair day at Ballyjamesduff, the 4th instant, all passed off perfectly quietly, until about seven o'clock P.M., when a party of Protestants, five in number, returning home towards Clandaugh, at about a quarter of a mile from Ballyjamesduff, had an altercation with a party of Roman Catholics, in which it does not clearly appear who were the first aggressors. From this, a report that the Protestants were being beaten seems to have spread to Clandaugh, a district distant about one mile from Ballyjamesduff, and inhabitated by low, violent Protestants, who immediately turned out, armed with sticks and other weapons near at hand, but no fire-arms. They then appear to have proceeded in two bodies of about twenty or twelve in each towards the town, beating indiscriminately and in detail every Roman Catholic whom they met on the road, and in so doing making use of the exclamation 'Papist dog.' Shortly after the altercation first mentioned, and near the spot where it took place, a serious attack was made upon a party of Roman Catholics, five or six in number, one of whom, John Carr, was so severely beaten as to cause his death. Ten persons are charged with this homicide, seven of whom are now in custody fully sworn to; the principal, William Donelly, with two others, have, I regret to say, hitherto eluded the vigilance of the police. The former is supposed to have gone to Liverpool, and the others to have left this part of the country. In the subsequent assaults, several Roman Catholics, men and women, appear to have been most unjustifiably wounded and beaten; none of whom, I am happy to say, are considered at present to be in a dangerous state.

"These disgraceful scenes of outrage appear to have been only eventually put an end to by the activity of the police in patrolling the roads, in doing which they came upon a party of Protestants, four of whom, after a chase, were taken prisoners and subsequently identified and committed to jail. Eleven are yet at large, and I greatly fear that there is no likelihood of their being made arraignable for the approaching assizes, although every effort has been, and still continues to be, made by the police."

Drummond's practice of putting Catholics into the police gave grave offence to the Ascendancy. He was examined on the subject. He stated that it was his desire to make the police popular; and as the population of the country was chiefly Catholic, that could best be done by making the police chiefly Catholic.

Committee—"Then in a Catholic population you would prefer having a Catholic police to a Protestant?"

Drummond—"Yes."

Committee—"Supposing that was carried into execution, do you think that persons of property in that district would have the same reliance on that police that they have now, they being generally Protestant?"

Drummond—"I feel persuaded that in the course of six months, from the manner in which the police did their duty, they would have that confidence."

Committee—"Do you think at first they would?"

Drummond—"I think there might be, and I know there is, a prejudice, and, therefore, that prejudice would have to be overcome."

Committee—"You think, in the short period of six months, they would open their eyes to see things differently?"

Drummond—"Yes; the more considerate at least would look at the manner in which the police discharged their duty; and I think they would be perfectly satisfied with that."

Committee—"Did you give the Committee to understand that you were perfectly certain that the Protestant portion of the resident gentry in Ireland, in six months, would have perfect confidence in the police being Roman Catholics?"

Drummond—"No; that was not what I stated. I stated that the manner in which I was confident the police would discharge their duties, even if there were a preponderance of Catholics in the force, would be such as to remove any prejudice that might exist on the part of the Protestant resident gentry."

It is needless to say how Drummond's opinion has been justified by events.

Since his time the Irish police have been chiefly a Catholic force. They have always possessed the confidence of the Ascendancy class.

The Roden Committee was specially appointed to prove that crime had increased in Ireland during Drummond's administration. Drummond demonstrated the contrary by the production of facts and figures, which the Committee scarcely attempted to deny or controvert. The Committee had manœuvred a good deal before coming to this crucial point. When they reached it, Drummond drew from his pockets a pile of papers, and said: "In dealing with this subject, I hope I may be permitted to refer to the official documents before me." The permission was granted, and the Under Secretary stated his case. He arranged his facts with marvellous skill, and handled his figures with scientific precision. He showed how convictions had increased, how offences had diminished, how trade had improved, how the price of land had risen, how respect for the law and sympathy with the Executive had grown up, how political agitation had comparatively ceased. Faction fights had been put down, Orangeism held in check, Ribbonism vigorously grappled with. He closed his case by handing in the official papers on which it was based.

Some of the facts and figures placed before the Committee by Drummond may be given here.

Orange Processions.

Year.	Number.
1836	27
1839	5

Disturbances in connection with Orange Processions.

Year.	Number.
1835	9
1836	5
1839	0

Murder or Manslaughter.

Year.	Committals.	
1832	620	
1833	687	
1834	575	
1835	712	Drummond's Administration.
1836	620	
1837	519	
1838	424	

Firing at the Person.

Year.	Committals.
1834	105
1838	47

Offences against Human Life, including the above.

Year.	Committals.
1832	772
1833	826
1834	729
1835	922
1836	843
1837	688
1838	575

Assaults on the Police.

Year.	Committals.	
1834	125	
1835	118	Drummond's Administration.
1836	119	
1837	91	
1838	94	

Cutting and Maiming.

Year.	Committals.
1835	1343
1838	944

Attacks on Houses.

Year.	Committals.
1835	818
1838	352

Illegal Notices.

Year.	Committals.
1835	755
1838	409

In fine, these facts were proved by Drummond:—Between 1834 and 1838, homicide had diminished 13 per cent.; firing at the person, 55 per cent.; incendiary fires, 17 per cent.; administration of unlawful oaths, 66 per cent.; stealing cattle, 46 per cent.; attacks upon houses, 63 per cent.; killing or maiming cattle, 12 per cent.; levelling houses, 65 per cent.; illegal meetings, 70 per cent. It was moreover shown that between 1834 and 1838, convictions had increased on committals from 40 to 47 per cent., while failures of justice by no bills, no prosecutions had diminished from 36 to 15 per cent.

The House of Lords, representing the Tory Orange party, had selected their own time and place for giving battle to the Irish Under Secretary. He had met them on their own ground, and beaten them. Some years afterwards Lord John Russell summed up effectively the work of the Lords' Committee. He said: "A Committee had been appointed in 1839 to show that crime had increased, and the security of life and property diminished; [but it] ended by proving that crime had diminished, and the increased security for property was demonstrated by this most conclusive test: five years' more purchase was given for land in 1839 than had been given for seven years before."[1]

When Drummond's examination was over, Lord Spencer said to him—"Your reputation has been immensely raised by your conduct in Ireland. It was good before, but it stands much higher now."

Drummond's appearance before the Lords' Committee was his last great victory over the Ascendancy faction. He proved that by justice and fair play, the Irish people might be made loyal to the English connection.

While the Committee was at work, Drummond was engaged in a warm controversy with Spring Rice and Lord Morpeth, respecting a delicate matter connected with his department. Mr (afterwards Sir) Matthew Barrington, Crown Solicitor on the Munster Circuit, was anxious to have his son joined with him in the office. Spring Rice and Morpeth favoured Barrington's proposal; Drummond opposed it. This correspondence took place:—

Spring Rice to Lord Morpeth.

"Downing Street, *11th May.*

"My Dear Morpeth,—Do you remember a letter I forwarded to you, in the early part of last month, from Barrington, applying to have his son joined with him in his office? Has anything been done upon it? It would be very desirable to arrange it as he wishes, if possible, and in the present position of affairs, with as little delay as possible.—Yours always, "T. Spring Rice."

[1] House of Commons, February 13, 1844.

Spring Rice to Drummond.

"Downing Street, *July 13th*, 1839.

"My Dear Drummond,—As I did not see you, I am obliged to trouble you with this letter, as the interests of another are concerned. At Barrington's desire, I asked Morpeth to appoint Barrington's son, in conjunction with himself, Crown Solicitor for the Munster Circuit—it being of course not only understood but expressed, that such appointments do not create any vested right that could make an impediment to the alterations of the office or its reforms. I thought this was not a very great favour for me to ask more especially on behalf of the best public servant of the Crown in Ireland, and one to whom Lord Melbourne's Government is under the deepest obligations. I believe Normanby was as anxious on the subject as I am.

"Morpeth told me that *you* had raised some objections which you would explain to me.

"As this explanation has not been given whilst you were here, allow me to ask for them now, that I may consider whether they can be surmounted or should be on the contrary acquiesced in.

"As a proof of the services which Barrington has rendered during his private stay here, I enclose an extract of a letter which I have just received from Lord Hatherton.

"Pray let me hear from you as soon as you can, and believe me, my dear Drummond, always yours,

"T. Spring Rice."

Lord Morpeth to Drummond.

"*July 26th*, 1839.

"My Dear Drummond,—I wish that you had seen Rice when you were in town, because in talking to each other you might have understood one another better, and I cannot conceal from you that he is much discomposed by the letter he has received from you about Barrington. I have no purpose now of combating your views, but, giving them their full force, I write to state why I am of opinion that we must concede this point. Rice holds that come when your proposition may before the Treasury, it will take a very considerable time before a matter of such extreme delicacy and importance can be finally decided; he tenders on the part of Barrington not only an understood, but an expressed agreement that the association of his son in partnership with himself shall give no claim or prescription in the future settlement of the office; he asks it as a feather in the young man's cap, and as a matter of paternal feeling. Be the force of all this what it may, the question which weighs with me is, does Barrington ask it under circumstances which admit of our refusing it. Rice sends to me the enclosed extract from a letter of Lord Hatherton to him; he looks upon Barrington's services to the public generally, and to this Government specially, both on the present and past occasions, as beyond all price, and if we refuse such a request as this, he will advise him to throw up his Crown Solicitorship. Lord Hatherton tells me that he thinks we ought to comply, and lastly and chiefly, Lord Normanby assures me that he *promised* Barrington it should be done. Well, then, I say we must take care afterwards that it is not suffered to interfere with the substantial benefits which our proposed arrangements may confer on the public service, but I will not care for any impressions or misconstructions which may be produced in the meanwhile. I will not take any step till you and the Lord Lieutenant (to whom I beg you to forward this note and the enclosure[1]) have had time to write to me, but I hope he will not then object to my stating to Rice and Barrington that at the close of the session, the request shall be complied with.—Very sincerely yours,

"MORPETH."

[1] Enclosure not kept.

"*P.S.*—I cannot omit to tell you how very deeply I consider the Government to be under obligation to Barrington for the services he has rendered in counteracting the designs of your opponents in the Committee. In shaping the course of the inquiry, in selecting and calling over the right witnesses, in preparing their examinations, instructing your friends in the Committee how to examine them, he has been indefatigable. He has written papers, analysed and digested the evidence taken, and promises much future useful service. He has to my knowledge worked night and day at it for the last month. He is really entitled to some very marked expression of your thanks. There is more practical good sense, usefulness, and zeal in him than in any man whose services I have ever had the good fortune to employ. I do not wish to say anything invidious of others, but if Barrington had not come over, we should have been in a great mess, and his stay here at present till after the Report appears is indispensable."

DRUMMOND TO LORD MORPETH.

"DUBLIN, *July 29th*, 1839.

"MY DEAR LORD MORPETH,—If Barrington's application were such as he represents it, merely for some honorary mark of distinction for his son with the sole view of putting a feather in the young man's cap and gratifying his own personal feelings, then would opposition on the part of any one connected with the Irish Government be most ungrateful and unjust. But while I have not a shadow of doubt that Barrington, in so representing his application, fully believes what he states, yet I do deny most emphatically that such would be the sole consequence and effect of complying with his application.

"If I should be able to prove to you that compliance with his request—even though accompanied by all the conditions proposed—would in fact be a violation of the very principle of the new arrangement which you were about to propose, and would inevitably lead to very inconvenient and probably mischievous consequences,—if I should be correct in this view, then surely it cannot be denied or concealed that the appointment would be a most indefensible and unjustifiable act on the part of the Government. What I ask under these circumstances is simply this: make no engagement—no promise actual or implied, but wait till you come over here yourself, and hear both parties: let Barrington state his own case, let those who object state their views: there need be no secrecy, no concealment: those who object are among the number who fully recognise and appreciate Barrington's claims and services. They are—they can be actuated only by one motive—an imperative sense of public duty. I can say for myself, that it is most painful to me to find myself in my present position with respect to Rice and Barrington—men whom I so sincerely esteem and value. I mentioned that the Attorney-General takes the same view of the case which I do: I believe so does Pigot, certainly Ball, who was Attorney-General when the new measure was framed. In the absence of the Lord Lieutenant, and without expressly referring to him, I do not venture to say what I believe his opinion to be, but I am much mistaken if he does not entertain quite as strong an opinion on the subject as Ball, Brady, and I. Under these circumstances the course which I suggest cannot surely be objected to by anyone. The last assizes for the year are over—no urgent public business calls for your immediate decision—defer then giving any pledge or promise until you have had personally and on the spot an opportunity of inquiring fully and deliberately into the merits of the case. Then if after such an inquiry you should advise the Lord Lieutenant to acquiesce in the application, I shall not say that I should rejoice in your decision even on Barrington's account—for if no alteration were in contemplation with respect to these offices, I am so strongly impressed with the mischievous impolicy and impropriety of making such important public offices hereditary, that I should nevertheless greatly regret the decision—but at least I should feel assured that it had been made with a full knowledge of the merits of the case, and that His Excellency and you were satisfied that the evil consequences which I anticipate were not to be apprehended.—Ever most truly yours,

"THOMAS DRUMMOND."

LORD MORPETH TO DRUMMOND.

"*August 1st*, 1839.

"MY DEAR DRUMMOND,—I tell you fairly I think I must give this boon to Barrington. The argument against hereditary appointments (good in itself) amounts to an eternal prohibition; we have disregarded it in the case of Mr Sampson in Clare, we have disregarded it in the instance of Moloney, and I therefore think it would be hardly handsome to raise it against Barrington. I am most unwilling, in anything, to act against your advice and judgment, for both of which I entertain such unfeigned esteem, but it is not only on the score of Barrington's recent and still continuing services, but also on the score of Lord Normanby's actual and parting promise, that we must now look on it as a matter of necessity, and make up our minds to it with a good grace. As a matter of policy too, I very much question whether with a view to our contemplated measure, it may not turn out of great advantage to carry Barrington with us, which our compliance now will inevitably give us a better chance of doing.—Ever yours,

"MORPETH."

"You must state all this to the Lord Lieutenant."

DRUMMOND TO LORD MORPETH.

"DUBLIN, *August 4th*, 1839.

"MY DEAR LORD MORPETH,—It distresses me to continue this subject, but I must add a few words, and if they have no effect, I have done.

"Our difference of opinion with respect to granting Barrington's request can only be explained by the very different views which we take of the nature and consequences of the appointment he asks. I may assume, that if you regarded it in the same light that I do, no consideration whatever would induce you to consent to it. Now, I am either right or wrong. If the latter, the only result of acceding to my request that you should not decide till you have heard both sides, would be, that the young Barrington would have to wait some three weeks—or it might be four —for his feather. Surely the excessive eagerness to reward the father's services might brook this delay, when it is recollected that the ink is scarcely yet dry which records his appointment to a highly valuable and lucrative office—that of solicitor to the Shannon Commissioners.

"Admitting all Barrington's claims, I ask, what officer under Government is rewarded and remunerated as he now is. £4000 a year the probable gain of his own situation—£800 per annum to his brother—and lastly, this appointment to the Shannon Commission, which I have reason to know will bring him in a very handsome sum. Surely this last consideration alone might enable you to bear up under the pressure of obligation for three weeks, especially when you consider that the question to be then tried is, whether this appointment will not peril the success of an important public measure—one which, if carried through with vigour, impartiality, and determination, will redound to your credit and to the improvement of the social condition of the country with regard to crime. If any but the most tried and approved men—men like Cahill, Ford, &c., who impressed the Committee with the highest opinion of their ability—be put into the new Department, failure or imperfect success must be the result, and what follows? An increase of crime—crime which is justly regarded as a test of the social state, and by which the efficiency of the Government will be, as it has been tried.

"Now I contend that Barrington's object is to get his son associated with him, and then, in due and decent time, to ask to retire, leaving us his son, an unfledged, inexperienced stripling of one and twenty or less, of whose competency you have not the slightest particle of proof, and of whose inexperience you have a positive certainty. The new regulations will require the attendance of the Crown Solicitors daily at the Castle during the usual office hours. Barrington will not like this. He will send his son, and will himself attend to the Shannon and his private business. I may remark by the way, that giving him this Shannon appointment is grossly at variance with the principles laid down and insisted upon in our new plan—namely, that the Crown Solicitors shall be placed on salaries, and shall then give up all private business, and devote themselves exclusively to their public duties, as the Solicitor of the Treasury now does, and as every Solicitor of any public department in England has been compelled to do. If the new plan should not be carried into effect, Barrington will in like manner avail himself of the first opportunity of resigning, his son remaining. This will seem a small favour to grant, and the circumstances under which it will be asked will be well chosen. An election for Limerick is about to take place. The Roches have no chance of being returned. Barrington is sure to carry it, and is ready to come forward. He only asks that his son should be continued in that office for which he has shown such singular fitness. Barrington told me some time ago that he was the only person that could carry Limerick at the next election ; and it required no great penetration to see the very natural connection between securing the representation of Limerick and appointing his son Crown Solicitor. Barrington, with all his merit, is a 'cunning little man.' These were Lord Normanby's words, and they were just and true. Is it conceivable that Lord Normanby, with a full knowledge of Barrington's propensities, and his own habitual caution as to giving promises, would have pledged himself to such an appointment, unless the nature of it had been partially, imperfectly, and unfairly represented to him, just as it has been represented to you, as a feather in the youth's cap—a gratification of paternal feeling—a mere honorary boon to a deserving public servant—whereas, if the object and effect had been honestly and fairly described, the appointment would have appeared as inadmissible in principle as it is likely to be mischievous and discreditable in its consequences. I really have not leisure to mention one half of the reasons that might be urged against it. It takes more time than I can possibly spare to do this in writing, and therefore I beseech you to let me have the opportunity of talking to you on the subject when you come over.

"One point I must however allude to. You say that my arguments against hereditary appointments lead to eternal exclusion. Assuredly they do, unless the candidate gives proof of his possessing qualifications equal to those of his competitors. He then rests on his own merit—not on his father's. It is against the untried, unknown youth, who has no other claim than being his father's son—it is against sacrificing the public interests by placing a most important office in such hands—that I protest.

"As to the precedents which you have quoted ; pray recollect that Sampson was an old man, and that the duties of his office had been for years practically performed by his son; but remember that there were objections made but overruled to the son being appointed to his father's place. Remember that this appointment was used by Mahony as the ground on which he placed his job; that Ball denounced it and resisted it, declaring that he could not hold up his head at the Four Courts if such a palpable job were attempted. It was given up. The upset of the Government came, and then it was directed. Now these two acts, both bad in themselves, are used to justify a third—a far more flagrant demand. The offices to which Sampson and Mahony have been appointed might be filled by any one who could read, and in natural capacity should be just above an idiot; but in the whole range of public offices intended for the administering and enforcing of the law, there cannot be named one, the efficiency of which is so important as the Crown Solicitors. What constitutes Barrington's claim on the Government? Superiority in this respect as compared with his brethren; but the very ground of his claim is a reason for not appointing any one who has not established clearly and unequivocally his own individual superiority. I was anxious before the Committee to prove the increase of convictions to committals in Lord Normanby's time. I was obliged to abandon it because the results of the Connaught Assizes, caused by the incompetency of the Crown Solicitor, were so bad that they vitiated the whole. Can any responsibility be greater than that of prolonging such a state of things by suffering yourself, under any consideration, to be led into the appointment to such offices of any but the very best men that are to be found? There are excellent men ready: are you to set them aside for a youth of whom you know nothing, good, bad, or indifferent?

"Nothing but my firm conviction that the step which

you have in view is wrong—essentially wrong—could justify or excuse what I feel to be very unbecoming pertinacity in pressing these opinions upon you. Most truly and sincerely do I acknowledge what you allude to in your note—the kind consideration which you have given on every occasion to any representation which I have had to make to you. On the other hand, if I have at any time pressed opinions upon you more perseveringly or warmly than even your indulgent nature thought right, I am sure you will do me the justice to believe that, however my judgment may have erred, my motives were not in fault.

"I am ashamed of the length of this note. I can only say that it is not a deliberate infliction, for I did not intend, when I began, to trouble you with more than a very few words.—Ever most truly yours,

"T. DRUMMOND."

SPRING RICE TO DRUMMOND.

"DOWNING STREET, *7th August* 1839.

"MY DEAR DRUMMOND,—I could not venture to allow myself to answer your letter of the 18th July, because it really vexed me so very much that I was afraid to trust myself, lest if I wrote or said all I felt I should go too far, and if I did not do so, that I should act with reserve or with a want of confidence towards you. Since then Morpeth has shown me your letter of the 29th, or rather, has communicated it to Barrington, and I must say, that I think this makes the case a still more disagreeable one. I cannot, however, any longer postpone my reply, which, however, I shall endeavour to keep within as moderate bounds as the circumstance will permit.

"The favour which I have earnestly solicited on the part of one who is among my best and most affectionate friends—one, too, whose services to our party and our

Government are undisputed, and whose private worth is as unquestionable as his public and official merit, was merely this:—

"That Barrington's son should be joined with him in his appointment as Crown Solicitor, that son having been regularly educated for the profession and office, but that no such appointment should stand in the way of any future alteration of the office, or should create any vested right in the young man, or add to the claims of Barrington himself, in the event of a reform of the system of Crown prosecutions.

"Consider well this limitation, without which neither Barrington nor I would have brought forward this application.

"I pass over altogether the fact of our not meeting. Lord Morpeth referred me expressly to you, by whom, as he informed me, an objection was raised to a compliance with my request. My belief, however, is that you felt disinclined to any adverse discussion, and therefore took no pains that we should meet, or rather took pains that we should not.

"Your reply to me from Dublin is that 'Barrington's proposal would be inconsistent with the spirit and the principles of an arrangement respecting Crown prosecutions, which the Irish Government are about to submit for the sanction of the Treasury.' Now, I do not think this is quite a candid objection, for the very terms of the application would have prevented the claims of young Barrington from standing for one hour in the way of such arrangements, if finally approved of. But if we are to be answered in reference to the recommendation contained in a paper which we have never seen, it amounts to an indefinite postponement, as well as to a most illogical objection.

"But this is not all. Your statement rests, and though

I thought your observations singularly inconclusive and inapplicable, still it was an obvious deduction that if you had not contemplated recommending to the Treasury a change of system, and if your promised paper was not in course of preparation, the appointment would have been made.

"Great was my astonishment, therefore, when in your letter to Lord Morpeth of the 29th you put forward a totally distinct objection irrespective of your contemplated reform. You now object, lest these important public offices should be made hereditary. This is an objection fatal to the arrangement altogether, and which, I think, you ought to have stated in your first communication to me. But is the objection a just one? or is it not rather a make-weight thrown in as an additional and insuperable difficulty to this request of mine? Next, whilst it would be an obvious absurdity to establish a claim to hereditary succession in public offices, is it prudent or rational to exclude the son of a deserving servant, if him self deserving? Further, can you with fairness urge this objection after other acts of your own? You appointed the son of a Mr Sampson, Clerk of the Crown in Clare, and never raised your dogma of hereditary succession. You appointed the son of Mr Mahony, and you had there no such scruple. I do not think that the claims of either were quite so strong as those of Barrington; however, the friends who urged those claims on the Irish Government might have been entitled to more consideration than it appears I possess.

"On the whole, I must say that a greater and more signal instance of ingratitude on the part of a Government never existed than will be found in this refusal, if persevered in. It will be ungrateful to the best public servant you have, independently of its extreme unkindness to me. But after the difficulties thrown in the way of the matter, I decline pressing the latter consideration. Besides which, if I had to consider this as the act of another Government, and the whole proceeded from men whom I did not know, I should say that these were to be found in the shifting of the objections—in the first statement of objection, that which was refuted by the proposed conditions; and in the second, a principle negatived by your own conduct in other cases—appearances of insincerity which it is difficult to remove.

"I shall show this letter to Morpeth, of course, and I prefer requesting you to ask him to bring the question before the Lord Lieutenant, rather than to trouble Lord Ebrington myself.

"As your paper has been some time prepared, and as you stated on the 18th July that it would shortly be submitted to the Treasury, I beg that you will send it officially to us, that we may have the advantage of reading it while Morpeth and Pigot are both here, who can give us any explanation which may be required.—Believe me, my dear Drummond, very faithfully yours,

"T. SPRING RICE."

DRUMMOND TO SPRING RICE.

"DUBLIN CASTLE, *22nd August* 1839.

"MY DEAR MR RICE,—I lost no time in placing your letter, as you desired, in the hands of the Lord Lieutenant, and His Excellency has written to Lord Morpeth on the subject. Having stated to the Lord Lieutenant and Lord Morpeth the objections which appeared to me to exist to the appointment which Barrington has applied for,—having explained that these objections are not the creations of my fancy, but are as strongly felt and expressed by others whose opinions in such a matter are especially entitled to attention—I mean the late and present Attorney-General—I have done my duty. It is for them now to decide; and seeing that personal feelings have been excited, I am unwilling to engage in any further discussion on this subject, without the express sanction or direction of my own immediate superiors.

"I am, indeed, most anxious that the objections which I have brought under the notice of the Lord Lieutenant should be inquired into;—that it should be ascertained, beyond all doubt, whether they are well or ill-founded; but in order that such inquiry may lead to a practical result, it should be made by those who have the power to decide, and on whom the whole responsibility of a wrong decision must rest. The proposition which I made to Lord Morpeth with this view seemed to me so plain, simple, and just, that I am really at a loss to conceive on what ground it could be objected to or complained of. The late Attorney-General (Ball), the then Solicitor, now Attorney-General (Brady), and myself, were engaged, under Lord Morpeth's direction, in drawing up a plan for improving the present mode of conducting Crown prosecutions in Ireland. That plan has been submitted to the Lord Lieutenant and Lord Morpeth, and in its most important particulars been approved by both. It appeared to us (Ball, Brady, and me) that the appointment asked by Barrington was altogether inconsistent with that plan,—that it would occasion much embarrassment and difficulty in carrying the arrangement into effect, and would assuredly expose the Government to deserved censure. Further, that the offer to accept the office, subject to any conditions or modifications which the new plan might render expedient, would not meet the difficulty, inasmuch as the appointment being, in our opinion, inconsistent with the very nature and objects of the measure, the revoking it, if previously made, could alone remove the objection. Such being our opinion, be it well or ill-founded, surely it was our duty to submit to the Lord Lieutenant that this step should not be taken without deliberate and careful inquiry. It was our anxious wish that everything should be done openly and above board—in the presence of Barrington himself, that he might have an opportunity of hearing, and, if he could, of answering our objections. Is there anything to complain of in this proceeding? We put it to Barrington, as a fair and reasonable man, to say whether there is. We hoped to convince him that we were right, and we could not pay him a higher compliment than to consider him open to conviction against his wishes and his interests. We have also urged that nothing should be done till after the proposed plan is carried into effect, and for this very obvious reason, that that alone will go a great way practically to settle the question. It will then be clearly seen whether the thing ought to be done at all, and, if done, under what conditions and restrictions. We have also stated, as an additional reason for the postponement and inquiry, we recommend that even if the new plan should not be adopted, there are other strong objections, but of a different nature, to this appointment. It will be recollected that it is represented as a mere feather in a young man's cap; would it then be decent to refuse the delay and inquiry sought, in the face of the strongly-expressed opinion of the Attorney-General, in reference to a matter belonging in a peculiar degree to his province as the responsible adviser of Crown prosecutions?

"You say my logic is bad, my arguments inconclusive, my sincerity questionable, and you quote two precedents as showing the unjustifiable character of our opposition. It is possible that the logic may be bad, but I am sure that the case is good nevertheless. But it is not quite fair to assume that a note written in the hurry of business should contain a complete and logical statement of our objections; with the daily duties of my office to dispose of, it is no easy matter to find time to write an elaborate argument; besides, the sole object of my note was to show the necessity of hearing before deciding, and, therefore, I merely alluded, and possibly not very methodically, to some of the prominent reasons for acceding to our application, reserving for the inquiry which we sought the full explanation of our objections. But without further attempting to defend our reasoning which you say is so bad, allow me to quote a passage in your own letter. You ask, 'Is it rational to exclude the son of a deserving public servant, if himself deserving?' Assuredly it would neither be just nor rational; who asserts that it would? No one; but of course you mean to apply this to the present case, and therein, permit me to say, you beg the whole question. It is purely because no one knows whether young Barrington is deserving or not, because he has not given, and indeed has not had time nor opportunity to give, proofs of his qualifications for an office which it would be a grievous sacrifice of the public interests to confer on anyone who had not proved himself beyond all doubt not only competent, but superior, or at least equal, to any other candidate. Can any one say that young Barrington has his father's capacity for business? It is very unlikely that he should, the probabilities are greatly against him; and yet a youth of twenty-one, wholly unknown, untried, and inexperienced, is to be appointed to a situation so important as regards the administration of the law, and the state of crime in this country, that less practical mischief would probably be done, though perhaps somewhat greater scandal might be occasioned, by associating the son of a judge with his father, than by acceding to this application.

"With regard to the two cases which you have referred to as precedents, I am satisfied that anxious as you must be for the credit of the Government, you would not have quoted these cases as examples to be followed, if you had been aware of the facts. Some excuse may be found for the first, but as to the second, it was strongly condemned and resisted by the Attorney-General (Ball). 'If this appointment should be made,' he said, 'I shall never be able to show my face again in the Four Courts.' It was stayed; some months afterwards came the resignation of the Government, and in the confusion Mahony carried his point. If we are to go on from bad to worse, these cases will be valuable as precedents; if from bad to better, they will be useful as beacons.

"With regard to our conduct in reference to this painful subject on which you seem disposed to reflect, I would put it to you, whether in advocating and supporting the wishes and interests of a 'dear and affectionate friend,' you are placed in the best position to do justice to the motives of those who feel themselves constrained by a strong sense of duty to oppose the application of your friend, though cordially concurring in your opinion of his valuable services and professional merits.

"You say my letter vexed you; believe me, if there be in that letter a single expression bearing the semblance of discourtesy or disrespect to you, nothing would give me greater pain; nothing could have been further from my intention. I have tasked my memory to recollect anything which I may have said that could by possibility bear any such construction, but in vain; and surely the sincere, though perhaps earnest, expression of opinion to a member of the Government in regard to a matter affecting, as I believe, the credit of the Government, ought not to have that effect.

"There are some things in your letter of which, I really think, I might have some reason to complain, though God knows, nothing is further from my intention. You accuse me of wishing to avoid you, notwithstanding my promise to Lord Morpeth that I should make a point of seeing you in reference to this matter before leaving London, and you attribute my motive for not calling to a disinclination to an adverse discussion. A very few words will, I hope, satisfy you how groundless these suspicions are.

"Some evidence having been given before the Committee which personally affected Alex. Macdonnell, he was anxious to be examined. His Excellency being also of opinion that this was desirable, I applied to Lord Wharncliffe, and ascertained there was but one day remaining on which this could be done. Under these circumstances I felt it incumbent on me to disregard my own personal convenience—to give up the few days to be allowed me, on concluding my evidence, for my own private business, even to leave unfinished everything of public business but what was absolutely indispensable, and to hurry off for Dublin, where I arrived the same evening on which Macdonnell had sailed a few hours before. Notwithstanding the extreme pressure upon me, I did make a point of calling on you the day before I left town at about three o'clock, for the express purpose of talking over this matter. I had the mortification of finding that you had gone to Tunbridge Wells. It was on a Friday, so that I had no reason to suppose you would be out of town. I saw Mr Bourke, and requested him to tell you how I was situated, and how impossible it would be for me to call again. This I hope is an answer. But why should I be disinclined to an adverse discussion with you? unless, indeed, I should think that no practical end was to be gained by it. Surely I am not wrong in supposing that though our discussion might have been adverse, it could not have been conducted in other than an amicable spirit. In truth, however, I did not then expect or even dream of an adverse discussion with you on this subject. I did think that the mere statement, that an extensive change in regard to the system of Crown prosecutions was in contemplation, and that the arrangements were nearly completed, would have produced an irresistible conviction of the propriety of postponing Barrington's application, either till that change had been effected or till a careful inquiry had shown that the strong opinions entertained with regard to the consequences of acceding to that application were erroneous.

"With respect to the 'minute' detailing and explaining the plan, there are some alterations which further consideration has suggested which must be submitted to the Lord Lieutenant and Lord Morpeth for their decision before it would be right to send it to the Treasury. Considerable opposition to this measure must of course be expected, and it is therefore essential that it should come before the Treasury in as perfect a state as possible. His Excellency is also desirous of going over the 'minute' with Lord Morpeth when he arrives, as he has done with the law officers. This revision will certainly be completed in a few days after Lord Morpeth's arrival, and the 'minute' thus revised will then be in Lord Morpeth's hands for transmission to the Treasury.

"I have now explained to you all my proceedings in regard to this matter. They have at least been open and undisguised; if they have given annoyance either to you or Barrington I am sorry for it, but on reviewing them calmly, I must candidly say that I am not aware of having said or done anything which I should wish to retract. I saw a letter from Barrington to Lord Morpeth yesterday, and I am happy to find that he is coming over soon, and most sincerely do I hope that the misunderstanding which appears to have arisen, from what cause I know not, will thereby be removed. I have been suffering for the last few days from a return of weakness in my eyes, which made it necessary for me to avoid all writing but what was absolutely indispensable; this is my excuse for not having immediately replied to your letter.—Always most faithfully and sincerely yours,

"T. DRUMMOND."

"The Chancellor of the Exchequer."

Drummond's arguments prevailed. Barrington's son was not joined with him in the office of Crown Solicitor during Drummond's lifetime, nor, I believe, after his death.[1]

It may be added that Barrington was a man of great ability, and decided popular views—reasons sufficient for inducing Drummond to keep him in active service, and to see that no one else did the duties of his important office.

In 1839, De Beaumont's "L'Irlande" was published. Dr Cooke Taylor, of Dublin University, set to work immediately on a translation. When it was nearly finished he wrote to Drummond.

DR COOKE TAYLOR TO DRUMMOND.

"[1839.]

"SIR,—I beg leave to send you by this day's post a number of the *Athenæum*, containing a notice of De Beaumont's 'Ireland,' with rather copious extracts. It was at first my purpose to dedicate my translation of the work, which is in a state of forwardness, to you, without going through the formality of asking your leave; for the book is, after all, only an extended commentary on 'property has its duties as well as its rights.' But De Beaumont's language is so very strong, that I deem it better to send you some specimens before asking you to connect your name with it in any way.

"May I take the liberty of asking whether there are any

[1] So I have recently been informed. Private letter *penès me.*

statistics of crime in Ireland which can be compared with statistics of ejectment. I am imprisoned by rheumatism in the face, united with the comforts of toothache, or I would not ask you to take any trouble in guiding my researches. But I will presume so much farther as to inquire how I could procure a copy of the Railway Report, part of which would go far to show that Ireland contains the elements of a middle class, which, if developed, would be the greatest of all checks to a landed aristocracy.—I have the honour to be, your obedient servant,

"W. C. TAYLOR."

No copy of Drummond's reply has been kept.

I shall close this chapter with letters from two eminent men who met Drummond in Ireland — Earl Fortescue, whose father succeeded Lord Normanby in the Lord Lieutenancy, and Sir C. Gavan Duffy.

EARL FORTESCUE TO MRS DRUMMOND.

"CASTLE HILL, NORTH DEVON,
"*April* 17, 1888.

"DEAR MRS DRUMMOND,—I have searched my father's portfolios in vain for any letters that could be of use to you in your pious work, or could throw any fresh light upon my father's relations, as Lord Lieutenant, with Mr Drummond—relations which, though constant while they lasted, which unfortunately was little more than one year, were almost always carried on *vivâ voce.* I have therefore to fall back on my sadly fading recollections of now nearly half a century ago.

"My father, with my late brother and myself, landed in Ireland on the first week of 1839, and forthwith commenced with Mr Drummond—of whose high character and valuable services he had already heard much—that official intercourse which speedily ripened into a sincere friendship, terminated only by Mr Drummond's lamented death.

"My father always spoke of him from the first with respect and esteem; but these were soon much enhanced when he realised, not only the ability, and indefatigable industry, but the singleness of purpose, and patriotic enthusiasm with which the Under Secretary laboured for the benefit of the country in which he had been called upon to serve. My father often spoke of the perfect straightforwardness, the dauntless moral courage, and the absolute unselfishness he had found in him; and being himself one of the sincerest, most fearless, most upright, and unselfish of men, he could well appreciate those qualities in his trusted friend and daily fellow-labourer in the Government of Ireland. I need hardly remind you that Lord Morpeth, a congenial spirit, loved and honoured by both, and in constant full communication with them, was detained in England by Cabinet and Parliamentary duties during the greater part of the time, and left them to transact between them on the spot much of the business that had to be done. My father had removed me from Cambridge, where I was reading rather slackly for honours, in order to make me his private secretary. But being then himself for the first time in office, and therefore without official experience, he found that he should do wisely to secure the services of his predecessor's aide-de-camp (C. Romilly), who was in some degree conversant with the routine of the business, and knew something besides of the officials and society in Dublin. He readily promised to let me see something of his work, and to show me how to help him in doing it; while my father, relying fully on my discretion, not only let me know all the confidential conversations,—I had all the confidential letters he had,—but after a little while got Mr Drummond's consent, and that of a few other officials at Dublin Castle, to my being present at their constant business interviews with my father, and hearing what passed.

"Mr Drummond very soon, in the kindest manner, encouraged me to question him freely, when he was not too busy, and seemed to take an amiable pleasure in eliciting my crude, youthful opinions on the current topics of the day. So I remember I speedily conceived a sort of affectionate reverence for him, which was kindled almost to enthusiasm by the abuse constantly showered upon him by the opponents of the Government.

"But I too soon, alas! lost for ever all further opportunities of strengthening that feeling by the personal intercourse which I prized so highly. I went abroad that autumn with my grandfather, Lord Harrowby, and several of his family, and was staying with them at Naples, when I was suddenly recalled in all haste by my father, and posted back to England day and night. This was for the purpose either of being a candidate at the dissolution, which was to have taken place if the Government were defeated, as at one moment seemed not improbable, on Sir John Yorke Buller's motion, or of becoming, as I did in February 1840, one of the Prime Minister's (Lord Melbourne) private secretaries, which kept me away from Ireland till some time after Mr Drummond's lamented death.

"But I never lost the feeling about him which I have described, and I cherish his memory still as that of one of the few men whom I consider it one of the privileges of my life to have known, and a high honour to have had the right to call my friend.

"Much regretting the meagreness of the information and recollections I have been able to write you, I remain, dear Mrs Drummond, yours sincerely,

"FORTESCUE."

SIR C. GAVAN DUFFY TO R. BARRY O'BRIEN.

"ST MARTIN LANTOSQUE, ALPES MARITIMES,
"*August* 1888.

"MY DEAR O'BRIEN,—I can be of little assistance to you, I fear, in furnishing personal impressions of Mr Drummond. It is true I saw him, and even transacted business with him once; but I was then a young journalist, barely escaped from boyhood, and he was an experienced and highly-placed official. And I am not sure that I understood in those days that the courtly Mulgrave was only the figurehead of the ship of State,—a gorgeously gilded and decorated, but ligneous figurehead as it seems to me by later lights,—and that the man at the wheel was Thomas Drummond.

"The popular Viceroy won my heart by a stroke of policy which was certainly concerted with Drummond, and, perhaps, prompted by him. In 1836 he made a tour through Ulster, and, for the first time in the memory of men then living, Catholics and Protestants were treated by the Sovereign's representative on an equal footing—a memorable and phenomenal transaction. I assisted at his reception in my native town. The gentry universally held away from him, and even the better class of Presbyterian shopkeepers were poorly represented on the Committee which prepared an Address. The great man of the town, the captain of a regiment of militia long disbanded, and the provost of a corporation which had not met for a quarter of a century, could not, as land agent of a Whig Peer, altogether withhold his countenance, but he intimated that he would visit the Viceroy on his own account, and not form part of any deputation. The men we mustered were the local doctor, attorney, woollen draper, and half a dozen country priests, headed, or rather heralded, by a handsome and stately old gentleman, who was a casual visitor to the town at the moment—Charles Hamilton Teeling of historic memory. Mr Teeling's name was a familiar one throughout the North, and it is probable that it was this unwonted spectacle of priest and rebel honouring the constituted authorities which is commemorated in Colonel Blacker's contemporary Orange ballad—

'Forth start the spawn of treason, the 'scaped of '98,
To bask in courtly favour, and sway the helm of State.
He comes, the open rebel fierce; *he* comes, the Jesuit sly,
But put your trust in God, my boys, and keep your powder dry.'

Lord Mulgrave received us as if we came in Court suits, and he did wisely, for these men were the leaders of the Liberal Club which ten years before had opened the county for the first time since the Union, by electing an emancipator against a combination of the gentry and the Government. A year later I was living in Dublin, and connected with the *Morning Register*—a journal which supported the Irish Government of Mulgrave, Woulfe, and Drummond, and I naturally heard much of their policy and proceedings.

"The first circumstance which fixed my eyes on Mr Drummond arose in my native county. There was a man there named Sam Gray, the Grand Master of an Orange Lodge, of whom it was notorious that he had murdered a Catholic neighbour in open day. He was tried, twice I think, by Orange juries, who refused to find a verdict against the Grand Master on any evidence, and he was at length set free. Some years after his trial a country gentleman, who was recommended by the Grand Jury of Monaghan for the office of High Sheriff of the county, in a freak of insolent bravado, appointed Sam Gray his sub-sheriff, authorised to impanel juries and control the administration of justice in his bailiwick. It was an outrage as gross as if James Carey, after his appearance in Green Street, had been selected by Mr Balfour for a similar employment; but, in the state of feeling in the north at that time, scarcely any one expected redress. Between the Union and the Mulgrave Administration the Ulster Grand Jurors might have raised Judas Iscariot to office, and any remonstrance of the Catholics would have been treated as an impertinence. But a young barrister from Belfast of exceptional independence of character, Thomas O'Hagan, destined in later times to become head of his profession in Ireland,[1] took the business in hand; and there was fortunately a strong, just man, fit to deal with such an emergency. Mr Drummond immediately wrote to the High Sheriff, pointing out the impropriety of the appointment which he had made, and requesting that he would substitute some unobjectionable person for Mr Gray. The High Sheriff replied that it was his undoubted right to select his deputy; neither law nor usage entitled the Executive to interfere with his choice, and by his choice he was determined to abide. Drummond replied, admitting the right of the Sheriff to select his deputy, but he pointed out that the right of the Lord Lieutenant to appoint and remove the High Sheriff was equally beyond controversy, and he informed the arrogant squire that His Excellency had thought proper to exercise that right by superseding him in office. The northern gentry were frantic with indignation, and, under the advice (as it was believed) of the leaders in Dublin (men who had grown grey in office before the coming of the Whigs), they resolved to checkmate the Administration,—to boycott it, as we would say just now. No gentleman of the county, it was resolved, would consent to hold the office from which the patron of Sam Gray had been removed. It was like a cordial to the heart of Ulster Catholics, who had never before had a taste of fairplay in such contests, to see how Drummond and his

[1] Afterwards Lord O'Hagan, and the first Catholic Lord Chancellor since the Revolution of '88.

colleagues dealt with this impediment. A Catholic gentleman of insignificant estate, but of good sense and good education, was immediately appointed High Sheriff, and, for the first time since a M'Mahon held the office under James II., a Catholic framed grand and petty panels, controlled prisons, and received the circuit judges in the 'gap of the north.'

"My slight personal communication with Drummond arose from another salutary stroke of authority. The citizens of Dublin were dexterously excluded from the franchise by an Act of Parliament, which required the payment of certain local taxes, in some cases as many as ten, before an elector was entitled to vote. But the Dublin corporation, in which no Catholic had been permitted to sit for five generations, were not content with such *chevaux de frise.* When an election was approaching, it was their habit, it was alleged, to instruct certain of their officers to keep out of the way, so that Catholic and Liberal electors might not have an opportunity of paying their taxes. This practice was brought under the notice of the Lord Lieutenant, and he appointed a Royal Commission to inquire into it. An official report of the proceedings was necessary, and the *Morning Register*, being requested to recommend a suitable person to furnish it, the editor selected me. Before the business was wound up I needed to call on Mr Drummond at the Castle—the sole visit I have made to that establishment in a long lifetime. After I had sat out a crowd of competitors for an interview, I was ushered into his room. I saw a grave, resolute man, with deep brow and a firm jaw, who was abrupt and brief of speech, and went straight to the point at issue. Though I was the last of a tedious train of clients who consumed his morning, the Secretary had an encouraging word for me. 'Well, my friend,' he said; 'what can I do for you?' When my business was considered, he asked for my address, with a view to a further communication. I proposed to write it. 'Give me your card,' he said rather brusquely. 'I have not got a card,' I replied. 'Good God!' exclaimed the overworked Secretary, in a tone which was a lesson to me, 'think of a sane man coming to transact business at a public department without a card of address.'

"During Drummond's career there was an organisation of the Liberals of Ulster under Sharman Crawford and Mr D. R. Ross, to keep rampant Orangeism in check, which he promoted if he did not project. But you have probably better information on this subject than I can supply.[1]

"Since that era, nearly half a century now, I have gathered and scattered libraries in widely separated countries; but, among a few books with which I have never parted, there is a copy of Drummond's 'Irish Railway Report,' given to me by a friend of his and a dear friend of mine as a cyclopædia of practical knowledge on Ireland. It was published at the same time as Gustave de Beaumont's 'L'Irlande, sociale, politique, et religieuse.' In a time of great intellectual barrenness, it is strange that a Frenchman and a Scotchman should have produced books which are still landmarks in the sluggish record of Irish progress.—Believe me to be, my dear O'Brien, very faithfully yours,

"C. GAVAN DUFFY."

[1] Sir Gavan Duffy is right in supposing that Drummond was interested in the formation of a Liberal party in Ulster; and so highly were his services recognised, that he was asked in 1839 to become a candidate for the representation of Belfast in the Imperial Parliament.

MR GIBSON TO DRUMMOND.

"BELFAST [1839].

"DEAR SIR,—I had the honour to-day of receiving a deputation from a very large and most respectable meeting of the Reform Society, requesting me to again stand for the town at the ensuing general election. This honour

The end of 1839 found Drummond a dying man, but resolved to remain at his post to the last. There were no personal reasons for this determination. Drummond's marriage with Miss Kinnaird had made him financially independent. But he had given himself up to Ireland, and he was ready to sacrifice life itself in the service of his adopted country. His friends urged him to retire from the public service for a time, but he would only promise to take another holiday early in the ensuing year. He thought that the weightiest duties of his office were done, that the most anxious period was past. He had the government of the country well in hand. He had survived the storms of abuse which the Ascendancy hoped would have overwhelmed him. He had won the respect of all classes, and gained the affections of the masses of the people. He believed he was in smooth water now, but he would not give up the helm until the ship was safely in port.

personal considerations have obliged me positively to decline, and I have been requested by a Committee appointed at the meeting (namely, Mr Sinnet, Mr Grimshaw, Mr Dunville, Mr Cranton, Mr Moorly), to state to you their conviction that you are the person most acceptable, under present circumstances, to the great body of the Liberal electors, and most likely to meet with their united support, and to inquire from you whether you are willing to entertain the proposal to become their candidate?

"I have not time, as the deputation have only just left me, to enter into any details. These can form matter of subsequent communication. Letters have been forwarded to Lord Belfast, to ascertain his Lordship's views, but until your answer is received no mention shall be made of this communication. Allow me to express the satisfaction I should feel if that answer should be favourable, and my hope, if so, that the town shall possess a representative so worthy of its highest confidence.—I remain, my dear Sir, yours faithfully,

"JAMES GIBSON."

CHAPTER XII.

1840.

DRUMMOND had promised to take a holiday early in the year 1840, but when the time came he put off the day. He was better, he said, and would gradually grow strong; moreover, he could ill be spared at the Castle just then. But his family and friends were not satisfied with these excuses; they urged him daily to leave Ireland and seek change and rest. He, however, made light of his ailments, and said it would be time enough to go away in the autumn. In January he wrote to his mother, to quiet her fears and cheer her by giving a good account of himself.

DRUMMOND TO HIS MOTHER.

"DUBLIN, *January* 29, 1840.

"MY DEAREST DEAR MOTHER,—My throat is so much better that I do not think I shall have to leave home at all; and the doing so would be very inconvenient at present. I am quite sure that if I do go, I should not go either to London or Edinburgh, or to anywhere I am like to meet anyone I know. Speaking is the thing to be avoided.

"If we are all spared till autumn, I shall propose running over to Scotland after Lord Morpeth comes over, or even before, and bring my Maria and little May, who will then be four years old, with me. This would be very delightful, and to this we may look forward with some confidence.

"Kindest love to my ever dear Eliza.—Believe me, dearest Mother, your ever affectionate son,

"T. D."

But his mother's fears were not quieted. She wrote an anxious letter, begging him to think more of himself, and to seek the change and rest which the physicians enjoined. He replied on Feb. 2:—

Drummond to his Mother.

"I do assure you, my dearest dear Mother, that you are distressing yourself very unnecessarily about me. I have carefully told you the whole extent of throat affection, which is really very trifling. It is so much diminished that I am going to the office to-morrow; but if it be not gone entirely by the end of the week I shall run over to Cheltenham for seven or eight days. I have no cough, and really very little discomfort.—Ever your affectionate son,

"T. Drummond."

But Drummond's wife, the best and most watchful of nurses, would not desist from urging her husband to yield to the advice of the doctors and the entreaties of friends until at length he consented to go to Cheltenham. On February 16 he wrote to his mother:—

Drummond to his Mother.

"My Dearest Dear Mother,—I have just time to say that we are on the point of starting to sail this evening by the half-past eleven o'clock packet for Liverpool. The night calm and pleasant. All well here—pets and all. We go by railway to Birmingham, and thence to Cheltenham, where we shall remain. Maria sends her kindest love to you.

"Adieu, my dearest dear Mother, and with kindest love to my ever dear Eliza, and affectionate remembrances to John, believe me, ever most affectionately,

"T. Drummond."

It was scarcely worth Drummond's while to have gone away. He was back again in less than a fortnight, and hard at work in Dublin Castle. Throughout March he continued at his post, and still remained the life and soul of the administration.

The Ascendancy did not trouble him much now. In 1839 they had put forth their whole strength to crush him, but failed ignominiously. They had not yet recovered from the effects of their defeat. The debates in the Commons, Drummond's evidence before the Lords' Committee, were fresh in their memory. They were demoralised. From the beginning of 1840 to the day of Drummond's death they scarcely stirred to attack him. Peace reigned throughout the land, and the Under Secretary gave himself up to the preparation of schemes for developing the resources of the country and improving the condition of the labouring poor. In the midst of this work he was struck down by fatal illness.

On Friday, April 10, he went to the Castle as usual. He always looked pallid and careworn now. His slender and graceful figure had grown very thin. His step had lost its elasticity. The genial and kindly smile which lighted up his handsome face was overcast. But his flashing eye still told of the energy and spirit that lived within. He never complained, and no one knew how he felt on any particular day. On this day he did not seem to suffer from any special illness. In the evening he entertained a number of friends at dinner. He was bright and cheery, and full of plans for the good of Ireland. On Saturday he went to the Castle again, and worked for nine hours. On Sunday morning he confessed to Mrs Drummond that he felt seriously unwell. The family physician, Dr Johnson, was at once sent for. He saw that Drummond was suffering from peritonitis. The case was one of the greatest gravity. On Monday, Drummond was worse, and Sir

Henry Marsh and Sir Philip Crampton were called in consultation with Dr Johnson. Sir Henry Marsh remained up with Drummond all Monday night.

On Tuesday afternoon the *Evening Post* contained a paragraph stating that the Under Secretary was lying dangerously ill at his lodge in the Phœnix Park. This was the first intelligence of his illness which reached the citizens of Dublin, and throughout Tuesday evening many inquiries were made at the Phœnix Park, and the newspaper offices in the city.

On Tuesday night Drummond began to sink. He suffered much pain, but was calm, placid, and resigned. He asked to see his children; but Dr Johnson told him that it would be better not. Drummond said: "Very well;" and asked the doctor to open a drawer, and hand him three little Bibles which were in it. He said: "Give these to my children, with their papa's blessing. It is the best legacy I can leave them." Later on, Dr Johnson broke the terrible news to him that he had not now long to live. He remained calm and unmoved, and whispered: "Doctor, all is peace; tell my dear mother that on my death-bed I remembered the instructions I had received from her in childhood." Mrs Drummond entered the room. Drummond called her to him, saying: "Dearest beloved Maria, you have been an angel wife to me. Your admonitions have blessed me."

On Wednesday morning he lay in a dying state, but perfectly conscious, and wearing that kindly loving smile which so well expressed the feelings of his tender, noble heart. The end was now near, and Dr Johnson asked Drummond where he would wish to be buried, "In Scotland or Ireland?" He answered quietly, slowly, and firmly: "I wish to be buried in Ireland, the country of my adoption—a country which I loved, which I have faithfully served, and for which I believe I have sacrificed my life."[1] Shortly after saying these words, Drummond died. He passed calmly away on Wednesday afternoon, April 15.

The intelligence of his death spread rapidly through Dublin, causing intense sorrow, and even consternation. No one had expected so sudden and fatal a termination to his illness. O'Connell had made preparations for a great public meeting to take place on April 16. But when the news of Drummond's death reached the agitator, he said: "There must be no meeting now; our first duty is to pay the last tribute of respect and esteem to the memory of Mr Drummond. Communicate with the Leinster delegates, and tell them not to come up. Nothing must be done till we have performed the melancholy duty of following Drummond to the grave." On Thursday the papers announced the sad event, which, it is scarcely an exaggeration to say, cast a dark shadow over the land. From the Liberal *Freeman's Journal* to the Orange *Evening Packet*, from the London *Morning Chronicle* to the *Mayo Mercury*, all bore testimony to the genius, uprightness, self-sacrificing patriotism of the man.

The *Morning Chronicle* questioned "whether in the whole range of the public service a loss could have been sustained more deeply to be deplored, and less easily to be supplied. How great his loss must prove will probably be felt by numbers, especially in that country to whose interests he had unreservedly attached himself, but can only be adequately measured by those who worked with him, or under him; and it is assuredly only they, with the inmates of his own domestic circle, who can at all appreciate the single-minded simplicity and fervour of his character, the unbroken and cheerful sweetness of his temper, and the high-minded delicacy of his conscience, from whose clear mirror every image of dishonesty, oppression, or meanness would have shrunk appalled."

[1] "The last words of Thomas Drummond," written down by Mrs Sharp.

The *Dublin Evening Post* declared: "No Irishman that ever lived was more thoroughly, more cordially, Irish than he—was more resolved, as far as his power went, and he was a man of the first mental capacity—as far as his influence extended, and that was, fortunately for the country, great indeed—to ameliorate her condition—to promote her prosperity—and, above all, to dispense equal and impartial justice amongst her people."

The *Freeman's Journal* asserted: "Mr Drummond was among the chief of those, whose anxiety to serve this country, reconciled the people to the continuance of the experimental policy [of giving the Union another trial], the long anticipated failure of which is now universally acknowledged."

The *Morning Register* thought that "it was not enough that we fix the memory of Mr Drummond in the nation's heart—the first English official, in the long centuries of our connection with England, so enshrined; we must testify to civilised Europe—to England—to our posterity, how we prize his rare and inestimable services. Where he has chosen a tomb, there also be his monument. Let our people, and their children, learn to look with pride upon the resting-place of one, whose love for Ireland presents an example to every patriot, and a model to every statesman."

Even the Orange *Evening Packet* bore grudging testimony to his powers: "He was, in fact, the sheet-anchor of the Irish Executive from the day of the Lichfield House compact to the day of his death; and it must not be denied that he filled office during a period of great difficulty. His commissioner's report[1] reflects the highest credit on his head, and proves him to have been a great man."

The provincial press joined in the general lamentation.

[1] The Railway Report.

The *Waterford Chronicle:* "The memory of Mr Drummond will live long embalmed in the fondest recollections of the people."

The *Newry Examiner:* "The ashes of Ireland's benefactor must not lie unhonoured by a public monument."

The *Kilkenny Journal:* "Seldom, if ever, has it devolved upon us to write an obituary for a public man, whose loss we so sincerely deplore, or whose death will be so universally felt."

The *Northern Whig:* "The Irish nation will join in a feeling of gratitude for the services, and of sorrow for the loss of so great a public benefactor."

Enlightened and liberal Scotsmen were proud of their fellow-countryman, and the *Scotsman* gave expression to their opinion: "His loss will be mourned from one end of Ireland to the other; for we venture to say, that never did an individual hold office in that unfortunate country who more faithfully devoted the energies of a vigorous understanding, and the virtues of a noble heart, to the advancement of her happiness and prosperity."

While the public press was thus testifying to Drummond's noble character, his bereaved mother and afflicted widow received letters from many sorrowing friends.

Lord Ebrington wrote to Drummond's mother:—

"How severe your affliction must be, I can but too well understand, after the opportunities which I derived from our daily and confidential intercourse of observing those noble and endearing qualities of heart and of mind which made me feel for him quite the affection of a brother."

Earl Spencer wrote:—

"If ever a man died for his country, he did so, and that country ought not, and, I believe, will not, be sparing in its expressions of gratitude to his memory. . . . When I saw him last I deceived myself, he looked so well and appeared so young, that I hoped the illness which he had suffered from before had passed away. But I still knew that the labour he was going through was beyond human endurance, and I urged upon him to take the first opportunity he could with honour to retire from his position in Ireland, to come into Parliament, and to apply himself to what is considered the higher, though it certainly is not a more useful or honourable, line of political life. I did so for the reasons I have given, and also because I was confident that in this, as in everything he had undertaken, his abilities and high character would soon place him in the most eminent position. He promised me he would do so, but I was obliged to agree with him, that unless some change took place in the Irish Government, he could not with honour to himself resign his office.

"My loss is great indeed, in the loss of such a friend; the loss of the country is great in the loss of such a public man; but yours, my dear Madam, is so much beyond all, that I can find no words to express it. It is not the loss of a mother merely, it is not even the loss of a mother in losing such a son, but my intimacy with him led me to know the peculiar attachment between you and him. I know he was to you everything. Had he fallen in his military profession, you would have had the consolation of feeling, in common with other mothers who have had to lament their sons who have died fighting for their country, that he died doing his duty; but you would not have had the consolation of knowing that he had left behind him works which will be beneficial to his fellow-creatures for ages, perhaps, to come. He has died for his country, and it is his extra official labours which have been the cause of his death; and you must reflect with satisfaction that, whenever Ireland does attain to the state of wealth and prosperity she will ultimately come to, it will be owing to Drummond's Report on the Railway System; that if disturbance is checked in that country, it will be owing to the able arrangements he has made with respect to the constabulary force. It was under the extra labour imposed on him by these two great works that his health broke down.

"He died, therefore, for his country, and he died doing her as great good as any one man ever effected."

His lordship also wrote to the unhappy widow:—

EARL SPENCER TO MRS DRUMMOND.

"ALTHORP.

"MY DEAR MADAM,—. . . Any memorial of one to whom I was so much attached as I was to him will be most gratifying to me, and I, therefore, thank you most sincerely for the prayer-book. To speak of gratitude between persons living on the terms he and I did, is impossible. The feeling between us was of an infinitely stronger nature; but if this were not so, I should say that there never existed anyone to whom I ever owed such a debt of gratitude as I did to him. I speak not merely of his assistance to me in my public life, but much more, for I feel it more, of the support, the comfort, the happiness I derived from his society as my private friend. To us who survive him, the honour in which his name is held, and the deep regret of everyone whose good opinion is worth having, is, undoubtedly, very gratifying.—Believe me, my dear Madam, yours most sincerely,

"SPENCER."

Sir George Philips, from whose house Mrs Drummond had been married, wrote to her:—

SIR GEORGE PHILIPS TO MRS DRUMMOND.

"MY DEAR MARIA,—. . . The death of your beloved husband, and of my invaluable friend, presents to us such a scene as it is impossible to contemplate without deep emotion, and the mind must be ill schooled and devoid of good feelings and principles that fails to derive enduring religious impressions from such an example of Christian hope, resignation, and fortitude. It may be truly said of him what was said of Addison, 'he taught us how to live; and (oh! too high the price for knowledge) he taught us how to die. . '

"If you have not seen the *Morning Chronicle*, I would recommend you to get it. It contains a short sketch of Mr Drummond's history, and is written with so much feeling, that I could not read it without shedding tears. I was curious to see what such unprincipled papers as the *Times* and *Morning Post* would say on the occasion. Their silence I consider as an unwilling tribute of respect and praise and deference to public opinion and feeling.

"My love to Mrs Sharp. God bless and preserve you both, and your dear children.—Ever, my dear Maria, your affectionate friend,

"G. PHILIPS."

On Wednesday, April 21, Drummond's remains were borne to their last resting place in Mount Jerome Cemetery, Dublin.

The funeral procession left the Under Secretary's Lodge in the Phœnix Park, at 9 A.M. It was accompanied by two hundred carriages belonging to the leading men of the country, and followed by a vast concourse of people. On entering the Cemetery, the pall was borne by the Lord Chancellor (Plunket), the Master of the Rolls (Sir Michael O'Loghlen), Judges Perrin and Ball, Baron Richards, and Major-General Sir J. F. Burgoyne. Among those who followed, close to the pail-bearers, the proud figure of O'Connell appeared pre-eminent. Never before, and never since, has an Irish leader, possessing the confidence of the vast majority of his fellow-countrymen, followed an English official to the grave.

When the services of the English Church for the dead had been read, Drummond's staff at the Castle asked permission to lower the coffin into the grave. This permission was granted, and, to use the language of an Irish journalist, who witnessed the sad ceremony, "shortly after one o'clock the tomb closed over the remains of as good a man in private life, and as efficient a public officer as ever the world produced."[1]

Two days after Drummond had been laid in the grave, a meeting was held in Dublin to consider the most fitting means of paying a lasting tribute of esteem to his memory. Foremost among the speakers at this meeting were Judge Moore and O'Connell.

It was unanimously resolved that a statue of Drummond should be erected to commemorate his public services and private virtues. This statue, executed by Hogan, was erected in 1843.

It now stands in the City Hall, Dublin, "side by side with the sculptured figures of Charles Lucas, Henry Grattan, and Daniel O'Connell."

Ireland to-day treasures the memory of the solitary English official who won the hearts of her people.

Drummond's fame rests on his administration of Ireland. It is idle to speculate what might have been his career had he followed the military profession or remained faithful to science. As a young engineer officer he showed soldierly qualities. He was self-reliant, courageous, cool: witness the incident told by General Larcom.[2] In science he made a name which still endures, and originated an invention which, it is scarcely an exaggeration to say, anticipated one of the most remarkable discoveries of our time—the

[1] *Dublin Evening Post*, April 21, 1840. [2] *Ante*, p. 19.

electric light. But he left the army, he gave up science for Ireland. Why? In answering this question it is only necessary to remember the distinguishing feature of Drummond's character—an intense sympathy for human suffering. The miseries of the Irish touched his heart, and he devoted his life to right the wrongs of an oppressed people.

He possessed exceptional qualities as an English ruler in Ireland. He was strong; he was just; he knew the country. He was not dependent on officials for his information, nor beholden to partizans for his policy. He was not swayed by the exigencies of party, nor fettered by the commands of incompetent superiors. He had studied the Irish question *au fond*. He held decided views upon it. He came to Ireland to carry out those views, and he allowed no one to interfere with his determination.

Those who entered into controversy with Drummond on Irish affairs found a man armed with facts, and fortified by an inflexible resolution and an intrepid spirit. He crushed his enemies on the Roden Committee by breadth of knowledge and readiness of wit. He defeated the Ascendancy in Ireland by strength of will and wealth of resource. He scattered the factions, curbed Orangeism, and restrained the excesses of the Ribbon Society by marvellous tact, matchless temper, and indomitable energy. He rebuked the landlords with dignity and force; controlled the magistracy with wisdom and caution; managed the police with vigour and skill. He made the Executive Government all-powerful by impressing his own character on the administration. He made public officials popular by teaching them to respect public opinion. He removed the obloquy which for centuries rested on Dublin Castle, by identifying the place with an impartial execution of the laws. Above all, he won the affections of the masses of the people by his love of justice, his hatred of oppression, his sympathy with poverty and suffering, his unfaltering championship of right.

The monument which stands over Drummond's grave in Mount Jerome Cemetery, Dublin, simply bears the inscription—

"THOMAS DRUMMOND."

But sometime in the near future, perhaps, his dying words, which epitomise the work of his life, may be engraved on the stone—

"Bury me in Ireland, the land of my adoption. I have loved her well and served her faithfully."

It remains but to add that in private life Drummond was the most lovable of men; a devoted husband, a tender father, a staunch friend; kind and genial to all around him, and ever ready to comfort, aid, and cheer those who sought his counsel and help.

His widow still lives, and remembers vividly the incidents of his eventful life. She, too, sympathises with the nation for whom her husband worked and died.

Drummond left three children—Mary, Fanny Eleanor, and Emily. Of these, Mary—who in 1863 married Joseph Kay, Q.C.—and Emily survive.

INDEX.

PRINTED BY

TURNBULL AND SPEARS,

EDINBURGH.

A LIST OF

KEGAN PAUL, TRENCH, & CO.'S PUBLICATIONS.

10.88

1 *Paternoster Square, London.*

A LIST OF KEGAN PAUL, TRENCH, & CO.'S PUBLICATIONS.

CONTENTS.

A. K. H. B.—From a Quiet Place. A New Volume of Sermons. Crown 8vo. 5*s.*

AINSWORTH (*F. W.*)—Personal Narrative of the Euphrates Expedition. 2 vols. 8vo. 30*s.*

ALEXANDER (*William, D.D., Bishop of Derry*)—The Great Question, and other Sermons. Crown 8vo. 6*s.*

ALLIES (*T. W.*) *M.A.*—Per Crucem ad Lucem. The Result of a Life. 2 vols. Demy 8vo. 25*s.*

A Life's Decision. Crown 8vo. 7*s.* 6*d.*

AMHERST (*Rev. W. J.*)—The History of Catholic Emancipation and the Progress of the Catholic Church in the British Isles (chiefy in England) from 1771–1820. 2 vols. Demy 8vo. 24*s.*

AMOS (*Prof. Sheldon*)—The History and Principles of the Civil Law of Rome. Demy 8vo. 16*s.*

ARISTOTLE—The Nicomachean Ethics of Aristotle. Translated by F. H. Peters, M.A. Third Edition. Crown 8vo. 6*s.*

AUBERTIN (*J. J.*)—A Flight to Mexico. With 7 full-page Illustrations and a Railway Map of Mexico. Crown 8vo. 7*s.* 6*d.*

Six Months in Cape Colony and Natal. With Illustrations and Map. Crown 8vo. 6*s.*

A Fight with Distances. With 8 Illustrations and 2 Maps. Crown 8vo. 7*s.* 6*d.*

Aucassin and Nicolette. Edited in Old French and rendered in Modern English by F. W. Bourdillon. Fcap. 8vo. 7*s.* 6*d.*

AUCHMUTY (*A. C.*)—Dives and Pauper, and other Sermons. Crown 8vo. 3*s.* 6*d.*

AZARIAS (*Brother*)—Aristotle and the Christian Church. Small crown 8vo. 3*s.* 6*d.*

BADGER (*George Percy*) *D.C.L.*—An English-Arabic Lexicon. In which the equivalents for English Words and Idiomatic Sentences are rendered into literary and colloquial Arabic. Royal 4to. 80*s.*

BAGEHOT (*Walter*)—THE ENGLISH CONSTITUTION. Fifth Edition. Crown 8vo. 7*s.* 6*d.*

LOMBARD STREET. A Description of the Money Market. Ninth Edition. Crown 8vo. 7*s.* 6*d.*

ESSAYS ON PARLIAMENTARY REFORM. Crown 8vo. 5*s.*

SOME ARTICLES ON THE DEPRECIATION OF SILVER, AND TOPICS CONNECTED WITH IT. Demy 8vo. 5*s.*

BAGOT (*Alan*) *C.E.*—ACCIDENTS IN MINES: Their Causes and Prevention. Crown 8vo. 6*s.*

THE PRINCIPLES OF COLLIERY VENTILATION. Second Edition, greatly enlarged, crown 8vo. 5*s.*

THE PRINCIPLES OF CIVIL ENGINEERING IN ESTATE MANAGEMENT. Crown 8vo. 7*s.* 6*d.*

BAIRD (*Henry M.*)—THE HUGUENOTS AND HENRY OF NAVARRE. 2 vols. 8vo. With Maps. 24*s.*

BALDWIN (*Capt. J. H.*)—THE LARGE AND SMALL GAME OF BENGAL AND THE NORTH-WESTERN PROVINCES OF INDIA. With 20 Illustrations. New and Cheaper Edition. Small 4to. 10*s.* 6*d.*

BALLIN (*Ada S. and F. L.*)—A HEBREW GRAMMAR. With Exercises selected from the Bible. Crown 8vo. 7*s.* 6*d.*

BALL (*John, F.R.S.*)—NOTES OF A NATURALIST IN SOUTH AMERICA. Crown 8vo. 8*s.* 6*d.*

BARCLAY (*Edgar*)—MOUNTAIN LIFE IN ALGERIA. Crown 4to. With numerous Illustrations by Photogravure. 16*s.*

BASU (*K. P.*) *M.A.*—STUDENTS' MATHEMATICAL COMPANION. Containing problems in Arithmetic, Algebra, Geometry, and Mensuration, for Students of the Indian Universities. Crown 8vo. 6*s.*

BAUR (*Ferdinand*) *Dr. Ph., Professor in Maulbronn.*—A PHILOLOGICAL INTRODUCTION TO GREEK AND LATIN FOR STUDENTS. Translated and adapted from the German by C. KEGAN PAUL, M.A., and the Rev. E. D. STONE, M.A. Third Edition. Crown 8vo. 6*s.*

BENN (*Alfred W.*)—THE GREEK PHILOSOPHERS. 2 vols. Demy 8vo. 28*s.*

BENSON (*A. C.*)—WILLIAM LAUD, SOMETIME ARCHBISHOP OF CANTERBURY. A Study. With Portrait. Crown 8vo. 6*s.*

BIBLE FOLK-LORE.—A STUDY IN COMPARATIVE MYTHOLOGY. Large crown 8vo. 10*s.* 6*d.*

BIRD (*Charles*) *F.G.S.*—HIGHER EDUCATION IN GERMANY AND ENGLAND: Being a Brief Practical Account of the Organisation and Curriculum of the German Higher Schools. With Critical Remarks and Suggestions with reference to those of England. Small crown 8vo. 2*s.* 6*d.*

BIRTH AND GROWTH OF RELIGION. A Book for Workers. Crown 8vo. cloth, 2*s.*; paper covers, 1*s.*

BLACKBURN (*Mrs. Hugh*)—BIBLE BEASTS AND BIRDS. A New Edition of 'Illustrations of Scripture by an Animal Painter.' With Twenty-two Plates, Photographed from the Originals, and Printed in Platinotype. 4to. cloth extra, gilt edges, 42*s.*

BLOOMFIELD (*The Lady*)—REMINISCENCES OF COURT AND DIPI MATIC LIFE. New and Cheaper Edition. With Frontispiece. Crown 8vo.

BLUNT (*The Ven. Archdeacon*)—THE DIVINE PATRIOT, AND OTH SERMONS, Preached in Scarborough and in Cannes. Crown 8vo. 4*s*. 6*d*.

BLUNT (*Wilfrid S.*)—THE FUTURE OF ISLAM. Crown 8vo. 6*s*.

IDEAS ABOUT INDIA. Crown 8vo. cloth, 6*s*.

BOSANQUET (*Bernard*)—KNOWLEDGE AND REALITY. A Criticism Mr. F. H. Bradley's 'Principles of Logic.' Crown 8vo. 9*s*.

BOUVERIE-PUSEY (*S. E. B.*)—PERMANENCE AND EVOLUTION. Inquiry into the supposed Mutability of Animal Types. Crown 8vo. 5*s*.

BOWEN (*H. C.*) *M.A.*—STUDIES IN ENGLISH, for the use of Mode Schools. 7th Thousand. Small crown 8vo. 1*s*. 6*d*.

ENGLISH GRAMMAR FOR BEGINNERS. Fcp. 8vo. 1*s*.

SIMPLE ENGLISH POEMS. English Literature for Junior Classes. Four Parts. Parts I., II., and III. 6*d*. each; Part IV. 1*s*.; complete, 3*s*.

BRADLEY (*F. H.*)—THE PRINCIPLES OF LOGIC. Demy 8vo. 16*s*.

BRADSHAW (*Henry*)—MEMOIR. By G. W. PROTHERO. 8vo. 16*s*.

BRIDGETT (*Rev. T. E.*)—HISTORY OF THE HOLY EUCHARIST GREAT BRITAIN. 2 vols. Demy 8vo. 18*s*.

BROOKE (*Rev. S. A.*)—LIFE AND LETTERS OF THE LATE REV. F. \ ROBERTSON, M.A. Edited by.

I. Uniform with Robertson's Sermons. 2 vols. With Steel Portrait, 7*s*. 6*d*.
II. Library Edition. 8vo. With Portrait, 12*s*.
III. A Popular Edition. In 1 vol. 8vo. 6*s*.

THE FIGHT OF FAITH. Sermons preached on various occasior Fifth Edition. Crown 8vo. 7*s*. 6*d*.

THE SPIRIT OF THE CHRISTIAN LIFE. Third Edition. Crown 8vo. 5

THEOLOGY IN THE ENGLISH POETS.—Cowper, Coleridge, Wordswort and Burns. Sixth Edition. Post 8vo. 5*s*.

CHRIST IN MODERN LIFE. Sixteenth Edition. Crown 8vo. 5*s*.

SERMONS. First Series. Thirteenth Edition. Crown 8vo. 5*s*.

SERMONS. Second Series. Sixth Edition. Crown 8vo. 5*s*.

BROWN (*Horatio F.*)—LIFE ON THE LAGOONS. With two Illustratio and a Map. Crown 8vo. 6*s*.

VENETIAN STUDIES. Crown 8vo. 7*s*. 6*d*.

BROWN (*Rev. J. Baldwin*) *B.A.*—THE HIGHER LIFE: its Reali Experience, and Destiny. Seventh Edition. Crown 8vo. 5*s*.

DOCTRINE OF ANNIHILATION IN THE LIGHT OF THE GOSPEL LOVE. Five Discourses. Fourth Edition. Crown 8vo. 2*s*. 6*d*.

THE CHRISTIAN POLICY OF LIFE. A Book for Young Men Business. Third Edition. Crown 8vo. 3*s*. 6*d*.

BURDETT (*Henry C.*)—HELP IN SICKNESS: Where to Go and Wh to Do. Crown 8vo. 1*s*. 6*d*.

HELPS TO HEALTH: The Habitation, The Nursery, The Schoolroo and The Person. With a Chapter on Pleasure and Health Resorts. Crov 8vo. 1*s*. 6*d*.

BURKE (Oliver J.)—SOUTH ISLES OF ARAN (COUNTY GALWAY). Crown 8vo. 2*s*. 6*d*.

BURKE (The late Very Rev. T. N.)—HIS LIFE. By W. J. FITZPATRICK. 2 vols. With Portrait. Demy 8vo. 30*s*.

BURTON (Mrs. Richard)—THE INNER LIFE OF SYRIA, PALESTINE, AND THE HOLY LAND. Post 8vo. 6*s*.

CANDLER (C.)—THE PREVENTION OF CONSUMPTION. A Mode of Prevention founded on a New Theory of the Nature of the Tubercle-Bacillus. Demy 8vo. 10*s*. 6*d*.

CARLYLE AND THE OPEN SECRET OF HIS LIFE. By HENRY LARKIN. Demy 8vo. 14*s*.

CARPENTER (W. B.) LL.D., M.D., F.R.S., &c.—THE PRINCIPLES OF MENTAL PHYSIOLOGY. With their Applications to the Training and Discipline of the Mind, and the Study of its Morbid Conditions. Illustrated. Sixth Edition. 8vo. 12*s*.

NATURE AND MAN: Essays, Scientific and Philosophical. With Memoir of the Author and Portrait. Large crown 8vo. 8*s*. 6*d*.

CATHOLIC DICTIONARY—Containing some account of the Doctrine, Discipline, Rites, Ceremonies, Councils, and Religious Orders of the Catholic Church. By WILLIAM E. ADDIS and THOMAS ARNOLD, M.A. Third Edition, demy 8vo. 21*s*.

CHEYNE (Rev. Canon, M.A., D.D., Edin.)—JOB AND SOLOMON; or, the Wisdom of the Old Testament. Demy 8vo. 12*s*. 6*d*.

THE PROPHECIES OF ISAIAH. Translated with Critical Notes and Dissertations. 2 vols. Fourth Edition. Demy 8vo. 25*s*.

THE BOOK OF PSALMS; or, THE PRAISES OF ISRAEL. A New Translation, with Commentary. Demy 8vo. 16*s*.

CHURGRESS, THE. By The Prig. Fcp. 8vo. 3*s*. 6*d*.

CLAIRAUT—ELEMENTS OF GEOMETRY. Translated by Dr. KAINES. With 145 Figures. Crown 8vo. 4*s*. 6*d*.

CLAPPERTON (Jane Hume)—SCIENTIFIC MELIORISM AND THE EVOLUTION OF HAPPINESS. Large crown 8vo. 8*s*. 6*d*.

CLODD (Edward) F.R.A.S.—THE CHILDHOOD OF THE WORLD: a Simple Account of Man in Early Times. Eighth Edition. Crown 8vo. 3*s*.
A Special Edition for Schools, 1*s*.

THE CHILDHOOD OF RELIGIONS. Including a Simple Account of the Birth and Growth of Myths and Legends. Eighth Thousand. Crown 8vo. 5*s*.
A Special Edition for Schools. 1*s*. 6*d*.

JESUS OF NAZARETH. With a brief sketch of Jewish History to the Time of His Birth. Second Edition. Small crown 8vo. 6*s*.

COGHLAN (J. Cole) D.D.—THE MODERN PHARISEE, AND OTHER SERMONS. Edited by the Very Rev. H. H. DICKINSON, D.D., Dean of Chapel Royal, Dublin. New and Cheaper Edition. Crown 8vo. 7*s*. 6*d*.

COLERIDGE (Sara)—MEMOIR AND LETTERS OF SARA COLERIDGE. Edited by her Daughter. With Index. Cheap Edition. With one Portrait. 7*s*. 6*d*.

COLERIDGE (The Hon. Stephen)—DEMETRIUS. Crown 8vo. 5*s*.

COOPER (James Fenimore)—LIFE. By T. R. LOUNDSBURY. W Portrait. Crown 8vo. 5*s*.

CORY (William)—A GUIDE TO MODERN ENGLISH HISTORY. Part I. MDCCCXV.–MDCCCXXX. Demy 8vo. 9*s*. Part II.—MDCCCXX MDCCCXXXV. 15*s*.

COTTERILL (H. B.)—AN INTRODUCTION TO THE STUDY OF POET Crown 8vo. 7*s*. 6*d*.

COTTON (H. J. S.)—NEW INDIA, OR INDIA IN TRANSITION. Th Edition. Crown 8vo. 4*s*. 6*d*. Popular Edition, paper covers, 1*s*.

COWIE (Right Rev. W. G.)—OUR LAST YEAR IN NEW ZEALAND. 18 Crown 8vo. 7*s*. 6*d*.

COX (Rev. Sir George W.) M.A., Bart.—THE MYTHOLOGY OF THE ARY NATIONS. New Edition. Demy 8vo. 16*s*.

TALES OF ANCIENT GREECE. New Edition. Small crown 8vo. 6*s*.

A MANUAL OF MYTHOLOGY IN THE FORM OF QUESTION AND ANSW New Edition. Fcp. 8vo. 3*s*.

AN INTRODUCTION TO THE SCIENCE OF COMPARATIVE MYTHOLO AND FOLK-LORE. Second Edition. Crown 8vo. 7*s*. 6*d*.

COX (Rev. Sir G. W.) M.A., Bart., and JONES (Eustace Hinton POPULAR ROMANCES OF THE MIDDLE AGES. Third Edition, in 1 Crown 8vo. 6*s*.

COX (Rev. Samuel) D.D.—A COMMENTARY ON THE BOOK OF JOB. V a Translation. Second Edition. Demy 8vo. 15*s*.

SALVATOR MUNDI; or, Is Christ the Saviour of all Men? Eleve Edition. Crown 8vo. 2*s*. 6*d*.

THE LARGER HOPE: a Sequel to 'SALVATOR MUNDI.' Second tion. 16mo. 1*s*.

THE GENESIS OF EVIL, AND OTHER SERMONS, mainly exposit Third Edition. Crown 8vo. 6*s*.

BALAAM: An Exposition and a Study. Crown 8vo. 5*s*.

MIRACLES. An Argument and a Challenge. Crown 8vo. 2*s*. 6*d*.

CRAVEN (Mrs.)—A YEAR'S MEDITATIONS. Crown 8vo. 6*s*.

CRAWEURD (Oswald)—PORTUGAL, OLD AND NEW. With Illustrati and Maps. New and Cheaper Edition. Crown 8vo. 6*s*.

CRUISE (F. R.) M.D.—THOMAS À KEMPIS. Notes of a Visit to Scenes in which his Life was spent, with some Account of the Examinatio his Relics. Demy 8vo. Illustrated. 12*s*.

CUNNINGHAM (W., B.D.)—POLITICS AND ECONOMICS: An Es on the Nature of the Principles of Political Economy, together with a Su of Recent Legislation. Crown 8vo. 5*s*.

DARMESTETER (Arsène)—THE LIFE OF WORDS AS THE SYMB OF IDEAS. Crown 8vo. 4*s*. 6*d*.

DAVIDSON (Rev. Samuel) D.D., LL.D.—CANON OF THE BIBLE: Formation, History, and Fluctuations. Third and revised Edition. S crown 8vo. 5*s*.

THE DOCTRINE OF LAST THINGS, contained in the New Testam compared with the Notions of the Jews and the Statements of Church Cre Small crown 8vo. 3*s*. 6*d*.

DAWSON (*Geo.*) *M.A.*—PRAYERS, WITH A DISCOURSE ON PRAYER. Edited by his Wife. First Series. New and Cheaper Edition. Crown 8vo. 3*s.* 6*d.*

PRAYERS, WITH A DISCOURSE ON PRAYER. Edited by GEORGE ST. CLAIR. Second Series. Crown 8vo. 6*s.*

SERMONS ON DISPUTED POINTS AND SPECIAL OCCASIONS. Edited by his Wife. Fourth Edition. Crown 8vo. 6*s.*

SERMONS ON DAILY LIFE AND DUTY. Edited by his Wife. Fifth Edition. Crown 8vo. 3*s.* 6*d.*

THE AUTHENTIC GOSPEL, and other Sermons. Edited by GEORGE ST. CLAIR. Third Edition. Crown 8vo. 6*s.*

EVERY-DAY COUNSELS. Edited by GEORGE ST. CLAIR, F.G.S. Crown 8vo. 6*s.*

BIOGRAPHICAL LECTURES. Edited by GEORGE ST. CLAIR, F.G.S. Second Edition. Large crown 8vo. 7*s.* 6*d.*

HAKESPEARE, and other Lectures. Edited by GEORGE ST. CLAIR, F.G.S. Large crown 8vo. 7*s.* 6*d.*

DE BURY (*Richard*)—THE PHILOBIBLON. Translated and Edited by ERNEST C. THOMAS.

DE JONCOURT (*Madame Marie*)—WHOLESOME COOKERY. Fourth Edition. Crown 8vo. cloth, 1*s.* 6*d.*; paper covers, 1*s.*

DENT (*H. C.*)—A YEAR IN BRAZIL. With Notes on Religion, Meteorology, Natural History, &c. Maps and Illustrations. Demy 8vo. 18*s.*

DOCTOR FAUST. The Old German Puppet Play, turned into English, with Introduction, etc., by T. C. H. HEDDERWICK. Large post 8vo. 7*s.* 6*d.*

DOWDEN (*Edward*) *LL.D.*—SHAKSPERE: a Critical Study of his Mind and Art. Eighth Edition. Post 8vo. 12*s.*

STUDIES IN LITERATURE, 1789–1877. Fourth Edition. Post 8vo. 6*s.*

TRANSCRIPTS AND STUDIES. Post 8vo. 12*s.*

DRUMMOND (*Thomas*)—LIFE. By R. BARRY O'BRIEN. 8vo. 14*s.*

DULCE DOMUM. Fcp. 8vo. 5*s.*

DU MONCEL (*Count*)—THE TELEPHONE, THE MICROPHONE, AND THE PHONOGRAPH. With 74 Illustrations. Third Edition. Small crown 8vo. 5*s.*

DUNN (*H. Percy*) *F.R.C.S.*—INFANT HEALTH. The Physiology and Hygiene of Early Life. Crown 8vo. 3*s.* 6*d.*

DURUY (*Victor*)—HISTORY OF ROME AND THE ROMAN PEOPLE. Edited by Professor MAHAFFY, with nearly 3,000 Illustrations. 4to. 6 Vols. in 12 Parts, 30*s.* each volume.

EDUCATION LIBRARY. Edited by Sir PHILIP MAGNUS:—

INDUSTRIAL EDUCATION. By Sir PHILIP MAGNUS.

AN INTRODUCTION TO THE HISTORY OF EDUCATIONAL THEORIES. By OSCAR BROWNING, M.A. Second Edition. 3*s.* 6*d.*

OLD GREEK EDUCATION. By the Rev. Prof. MAHAFFY, M.A. Second Edition. 3*s.* 6*d.*

SCHOOL MANAGEMENT; including a General View of the Work of Education. By JOSEPH LANDON. Sixth Edition. 6*s.*

EDWARDES (*Major-General Sir Herbert B.*)—MEMORIALS OF HIS LIFE. By his WIFE. With Portrait and Illustrations. 2 vols. 8vo. 36*s.*

EIGHTEENTH CENTURY ESSAYS. Selected and Edited by AUSTIN DOBSO
Fcp. 8vo. 1*s*. 6*d*.

ELSDALE (*Henry*)—STUDIES IN TENNYSON'S IDYLLS. Crown 8vo. 5*s*

EMERSON'S (*Ralph Waldo*) LIFE. By OLIVER WENDELL HOLM
[English Copyright Edition.] With Portrait. Crown 8vo. 6*s*.

ERANUS. A COLLECTION OF EXERCISES IN THE ALCAIC AND SAPPH
METRES. Edited by F. W. CORNISH, Assistant Master at Eton. Secc
Edition. Crown 8vo. 2*s*.

FIVE O'CLOCK TEA. Containing Receipts for Cakes of every descriptic
Savoury Sandwiches, Cooling Drinks, &c. Fcp. 8vo. 1*s*. 6*d*., or 1*s*. sewed.

FLINN (*D. Edgar*)—IRELAND: its Health Resorts and Watering-Plac
With Frontispiece and Maps. Demy 8vo. 5s.

FORBES (*Bishop*)—A MEMOIR, by the Rev. DONALD J. MACK
Portrait and Map. Crown 8vo. 7*s*. 6*d*.

FORDYCE (*John*)—THE NEW SOCIAL ORDER. Crown 8vo. 3*s*. 6*d*.

FOTHERINGHAM (*James*)—STUDIES IN THE POETRY OF ROBE
BROWNING. Crown 8vo. 6*s*.

FRANKLIN (*Benjamin*)—AS A MAN OF LETTERS. By J. B. MCMASTE
Crown 8vo. 5*s*.

FROM WORLD TO CLOISTER; or, My Novitiate. By BERNARD. Cro
8vo. 5*s*.

GARDINER (*Samuel R.*) *and J. BASS MULLINGER, M.A.*
INTRODUCTION TO THE STUDY OF ENGLISH HISTORY Second Editic
Large crown 8vo. 9*s*.

GEORGE (*Henry*)—PROGRESS AND POVERTY: an Inquiry into t
Causes of Industrial Depressions, and of Increase of Want with Increase
Wealth. The Remedy. Library Edition. Post 8vo. 7*s*. 6*d*. Cabinet E
tion, crown 8vo. 2*s*. 6*d*.

SOCIAL PROBLEMS. Crown 8vo. 5*s*.

PROTECTION, OR FREE TRADE. An Examination of the Tar
Question, with especial regard to the Interests of Labour. Second Editic
Crown 8vo. 5*s*.

*** Also Cheap Editions of each of the above, limp cloth, 1*s*. 6*d*.; paper covers, 1*s*

GILBERT (*Mrs.*)—AUTOBIOGRAPHY, and other Memorials. Edited
JOSIAH GILBERT. Fifth Edition. Crown 8vo. 7*s*. 6*d*.

GILLMORE (*Col. Parker*)—DAYS AND NIGHTS BY THE DESERT. Wi
numerous Illustrations. Demy 8vo. 10*s*. 6*d*.

GLANVILL (*Joseph*)—SCEPSIS SCIENTIFICA; or, Confest Ignorance, t
Way to Science; in an Essay of the Vanity of Dogmatising and Confide
Opinion. Edited, with Introductory Essay, by JOHN OWEN. Elzevir 8v
printed on hand-made paper, 6*s*.

GLASS (*Henry Alex.*)—THE STORY OF THE PSALTERS. Crown 8vo. 5

GLOSSARY OF TERMS AND PHRASES. Edited by the Rev. H. PERCY SMI
and others. Medium 8vo. 7*s*. 6*d*.

GLOVER (*F.*) *M.A.*—EXEMPLA LATINA. A First Construing Book, wi
Short Notes, Lexicon, and an Introduction to the Analysis of Sentences. Seco
Edition. Fcp. 8vo. 2*s*.

GOODENOUGH (*Commodore J. G.*)—MEMOIR OF, with Extracts fro
his Letters and Journals. Edited by his Widow. With Steel Engrav
Portrait. Third Edition. Crown 8vo. 5*s*.

GORDON (*Major-Gen. C. G.*)—HIS JOURNALS AT KARTOUM. Printed from the Original MS. With Introduction and Notes by A EGMONT HAKE. Portrait, 2 Maps, and 30 Illustrations. 2 vols. Demy 8vo. 21*s.* Also a Cheap Edition in 1 vol., 6*s.*

GORDON'S (GENERAL) LAST JOURNAL. A Facsimile of the last Journal received in England from General Gordon. Reproduced by Photo-lithography. Imperial 4to. £3. 3*s.*

EVENTS IN HIS LIFE. From the Day of his Birth to the Day of his Death. By Sir H. W. GORDON. With Maps and Illustrations. Demy 8vo. 7*s.* 6*d.*

GOSSE (*Edmund*) — SEVENTEENTH CENTURY STUDIES. A Contribution to the History of English Poetry. Demy 8vo. 10*s.* 6*d.*

GOULD (*Rev. S. Baring*) *M.A.*—GERMANY, PRESENT AND PAST. New and Cheaper Edition. Large crown 8vo. 7*s.* 6*d.*

THE VICAR OF MORWENSTOW: a Life of Robert Stephen Hawker, M.A. New and Cheaper Edition. Crown 8vo. 5*s.*

GOWAN (*Major Walter E.*) — A. IVANOFF'S RUSSIAN GRAMMAR. (16th Edition). Translated, enlarged, and arranged for use of Students of the Russian Language. Démy 8vo. 6*s.*

GOWER (*Lord Ronald*)—MY REMINISCENCES. Limp Parchment, Antique, with Etched Portrait, 10*s.* 6*d.*

BRIC-À-BRAC. Being some Photoprints illustrating Art objects at Gower Lodge, Windsor. Super royal 8vo. 15*s.*; Persian leather, 21*s.*

LAST DAYS OF MARY ANTOINETTE. An Historical Sketch. With Portrait and Facsimiles. Fcp. 4to. 10*s.* 6*d.*

NOTES OF A TOUR FROM BRINDISI TO YOKOHAMA, 1883–1884. Fcp. 8vo. 2*s.* 6*d.*

GRAHAM (*William*) *M.A.*—THE CREED OF SCIENCE, Religious, Moral, and Social. Second Edition, revised. Crown 8vo. 6*s.*

THE SOCIAL PROBLEM IN ITS ECONOMIC, MORAL, AND POLITICAL ASPECTS. Demy 8vo. 14*s.*

GRIMLEY (*Rev. H. N.*) *M.A.*—TREMADOC SERMONS, CHIEFLY ON THE SPIRITUAL BODY, THE UNSEEN WORLD, AND THE DIVINE HUMANITY. Fourth Edition. Crown 8vo. 6*s.*

THE TEMPLE OF HUMANITY, and other Sermons. Crown 8vo. 6*s.*

GURNEY (*Edmund*)—TERTIUM QUID: Chapters on various Disputed Questions. 2 vols. Crown 8vo. 12*s.*

HADDON (*Caroline*)—THE LARGER LIFE, STUDIES IN HINTON'S ETHICS. Crown 8vo. 5*s.*

HAECKEL (*Prof. Ernst*)—THE HISTORY OF CREATION. Translation revised by Professor E. RAY LANKESTER, M.A., F.R.S. With Coloured Plates and Genealogical Trees of the various groups of both plants and animals. 2 vols. Third Edition. Post 8vo. 32*s.*

THE HISTORY OF THE EVOLUTION OF MAN. With numerous Illustrations. 2 vols. Post 8vo. 32*s.*

A VISIT TO CEYLON. Post 8vo. 7*s.* 6*d.*

FREEDOM IN SCIENCE AND TEACHING. With a Prefatory Note by T. H. HUXLEY, F.R.S. Crown 8vo. 5*s.*

HALCOMBE (*J. J.*)—Gospel Difficulties due to a Displac Section of St. Luke. Second Edition. Crown 8vo. 6*s.*

Hamilton, Memoirs of Arthur, B.A., of Trinity College, Cambrid Crown 8vo. 6*s.*

Handbook of Home Rule, being Articles on the Irish Question Various Writers. Edited by James Bryce, M.P. Second Edition. Cro 8vo. 1*s.* sewed, or 1*s.* 6*d.* cloth.

HART (*Rev. J. W. T.*)—Autobiography of Judas Iscariot. A Ch acter-Study. Crown 8vo. 3*s.* 6*d.*

HAWEIS (*Rev. H. R.*) *M.A.*—Current Coin. Materialism—T Devil—Crime—Drunkenness—Pauperism—Emotion—Recreation—T Sabbath. Fifth Edition. Crown 8vo. 5*s.*

Arrows in the Air. Fifth Edition. Crown 8vo. 5*s.*

Speech in Season. Fifth Edition. Crown 8vo. 5*s.*

Thoughts for the Times. Fourteenth Edition. Crown 8vo. 5*s*

Unsectarian Family Prayers. New Edition. Fcp. 8vo. 1*s.* 6*d.*

HAWTHORNE (*Nathaniel*)—Works. Complete in 12 vols. Lar post 8vo. each vol. 7*s.* 6*d.*

Vol. I. Twice-Told Tales.
II. Mosses from an Old Manse.
III. The House of the Seven Gables, and The Snow Image.
IV. The Wonder Book, Tanglewood Tales, and Grandfather's Cha
V. The Scarlet Letter, and The Blithedale Romance.
VI. The Marble Faun. (Transformation.)
VII. & VIII. Our Old Home, and English Note-Books.
IX. American Note-Books.
X. French and Italian Note-Books.
XI. Septimius Felton, The Dolliver Romance, Fanshawe, a in an appendix, The Ancestral Footstep.
XII. Tales and Essays, and other Papers, with a Biographic Sketch of Hawthorne.

HEATH (*Francis George*)—Autumnal Leaves. Third and Chea Edition. Large crown 8vo. 6*s.*

Sylvan Winter. With 70 Illustrations. Large crown 8vo. 14*s.*

HEGEL—The Introduction to Hegel's Philosophy of Fine A Translated from the German, with Notes and Prefatory Essay, by Berna Bosanquet, M.A. Crown 8vo. 5*s.*

HEIDENHAIN (*Rudolph*) *M.D.*—Hypnotism; or Animal Magnetis With Preface by G. J. Romanes, F.R.S. Second Edition. Small cro 8vo. 2*s.* 6*d.*

HENNESSY (*Sir John Pope*)—Ralegh in Ireland, with his Lett on Irish Affairs and some Contemporary Documents. Large cro 8vo. printed on hand-made paper, parchment, 10*s.* 6*d.*

HENRY (*Philip*)—Diaries and Letters. Edited by Matthew Hen Lee, M.A. Large crown 8vo. 7*s.* 6*d.*

HINTON (*J.*)—The Mystery of Pain. New Edition. Fcp. 8vo. 1*s*

Life and Letters. With an Introduction by Sir W. W. Gu Bart., and Portrait engraved on Steel by C. H. Jeens. Fifth Editi Crown 8vo. 8*s.* 6*d.*

INTON (J.)—continued.

PHILOSOPHY AND RELIGION. Selections from the MSS. of the late JAMES HINTON. Edited by CAROLINE HADDON. Second Edition. Crown 8vo. 5*s*.

THE LAW BREAKER AND THE COMING OF THE LAW. Edited by MARGARET HINTON. Crown 8vo. 6*s*.

OOPER (Mary)—LITTLE DINNERS: HOW TO SERVE THEM WITH ELEGANCE AND ECONOMY. Twentieth Edition. Crown 8vo. 2*s*. 6*d*.

COOKERY FOR INVALIDS, PERSONS OF DELICATE DIGESTION, AND CHILDREN. Fifth Edition. Crown 8vo. 2*s*. 6*d*.

EVERY-DAY MEALS. Being Economical and Wholesome Recipes for Breakfast, Luncheon, and Supper. Seventh Edition. Crown 8vo. 2*s*. 6*d*.

OPKINS (Ellice)—WORK AMONGST WORKING MEN. Fifth Edition. Crown 8vo. 3*s*. 6*d*.

ORNADAY (W. T.)—TWO YEARS IN A JUNGLE. With Illustrations. Demy 8vo. 21*s*.

OSPITALIER (E.)—THE MODERN APPLICATIONS OF ELECTRICITY. Translated and Enlarged by JULIUS MAIER, Ph.D. 2 vols. Second Edition, revised, with many additions and numerous Illustrations. Demy 8vo. 12*s*. 6*d*. each volume.

VOL. I.—Electric Generators, Electric Light.
II.—Telephone: Various Applications: Electrical Transmission of Energy.

W (Robert) M.A.—THE CHURCH OF ENGLAND AND OTHER RELIGIOUS COMMUNIONS. A Course of Lectures delivered in the Parish Church of Clapham. Crown 8vo. 7*s*. 6*d*.

OW TO MAKE A SAINT; or, The Process of Canonisation in the Church of England. By The Prig. Fcp. 8vo. 3*s*. 6*d*.

YNDMAN (H. M.)—THE HISTORICAL BASIS OF SOCIALISM IN ENGLAND. Large crown 8vo. 8*s*. 6*d*.

M THURN (Everard F.)—AMONG THE INDIANS OF GUIANA. Being Sketches, chiefly Anthropologic, from the Interior of British Guiana. With 53 Illustrations and a Map. Demy 8vo. 18*s*.

XORA: A Mystery. Crown 8vo. 6*s*.

ACCOUD (Prof. S.)—THE CURABILITY AND TREATMENT OF PULMONARY PHTHISIS. Translated and Edited by M. LUBBOCK, M.D. 8vo. 15*s*.

AUNT IN A JUNK: A Ten Days' Cruise in Indian Seas. Large crown 8vo. 7*s*. 6*d*.

ENKINS (E.) and RAYMOND (J.)—THE ARCHITECT'S LEGAL HANDBOOK. Third Edition, Revised. Crown 8vo. 6*s*.

ENKINS (Rev. Canon R. C.)—HERALDRY: English and Foreign. With a Dictionary of Heraldic Terms and 156 Illustrations. Small crown 8vo. 3*s*. 6*d*.

STORY OF THE CARAFFA. Small crown 8vo. 3*s*. 6*d*.

EROME (Saint)—LIFE, by Mrs. CHARLES MARTIN. Large cr. 8vo. 6*s*.

OEL (L.)—A CONSUL'S MANUAL AND SHIPOWNER'S AND SHIPMASTER'S PRACTICAL GUIDE IN THEIR TRANSACTIONS ABROAD. With Definitions of Nautical, Mercantile, and Legal Terms; a Glossary of Mercantile Terms in English, French, German, Italian, and Spanish; Tables of the Money, Weights, and Measures of the Principal Commercial Nations and their Equivalents in British Standards; and Forms of Consular and Notarial Acts. Demy 8vo. 12*s*.

ORDAN (Furneaux) F.R.C.S.—ANATOMY AND PHYSIOLOGY IN CHARACTER. Crown 8vo. 5*s*.

KAUFMANN (Rev. M.) M.A.—SOCIALISM: its Nature, its Dangers, ai its Remedies considered. Crown 8vo. 7*s.* 6*d.*

UTOPIAS; or, Schemes of Social Improvement, from Sir Thomas Mo to Karl Marx. Crown 8vo. 5*s.*

CHRISTIAN SOCIALISM. Crown 8vo. 4*s.* 6*d.*

KAY (David)—EDUCATION AND EDUCATORS. Crown 8vo. 7*s.* 6*d.*

MEMORY: What it is, and how to improve it. Crown 8vo. 6*s.*

KAY (Joseph)—FREE TRADE IN LAND. Edited by his Widow. Wi Preface by the Right Hon. JOHN BRIGHT, M.P. Seventh Edition. Cro 8vo. 5*s.*

*** Also a cheaper edition, without the Appendix, but with a Review of Rec Changes in the Land Laws of England, by the Right Hon. G. OSBOR MORGAN, Q.C., M.P. Cloth, 1*s.* 6*d.*; Paper covers, 1*s.*

KELKE (W. H. H.)—AN EPITOME OF ENGLISH GRAMMAR FOR T USE OF STUDENTS. Adapted to the London Matriculation Course and Si lar Examinations. Crown 8vo. 4*s.* 6*d.*

KEMPIS (Thomas à)—OF THE IMITATION OF CHRIST. Parchme Library Edition, parchment or cloth, 6*s.*; vellum, 7*s.* 6*d.* The Red Li Edition, fcp. 8vo. cloth extra, 2*s.* 6*d.* The Cabinet Edition, small 8v cloth limp, 1*s.*; or cloth boards, red edges, 1*s.* 6*d.* The Miniature Editio 32mo. cloth limp, 1*s.*; or with red lines, 1*s.* 6*d.*

*** All the above Editions may be had in various extra bindings.

KENNARD (Rev. H. B.)—MANUAL OF CONFIRMATION. 16mo. clot 1*s.* Sewed, 3*d.*

KENDALL (Henry)—THE KINSHIP OF MEN: Genealogy viewed as Science. Crown 8vo. 5*s.*

KETTLEWELL (Rev. S.) M.A.—THOMAS À KEMPIS AND T BROTHERS OF COMMON LIFE. 2 vols. With Frontispieces. Demy 8v 30*s.*

*** Also an Abridged Edition in 1 vol. With Portrait. Crown 8vo. 7*s.* 6*d.*

KIDD (Joseph) M.D.—THE LAWS OF THERAPEUTICS; or, the Scien and Art of Medicine. Second Edition. Crown 8vo. 6*s.*

KINGSFORD (Anna) M.D.—THE PERFECT WAY IN DIET. A Treati advocating a Return to the Natural and Ancient Food of Race. Small cro 8vo. 2*s.*

KINGSLEY (Charles) M.A.—LETTERS AND MEMORIES OF HIS LIF Edited by his WIFE. With Two Steel Engraved Portraits and Vignett Sixteenth Cabinet Edition, in 2 vols. Crown 8vo. 12*s.*

*** Also a People's Edition in 1 vol. With Portrait. Crown 8vo. 6*s.*

ALL SAINTS' DAY, and other Sermons. Edited by the Rev. V HARRISON. Third Edition. Crown 8vo. 7*s.* 6*d.*

TRUE WORDS FOR BRAVE MEN. A Book for Soldiers' and Sailo Libraries. Fourteenth Edition. Crown 8vo. 2*s.* 6*d.*

KNOX (Alexander A.)—THE NEW PLAYGROUND; or, Wanderings i Algeria. New and Cheaper Edition. Large crown 8vo. 6*s.*

LAMARTINE (Alphonse de). By Lady MARGARET DOMVILE. Lar crown 8vo., with Portrait, 7*s.* 6*d.*

LAND CONCENTRATION AND IRRESPONSIBILITY OF POLITICAL POWER, as causing the Anomaly of a Widespread State of Want by the Side of the Vast Supplies of Nature. Crown 8vo. 5*s*.

LANDON (*Joseph*)—SCHOOL MANAGEMENT; including a General View of the Work of Education, Organisation, and Discipline. Sixth Edition. Crown 8vo. 6*s*.

LAURIE (*S. S.*)—LECTURES ON THE RISE AND EARLY CONSTITUTION OF UNIVERSITIES. With a Survey of Mediæval Education. Crown 8vo. 6*s*.

LEE (*Rev. F.* G.) *D.C.L.*—THE OTHER WORLD; or, Glimpses of the Supernatural. 2 vols. A New Edition. Crown 8vo. 15*s*.

LEFEVRE (*Right Hon. G. Shaw*)—PEEL AND O'CONNELL. Demy 8vo. 10*s*. 6*d*.

INCIDENTS OF COERCION. A Journal of Visits to Ireland. Crown 8vo. 1*s*.

LETTERS FROM AN UNKNOWN FRIEND. By the Author of 'Charles Lowder.' With a Preface by the Rev. W. H. Cleaver. Fcp. 8vo. 1*s*.

LEWARD (*Frank*)—Edited by CHAS. BAMPTON. Crown 8vo. 7*s*. 6*d*.

LIFE OF A PRIG. By ONE. Third Edition. Fcp. 8vo. 3*s*. 6*d*.

LILLIE (*Arthur*) *M.R.A.S.*—THE POPULAR LIFE OF BUDDHA. Containing an Answer to the Hibbert Lectures of 1881. With Illustrations. Crown 8vo. 6*s*.

BUDDHISM IN CHRISTENDOM; or, Jesus, the Essene. Demy 8vo. with Illustrations. 15*s*.

LOCHER (*Carl*)—EXPLANATION OF THE ORGAN STOPS, with Hints for Effective Combinations. Illustrated. Demy 8vo. 5*s*.

LONGFELLOW (*H. Wadsworth*)—LIFE. By his Brother, SAMUEL LONGFELLOW. With Portraits and Illustrations. 3 vols. Demy 8vo. 42*s*.

LONSDALE (*Margaret*)—SISTER DORA: a Biography. With Portrait. Cheap Edition. Crown 8vo. 2*s*. 6*d*.

GEORGE ELIOT: Thoughts upon her Life, her Books, and Herself. Second Edition. Small crown 8vo. 1*s*. 6*d*.

LOWDER (*Charles*)—A BIOGRAPHY. By the Author of 'St. Teresa.' New and Cheaper Edition. Crown 8vo. With Portrait. 3*s*. 6*d*.

LÜCKES (*Eva C. E.*)—LECTURES ON GENERAL NURSING, delivered to the Probationers of the London Hospital Training School for Nurses. Second Edition. Crown 8vo. 2*s*. 6*d*.

LYTTON (*Edward Bulwer, Lord*)—LIFE, LETTERS, AND LITERARY REMAINS. By his Son the EARL OF LYTTON. With Portraits, Illustrations, and Facsimiles. Demy 8vo. cloth. Vols. I. and II. 32*s*.

MACHIAVELLI (*Niccolò*)—HIS LIFE AND TIMES. By Prof. VILLARI. Translated by LINDA VILLARI. 4 vols. Large post 8vo. 48*s*.

DISCOURSES ON THE FIRST DECADE OF TITUS LIVIUS. Translated from the Italian by NINIAN HILL THOMSON, M.A. Large crown 8vo. 12*s*.

THE PRINCE. Translated from the Italian by N. H. T. Small crown 8vo. printed on hand-made paper, bevelled boards, 6*s*.

MACNEILL (*J.* G. *Swift*)—HOW THE UNION WAS CARRIED. Crown 8vo. cloth, 1*s*. 6*d*.; paper covers, 1*s*.

MAGNUS (*Lady*)—ABOUT THE JEWS SINCE BIBLE TIMES. From the Babylonian Exile till the English Exodus. Small crown 8vo. 6*s*.

MAGUIRE (*Thomas*)—LECTURES ON PHILOSOPHY. Demy 8vo. 9*s.*

MAINTENON (*Madame de*). By EMILY BOWLES. With Portra Large crown 8vo. 7*s.* 6*d.*

MANY VOICES.—Extracts from Religious Writers, from the First to t Sixteenth Century. With Biographical Sketches. Crown 8vo. cloth extra,

MARKHAM (*Capt. Albert Hastings*) *R.N.*—THE GREAT FROZEN SE a Personal Narrative of the Voyage of the *Alert* during the Arctic Expediti of 1875–6. With 33 Illustrations and Two Maps. Sixth Edition. Crown 8vo.

MARTINEAU (*Gertrude*)—OUTLINE LESSONS ON MORALS. Sm crown 8vo. 3*s.* 6*d.*

MASON (*Charlotte M.*)—HOME EDUCATION. A Course of Lectures Ladies, delivered in Bradford in the winter of 1885–1886. Crown 8vo. 3*s.* 6

MATTER AND ENERGY: An Examination of the Fundamental Conce tions of Physical Force. By B. L. L. Small crown 8vo. 2*s.*

MATUCE (*H. Ogram*)—A WANDERER. Crown 8vo. 5*s.*

MAUDSLEY (*H.*) *M.D.*—BODY AND WILL. Being an Essay Concerni Will, in its Metaphysical, Physiological, and Pathological Aspects. 8vo. 12

NATURAL CAUSES AND SUPERNATURAL SEEMINGS. Second Editic Crown 8vo. 6*s.*

McGRATH (*Terence*)—PICTURES FROM IRELAND. New and Cheap Edition. Crown 8vo. 2*s.*

McKINNEY (*S. B. G.*)—THE SCIENCE AND ART OF RELIGIO Crown 8vo. 8*s.* 6*d.*

MILLER (*Edward*)—THE HISTORY AND DOCTRINES OF IRVINGISM or, the so-called Catholic and Apostolic Church. 2 vols. Large post 8vo. 1

THE CHURCH IN RELATION TO THE STATE. Large crown 8vo. 4*s.*

MILLS (*Herbert*)—POVERTY AND THE STATE; or, Work for the Une ployed. An Enquiry into the Causes and Extent of Enforced Idleness. Cr. 8vo.

MINTON (*Rev. Francis*)—CAPITAL AND WAGES. 8vo. 15*s.*

MITCHELL (*John*)—LIFE. By WILLIAM DILLON. With Portra Demy 8vo.

MITCHELL (*Lucy M.*)—A HISTORY OF ANCIENT SCULPTURE. Wi numerous Illustrations, including six Plates in Phototype. Super royal, 42*s.*

SELECTIONS FROM ANCIENT SCULPTURE. Being a Portfolio contai ing Reproductions in Phototype of 36 Masterpieces of Ancient Art, to illu trate Mrs. MITCHELL'S 'History of Ancient Sculpture.' 18*s.*

MIVART (*St. George*)—ON TRUTH. 8vo. 16*s.*

MOCKLER (*E.*)—A GRAMMAR OF THE BALOOCHEE LANGUAGE, as it spoken in Makran (Ancient Gedrosia), in the Persia-Arabic and Rom characters. Fcp. 8vo. 5*s.*

MOHL (*Julius and Mary*)—LETTERS AND RECOLLECTIONS OF. M. C. M. SIMPSON. With Portraits and Two Illustrations. Demy 8vo. 1

MOLESWORTH (*W. Nassau*)—HISTORY OF THE CHURCH OF EN LAND FROM 1660. Large crown 8vo. 7*s.* 6*d.*

MORELL (J. R.)—EUCLID SIMPLIFIED IN METHOD AND LANGUAGE. Being a Manual of Geometry. Compiled from the most important French Works, approved by the University of Paris and the Minister of Public Instruction. Fcp. 8vo. *2s. 6d.*

MORISON (James Cotter)—THE SERVICE OF MAN. An Essay towards the Religion of the Future. Demy 8vo. *10s. 6d.*; Cheap Edition, crown 8vo. *5s.*

MORSE (E. S.) Ph.D.—FIRST BOOK OF ZOOLOGY. With numerous Illustrations. New and Cheaper Edition. Crown 8vo. *2s. 6d.*

MY LAWYER: A Concise Abridgment of the Laws of England. By a Barrister-at-Law. Crown 8vo. *6s. 6d.*

NELSON (J. H.) M.A.—A PROSPECTUS OF THE SCIENTIFIC STUDY OF THE HINDÛ LAW. Demy 8vo. *9s.*

INDIAN USAGE AND JUDGE-MADE LAW IN MADRAS. Demy 8vo. *12s.*

NEW SOCIAL TEACHINGS. By POLITICUS. Small crown 8vo. *5s.*

NEWMAN (Cardinal)—CHARACTERISTICS FROM THE WRITINGS OF. Being Selections from his various Works. Arranged with the Author's personal Approval. Seventh Edition. With Portrait. Crown 8vo. *6s.*

*** A Portrait of Cardinal Newman, mounted for framing, can be had, *2s. 6d.*

NEWMAN (Francis William)—ESSAYS ON DIET. Small crown 8vo. *2s.*

MISCELLANIES. Vol. II.: Essays, Tracts, and Addresses, Moral and Religious. Demy 8vo. *12s.*

REMINISCENCES OF TWO EXILES AND TWO WARS. Crown 8vo. *3s. 6d.*

NICOLS (Arthur) F.G.S., F.R.G.S.—CHAPTERS FROM THE PHYSICAL HISTORY OF THE EARTH: an Introduction to Geology and Palæontology. With numerous Illustrations. Crown 8vo. *5s.*

NIHILL (Rev. H. D.)—THE SISTERS OF ST. MARY AT THE CROSS: SISTERS OF THE POOR AND THEIR WORK. Crown 8vo. *2s. 6d.*

NOEL (The Hon. Roden)—ESSAYS ON POETRY AND POETS. Demy 8vo. *12s.*

NOPS (Marianne)—CLASS LESSONS ON EUCLID. Part I. containing the First Two Books of the Elements. Crown 8vo. *2s. 6d.*

NUCES: EXERCISES ON THE SYNTAX OF THE PUBLIC SCHOOL LATIN PRIMER. New Edition in Three Parts. Crown 8vo. each *1s.*

*** The Three Parts can also be had bound together in cloth, *3s.*

OATES (Frank) F.R.G.S.—MATABELE LAND AND THE VICTORIA FALLS. A Naturalist's Wanderings in the Interior of South Africa. Edited by C. G. OATES, B.A. With numerous Illustrations and 4 Maps. Demy 8vo. *21s.*

O'BRIEN (R. Barry)—IRISH WRONGS AND ENGLISH REMEDIES, with other Essays. Crown 8vo. *5s.*

OGLE (W.) M.D., F.R.C.P.—ARISTOTLE ON THE PARTS OF ANIMALS. Translated, with Introduction and Notes. Royal 8vo. *12s. 6d.*

OLIVER (Robert)—UNNOTICED ANALOGIES. A Talk on the Irish Question. Crown 8vo. *3s. 6d.*

O'MEARA (Kathleen)—HENRI PERREYVE AND HIS COUNSELS TO THE SICK. Small crown 8vo. *5s.*

ONE AND A HALF IN NORWAY. A Chronicle of Small Beer. By Either and Both. Small crown 8vo. *3s. 6d.*

O'NEIL (The late Rev. Lord).—SERMONS. With Memoir and Portrait. Crown 8vo. *6s.*

ESSAYS AND ADDRESSES. Crown 8vo. *5s.*

OTTLEY (*Henry Bickersteth*)—THE GREAT DILEMMA: Christ His o Witness or His own Accuser. Six Lectures. Second Edition. Crown 8\ 3*s.* 6*d.*

OUR PRIESTS AND THEIR TITHES. By a Priest of the Province Canterbury. Crown 8vo. 5*s.*

OUR PUBLIC SCHOOLS—ETON, HARROW, WINCHESTER, RUGBY, WES MINSTER, MARLBOROUGH, THE CHARTERHOUSE. Crown 8vo. 6*s.*

OWEN (*F. M.*)—JOHN KEATS: a Study. Crown 8vo. 6*s.*

PADGHAM (*Richard*)—IN THE MIDST OF LIFE WE ARE IN DEAT Crown 8vo. 5*s.*

PALMER (*the late William*)—NOTES OF A VISIT TO RUSSIA IN 1840-4 Selected and arranged by JOHN H. CARDINAL NEWMAN. With Portrait. Cro 8vo. 8*s.* 6*d.*

EARLY CHRISTIAN SYMBOLISM. A series of Compositions from Fresc Paintings, Glasses, and Sculptured Sarcophagi. Edited by the Rev. PROVO NORTHCOTE, D.D., and the Rev. CANON BROWNLOW, M.A. With Colour Plates, folio, 42*s.*; or with plain plates, folio, 25*s.*

PARCHMENT LIBRARY. Choicely printed on hand-made paper, limp parc ment antique or cloth, 6*s.*; vellum, 7*s.* 6*d.* each volume.

CARLYLE'S SARTOR RESARTUS.

MILTON'S POETICAL WORKS. 2 vols.

CHAUCER'S CANTERBURY TALES. 2 vols. Edited by ALFRED V POLLARD.

SELECTIONS FROM THE PROSE WRITINGS OF JONATHAN SWIFT. Wi a Preface and Notes by STANLEY LANE-POOLE, and Portrait.

ENGLISH SACRED LYRICS.

SIR JOSHUA REYNOLDS' DISCOURSES. Edited by EDMUND GOSSE.

SELECTIONS FROM MILTON'S PROSE WRITINGS. Edited by ERNES MYERS.

THE BOOK OF PSALMS. Translated by the Rev. Canon CHEYNE, D.

THE VICAR OF WAKEFIELD. With Preface and Notes by AUSTI DOBSON.

ENGLISH COMIC DRAMATISTS. Edited by OSWALD CRAWFURD.

ENGLISH LYRICS.

THE SONNETS OF JOHN MILTON. Edited by MARK PATTISO With Portrait after Vertue.

FRENCH LYRICS. Selected and Annotated by GEORGE SAINTSBUR With miniature Frontispiece, designed and etched by H. G. Glindoni.

FABLES by MR. JOHN GAY. With Memoir by AUSTIN DOBSO and an etched Portrait from an unfinished Oil-sketch by Sir Godfrey Kneller

SELECT LETTERS OF PERCY BYSSHE SHELLEY. Edited, with an Intr tion, by RICHARD GARNETT.

THE CHRISTIAN YEAR; Thoughts in Verse for the Sundays ar Holy Days throughout the Year. With etched Portrait of the Rev. J. Keb after the Drawing by G. Richmond, R.A.

SHAKSPERE'S WORKS. Complete in Twelve Volumes.

EIGHTEENTH CENTURY ESSAYS. Selected and Edited by AUST DOBSON. With a Miniature Frontispiece by R. Caldecott.

PARCHMENT LIBRARY—continued.

Q. HORATI FLACCI OPERA. Edited by F. A. CORNISH, Assistant Master at Eton. With a Frontispiece after a design by L. ALMA TADEMA. Etched by LEOPOLD LOWENSTAM.

EDGAR ALLAN POE'S POEMS. With an Essay on his Poetry by ANDREW LANG, and a Frontispiece by Linley Sambourne.

SHAKSPERE'S SONNETS. Edited by EDWARD DOWDEN. With a Frontispiece etched by Leopold Lowenstam, after the Death Mask.

ENGLISH ODES. Selected by EDMUND GOSSE. With Frontispiece on India paper by Hamo Thornycroft, A.R.A.

OF THE IMITATION OF CHRIST. By THOMAS À KEMPIS. A revised Translation. With Frontispiece on India paper, from a Design by W. B. Richmond.

POEMS: Selected from PERCY BYSSHE SHELLEY. Dedicated to Lady Shelley. With Preface by RICHARD GARNETT and a Miniature Frontispiece.

LETTERS AND JOURNALS OF JONATHAN SWIFT. Selected and edited, with a Commentary and Notes, by STANLEY LANE POOLE.

DE QUINCEY'S CONFESSIONS OF AN ENGLISH OPIUM EATER. Reprinted from the First Edition. Edited by RICHARD GARNETT.

THE GOSPEL ACCORDING TO MATTHEW, MARK, AND LUKE.

ARSLOE (Joseph) — OUR RAILWAYS. Sketches, Historical and Descriptive. With Practical Information as to Fares and Rates, &c., and a Chapter on Railway Reform. Crown 8vo. 6*s*.

ASCAL (Blaise)—THE THOUGHTS OF. Translated from the Text of AUGUSTE MOLINIER by C. KEGAN PAUL. Large crown 8vo. with Frontispiece, printed on hand-made paper, parchment antique, or cloth, 12*s*.; vellum, 15*s*. New Edition, crown 8vo. 6*s*.

ATON (W. A.)—DOWN THE ISLANDS; a Voyage to the Caribbees. Illustrations. Demy 8vo. 16*s*.

AUL (C. Kegan)—BIOGRAPHICAL SKETCHES. Printed on hand-made paper, bound in buckram. Second Edition. Crown 8vo. 7*s*. 6*d*.

EARSON (Rev. S.)—WEEK-DAY LIVING. A Book for Young Men and Women. Second Edition. Crown 8vo. 5*s*.

ENRICE (Major J.)—ARABIC AND ENGLISH DICTIONARY OF THE KORAN. 4to. 21*s*.

ESCHEL (Dr. Oscar)—THE RACES OF MAN AND THEIR GEOGRAPHICAL DISTRIBUTION. Second Edition, large crown 8vo. 9*s*.

ETERS (F. H.)—THE NICOMACHEAN ETHICS OF ARISTOTLE. Translated by. Crown 8vo. 6*s*.

IDGEON (D.)—AN ENGINEER'S HOLIDAY; or, Notes of a Round Trip from Long. 0° to 0°. New and Cheaper Edition. Large crown 8vo. 7*s*. 6*d*.

OLD WORLD QUESTIONS AND NEW WORLD ANSWERS. Large crown 8vo. 7*s*. 6*d*.

LAIN THOUGHTS FOR MEN. Eight Lectures delivered at the Foresters' Hall, Clerkenwell, during the London Mission, 1884. Crown 8vo. 1*s*. 6*d*.; paper covers, 1*s*.

LOWRIGHT (C. B.)—THE BRITISH UREDINEÆ AND USTILAGINEÆ. With Illustrations. Demy 8vo. 10*s*. 6*d*.

OE (*Edgar Allan*)—WORKS OF. With an Introduction and a Memoir by RICHARD HENRY STODDARD. In 6 vols. with Frontispieces and Vignettes. Large crown 8vo. 6*s*. each vol.

RICE (*Prof. Bonamy*)—CHAPTERS ON PRACTICAL POLITICAL ECONOMY. Being the Substance of Lectures delivered before the University of Oxford. New and Cheaper Edition. Large post 8vo. 5*s*.

RIG'S BEDE: The Venerable Bede Expurgated, Expounded, and Exposed. By the PRIG, Author of 'The Life of a Prig.' Fcp. 8vo. 3*s*. 6*d*.

RIGMENT (THE). A Collection of 'The Prig' Books. Crown 8vo. 6*s*.

ULPIT COMMENTARY (THE). Old Testament Series. Edited by the Rev. J. S. EXELL and the Very Rev. Dean H. D. M. SPENCE.

GENESIS. By Rev. T. WHITELAW, M.A. With Homilies by the Very Rev. J. F. MONTGOMERY, D.D., Rev. Prof. R. A. REDFORD, M.A., LL.B., Rev. F. HASTINGS, Rev. W. ROBERTS, M.A.; an Introduction to the Study of the Old Testament by the Venerable Archdeacon FARRAR, D.D., F.R.S.; and Introductions to the Pentateuch by the Right Rev. H. COTTERILL, D.D., and Rev. T. WHITELAW, M.A. Eighth Edition. One vol. 15*s*.

EXODUS. By the Rev. Canon RAWLINSON. With Homilies by Rev. J. ORR, Rev. D. YOUNG, Rev. C. A. GOODHART, Rev. J. URQUHART, and Rev. H. T. ROBJOHNS. Fourth Edition. Two vols. each 9*s*.

LEVITICUS. By the Rev. Prebendary MEYRICK, M.A. With Introductions by Rev. R. COLLINS, Rev. Professor A. CAVE, and Homilies by Rev. Prof. REDFORD, LL.B., Rev. J. A. MACDONALD, Rev. W. CLARKSON, Rev. S. R. ALDRIDGE, LL.B., and Rev. MCCHEYNE EDGAR. Fourth Edition. 15*s*.

NUMBERS. By the Rev R. WINTERBOTHAM, LL.B. With Homilies by the Rev. Professor W. BINNIE, D.D., Rev. E. S. PROUT, M.A., Rev. D. YOUNG, Rev. J. WAITE; and an Introduction by the Rev. THOMAS WHITELAW, M.A. Fifth Edition. 15*s*.

DEUTERONOMY. By Rev. W. L. ALEXANDER, D.D. With Homilies by Rev. D. DAVIES, M.A., Rev. C. CLEMANCE, D.D., Rev. J. ORR, B.D., and Rev. R. M. EDGAR, M.A. Fourth Edition. 15*s*.

JOSHUA. By Rev. J. J. LIAS, M.A. With Homilies by Rev. S. R. ALDRIDGE, LL.B., Rev. R. GLOVER, Rev. E. DE PRESSENSÉ, D.D., Rev. J. WAITE, B.A. Rev. W. F. ADENEY, M.A.; and an Introduction b the Rev. A. PLUMMER, M.A. Fifth Edition. 12*s*. 6*d*.

JUDGES AND RUTH. By the Bishop of Bath and Wells and Rev. J. MORISON, D.D. With Homilies by Rev. A. F. MUIR, M.A., Rev. W. F. ADENEY, M.A., Rev. W. M. STATHAM, and Rev. Professor J. THOMSON, M.A. Fifth Edition. 10*s*. 6*d*.

1 and 2 SAMUEL. By the Very Rev. R. P. SMITH, D.D. Wit Homilies by Rev. DONALD FRASER, D.D., Rev. Prof. CHAPMAN, Rev. B. DALE, and Rev G. WOOD. Vol. I. Sixth Edition, 15*s*. Vol. II. 15*s*.

1 KINGS. By the Rev. JOSEPH HAMMOND, LL.B. With Homilies by the Rev. E DE PRESSENSÉ, D.D., Rev. J. WAITE, B.A., Rev. A. ROWLAND, LL.B., Rev. J. A. MACDONALD, and Rev. J. URQUHART. Fifth Edition. 15*s*.

1 CHRONICLES. By the Rev. Prof. P. C. BARKER, M.A., LL.B. With Homilies by Rev. Prof. J. R. THOMSON, M.A., Rev. R. TUCK, B.A., Rev. W. CLARKSON, B.A., Rev. F. WHITFIELD, M A., and Rev. RICHARD GLOVER. 15*s*.

ULPIT COMMENTARY (THE). Old Testament Series—continued.

EZRA, NEHEMIAH, AND ESTHER. By Rev. Canon G. RAWLINSON, M.A. With Homilies by Rev. Prof. J. R. THOMSON, M.A., Rev. Prof. R. A. REDFORD, LL.B., M.A., Rev. W. S. LEWIS, M.A., Rev. J. A. MACDONALD, Rev. A. MACKENNAL, B.A., Rev. W. CLARKSON, B.A., Rev. F. HASTINGS, Rev. W. DINWIDDIE, LL.B., Rev. Prof. ROWLANDS, B.A., Rev. G. WOOD, B.A., Rev. Prof. P. C. BARKER, LL.B., M.A., and Rev. J. S. EXELL, M.A. Sixth Edition. One vol. 12*s.* 6*d.*

ISAIAH. By the Rev. Canon G. RAWLINSON, M.A. With Homilies by Rev. Prof. E. JOHNSON, M.A., Rev. W. CLARKSON, B.A., Rev. W. M. STATHAM, and Rev. R. TUCK, B.A. Second Edition. 2 vols. each 15*s.*

JEREMIAH (Vol. I.). By the Rev. Canon CHEYNE, D.D. With Homilies by the Rev W. F. ADENEY, M.A., Rev. A. F. MUIR, M.A., Rev. S. CONWAY, B.A., Rev. J. WAITE, B.A., and Rev. D. YOUNG, B.A. Third Edition. 15*s.*

JEREMIAH (Vol. II.), AND LAMENTATIONS. By the Rev. Canon CHEYNE, D.D. With Homilies by Rev. Prof. J. R. THOMSON, M.A., Rev. W. F. ADENEY, M.A., Rev. A. F. MUIR, M.A., Rev. S. CONWAY, B.A., Rev. D. YOUNG, B.A. 15*s.*

HOSEA AND JOEL. By the Rev. Prof. J. J. GIVEN, Ph.D., D.D. With Homilies by the Rev. Prof. J. R. THOMSON, M.A., Rev. A. ROWLAND, B.A., LL.B., Rev. C. JERDAN, M.A., LL.B., Rev. J. ORR, M.A., B.D., and Rev. D. THOMAS, D.D. 15*s.*

ULPIT COMMENTARY (THE). New Testament Series.

ST. MARK. By the Very Rev. E. BICKERSTETH, D.D., Dean of Lichfield. With Homilies by the Rev. Prof. THOMSON, M.A., Rev. Prof. GIVEN, M.A., Rev. Prof. JOHNSON, M.A., Rev. A. ROWLAND, LL.B., Rev. A. MUIR, M.A., and Rev. R. GREEN. Fifth Edition. 2 vols. each 10*s.* 6*d.*

ST. JOHN. By the Rev. Prof. H. R. REYNOLDS, D.D. With Homilies by Rev. Prof. T. CROSKERY, D.D., Rev. Prof. J. R. THOMSON, Rev. D. YOUNG, Rev. B. THOMAS, and Rev. G. BROWN. 2 vols. each 15*s.*

THE ACTS OF THE APOSTLES. By the Bishop of BATH AND WELLS. With Homilies by Rev. Prof. P. C. BARKER, M.A., Rev. Prof. E. JOHNSON, M.A., Rev. Prof. R. A. REDFORD, M.A., Rev. R. TUCK, B.A., Rev. W. CLARKSON, B.A. Fourth Edition. Two vols. each 10*s.* 6*d.*

I CORINTHIANS. By the Ven. Archdeacon FARRAR, D.D. With Homilies by Rev. Ex-Chancellor LIPSCOMB, LL.D., Rev. DAVID THOMAS, D.D., Rev. DONALD FRASER, D.D., Rev. Prof. J. R. THOMSON, M.A., Rev. R. TUCK, B.A., Rev. E. HURNDALL, M.A., Rev. J. WAITE, B.A., Rev. H. BREMNER, B.D. Third Edition. 15*s.*

II CORINTHIANS AND GALATIANS. By the Ven. Archdeacon FARRAR, D.D., and Rev. Preb. E. HUXTABLE. With Homilies by Rev. Ex-Chancellor LIPSCOMB, LL.D., Rev. DAVID THOMAS, D.D., Rev. DONALD FRASER, D.D., Rev. R. TUCK, B.A., Rev. E. HURNDALL, M.A., Rev. Prof. J. R. THOMSON, M.A., Rev. R. FINLAYSON, B.A., Rev. W. F. ADENEY, M.A., Rev. R. M. EDGAR, M.A., and Rev. T. CROSKERY, D.D. 21*s.*

EPHESIANS, PHILIPPIANS, AND COLOSSIANS. By the Rev. Prof. W. G. BLAIKIE, D.D., Rev. B. C. CAFFIN, M.A., and Rev. G. G. FINDLAY, B.A. With Homilies by Rev. D. THOMAS, D.D., Rev. R. M. EDGAR, M.A., Rev. R. FINLAYSON, B.A., Rev. W. F. ADENEY, M.A., Rev. Prof. T. CROSKERY, D.D., Rev. E. S. PROUT, M.A., Rev. Canon VERNON HUTTON, and Rev. U. R. THOMAS, D.D. Second Edition. 21*s.*

PULPIT COMMENTARY (THE). New Testament Series—continued.

THESSALONIANS, TIMOTHY, TITUS, AND PHILEMON. By the BISH OF BATH AND WELLS, Rev. Dr. GLOAG, and Rev. Dr. EALES. Wi Homilies by the Rev. B. C. CAFFIN, M.A., Rev. R. FINLAYSON, B.A., Re Prof. T. CROSKERY, D.D., Rev. W. F. ADENEY, M.A., Rev. W. I STATHAM, and Rev. D. THOMAS, D.D. 15*s.*

HEBREWS AND JAMES. By the Rev. J. BARMBY, D.D., and Re Prebendary E. C. S. GIBSON, M.A. With Homiletics by the Rev. C. JERDA M.A., LL.B., and Rev. Prebendary E. C. S. GIBSON. And Homilies by t Rev. W. JONES, Rev. C. NEW, Rev. D. YOUNG, B.A., Rev. J. S. BRIGH Rev. T. F. LOCKYER, B.A., and Rev. C. JERDAN, M.A., LL.B. Seco Edition. Price 15*s.*

PUSEY (Dr.)—SERMONS FOR THE CHURCH'S SEASONS FROM ADVE TO TRINITY. Selected from the published Sermons of the late EDWA BOUVERIE PUSEY, D.D. Crown 8vo. 5*s.*

QUEKETT (Rev. William)—MY SAYINGS AND DOINGS, WITH R MINISCENCES OF MY LIFE. Demy 8vo. 18*s.*

RANKE (Leopold von)—UNIVERSAL HISTORY. The Oldest Histori Group of Nations and the Greeks. Edited by G. W. PROTHERO. Demy 8vo. 1

RENDELL (J. M.)—CONCISE HANDBOOK OF THE ISLAND OF MADEI With Plan of Funchal and Map of the Island. Fcp. 8vo. 1*s.* 6*d.*

REYNOLDS (Rev. J. W.)—THE SUPERNATURAL IN NATURE. Verification by Free Use of Science. Third Edition, revised and enlarg Demy 8vo. 14*s.*

THE MYSTERY OF MIRACLES. Third and Enlarged Edition. Cro 8vo. 6*s.*

THE MYSTERY OF THE UNIVERSE: Our Common Faith. De 8vo. 14*s.*

THE WORLD TO COME: Immortality a Physical Fact. Crown 8vo.

RIBOT (Prof. Th.)—HEREDITY: a Psychological Study on its Phenome its Laws, its Causes, and its Consequences. Second Edition. Large cro 8vo. 9*s.*

RIVINGTON (Luke)—AUTHORITY, OR A PLAIN REASON FOR JOINI THE CHURCH OF ROME. Crown 8vo. 3*s.* 6*d.*

ROBERTSON (The late Rev. F. W.) M.A.—LIFE AND LETTERS Edited by the Rev. Stopford Brooke, M.A.

I. Two vols., uniform with the Sermons. With Steel Portrait. Cro 8vo. 7*s.* 6*d.*

II. Library Edition, in demy 8vo. with Portrait. 12*s.*

III. A Popular Edition, in 1 vol. Crown 8vo. 6*s.*

SERMONS. Four Series. Small crown 8vo. 3*s.* 6*d.* each.

THE HUMAN RACE, and other Sermons. Preached at Cheltenha Oxford, and Brighton. New and Cheaper Edition. Small crown 8vo. 3*s.*

NOTES ON GENESIS. New and Cheaper Edition. Small crown 8 3*s.* 6*d.*

EXPOSITORY LECTURES ON ST. PAUL'S EPISTLES TO THE CORINTHIA A New Edition. Small crown 8vo. 5*s.*

LECTURES AND ADDRESSES, with other Literary Remains. A N Edition. Small crown 8vo. 5*s.*

AN ANALYSIS OF TENNYSON'S 'IN MEMORIAM.' (Dedicated Permission to the Poet-Laureate.) Fcp. 8vo. 2*s.*

THE EDUCATION OF THE HUMAN RACE. Translated from the Gc of Gotthold Ephraim Lessing. Fcp. 8vo. 2*s.* 6*d.*

*** A Portrait of the late Rev. F. W. Robertson, mounted for framing, be had, 2*s.* 6*d.*

ROGERS (William)—REMINISCENCES. Compiled by R. H. HADDEN. With Portrait. Third Edition. Crown 8vo. 6*s*.

ROMANCE OF THE RECUSANTS. By the Author of 'Life of a Prig.' Cr. 8vo. 5*s*.

ROMANES (G. J.)—MENTAL EVOLUTION IN ANIMALS. With a Posthumous Essay on Instinct, by CHARLES DARWIN, F.R.S. Demy 8vo. 12*s*.

MENTAL EVOLUTION IN MAN. Vol. I. 8vo. 14*s*.

ROSMINI SERBATI (A.) Founder of the Institute of Charity—LIFE. By FATHER LOCKHART. 2 vols. Crown 8vo. 12*s*.

ROSMINI'S ORIGIN OF IDEAS. Translated from the Fifth Italian Edition of the Nuovo Saggio. *Sull' origine delle idee.* 3 vols. Demy 8vo. 10*s*. 6*d*. each.

ROSMINI'S PSYCHOLOGY. 3 vols. Demy 8vo. [Vols. I. & II. now ready, 10*s*. 6*d*. each.

ROSS (Janet)—ITALIAN SKETCHES. With 14 full-page Illustrations. Crown 8vo. 7*s*. 6*d*.

RULE (Martin) M.A.—THE LIFE AND TIMES OF ST. ANSELM, ARCHBISHOP OF CANTERBURY AND PRIMATE OF THE BRITAINS. 2 vols. Demy 8vo. 32*s*.

SAMUEL (Sydney M.)—JEWISH LIFE IN THE EAST. Small crown 8vo. 3*s*. 6*d*.

SAYCE (Rev. Archibald Henry)—INTRODUCTION TO THE SCIENCE OF LANGUAGE. 2 vols. Second Edition. Large post 8vo. 21*s*.

SCOONES (W. Baptiste)—FOUR CENTURIES OF ENGLISH LETTERS A Selection of 350 Letters by 150 Writers, from the Period of the Paston Letters to the Present Time. Third Edition. Large crown 8vo. 6*s*.

SÉE (Prof. Germain)—BACILLARY PHTHISIS OF THE LUNGS. Translated and Edited for English Practitioners, by WILLIAM HENRY WEDDELL, M.R.C.S. Demy 8vo. 10*s*. 6*d*.

SELWYN (Augustus) D.D.—LIFE. By Canon G. H. CURTEIS. Crown 8vo. 6*s*.

SEYMOUR (W. Digby)—HOME RULE AND STATE SUPREMACY. Crown 8vo. 3*s*. 6*d*.

SHAKSPERE—WORKS. The Avon Edition, 12 vols. fcp. 8vo. cloth, 18*s*.; in cloth box, 21*s*.; bound in 6 vols., cloth, 15*s*.

SHAKSPERE—WORKS (An Index to). By EVANGELINE O'CONNOR. Crown 8vo. 5*s*.

SHELLEY (Percy Bysshe).—LIFE. By EDWARD DOWDEN, LL.D. With Portraits and Illustrations, 2 vols., demy 8vo. 36*s*.

SHILLITO (Rev. Joseph)—WOMANHOOD: its Duties, Temptations, and Privileges. A Book for Young Women. Third Edition. Crown 8vo. 3*s*. 6*d*.

SHOOTING, PRACTICAL HINTS ON. Being a Treatise on the Shot Gun and its Management. By '20-Bore.' With 55 Illustrations. Demy 8vo. 12*s*.

SISTER AUGUSTINE, Superior of the Sisters of Charity at the St. Johannis Hospital at Bonn. Cheap Edition. Large crown 8vo. 4*s*. 6*d*.

SKINNER (JAMES). A Memoir. By the Author of 'Charles Lowder.' With a Preface by Canon CARTER, and Portrait. Large crown 8vo. 7*s*. 6*d*.
* Also a Cheap Edition, with Portrait. Crown 8vo. 3*s*. 6*d*.

SMEATON (Donald).—THE LOYAL KARENS OF BURMAH. Crown 8vo. 4*s*. 6*d*.

SMITH (Edward) M.D., LL.B., F.R.S.—TUBERCULAR CONSUMPTION IN ITS EARLY AND REMEDIABLE STAGES. Second Edition. Crown 8vo. 6*s*.

SMITH (*L. A.*)—MUSIC OF THE WATERS: Sailors' Chanties, or Wo ing Songs of the Sea of all Maritime Nations. Demy 8vo. 12*s.*

SMITH (*Sir W. Cusack, Bart.*)—OUR WAR SHIPS. A Naval Ess Crown 8vo. 5*s.*

SPANISH MYSTICS. By the Editor of 'Many Voices.' Crown 8vo. 5*s.*

SPECIMENS OF ENGLISH PROSE STYLE FROM MALORY TO MACAULA Selected and Annotated, with an Introductory Essay, by GEORGE SAINTSBUR Large crown 8vo., printed on hand-made paper, parchment antique, or clot 12*s.*; vellum, 15*s.*

SPEDDING (*James*)—REVIEWS AND DISCUSSIONS, LITERARY, POLITICA AND HISTORICAL NOT RELATING TO BACON. Demy 8vo. 12*s.* 6*d.*

EVENINGS WITH A REVIEWER; or, Bacon and Macaulay. With Prefatory Notice by G. S. VENABLES, Q.C. 2 vols. Demy 8vo. 18*s.*

STRACHEY (*Sir John*)—LECTURES ON INDIA. 8vo. 15*s.*

STRAY PAPERS ON EDUCATION AND SCENES FROM SCHOOL LIFE. By B. Second Edition. Small crown 8vo. 3*s.* 6*d.*

STREATFEILD (*Rev. G. S.*) *M.A.*—LINCOLNSHIRE AND THE DANE Large crown 8vo. 7*s.* 6*d.*

STRECKER-WISLICENUS—ORGANIC CHEMISTRY. Translated a Edited, with Extensive Additions, by W. R. HODGKINSON, Ph.D., and A. GREENAWAY, F.I.C. Demy 8vo. 12*s.* 6*d.*

SUAKIN, 1885; being a Sketch of the Campaign of this Year. By Officer who was there. Second Edition. Crown 8vo. 2*s.* 6*d.*

SULLY (*James*) *M.A.*—PESSIMISM: a History and a Criticism. Secor Edition. Demy 8vo. 14*s.*

TARRING (*Charles James*) *M.A.*—A PRACTICAL ELEMENTARY TURKIS GRAMMAR. Crown 8vo. 6*s.*

TAYLOR (*Hugh*)—THE MORALITY OF NATIONS. A Study in th Evolution of Ethics. Crown 8vo. 6*s.*

TAYLOR (*Rev. Isaac*)—THE ALPHABET. An Account of the Origi and Development of Letters. Numerous Tables and Facsimiles. 2 vols. 8vo. 36

LEAVES FROM AN EGYPTIAN NOTE-BOOK. Crown 8vo. 5*s.*

TAYLOR (*Reynell*) *C.B.*, *C.S.I.*—A BIOGRAPHY. By E. GAMBIE PARRY. With Portrait and Map. Demy 8vo. 14*s.*

THOM (*John Hamilton*)—LAWS OF LIFE AFTER THE MIND OF CHRIS Two Series. Crown 8vo. 7*s.* 6*d.* each.

THOMPSON (*Sir H.*)—DIET IN RELATION TO AGE AND ACTIVIT Fcp. 8vo. cloth, 1*s.* 6*d.*; Paper covers, 1*s.*

TIDMAN (*Paul F.*)—GOLD AND SILVER MONEY. Part I.—A Plai Statement. Part II.—Objections Answered. Third Edition. Crown 8vo. 1

MONEY AND LABOUR. 1*s.* 6*d.*

TODHUNTER (*Dr. J.*)—A STUDY OF SHELLEY. Crown 8vo. 7*s.*

TOLSTOI (*Count Leo*)—CHRIST'S CHRISTIANITY. Translated from th Russian. Large crown 8vo. 7*s.* 6*d.*

TRANT (*William*)—TRADE UNIONS; Their Origin and Objects, Infl ence and Efficacy. Small crown 8vo. 1*s.* 6*d.*; paper covers, 1*s.*

TRENCH (*The late R. C., Archbishop*)—LETTERS AND MEMORIALS. Edited by the Author of 'Charles Lowder, a Biography,' &c. With two Portraits. 2 vols. demy 8vo. 21*s.*

SERMONS NEW AND OLD. Crown 8vo. 6*s.*

WESTMINSTER AND DUBLIN SERMONS. Crown 8vo. 6*s.*

NOTES ON THE PARABLES OF OUR LORD. Fourteenth Edition. 8vo. 12*s.*; Popular Edition, crown 8vo. 7*s.* 6*d.*

NOTES ON THE MIRACLES OF OUR LORD. Twelfth Edition. 8vo. 12*s.*; Popular Edition, crown 8vo. 7*s.* 6*d.*

STUDIES IN THE GOSPELS. Fifth Edition, Revised. 8vo. 10*s.* 6*d.*

BRIEF THOUGHTS AND MEDITATIONS ON SOME PASSAGES IN HOLY Scripture. Third Edition. Crown 8vo. 3*s.* 6*d.*

SYNONYMS OF THE NEW TESTAMENT. Tenth Edition, Enlarged. 8vo. 12*s.*

ON THE AUTHORISED VERSION OF THE NEW TESTAMENT. Second Edition. 8vo. 7*s.*

COMMENTARY ON THE EPISTLE TO THE SEVEN CHURCHES IN ASIA. Fourth Edition, Revised. 8vo. 8*s.* 6*d.*

THE SERMON ON THE MOUNT. An Exposition drawn from the Writings of St. Augustine, with an Essay on his Merits as an Interpreter of Holy Scripture. Fourth Edition, Enlarged. 8vo. 10*s.* 6*d.*

SHIPWRECKS OF FAITH. Three Sermons preached before the University of Cambridge in May 1867. Fcp. 8vo. 2*s.* 6*d.*

LECTURES ON MEDIÆVAL CHURCH HISTORY. Being the Substance of Lectures delivered at Queen's College, London. Second Edition. 8vo. 12*s.*

ENGLISH, PAST AND PRESENT. Thirteenth Edition, Revised and Improved. Fcp. 8vo. 5*s.*

ON THE STUDY OF WORDS. Nineteenth Edition, Revised. Fcp. 8vo. 5*s.*

SELECT GLOSSARY OF ENGLISH WORDS USED FORMERLY IN SENSES DIFFERENT FROM THE PRESENT. Sixth Edition, Revised and Enlarged. Fcp. 8vo. 5*s.*

PROVERBS AND THEIR LESSONS. Seventh Edition, Enlarged. Fcp. 8vo. 4*s.*

POEMS. Collected and Arranged Anew. Ninth Edition. Fcp. 8vo. 7*s.* 6*d.*

POEMS. Library Edition. 2 vols. Small crown 8vo. 10*s.*

SACRED LATIN POETRY. Chiefly Lyrical, Selected and Arranged for Use. Third Edition, Corrected and Improved. Fcp. 8vo. 7*s.*

A HOUSEHOLD BOOK OF ENGLISH POETRY. Selected and Arranged, with Notes. Fourth Edition, Revised. Extra fcp. 8vo. 5*s.* 6*d.*

AN ESSAY ON THE LIFE AND GENIUS OF CALDERON. With Translations from his 'Life's a Dream' and 'Great Theatre of the World.' Second Edition, Revised and Improved. Extra fcp. 8vo. 5*s.* 6*d*,

GUSTAVUS ADOLPHUS IN GERMANY, AND OTHER LECTURES ON THE THIRTY YEARS' WAR. Third Edition, Enlarged. Fcp. 8vo. 4*s.*

PLUTARCH: HIS LIFE, HIS LIVES, AND HIS MORALS. Second Edition, Enlarged. Fcap. 8vo. 3*s.* 6*d.*

REMAINS OF THE LATE MRS. RICHARD TRENCH. Being Selections from her Journals, Letters, and other Papers. New and Cheaper Issue. With Portrait. 8vo. 6*s.*

TUTHILL (*C. A. H.*)—ORIGIN AND DEVELOPMENT OF CHRISTI DOGMA. Crown 8vo. 3*s.* 6*d.*

TWINING (*Louisa*)—WORKHOUSE VISITING AND MANAGEMENT DURI TWENTY-FIVE YEARS. Small crown 8vo. 2*s.*

TWO CENTURIES OF IRISH HISTORY. Edited by JAMES BRYCE, M. 8vo. 16*s.*

UMLAUFT (*F.*)—THE ALPS. Illustrated. 8vo.

VAL D'EREMAO (*J. P.*) *D.D.*—THE SERPENT OF EDEN. Cro 8vo. 4*s.* 6*d.*

VAUGHAN (*H. Halford*)—NEW READINGS AND RENDERINGS SHAKESPEARE'S TRAGEDIES. 3 vols. Demy 8vo. 12*s.* 6*d.* each.

VICARY (*J. Fulford*)—SAGA TIME. With Illustrations. Cr. 8vo. 7*s.*

VOLCKXSOM (*E. W. v.*)—CATECHISM OF ELEMENTARY MODE CHEMISTRY. Small crown 8vo. 3*s.*

WALPOLE (*Chas. George*)—A SHORT HISTORY OF IRELAND FROM T EARLIEST TIMES TO THE UNION WITH GREAT BRITAIN. With 5 Maps a Appendices. Third Edition. Crown 8vo. 6*s.*

WARD (*William George*) *Ph.D.* — ESSAYS ON THE PHILOSOPHY THEISM. Edited, with an Introduction, by WILFRID WARD. 2 vols. de 8vo. 21*s.*

WARD (*Wilfrid*)—THE WISH TO BELIEVE: A Discussion concerni the Temper of Mind in which a reasonable Man should undertake Religi Inquiry. Small crown 8vo. 5*s.*

WARNER (*Francis*) *M.D.*—LECTURES ON THE ANATOMY OF MOV MENT. Crown 8vo. 4*s.* 6*d.*

WARTER (*J. W.*)—AN OLD SHROPSHIRE OAK. 2 vols. demy 8vo. 2

WEDMORE (*Frederick*)—THE MASTERS OF GENRE PAINTING. W Sixteen Illustrations. Post 8vo. 7*s.* 6*d.*

WHIBLEY (*Charles*)—CAMBRIDGE ANECDOTES. Crown 8vo. 7*s.* 6*d.*

WHITMAN (*Sidney*)—CONVENTIONAL CANT: Its Results and Reme Crown 8vo. 6*s.*

WHITNEY (*Prof. William Dwight*)—ESSENTIALS OF ENGLISH GRAMM for the Use of Schools. Second Edition, crown 8vo. 3*s.* 6*d.*

WHITWORTH (*George Clifford*)—AN ANGLO-INDIAN DICTIONAR a Glossary of Indian Terms used in English. Demy 8vo. cloth, 12*s.*

WILBERFORCE (*Samuel*) *D.D.*—LIFE. By R. G. WILBERFOR Crown 8vo. 6*s.*

WILSON (*Mrs. R. F.*)—THE CHRISTIAN BROTHERS: THEIR ORIG AND WORK. Crown 8vo. 6*s.*

WOLTMANN (*Dr. Alfred*), *and WOERMANN* (*Dr. Karl*) HISTORY OF PAINTING. Vol. I. Ancient, Early, Christian, and Media Painting. With numerous Illustrations. Super-royal 8vo. 28*s.*; bevel boards, gilt leaves, 30*s.* Vol. II. The Painting of the Renascence. Cl 42*s.*; cloth extra, bevelled boards, 45*s.*

WORDS OF JESUS CHRIST TAKEN FROM THE GOSPELS. Small crown 8 2*s.* 6*d.*

YOUMANS (*Eliza A.*)—FIRST BOOK OF BOTANY. Designed to cultiv the Observing Powers of Children. With 300 Engravings. New and Chea Edition. Crown 8vo. 2*s.* 6*d.*

YOUMANS (*Edward L.*) *M.D.*—A CLASS BOOK OF CHEMISTRY, on Basis of the New System. With 200 Illustrations. Crown 8vo. 5*s.*

YOUNG (*Arthur*).—AXIAL POLARITY OF MAN'S WORD-EMBOD IDEAS, AND ITS TEACHING. Demy 4to. 15*s.*

THE INTERNATIONAL SCIENTIFIC SERIES.

I. FORMS OF WATER: a Familiar Exposition of the Origin and Phenomena of Glaciers. By J. Tyndall, LL.D., F.R.S. With 25 Illustrations. Ninth Edition. Crown 8vo. 5*s.*

II. PHYSICS AND POLITICS; or, Thoughts on the Application of the Principles of 'Natural Selection' and 'Inheritance' to Political Society. By Walter Bagehot. Eighth Edition. Crown 8vo. 5*s.*

III. FOODS. By Edward Smith, M.D., LL.B., F.R.S. With numerous Illustrations. Ninth Edition. Crown 8vo. 5*s.*

IV. MIND AND BODY: the Theories and their Relation. By Alexander Bain, LL.D. With Four Illustrations. Eighth Edition. Crown 8vo. 5*s.*

V. THE STUDY OF SOCIOLOGY. By Herbert Spencer. Thirteenth Edition. Crown 8vo. 5*s.*

VI. ON THE CONSERVATION OF ENERGY. By Balfour Stewart, M.A., LL.D., F.R.S. With 14 Illustrations. Seventh Edition. Crown 8vo. 5*s.*

VII. ANIMAL LOCOMOTION; or, Walking, Swimming, and Flying. By J. B. Pettigrew, M.D., F.R.S., &c. With 130 Illustrations. Third Edition. Crown 8vo. 5*s.*

VIII. RESPONSIBILITY IN MENTAL DISEASE. By Henry Maudsley, M.D. Fourth Edition. Crown 8vo. 5*s.*

IX. THE NEW CHEMISTRY. By Professor J. P. Cooke. With 31 Illustrations. Ninth Edition, remodelled and enlarged. Crown 8vo. 5*s.*

X. THE SCIENCE OF LAW. By Professor Sheldon Amos. Sixth Edition. Crown 8vo. 5*s.*

XI. ANIMAL MECHANISM: a Treatise on Terrestrial and Aërial Locomotion. By Professor E. J. Marey. With 117 Illustrations. Third Edition. Crown 8vo. 5*s.*

XII. THE DOCTRINE OF DESCENT AND DARWINISM. By Professor Oscar Schmidt. With 26 Illustrations. Seventh Edition. Crown 8vo. 5*s.*

XIII. THE HISTORY OF THE CONFLICT BETWEEN RELIGION AND SCIENCE. By J. W. Draper, M.D., LL.D. Twentieth Edition. Crown 8vo. 5*s.*

XIV. FUNGI: their Nature, Influences, Uses, &c. By M. C. Cooke, M.D., LL.D. Edited by the Rev. M. J. Berkeley, M.A., F.L.S. With numerous Illustrations. Fourth Edition. Crown 8vo. 5*s.*

XV. THE CHEMICAL EFFECTS OF LIGHT AND PHOTOGRAPHY. By Dr. Hermann Vogel. Translation thoroughly revised. With 100 Illustrations. Fifth Edition. Crown 8vo. 5*s.*

XVI. THE LIFE AND GROWTH OF LANGUAGE. By Professor William Dwight Whitney. Fifth Edition. Crown 8vo. 5*s.*

XVII. MONEY AND THE MECHANISM OF EXCHANGE. By W. Stanley Jevons, M.A., F.R.S. Eighth Edition. Crown 8vo. 5*s.*

XVIII. THE NATURE OF LIGHT. With a General Account of Physical Optics. By Dr. Eugene Lommel. With 188 Illustrations and a Table of Spectra in Chromo-lithography. Fourth Edit. Crown 8vo. 5*s.*

XIX. ANIMAL PARASITES AND MESSMATES. By P. J. Van Beneden. With 83 Illustrations. Third Edition. Crown 8vo. 5*s.*

XX. FERMENTATION. By Professor Sehützenberger. With 28 Illustrations. Fourth Edition. Crown 8vo. 5*s.*

XXI. THE FIVE SENSES OF MAN. By Professor Bernstein. With 91 Illustrations. Fifth Edition. Crown 8vo. 5*s.*

XXII. THE THEORY OF SOUND IN ITS RELATION TO MUSIC. By Professor Pietro Blaserna. With numerous Illustrations. Third Edition. Crown 8vo. 5*s.*

XXIII. STUDIES IN SPECTRUM ANALYSIS. By J. Norman Lockyer, F.R.S. Fourth Edition. With six Photographie Illustrations of Spectra, and numerous Engravings on Wood. Crown 8vo. 6*s.* 6*d.*

XXIV. A History of the Growth of the Steam Engine. By Professor R. H. Thurston. With numerous Illustrations. Fourth Edition. Crown 8vo. 5*s*.

XXV. Education as a Science. By Alexander Bain, LL.D. Sixth Edition. Crown 8vo. 5*s*.

XXVI. The Human Species. By Prof. A. De Quatrefages. Fourth Edition. Crown 8vo. 5*s*.

XXVII. Modern Chromatics. With Applications to Art and Industry. By Ogden N. Rood. With 130 original Illustrations. Second Edition. Crown 8vo. 5*s*.

XXVIII. The Crayfish: an Introduction to the Study of Zoology. By Professor T. H. Huxley. With 82 Illustrations. Fourth Edition. Crown 8vo. 5*s*.

XXIX. The Brain as an Organ of Mind. By H. Charlton Bastian, M.D. With numerous Illustrations. Third Edition. Crown 8vo. 5*s*.

XXX. The Atomic Theory. By Prof. Wurtz. Translated by G. Cleminshaw, F.C.S. Fifth Edition. Crown 8vo. 5*s*.

XXXI. The Natural Conditions of Existence as they affect Animal Life. By Karl Semper. With 2 Maps and 106 Woodcuts. Third Edition. Crown 8vo. 5*s*.

XXXII. General Physiology of Muscles and Nerves. By Prof. J. Rosenthal. Third Edition. With Illustrations. Crown 8vo. 5*s*.

XXXIII. Sight: an Exposition of the Principles of Monocular and Binocular Vision. By Joseph Le Conte, LL.D. Second Edition. With 132 Illustrations. Crown 8vo. 5*s*.

XXXIV. Illusions: a Psychological Study. By James Sully. Third Edition. Crown 8vo. 5*s*.

XXXV. Volcanoes: what they are and what they teach. By Professor J. W. Judd, F.R.S. With 92 Illustrations on Wood. Fourth Edition. Crown 8vo. 5*s*.

XXXVI. Suicide: an Essay on Comparative Moral Statistics. By Prof. H. Morselli. Second Edition. With Diagrams. Crown 8vo. 5*s*.

XXXVII. The Brain and its Fu tions. By J. Luys. Second Editi With Illustrations. Crown 8vo. 5*s*.

XXXVIII. Myth and Science: Essay. By Tito Vignoli. Tb Edition. Crown 8vo. 5*s*.

XXXIX. The Sun. By Professor Yo With Illustrations. Third Editi Crown 8vo. 5*s*.

XL. Ants, Bees, and Wasps: a Rec of Observations on the Habits of Social Hymenoptera. By Sir J Lubbock, Bart., M.P. With 5 Chro lithographic Illustrations. Ni Edition. Crown 8vo 5*s*.

XLI. Animal Intelligence. By G. Romanes, LL.D., F.R.S. Fou Edition. Crown 8vo. 5*s*.

XLII. The Concepts and Theories Modern Physics. By J. B. Sta Third Edition. Crown 8vo. 5*s*.

XLIII. Diseases of Memory: an Es in the Positive Pyschology. By P Th. Ribot. Third Edition. Cro 8vo. 5*s*.

XLIV. Man before Metals. By Joly. Fourth Edition. Crown 8vo.

XLV. The Science of Politics. Prof. Sheldon Amos. Third Ec Crown. 8vo. 5*s*.

XLVI. Elementary Meteorolo By Robert H. Scott. Fourth Editi With numerous Illustrations. Cro 8vo. 5*s*.

XLVII. The Organs of Speech a their Application in the F mation of Articulate Soun By Georg Hermann von Mey With 47 Woodcuts. Crown 8vo. 5*s*.

XLVIII. Fallacies: a View of Lo from the Practical Side. By Alfi Sidgwick. Second Edition. Cro 8vo. 5*s*.

XLIX. Origin of Cultivated Plan By Alphonse de Candolle. Seco Edition. Crown 8vo. 5*s*.

L. Jelly Fish, Star Fish, and S Urchins. Being a Research Primitive Nervous Systems. G. J. Romanes. Crown 8vo. 5*s*.

LI. The Common Sense of the Exa Sciences. By the late William Kir don Clifford. Second Edition. Wi 100 Figures. 5*s*.

LII. PHYSICAL EXPRESSION: ITS MODES AND PRINCIPLES. By Francis Warner, M.D., F.R.C.P. With 50 Illustrations. 5*s*.

LIII. ANTHROPOID APES. By Robert Hartmann. With 63 Illustrations. 5*s*.

LIV. THE MAMMALIA IN THEIR RELATION TO PRIMEVAL TIMES. By Oscar Schmidt. With 51 Woodcuts. 5*s*.

LV. COMPARATIVE LITERATURE. By H. Macaulay Posnett, LL.D. 5*s*.

LVI. EARTHQUAKES AND OTHER EARTH MOVEMENTS. By Prof. JOHN MILNE. With 38 Figures. Second Edition. 5*s*.

LVII. MICROBES, FERMENTS, AND MOULDS. By E. L. TROUESSART. With 107 Illustrations. 5*s*.

LVIII. GEOGRAPHICAL AND GEOLOGICAL DISTRIBUTION OF ANIMALS. By Professor A. Heilprin. With Frontispiece. 5*s*.

LIX. WEATHER. A Popular Exposition of the Nature of Weather Changes from Day to Day. By the Hon. Ralph Abercromby. With 96 Illustrations. Second Edition. 5*s*.

LX. ANIMAL MAGNETISM. By Alfred Binet and Charles Féré. 5*s*.

LXI. MANUAL OF BRITISH DISCOMYCETES, with descriptions of all the Species of Fungi hitherto found in Britain included in the Family, and Illustrations of the Genera. By William Phillips, F.L.S. 5*s*.

LXII. INTERNATIONAL LAW. With Materials for a Code of International Law. By Professor Leone Levi. 5*s*.

LXIII. THE GEOLOGICAL HISTORY OF PLANTS. By Sir J. William Dawson. With 80 Illustrations. 5*s*.

LXIV. THE ORIGIN OF FLORAL STRUCTURES THROUGH INSECT AND OTHER AGENCIES. By Professor G. Henslow.

LXV. ON THE SENSES, INSTINCTS, AND INTELLIGENCE OF ANIMALS. With special Reference to Insects. By Sir John Lubbock, Bart., M.P. 100 Illustrations. 5*s*.

MILITARY WORKS.

BARRINGTON (*Capt. J. T.*)—ENGLAND ON THE DEFENSIVE; or, the Problem of Invasion Critically Examined. Large crown 8vo. with Map, 7*s*. 6*d*.

BRACKENBURY (*Col. C. B.*) *R.A.*—MILITARY HANDBOOKS FOR REGIMENTAL OFFICERS:

I. MILITARY SKETCHING AND RECONNAISSANCE. By Colonel F. J. Hutchison and Major H. G. MacGregor. Fifth Edition. With 15 Plates. Small crown 8vo. 4*s*.

II. THE ELEMENTS OF MODERN TACTICS PRACTICALLY APPLIED TO ENGLISH FORMATIONS. By Lieut.-Col. Wilkinson Shaw. Sixth Edit. With 25 Plates and Maps. Small crown 8vo. 9*s*.

III. FIELD ARTILLERY: its Equipment, Organisation, and Tactics. By Major Sisson C. Pratt, R.A. With 12 Plates. Third Edition. Small crown 8vo. 6*s*.

IV. THE ELEMENTS OF MILITARY ADMINISTRATION. First Part: Permanent System of Administration. By Major J. W. Buxton. Small crown 8vo. 7*s*. 6*d*.

BRACKENBURY (*Col. C. B.*) *R.A.*—continued.

V. MILITARY LAW: its Procedure and Practice. By Major Sisson C. Pratt, R.A. Third Edition. Small crown 8vo. 4*s*. 6d.

VI. CAVALRY IN MODERN WAR. By Major-General F. Chenevix Trench. Small crown 8vo. 6*s*.

VII. FIELD WORKS. Their Technical Construction and Tactical Application. By the Editor, Col. C. B. Brackenbury, R.A. Small crown 8vo.

BROOKE (*Major C. K.*)—A SYSTEM OF FIELD TRAINING. Small crown 8vo. 2*s*.

CLERY (*Col. C. Francis*) *C.B.*—MINOR TACTICS. With 26 Maps and Plans. Eighth Edition. Crown 8vo. 9*s*.

COLVILE (*Lieut.-Col. C. F.*)—MILITARY TRIBUNALS. Sewed, 2*s*. 6*d*.

CRAUFURD (*Capt. H. J.*)—SUGGESTIONS FOR THE MILITARY TRAINING OF A COMPANY OF INFANTRY. Crown 8vo. 1*s*. 6*d*.

HAMILTON (*Capt. Ian*) *A.D.C.*—The Fighting of the Future. 1*s*.

HARRISON (*Lieut.-Col. R.*) — The Officer's Memorandum Book for Peace and War. Fourth Edition. Oblong 32mo. roan, with pencil, 3*s*. 6*d*.

Notes on Cavalry Tactics, Organisation, &c. By a Cavalry Officer. With Diagrams. Demy 8vo. 12*s*.

PARR (*Col. H. Hallam*) *C.M.G.*—The Dress, Horses, and Equipment of Infantry and Staff Officers. Crown 8vo. 1*s*.

Further Training and Equipment of Mounted Infantry. Crown 8vo. 1*s*.

SCHAW (*Col. H.*)—The Defence a Attack of Positions and Loca ties. Third Edition, revised a corrected. Crown 8vo. 3*s*. 6*d*.

STONE (*Capt. F. Gleadowe*) *R.A.*—T tical Studies from the Fran German War of 1870–71. W 22 Lithographic Sketches and Ma Demy 8vo. 10*s*. 6*d*.

The Campaign of Fredericksbu November-December, 1862: a Stu for Officers of Volunteers. By Line Officer. Second Edition. Cro 8vo. With Five Maps and Plans.

WILKINSON (*H. Spenser*) *Capt.* 2 *Lancashire R.V.*—Citizen Soldie Essays towards the Improvement the Volunteer Force. Cr. 8vo. 2*s*.

POETRY.

ADAM OF ST. VICTOR—The Liturgical Poetry of Adam of St. Victor. From the text of Gautier. With Translations into English in the Original Metres, and Short Explanatory Notes. By Digby S. Wrangham, M.A. 3 vols. Crown 8vo. printed on hand-made paper, boards, 21*s*.

ALEXANDER (*William*) *D.D.*, *Bishop of Derry*—St. Augustine's Holiday, and other Poems. Crown 8vo. 6*s*.

AUCHMUTY (*A. C.*)—Poems of English Heroism: From Brunanburgh to Lucknow; from Athelstan to Albert. Small crown 8vo. 1*s*. 6*d*.

BARNES (*William*)—Poems of Rural Life, in the Dorset Dialect. New Edition, complete in one vol. Crown 8vo. 6*s*.

BAYNES (*Rev. Canon H. R.*)—Home Songs for Quiet Hours. Fourth and cheaper Edition. Fcp. 8vo. 2*s*. 6*d*.

BEVINGTON (*L. S.*)—Key Notes. Small crown 8vo. 5*s*.

BLUNT (*Wilfrid Scawen*)—The Wind and the Whirlwind. Demy 8vo. 1*s*. 6*d*.

The Love Sonnets of Proteus. Fifth Edition. 18mo. cloth extra, gilt top, 5*s*.

BOWEN (*H. C.*) *M.A.*—Simple English Poems. English Literature for Junior Classes. In Four Parts. Parts I. II. and III. 6*d*. each, and Part IV. 1*s*., complete 3*s*.

BRYANT (*W. C.*) — Poems. Ch Edition, with Frontispiece. S crown 8vo. 3*s*. 6*d*.

Calderon's Dramas: the Won working Magician—Life is a Dre —the Purgatory of St. Patrick. Tr lated by Denis Florence MacCart Post 8vo. 10*s*.

CAMPBELL (*Lewis*)—Sophocles. Seven Plays in English Verse. Cro 8vo. 7*s*. 6*d*.

CERVANTES.—Journey to P nassus. Spanish Text, with Tra lation into English Tercets, Prefa and Illustrative Notes, by James Gibson. Crown 8vo. 12*s*.

Numantia; a Tragedy. Transla from the Spanish, with Introduct and Notes, by James Y. Gibs Crown 8vo., printed on hand-m paper, 5*s*.

Cid Ballads, and other Poems. Tra lated from Spanish and German J. Y. Gibson. 2 vols. Crown 8vo. 1

CHRISTIE (*A. J.*)—The End of M Fourth Edition. Fcp. 8vo. 2*s*. 6

COXHEAD (*Ethel*)—Birds and Babi Imp. 16mo. With 33 Illustrations.

DANTE—The Divina Commedia Dante Alighieri. Translated, l for line, in the 'Terza Rima' of original, with Notes, by Freder K. H. Haselfoot, M.A. Demy 8 16*s*.

DE BERANGER.—A SELECTION FROM HIS SONGS. In English Verse. By WILLIAM TOYNBEE. Small crown 8vo. 2*s*. 6*d*.

D*ENNIS* (*J.*)—ENGLISH SONNETS. Collected and Arranged by. Small crown 8vo. 2*s*. 6*d*.

DE VERE (*Aubrey*)—POETICAL WORKS:

I. THE SEARCH AFTER PROSERPINE, &c. 6*s*.

II. THE LEGENDS OF ST. PATRICK, &c. 6*s*.

III. ALEXANDER THE GREAT, &c. 6*s*.

THE FORAY OF QUEEN MEAVE, and other Legends of Ireland's Heroic Age. Small crown 8vo. 5*s*.

LEGENDS OF THE SAXON SAINTS. Small crown 8vo. 6*s*.

LEGENDS AND RECORDS OF THE CHURCH AND THE EMPIRE. Small crown 8vo. 6*s*.

DOBSON (*Austin*)—OLD WORLD IDYLLS, and other Verses. Eighth Edition. Elzevir 8vo. cloth extra, gilt tops, 6*s*.

AT THE SIGN OF THE LYRE. Fifth Edition. Elzevir 8vo., gilt top, 6*s*.

DO*WDEN* (*Edward*) *LL.D.*—SHAKSPERE'S SONNETS. With Introduction and Notes. Large post 8vo. 7*s*. 6*d*.

*DU*TT (*Toru*)—A SHEAF GLEANED IN FRENCH FIELDS. New Edition. Demy 8vo. 10*s*. 6*d*.

ANCIENT BALLADS AND LEGENDS OF HINDUSTAN. With an Introductory Memoir by EDMUND GOSSE. Second Edition. 18mo. Cloth extra, gilt top, 5*s*.

ELL*IO*TT (*Ebenezer*), *The Corn Law Rhymer*—POEMS. Edited by his Son, the Rev. Edwin Elliott, of St. John's, Antigua. 2 vols. crown 8vo. 18*s*.

ENGLISH VERSE. Edited by W. J. LINTON and R. H. STODDARD. In 5 vols. Crown 8vo. each 5*s*.

1. CHAUCER TO BURNS.
2. TRANSLATIONS.
3. LYRICS OF THE NINETEENTH CENTURY.
4. DRAMATIC SCENES AND CHARACTERS.
5. BALLADS AND ROMANCES.

EVANS (*Anne*)—POEMS AND MUSIC. With Memorial Preface by ANN THACKERAY RITCHIE. Large crown 8vo. 7*s*.

GOSSE (*Edmund W.*)—NEW POEMS. Crown 8vo. 7*s*. 6*d*.

FIRDAUSI IN EXILE, and other Poems. Elzevir 8vo. gilt top, 6*s*.

GURNEY (*Rev. Alfred*)—THE VISION OF THE EUCHARIST, and other Poems. Crown 8vo. 5*s*.

A CHRISTMAS FAGGOT. Small crown 8vo. 5*s*.

HARRISON (*Clifford*)—IN HOURS OF LEISURE. Second Edition. Crown 8vo. 5*s*.

KEATS (*John*)—POETICAL WORKS. Edited by W. T. ARNOLD. Large crown 8vo. choicely printed on hand-made paper, with Portrait in *eau forte*. Parchment, or cloth, 12*s*.; vellum, 15*s*.

Also, a smaller Edition. Crown 8vo. 3*s*. 6*d*.

KING (*Mrs. Hamilton*)—THE DISCIPLES. Eighth Edition, with Portrait and Notes. Crown 8vo. 5*s*. Elzevir Edition, 6*s*.

A BOOK OF DREAMS. Third Edition. Crown 8vo. 3*s*. 6*d*.

THE SERMON IN THE HOSPITAL. Reprinted from 'The Disciples.' Fcp. 8vo. 1*s*. Cheap Edition, 3*d*., or 20*s*. per 100.

KNOX (*The Hon. Mrs. O. N.*)—FOUR PICTURES FROM A LIFE, and other Poems. Small crown 8vo. 3*s*. 6*d*.

L*ANG* (*A.*)—XXXII BALLADES IN BLUE CHINA. Elzevir 8vo. parchment, or cloth, 5*s*.

RHYMES À LA MODE. With Frontispiece by E. A. Abbey. Elzevir 8vo. cloth extra, gilt top, 5*s*.

L*AWSON* (*Right Hon. Mr. Justice*)—HYMNI USITATI LATINE REDDITI, with other Verses. Small 8vo. parchment, 5*s*.

LIVING ENGLISH POETS. MDCCCLXXXII. With Frontispiece by Walter Crane. Second Edition. Large crown 8vo. printed on hand-made paper. Parchment, or cloth, 12*s*.; vellum, 15*s*.

L*OCKER* (*F.*)—LONDON LYRICS. New Edition, with Portrait. 18mo. cloth extra, gilt tops, 5*s*.

LOVE IN IDLENESS. A Volume of Poems. With an etching by W. B. Scott. Small crown 8vo. 5*s*.

LUMSDEN (*Lieut.-Col. H. W.*)—BEOWULF: an Old English Poem. Translated into Modern Rhymes. Second and revised Edition. Small crown 8vo. 5*s.*

MAGNUSSON (*Eirikr*) *M.A., and PALMER* (*E. H.*) *M.A.*—JOHAN LUDVIG RUNEBERG'S LYRICAL SONGS, IDYLLS, AND EPIGRAMS. Fcp. 8vo. 5*s.*

MEREDITH (*Owen*) [*The Earl of Lytton*]—LUCILE. New Edition. With 32 Illustrations. 16mo. 3*s.* 6*d.*; cloth extra, gilt edges, 4*s.* 6*d.*

MORRIS (*Lewis*)—POETICAL WORKS. New and Cheaper Editions, with Portrait, complete in 4 vols. 5*s.* each.

Vol. I. contains Songs of Two Worlds. Twelfth Edition.

Vol. II. contains The Epic of Hades. Twenty-second Edition.

Vol. III. contains Gwen and the Ode of Life. Seventh Edition.

Vol. IV. contains Songs Unsung and Gycia. Fifth Edition.

SONGS OF BRITAIN. Third Edition. Fcp. 8vo. 5*s.*

THE EPIC OF HADES. With 16 Autotype Illustrations after the drawings by the late George R. Chapman. 4to. cloth extra, gilt leaves, 21*s.*

THE EPIC OF HADES. Presentation Edit. 4to. cloth extra, gilt leaves, 10*s.* 6*d.*

THE LEWIS MORRIS BIRTHDAY BOOK. Edited by S. S. Copeman. With Frontispiece after a design by the late George R. Chapman. 32mo. cloth extra, gilt edges, 2*s.*; cloth limp, 1*s.* 6*d.*

MORSHEAD (*E. D. A.*)—THE HOUSE OF ATREUS. Being the Agamemnon, Libation-Bearers, and Furies of Æschylus. Translated into English Verse. Crown 8vo. 7*s.*

THE SUPPLIANT MAIDENS OF ÆSCHYLUS. Crown 8vo. 3*s.* 6*d.*

MULHOLLAND (*Rosa*).—VAGRANT VERSES. Small crown 8vo. 5*s.*

NADEN (*Constance C. W.*)—A MODERN APOSTLE, and other Poems. Small crown 8vo. 5*s.*

NOEL (*The Hon. Roden*)—A LITTLE CHILD'S MONUMENT. Third Edition. Small crown 8vo. 3*s.* 6*d.*

THE RED FLAG, and other Poems. New Edition. Small crown 8vo. 6*s.*

THE HOUSE OF RAVENSBURG. New Edition. Small crown 8vo. 6*s.*

NOEL (*The Hon. Roden*)—continued.

SONGS OF THE HEIGHTS AND DEE Crown 8vo. 6*s.*

A MODERN FAUST. Small crown 8

O'BRIEN (*Charlotte Grace*)—LYRI Small crown 8vo. 3*s.* 6*d.*

O'HAGAN (*John*)—THE SONG ROLAND. Translated into Engl Verse. New and Cheaper Editi Crown 8vo. 5*s.*

PFEIFFER (*Emily*)—THE RHYME THE LADY OF THE ROCK AND H IT GREW. Small crown 8vo. 3*s.*

GERARD'S MONUMENT, and other Poe Second Edition. Crown 8vo. 6*s.*

UNDER THE ASPENS: Lyrical Dramatic. With Portrait. Cro 8vo. 6*s.*

PIATT (*J. J.*)—IDYLS AND LYRICS THE OHIO VALLEY. Crown 8vo.

PIATT (*Sarah M. B.*)—A VOYAGE THE FORTUNATE ISLES, and ot Poems. 1 vol. Small crown 8 gilt top, 5*s.*

IN PRIMROSE TIME. A New I Garland. Small crown 8vo. 2*s.* 6

RARE POEMS OF THE 16TH AND 17 CENTURIES. Edited by W. J. Lint Crown 8vo. 5*s.*

RHOADES (*James*)—THE GEORGICS VIRGIL. Translated into Eng Verse. Small crown 8vo. 5*s.*

ROBINSON (*A. Mary F.*)—A HAND OF HONEYSUCKLE. Fcp. 8vo. 3*s.*

THE CROWNED HIPPOLYTUS. Tr lated from Euripides. With N Poems. Small crown 8vo. cloth,

SHAKSPERE'S WORKS. The Avon Editi 12 vols. fcp. 8vo. cloth, 18*s.*; and box, 21*s.*; bound in 6 vols. cloth,

SOPHOCLES: The Seven Plays in Eng Verse. Translated by Lewis Ca bell. Crown 8vo. 7*s.* 6*d.*

SYMONDS (*John Addington*)—VA BUNDULI LIBELLUS. Crown 8vo.

TAYLOR (*Sir H.*)—Works Complet Five Volumes. Crown 8vo. 30*s.*

PHILIP VAN ARTEVELDE. Fcp. 3*s.* 6*d.*

THE VIRGIN WIDOW, &c. Fcp. 3*s.* 6*d.*

THE STATESMAN. Fcp. 8vo. 3*s.*

TODHUNTER (*Dr. J.*)—LAURELLA, and other Poems. Crown 8vo. 6*s.* 6*d.*

FOREST SONGS. Small crown 8vo. 3*s.* 6*d.*

THE TRUE TRAGEDY OF RIENZI: a Drama. Crown 8vo. 3*s.* 6*d.*

ALCESTIS: a Dramatic Poem. Extra fcp. 8vo. 5*s.*

HELENA IN TROAS. Small crown 8vo. 2*s.* 6*d.*

TYNAN (*Katherine*)—LOUISE DE LA VALLIERE, and other Poems. Small crown 8vo. 3*s.* 6*d.*

SHAMROCKS. Small crown 8vo. 5*s.*

VICTORIAN HYMNS: English Sacred Songs of Fifty Years. Dedicated to the Queen. Large post 8vo. 10*s.* 6*d.*

WATTS (*Alaric Alfred and Emma Mary Howitt*)—AURORA: a Medley of Verse. Fcp. 8vo. 5*s.*

WORDSWORTH—SELECTIONS. By Members of the Wordsworth Society. Large crown 8vo. parchment, 12*s.*; vellum, 15*s.* Also, cr. 8vo. cl. 4*s.* 6*d.*

WORDSWORTH BIRTHDAY BOOK, THE. Edited by ADELAIDE and VIOLET WORDSWORTH. 32mo. limp cloth, 1*s.* 6*d.*; cloth extra, 2*s.*

WORKS OF FICTION.

'ALL BUT:' a Chronicle of Laxenford Life. By PEN OLIVER, F.R.C.S. With 20 Illustrations. Second Edit. Crown 8vo. 6*s.*

BANKS (*Mrs. G. L.*)—GOD'S PROVIDENCE HOUSE. New Edition. Crown 8vo. 6*s.*

CHICHELE (*Mary*)—DOING AND UNDOING: a Story. Crown 8vo. 4*s.* 6*d.*

CRAWFURD (*Oswald*)—SYLVIA ARDEN. Crown 8vo. 6*s.*

GARDINER (*Linda*)—HIS HERITAGE. Crown 8vo. 6*s.*

GRAY (*Maxwell*)—THE SILENCE OF DEAN MAITLAND. Fourth Edition. Crown 8vo. 6*s.*

GREY (*Rowland*)—BY VIRTUE OF HIS OFFICE. Crown 8vo. 6*s.*

IN SUNNY SWITZERLAND. Small crown 8vo. 5*s.*

LINDENBLUMEN, and other Stories. Small crown 8vo. 5*s.*

HUNTER (*Hay*)—CRIME OF CHRISTMAS DAY. A Tale of the Latin Quarter. By the Author of 'My Ducats and My Daughter.' 1*s.*

HUNTER (*Hay*) *and WHYTE* (*Walter*) MY DUCATS AND MY DAUGHTER. New and Cheaper Edition. With Frontispiece. Crown 8vo. 6*s.*

INGELOW (*Jean*)—OFF THE SKELLIGS. A Novel. With Frontispiece. Second Edition. Crown 8vo. 6*s.*

IXORA. A Mystery. Crown 8vo. 6*s.*

JENKINS (*Edward*)—A SECRET OF TWO LIVES. Crown 8vo. 2*s.* 6*d.*

KIELLAND (*Alexander L.*)—GARMAN AND WORSE. A Norwegian Novel. Authorised Translation by W. W. Kettlewell. Crown 8vo. 6*s.*

LANG (*Andrew*)—IN THE WRONG PARADISE, and other Stories. Crown 8vo. 6*s.*

MACDONALD (*G.*)—DONAL GRANT. Crown 8vo. 6*s.*

CASTLE WARLOCK. Crown 8vo. 6*s.*

MALCOLM. With Portrait of the Author engraved on Steel. Crown 8vo. 6*s.*

THE MARQUIS OF LOSSIE. Crown 8vo. 6*s.*

ST. GEORGE AND ST. MICHAEL. Crown 8vo. 6*s.*

PAUL FABER, SURGEON. Crown 8vo. 6*s.*

THOMAS WINGFOLD, CURATE. Crown 8vo. 6*s.*

WHAT'S MINE'S MINE. Second Edition. Crown 8vo. 6*s.*

ANNALS OF A QUIET NEIGHBOURHOOD. Crown 8vo. 6*s.*

THE SEABOARD PARISH: a Sequel to 'Annals of a Quiet Neighbourhood.' Crown 8vo. 6*s.*

WILFRED CUMBERMEDE. An Autobiographical Story. Crown 8vo. 6*s.*

THE ELECT LADY. Crown 8vo. 6*s.*

MALET (*Lucas*)—COLONEL ENDERBY'S WIFE. Crown 8vo. 6*s.*

A COUNSEL OF PERFECTION. Crown 8vo. 6*s.*

MULHOLLAND (*Rosa*)—MARCELLA GRACE. An Irish Novel. Crown 8vo. 6*s.*

A FAIR EMIGRANT. Crown 8vo. 6*s.*

OGLE (*A. C.*) ('*Ashford Owen.*') A LOST LOVE. Small crown 8vo. 2*s.* 6*d.*

PALGRAVE (*W. Gifford*)—HERMANN AGHA: an Eastern Narrative. Third Edition. Crown 8vo. 6*s.*

SEVERNE (*Mrs.*)—THE PILLAR HOUSE. With Frontispiece. Crown 8vo. 6*s.*

SHAW (*Flora L.*)—CASTLE BLAIR; a Story of Youthful Days. New and Cheaper Edition. Crown 8vo. 3*s.* 6*d.*

STRETTON (*Hesba*) — THROUGH A NEEDLE'S EYE. A Story. New and Cheaper Edition, with Frontispiece. Crown 8vo. 6*s.*

TAYLOR (*Col. Meadows*) *C.S.I., M.R.I.A.*
SEETA. A Novel. New and Cheaper Edition. With Frontispiece. Crown 8vo. 6*s.*

TAYLOR (*Col. Meadows*) *C.S.I., M.R.I.*—continued.

TIPPOO SULTAUN: a Tale of the Mys War. New Edition, with Frontispie Crown 8vo. 6*s.*

RALPH DARNELL. New and Chea Edition. With Frontispiece. Cro 8vo. 6*s.*

A NOBLE QUEEN. New and Chea Edition. With Frontispiece. Cro 8vo. 6*s.*

THE CONFESSIONS OF A THI Crown 8vo. 6*s.*

TARA: a Mahratta Tale. Crown 8vo.

WITHIN SOUND OF THE SEA. N and Cheaper Edition, with Fron piece. Crown 8vo. 6*s.*

BOOKS FOR THE YOUNG.

BRAVE MEN'S FOOTSTEPS. A Book of Example and Anecdote for Young People. By the Editor of 'Men who have Risen.' With Four Illustrations by C. Doyle. Eighth Edition. Crown 8vo. 2*s.* 6*d.*

COXHEAD (*Ethel*)—BIRDS AND BABIES. With 33 Illustrations. Imp. 16mo. cloth gilt, 1*s.*

DAVIES (*G. Christopher*) — RAMBLES AND ADVENTURES OF OUR SCHOOL FIELD CLUB. With Four Illustrations. New and Cheaper Edition. Crown 8vo. 3*s.* 6*d.*

EDMONDS (*Herbert*) — WELL-SPENT LIVES: a Series of Modern Biographies. New and Cheaper Edition. Crown 8vo. 3*s.* 6*d.*

EVANS (*Mark*)—THE STORY OF OUR FATHER'S LOVE, told to Children. Sixth and Cheaper Edition of Theology for Children. With Four Illustrations. Fcp. 8vo. 1*s.* 6*d.*

MAC KENNA (*S. J.*)—PLUCKY FELLOWS. A Book for Boys. With Six Illustrations. Fifth Edition. Crown 8vo. 3*s.* 6*d.*

MALET (*Lucas*)—LITTLE PETER. A Christmas Morality for Children of any Age. With numerous Illustrations. 5*s.*

REANEY (*Mrs. G. S.*)—WAKING A WORKING; or, From Girlhood Womanhood. New and Chea Edition. With a Frontispiece. 8vo. 3*s.* 6*d.*

BLESSING AND BLESSED: a Sketch Girl Life. New and Cheaper Editic Crown 8vo. 3*s.* 6*d.*

ROSE GURNEY'S DISCOVERY. A Bo for Girls. Dedicated to their Mothe Crown 8vo. 3*s.* 6*d.*

ENGLISH GIRLS: Their Place and Pow With Preface by the Rev. R. W. Dal Fourth Edition. Fcp. 8vo. 2*s.* 6*d.*

JUST ANYONE, and other Stories. Thr Illustrations. Royal 16mo. 1*s.* 6*d.*

SUNBEAM WILLIE, and other Stori Three Illustrations. Royal 16m 1*s.* 6*d.*

SUNSHINE JENNY, and other Storie Three Illustrations. Royal 16m 1*s.* 6*d.*

STORR (*Francis*) *and TURNER* (*Hawe* CANTERBURY CHIMES; or, Chauc Tales Re-told to Children. With S Illustrations from the Ellesmere M Third Edition. Fcp. 8vo. 3*s.* 6*d.*

STRETTON (*Hesba*)—DAVID LLOYD LAST WILL. With Four Illustr tions. New Edition. Royal 16m 2*s.* 6*d.*

WHITAKER (*Florence*)—CHRISTY'S I HERITANCE: A London Story. Illu trated. Royal 16mo. 1*s.* 6*d.*

Spottiswoode & Co. Printers, New-street Square, London.

Lightning Source UK Ltd.
Milton Keynes UK
UKOW05f1957100317
296393UK00020B/461/P